An Introduction to
Formal Specification and Z

Prentice Hall International Series in Computer Science

C.A.R. Hoare, Series Editor

ARNOLD, A., *Finite Transition Systems*
ARNOLD, A. and GUESSARIAN, I., *Mathematics for Computer Science*
BARR, M. and WELLS, C., *Category Theory for Computing Science* (2nd edn)
BEN-ARI, M., *Principles of Concurrent and Distributed Programming*
BEN-ARI, M., *Mathematical Logic for Computer Science*
BEST, E., *Semantics of Sequential and Parallel Programs*
BIRD, R. and WADLER, P., *Introduction to Functional Programming*
BOVET, D.P. and CRESCENZI, P., *Introduction to the Theory of Complexity*
DE BROCK, B., *Foundations of Semantic Databases*
BRODA, EISENBACH, KHOSHNEVISAN and VICKERS, *Reasoned Programming*
BURKE, E. and FOXLEY, E., *Logic and Its Applications*
DAHL, O.-J., *Verifiable Programming*
DAVIES, J. and WOODCOCK, J., *Using Z: Specification, refinement and proof*
DUNCAN, E., *Microprocessor Programming and Software Development*
ELDER, J., *Compiler Construction*
ELLIOTT, R.J. and HOARE, C.A.R. (eds), *Scientific Applications of Multiprocessors*
FREEMAN, T.L. and PHILLIPS, R.C., *Parallel Numerical Algorithms*
GOLDSCHLAGER, L. and LISTER, A., *Computer Science: A modern introduction* (2nd edn)
GORDON, M.J.C., *Programming Language Theory and Its Implementation*
GRAY, P.M.D., KULKARNI, K.G. and PATON, N.W., *Object-oriented Databases*
HAYES, I. (ed.), *Specification Case Studies* (2nd edn)
HEHNER, E.C.R., *The Logic of Programming*
HINCHEY, M.G. and BOWEN, J.P., *Applications of Formal Methods*
HOARE, C.A.R., *Communicating Sequential Processes*
HOARE, C.A.R. and GORDON, M.J.C. (eds), *Mechanized Reasoning and Hardware Design*
HOARE, C.A.R. and JONES, C.B. (eds), *Essays in Computing Science*
HOARE, C.A.R. and SHEPHERDSON, J.C. (eds), *Mechanical Logic and Programming Languages*
HUGHES, J.G., *Database Technology: A software engineering approach*
HUGHES, J.G., *Object-oriented Databases*
INMOS LTD, *Occam 2 Reference manual*
JACKSON, M.A., *System Development*
JONES, C.B., *Systematic Software Development Using VDM* (2nd edn)
JONES, C.B. and SHAW, R.C.F. (eds), *Case Studies in Systematic Software Development*
JONES, G., *Programming in Occam*
JONES, G. and GOLDSMITH, M., *Programming in Occam 2*
JONES, N.D., GOMARD, C.K. and SESTOFT, P., *Partial Evaluation and Automatic Program Generation*
JOSEPH, M., *Real-time Systems: Specification, verification and analysis*
JOSEPH, M., PRASAD, V.R. and NATARAJAN, N., *A Multiprocessor Operating System*
KALDEWAIJ, A., *Programming: The derivation of algorithms*
KING, P.J.B., *Computer and Communications Systems Performance Modelling*
LALEMENT, R., *Computation as Logic*
McCABE, F.G., *Logic and Objects*
McCABE, F.G., *High-level Programmer's Guide to the 68000*
MEYER, B., *Introduction to the Theory of Programming Languages*
MEYER, B., *Object-oriented Software Construction*
MILNER, R., *Communication and Currency*

An Introduction to
Formal Specification and Z

Second edition

Ben Potter
University of Hertfordshire

Jane Sinclair
Open University

David Till
City University, London

PRENTICE HALL

London New York Toronto Sydney Tokyo Singapore
Madrid Mexico City Munich

First published 1996 by
Prentice Hall Europe
Campus 400, Maylands Avenue
Hemel Hempstead
Hertfordshire, HP2 7EZ
A division of
Simon & Schuster International Group

Printed and bound in Great Britain by Redwood Books,
Trowbridge, Wiltshire

Library of Congress Cataloging-in-Publication Data

Potter, Ben.
  Introduction to formal specification and Z / Ben Potter, Jane
Sinclair, and David Till. -- 2nd ed.
      p.   cm.
  Includes bibliographical references and index.
  ISBN 0-13-242207-7 (pbk.)
    1. Computer software--Development. 2. Z (Computer program
  language) I. Sinclair, Jane II. Till, David. III. Title.
QA76.76.D47P68 1996
005.1'2--dc20   96-15929
                                                         CIP

British Library Cataloguing-in-Publication Data

A catalogue record for this book is available
from the British Library

ISBN 0-13-242207-7

---

1 2 3 4 5   00 99 98 97 96

Contents

Preface to the Second Edition

There are many books which address the topic of computer system design. No small number of these describe the process of design and implementation of such systems by the application of systematic methodologies of various kinds, often with the intent of realising the design according to some particular programming paradigm.

This book takes as its primary focus the issue of specification of computer systems. We approach the subject by considering simple practical systems to which, we hope, most people will be able to relate immediately.

By specification we refer to the process of defining the behaviour of a system as viewed from the outside. Due concern for the inner workings of a system must clearly be given in order to achieve a working implementation, but we believe this to be a consideration subsequent to the achievement of a correct specification of the desired system. To take some analogies: a bridge might be specified by its average and maximum load-carrying capacities along with its length and width, whereas the choice of planks of wood, steel cables or reinforced concrete with which to build its spans or arches are matters of implementation. An airline will express its need for a new airliner in terms of desired range, carrying capacity, operating cost and so forth, rather than an expression of the size of wing and number of engines and choice of materials to be used during construction. Nearer home, perhaps, most of us will choose a car on the basis of the number of doors and seats, speed, acceleration and fuel consumption figures, along with subjective measures of comfort, style and colour. Undue concern for the kind of metal from which the engine block has been cast is not usual for the average buyer. In short, the concerns of specifications are the issues which describe *what* a system must offer rather than the prescription of *how* these things are to be achieved.

There are now many methods and languages by means of which computer-based systems may be crafted. Only recently has attention turned to the topics of notations and methods for specification of systems; in particular to the specification of systems before the attempt to construct them is begun.

Within this book we describe a toolkit of notation based on well-founded mathematical concepts and a method for using the toolkit in order to describe the behaviour of computer-based information systems. No particular mathematical background will be assumed other than a familiarity with algebraic notation as used in school; we shall however assume willingness to work through the exercises. Also on offer will be methods of proof by logical argument that the systems so described possess certain desirable properties, and methods by which we may proceed from pure specification towards executable systems in a controlled manner.

Throughout the book we have attempted to draw on material for examples which can be easily related to real-life experience by the reader, eschewing the mysteries of text-editors, symbol tables and the like. Nevertheless the techniques described here are quite equal to the task of specifying a wide range of systems. For some examples of these reference may be made to [Hay93].

The intention of this book is to provide a graduated introductory text suitable for study as part of a first or second year undergraduate course, and also for use by experienced software practitioners. As such, the text may be considered to fall into three parts.

To begin, we set the context for the use of Z. Chapter 2 provides an easy introduction to the principles underlying the Z notation, and Chapter 3 presents a first specification using only these basics. The first three chapters thus constitute an informal introduction to the subject matter, and should be found quite straightforward.

The second part of the book is slightly more dense, as it sets out to provide a largely complete tutorial for the Z notation via Chapters 4, 5 and 6. These consist of a substantial body of material which must be mastered in order to write specifications. Many exercises have been provided to encourage the achievement of this. In the second edition, solutions to a large selection of the exercises have been included. Those exercises to which suggested solutions have been given at the end of the book are indicated by a ◇ sign. Chapter 7 then seeks to clarify matters by demonstrating how the notation may be used, and it does this by re-casting the simple specification given in Chapter 3. An extended case study is presented in Chapter 8, with much of the material included in the solutions.

Finally, in the third section we offer overviews of the scope for logical reasoning and rigorous production of software made feasible by the notation used in Chapters 9, 10 and 11. These are intended to survey and mark out the possibilities, rather than offer complete tutorials; they may thus be found a steeper climb than the earlier sections. We offer no apology for this, as we would expect further study to be necessary to achieve competence in these more advanced areas, bearing in mind the introductory nature of this book. For the second edition, we have modified some of our refinement rules in the light of a similar treatment of refinement in Wordsworth's *Software Development with Z* [Wor93]. The final chapter offers a distillation of some experiences of applying Z to projects in the field.

We have deliberately sought to produce an introductory text rather than a reference manual or a volume of industrial case studies, believing both these topics to have been already addressed more than adequately elsewhere [Spi92, Hay93].

In some senses, then, this volume may be considered complementary to the afore-mentioned.

Since publication of the first edition the Z community has been moving towards a British Standard for Z, and this has led to some revision of the notation. At the time of writing of the second edition this work is not complete but we have sought to include our best understanding of the contents of the Standard. Readers using this book may take it that the second edition of Spivey's *Z Reference Manual* [Spi92] is sufficiently close to the Standard which will be adopted as to make no real difference for present purposes. The syntax of Z, corresponding to Spivey's second edition, is included in Appendix B. Of course, the Standard is intended to serve as definitive for those who wish to create Z support tools or to develop high-integrity systems using Z as specification language; any reader who needs that kind of detail can consult the currently available versions of the Standard [BN92].

Summary of differences from first edition

The second edition differs from the first in the following areas:

- alignment of the notation with the standard version of the language, insofar as is possible prior to publication of the standard

- additional notation, particularly promotion

- provision of solutions to selected exercises

- an additional case study

- presentation of further work on refinement.

Naturally, all known errors have been corrected.

Acknowledgements

This book draws almost entirely on the work of the developers of the Z notation and technique for its basic material. We thank them gratefully for all their work, not only in creating the notation but also in presenting it via numerous courses and papers. We are especially grateful to Tony Hoare, Jim Woodcock, Steve King, John Nicholls, Paul Gardiner, Jeff Sanders and Bernard Sufrin, all of Oxford University, for their help and encouragement.

We also thank all those who have offered comment on the text of both editions, pointed out errors and deficiencies, and suggested improvements. Some of these reviewers have been anonymous, but we would like to offer particular thanks to Tim Clement, of the University of Manchester, and John Derrick, of the University of Kent. The typographic task was greatly aided by Mike Spivey, and we are also indebted to him for the syntax tables which appear at the end of the book. Our thanks are due to Vitoria Cunningham-Smith for the Camp Energy case study.

Finally, we offer thanks to all colleagues, friends and families who have provided help, support and encouragement with this venture. We also thank our readers who have made suggestions concerning the first edition. We hope that they will do the same for this new edition.

Chapter 1

Formal specification in the context of software engineering

The design and construction of information processing systems which incorporate computers is a new branch of engineering. The first programmable digital computers appeared during the 1940s, but the widespread use of computers did not really begin until the 1960s. Thus the challenge of learning how to produce systems and software, as a major engineering activity, has only been with us for perhaps thirty years.

By contrast, the building of ships has been practised for over two thousand years, and the construction of houses and bridges for considerably longer. Small wonder, then, that many of the principles of civil, nautical, structural and mechanical engineering have become part of our collective consciousness. For instance, few would begin to build even a model boat without a set of drawings, and one hardly remarks on the need for plans to be prepared for a new house or even an extension to an old one.

Time has not yet allowed us to acquire the equivalent body of expertise with which to surround and support the development of software-based systems. Consequently many systems are constructed with little or no overt attention to any underlying theory, and without the benefit of centuries of experience in the selection of those techniques which are most likely to confer success. As a result, many large endeavours run late and exceed their budgets, yet are still faulty when declared complete.

For example, modern banks rely on computers to support networks of cash dispensing machines. There have been cases where a fault in software has forced the network of cash dispensers to be closed down, resulting in inconvenience to thousands of customers and loss of business to the bank which could rapidly amount to hundreds of thousands of pounds [Neu89]. Cases where public utilities have delivered incorrect bills for services for huge cash amounts, sometimes millions of pounds, are now part of the folklore associated with the penetration of computer

1

systems or their effects into almost every corner of modern life.

As computing technology becomes a cheap alternative to mechanical or electronic control systems these problems spread from the realms of simple nuisance or financial penalty to areas where safety of property and even life itself is threatened. Computers and their associated software are now to be found in robots, aircraft control systems, motor cars and nuclear power plant control systems. Even a casual study of the Risks section in *IEEE Software Engineering Notes* [Neu89] should be sufficient to raise immediate concerns over the safety of such systems. The likelihood of a major accident directly attributable to faulty software is a worry which is not to be easily dismissed.

1.1   Software engineering

Recognition of the problems of the industry has led to efforts to improve upon the current craft methods. These improvements are generally known by the name software engineering. The title covers many facets of the problem, ranging from techniques to help with the initial definition of the problem to be addressed, through to the production of documentation to support a completed system.

Before examining software engineering more closely it may be helpful to compare and contrast the software industry with other, 'hard' engineering disciplines, in order to gain some understanding of why techniques for engineering software systems may need to be different from techniques used in other branches of engineering.

To begin with, software design is not distinguished from software production. Compare this situation with the motor industry, where the costs of designing a new car are enormous, especially when the costs of tooling are included. However, even when a car has been designed the production of each unit still requires a substantial amount of energy, skill and raw material. By contrast, the task of producing a million identical software packages requires one major act of design and then simple repetition of a copying task, which can be made completely automatic. (Issues of documentation and distribution are conveniently neglected here, as they are common to most engineering products.) From this we can see that the engineering of software has a large creative design phase and a trivial manufacturing phase, but a substantial testing requirement.

Further, even after software has been delivered to the customer the apparent ease with which it can be changed leads to a process known as maintenance, where new facilities and corrections are applied to the working system. Contrast this with a motor car: this is also an object which has been produced by an engineering process, but it is seldom enhanced in service. Eventually, despite maintenance, it will wear out through use. By contrast, software suffers no wear at all from use; it may be executed and thus do useful work millions of times without any ill effects. However, as has been noted, it is liable to be changed in service to reflect the additional functions expected of it and to correct faults in the original structure. Eventually, making changes becomes effectively impossible, as successive alterations destroy the original structure and hence the understanding required to permit successful change. It is thus the maintenance process itself which wears out software, rather than use.

Software is also apparently much more amenable to change than other engineering technologies. For example, it seems to be much simpler to change one line of a program in the software controlling a car ignition system than to alter the tooling in order to change the shape of a component in the engine to achieve the same ends. This very flexibility can lead to a failure to understand the cost of changes to software and thus the need for control of the process whereby these changes are made.

The accumulated public perception of computer systems is that they are inherently faulty. In the very early days, computer hardware was notoriously unreliable. Computers required many thousands, even hundreds of thousands, of individual valves, and eventually transistors. Even with a mean time between failures (MTBF) of 1 million hours for a transistor, it is easy to see how an MTBF of 45 minutes for a large computer might represent success. Since then, the MTBF of hardware has risen by orders of magnitude, with the integrated circuit being inherently more reliable and also greatly reducing the number of wired or soldered interconnections, which further hinder continuous operation. Poor reliability of software would now appear to be the dominant problem in the battle to build reliable systems. Indeed, the prevailing condition might be characterised by observing that we have moved from a situation where the hardware was the limiting technology to the point where our ability to produce reliable software now places a serious limit on progress. However, as Bowen and Stavridou have noted [BS93], some 35% of software failures are still caused by hardware-induced problems, so scope for improvement in both hardware performance and the construction of resilient software remains.

Errors in software are casually referred to as 'bugs', whereas the equivalent term in other engineering disciplines is 'faulty component'. This has led to a rather sloppy situation, where low standards are generally accepted as normal. This is not the case in other branches of engineering. If the design of an aircraft is incorrect in some major way then the maker stands to lose large amounts of money and goodwill, and is seen to do so publicly. Claims may be made for loss of property, personal injury or loss of life. By contrast, the architects of a software system may risk some legal action from an irate customer, but the conventions of the industry usually restrict the action required to that of issuing a correction to be applied to the faulty system. This has begun to change, at least in certain sectors of the industry. For example, the UK Ministry of Defence has issued a draft standard for software in safety critical systems [UMoD89] which mandates the use of formal methods, although it must be said that the response to this has been less than wholehearted. In secure systems, too, there is increasing evidence of some movement towards increased adoption of formalism [CCEBUE94]. Furthermore, in the UK at least, suppliers of systems are legally liable for the software which they produce, both under contractual provisions covered by the law of civil liability and also by the Consumer Protection Act of 1987. Apart from any desire to be able to claim use of best current practice, the prospect of lengthy and expensive litigation may yet encourage system developers to apply risk reducing techniques for their own protection.

Digital computing is based on the concept of binary logic, where circuits are definitely in one state or another. This is quite unlike other kinds of engineering, where materials are subject to continuously varying forces and respond in a similarly continuous fashion, up to the point of complete failure. Despite the apparently greater simplicity, this makes the prediction of the outcome of a combination of components based on binary logic quite difficult as compared with the task of modelling the behaviour of, say, a system of beams in a structure. This is due to the combinatorial nature of digital systems making extrapolation of expected behaviour unrealistic. One consequence of this is the reliance of developers of computer systems on the notion of testing, whereby a program is written and then executed to check that it exhibits the desired behaviour. Now it is an unfortunate fact, pointed out many years ago by Dijkstra [Dij72], that testing can only reveal errors and never demonstrate the absence of them. In the case of a physical structure, it may be adequate to define the system of interconnected beams to be used, calculate the stresses in critical cases and then perhaps test the structure to six times the desired load. By such a process we can be reasonably sure that the structure will carry out the task intended. Much of our confidence in this fact lies in the continuous nature of the behaviour of beams, which allows us to interpolate many intermediate cases from the calculations and tests actually carried out. However a software system will be making perhaps hundreds of thousands of independent logical tests and decisions to allow the correct functioning of, say, a supermarket checkout. In order to be confident that even such a simple system is correct it would be necessary to devise a test scheme which exercised some minimal combination of all the decisions to be made by the software; in this case it would need to include combinations of key depressions, prices of items, amounts of change to be given and so on. This is extremely hard, and for a medium sized system containing 1000 decisions would require 10^{300} test cases. The time required to do this renders it simply impractical; even if the tests could be executed at a rate of one per microsecond, such a system could not be exhaustively tested during the lifetime of the universe. However, the alternative may be terrifying; a nuclear reactor control system might exhibit a catastrophic error due to a combination of circumstances encountered only after six months of operation, for example.

This is where mathematical proof of theorems identified in a specification may be of assistance. In terms of the eventual implementation, proof of one property at the specification stage may yield a result which corresponds to the behaviour of a very large number of possible execution sequences, offering an increased level of confidence with the opportunity of reducing test cases. If, for example, it could be shown that the effect of causing the opening and then subsequent closing of a valve in our reactor control system will result in the system returning to its original state, then we may be more confident about the behaviour of the system.

Further, proofs at specification time which demonstrate that assumptions made concerning the system are, in actual fact, faulty may well pre-empt the implementation of programs based on such assumptions. This can save effort and also avoid designing errors into the system which must, if discovered at all, be found by extensive (and expensive) testing and subsequent rectification.

It seems clear, then, that attention to the problems and challenges of engineering software systems is urgently needed.

1.2   Life-cycles and processes

Every product, be it hardware or software, exhibits a life-cycle – it is conceived, developed, leads a (more or less) productive life, reaches maturity, and eventually is retired. Equally, any organisation which produces software will perform a number of distinct activities. Many models of these life-cycles and processes, and their possible organisation and interaction, have been proposed, and we do not seek to continue this work here, except perhaps to note that some conflation of the two concepts has occurred. We suggest that most of the work done on any project takes the form of model building, and that these models are made progressively though not monotonically more concrete as the implementation is achieved. There are those who argue for a process based on the building of working models, and others who justify a more considered approach. We attempt here to distinguish the processes which must take place in any software project, however large or small, regardless of the process model adopted, and thus facilitate discussion of those tasks and increase understanding of the particular needs of each part of the process. Obviously the emphasis may shift from project to project, depending on the nature of the project and on the particular characteristics of the development team and their working environment, but broadly the activities are as follows:

- **Requirements Analysis:** the customer and supplier work together to identify, understand and define the actual problems for which a solution is sought.

- **System Specification:** the requirements which the system must meet are set down in an agreed form. This will include functions to be performed by the system along with other attributes such as performance, reliability and usability criteria.

- **Design:** alternative ways of satisfying the specification are explored, depending on the types of equipment involved and the performance required. This represents the crucial bridge between the earlier phases, which should be characterised by asking 'what is to be done?', and the later phases which are more concerned with the 'how?'

- **Implementation:** the chosen design must now be translated into executable programs; all outstanding details concerning functions to be performed and the nature of the data involved must be settled to allow this phase to be completed.

- **Test and Integration:** following testing of the parts, the system can be assembled into a whole and tested to see that the component parts fit and work together correctly.

- **Support and Enhancement:** the completed system must be delivered to the ultimate user; throughout its life it may be subject to correction of errors, and the addition of new features brought about by changes to the environment in which it is used.

The breakdown given here is very general. More detailed subdivisions of the processes have been given, and an iterative development approach might seek to subsume a number of tasks within each cycle, but in our view the most important issue is the recognition of the different needs of each part of the process rather than a detailed debate concerning the relative merits of the competing process models.

1.3   The importance of specification

Experience in a number of large projects has shown that the vast bulk of the costs of a software project lies with the fixing of errors at the implementation and test stages of the work. However, more detailed investigation reveals that a very large percentage of these errors are traceable to imprecision in the early stages of the project. That is, the high costs during the implementation and test phases are largely caused by false economies at the specification and design phases. (See Figure 1.1.) This occurs because of loose wording or lack of essential detail at the specification phase; this often results in faulty design decisions being taken at later stages when fewer checks are applied. Eventually, the detection

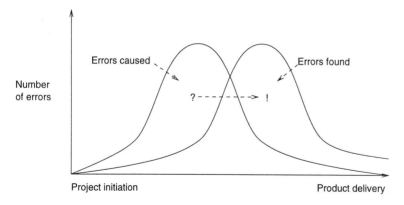

Figure 1.1: Cause and discovery of errors throughout the life-cycle

and rectification of these errors can involve a large team (which may have already made yet further design decisions) causing major re-work. It is important to stress this point: whilst the bulk of the errors appear at later stages in the process, the cause rate has peaked earlier in the cycle.

The cost of correcting an error in a software product which has been delivered to the customer has been measured at figures up to $10,000 [Fag76], and these were 1970s dollars. In a reasonably large system, delivered to many customers, only 100 errors need to slip through the net to add $1,000,000 to the cost of developing the product. This combination of steeply rising costs of rectification and the bulk of errors being caused early in the life-cycle leads to the argument that extra effort and the use of more powerful techniques at those early stages could well lead to a reduced error rate, which will feed forward to provide a reduction in the total number of errors and perhaps substantial cost savings.

1.4   The need for formality and abstraction

From the early days of data processing when analysts drew systems flowcharts and wrote program specifications in natural language, there has developed a body of methods and techniques, many of them graphical in nature. Typically these address the problem by decomposition into manageable sub-systems, by capturing static relationships between the data to be operated on by the system, and by identifying the logical information flows through the system. More recent trends link the data and the processing more intimately in the object-oriented style. In most approaches, however, the analyst is required to use natural language or some loosely defined subset of it to attempt the actual precise description of the functions of the system.

It is apparent that the use of natural language alone for specification purposes is inadequate due to its lack of precision. This imprecision, a characteristic of language sometimes deliberately exploited in everyday life, is a prime culprit in the production of ambiguous and incomplete specifications. Only later, when the precision of a programming language is brought to bear, does it become clear that there are major omissions and inconsistencies in the specification. Perhaps, then, we should look to programming languages for a solution to this problem.

It would seem possible to use existing programming languages in order to express specifications: indeed, programs are used as specifications for the behaviour of the computers which execute them. However, the very nature of current digital computers requires the program of instructions to be absolutely unambiguous and precise to the last detail, both with regard to the data items and their encodings as well as the explicit description of the means by which the data are to be manipulated; this forces us to describe *how* the task is to be accomplished, rather than concentrate on the description of *what* it is that we want to be accomplished. Thus current programming languages would seem unsuitable as specification languages. What is needed is a vehicle which offers the precision of a programming language, but without the fine details of data structure and algorithm. We also want to be able to conduct rigorous arguments to establish desirable properties of our specifications. This combination of precision and the ability to argue rigorously is what we mean by formality. Being able to say what is required without commitment to details of how it is to be achieved is what we mean by abstraction.

With all this in mind, we choose to use a mathematical notation based on the principles of set theory, predicate logic, relations and functions for specification purposes. This has several advantages over both natural language and conventional programming languages. First of all, the meanings are clear and can always be disambiguated by appealing to the underlying mathematics. Second, the concepts used allow far greater precision than natural language without sacrificing brevity for the mass of detail required by current programming languages. Finally, rigorous demonstration of properties of the specification is made possible by the application of mathematical proof techniques.

Use of such techniques offers the possibility of producing clear specifications of the functions expected of a computer system. Used in conjunction with sufficient prose, formal specifications can be of enormous value both in clarifying the statement of the user requirements and also as a precise expression of the fundamental aspects of the designer's task. Obviously, other techniques should be called into play where they are applicable: the user's interface, for instance, must be considered with due regard to the physiological and psychological aspects of the system's use. Other aspects such as documentation requirements, performance and the like may be better described by reference to appropriate standards, or through the use of natural language or diagrams or other formalisms.

For those concerned about the novelty of this formal approach, it may be worth reflecting that formal statements concerning systems are already frequently made, as in 'The system should respond to 90% of enquiries within 10 seconds' or 'The hand-held terminal shall weigh less than 2 kilograms', for these are both formal statements whose truth or falsehood may be readily determined. Programming languages are themselves very formal, although this fact is often overlooked. As we have noted above, the problem here is that the level of detail required is too fine for the needs of the specifier.

The use of formal techniques should be seen as a way of achieving a high degree of confidence that a system will conform to its specification. There can never be an absolute guarantee of correctness, for the system will be embedded in an informal world, where absolute correctness has no meaning. These techniques have little to offer directly to the problems of managing software projects, although the benefit to be gained from gaining a clear understanding of the task at an early stage should not be underestimated.

1.5   The notation we shall use

Growing awareness of the need for formal specification has led to the development of various specification languages. Some of these take as their starting point a large body of standard mathematical concepts and notation, including set theory, and use these to build models of systems, the best known exemplars of this approach being Z and VDM, the Vienna Development Method [Jon86]. The family of process algebras represented by CSP (Communicating Sequential Processes) [Hoa85] and the Calculus of Communicating Systems, CCS [Mil89], build on similar mathematical foundations, but provide notations which capture the permissible ordering of the events with which a system is concerned. There are also property-based styles of specification, where equations are used to capture facets of desired system behaviour directly, without any attempt to build a model in an intermediate mathematical notation.

The relative merits of the different styles of specification are far from clear at the moment, and much research is currently being devoted to the development and application of notations. We have chosen to use the Z notation for the reasons which we shall now rehearse, aware that these are by no means conclusive.

The experience gained over the past 15 years from case studies in Z specification has demonstrated that a large variety of specification problems may be successfully addressed in Z and that set theory forms an adequate basis for building the more complex data structures which are needed in specifications. Furthermore, the purely notational devices of Z make a significant contribution to our ability to construct comprehensible specifications, just as good typography makes a book more readable. An important practical issue which arises when considering the adoption of a new notation is that of standardisation. Z now has quite a long history and is, at this writing, the subject of BSI standardisation. Such activity gives encouragement to the developers of the software tools which allow us to create, manipulate and verify Z specifications. Pending the arrival of the ratified BSI standard, and on the basis that it will not be very dissimilar, we shall take *The Z Notation: A Reference Manual* (2nd edition) [Spi92] as definitive.

Some useful contacts and sources of information on Z will be found in Chapter 12, along with brief references to some of its applications.

1.6   Further reading

More general information about software engineering may be found in *Software Engineering* by Ian Somerville [Som92] and also in *A Practical Handbook for Software Development* by N. D. Birrell and M. Ould [BO85], and *Software Engineering: A Practitioner's Approach* by R.S. Pressman [Pre92]. A compendium of useful items may be found in *The Software Engineer's Reference Book*, edited by J. A. McDermid [MS91]. The issues of cost are addressed in *Software Engineering Economics* by B.W. Boehm [Boe81].

Chapter 2

An informal introduction
to logic and set theory

A specification written in Z is a mixture of formal, mathematical statements and informal explanatory text. Both are important: the formal part gives a precise description of the system being specified while the informal text makes the document more readable and comprehensible, linking the mathematics to the real world.

The formal component of Z is based on set theory, a subject now often taught in schools from an early age, though readers of mature years may not have encountered it. To the basic notions of set theory, Z adds the idea that the objects in its universe may be categorised into different kinds, and that there is no overlap between distinct kinds: we say that the set theory is a typed set theory. A second most important distinguishing feature of Z is a device, known as the schema, which allows us to group together descriptions of objects into named units which can be referred to throughout the specification: this aspect of Z will not be discussed until Chapter 6.

In the present chapter we take a first look at sets and how to define them. In order to construct all but the simplest of sets, or to make any statement about the objects we define, we need to be able to make assertions using elementary logic. We see how this may be done here, while deferring to a later chapter discussion of how reasoning may be conducted within the logic.

Our aim in this chapter is to introduce just enough notation to be able to make a first attempt at specification in a style rather like that of Z. This first specification is the subject of the following chapter; the example used there will be revisited later on when we have the full Z notation at our disposal, enabling us to describe it more neatly and to add further features.

2.1   Sets

The idea of forming sets, collections, aggregates or classes of distinct objects seems to be a very basic item of equipment in our mental toolbox. There are many more words in the English language which denote the same idea when applied to certain kinds of objects; for example, pack, pride, swarm, flock, covey, and so on. There is no need to bring together physically the members of a set; all that is necessary is that they be grouped together mentally, usually as examples of objects which share some particular property or attribute. For our purposes we shall only consider sets whose elements are chosen from bigger sets which may be thought of as the largest sets of objects of particular kinds. Thus it might be quite reasonable to regard as a conceptual unit the collection of objects listed between the curly brackets here:

$$\{ClementAttlee,\ UnitedKingdom,\ 1945,\ 10DowningStreet\}$$

but we shall not regard this as a set because the four elements are quite different kinds of objects, that is to say, a person, a country, a year and a house. We shall of course need to be able to group together such disparate items, but they will not be called sets. Moreover it would be possible to invent a concept which included persons, countries, years and houses, but it would be of such generality that it would be of little use to us. In this case it might be something like 'entity', for it has to embrace the concrete and the abstract, the animate and the inanimate. The collective nouns mentioned earlier lead us in the right direction. We talk of packs of wolves, prides of lions, swarms of bees and so on; a particular pack of wolves is a set because each of its members is a wolf.

2.1.1   Basic ideas of sets

In order to give examples of sets it is helpful to refer to objects which have commonly used names. Thus we might define various sets of countries as follows:

$EU ==$
  $\{Belgium, France, Germany, Italy,$
  $Luxemburg, Netherlands, Denmark, Greece,$
  $Ireland, United\ Kingdom, Spain, Portugal\}$
$NATO ==$
  $\{Belgium, Canada, Denmark, France, Iceland, Italy,$
  $Luxemburg, Netherlands, Norway, Portugal, United\ Kingdom,$
  $United\ States, Greece, Turkey, Spain, Germany\}$
$Scandinavia == \{Denmark, Finland, Norway, Sweden, Iceland\}$
$Benelux == \{Belgium, Netherlands, Luxemburg\}$

CentralAmerica ==
        {*Costa Rica, Honduras, El Salvador,*
         Guatemala, Nicaragua, Belize, Panama}

where the symbol == may be read 'is defined as' or 'is a name for'[1]. Here we see that a set may be specified by listing its members, enclosing the list in curly braces. Notice that in each case the list contains no duplicates; to list a member twice is harmless but redundant since the set is not changed because it consists of its distinct members. No significance is to be attached to the order in which the members are specified in the list; of course it could be helpful to list them in alphabetical order to ensure that none is left out, but again, the set is the same whatever the order of listing may be. As an example of a set of a different kind:

TextsConsulted ==
        {*Naive Set Theory by Halmos ,*
         Introduction to Mathematical Logic by Mendelson,
         Axiomatic Set Theory by Suppes,
         Sets Logic and Axiomatic Theories by Stoll,
         Logic and Algorithms by Korfhage}

Clearly we want to be able to ask of a set whether a particular object is a member or not. For example, we might want to know if the following statement is true or false:

Belgium is a member of the EU

The symbol used for membership is ∈, so that this becomes:

Belgium ∈ *EU*

In this case the statement is true, according to our earlier definitions. Here is an example of a similar statement which happens to be false:

The Periodic Table by Levi ∈ *TextsConsulted*

There are statements which can be written down which we shall regard as neither true nor false, but meaningless; for example:

Finland ∈ *TextsConsulted*

What renders this meaningless, for our purposes, is that *Finland* is not the same kind of object as the members of *TextsConsulted*, because it is a country not a

---

[1]This is not the usual mathematical symbol. Indeed, it often happens that in mathematics textbooks the ordinary = symbol is used, but as part of a phrase such as 'let $x = 2^y$'; if a distinction is made then the symbols ≡ or $=_d$ are often used. We use == because that is the Z symbol.

book. It could be argued that such a statement is false, but we shall find that it helps to eliminate certain kinds of errors if we treat it as nonsense; the presumption is that if such a statement is made then there must be some confusion. Thus, in order to be taken seriously, a statement involving $\in$ must relate an object and a set whose members are objects of the same kind.

It is sometimes useful to be able to say that an object is not an element of some set; the symbol $\notin$ is used in such cases, so that we may say for example:

> *The Periodic Table by Levi $\notin$ TextsConsulted*

Note that:

> *Finland $\notin$ TextsConsulted*

is again meaningless, for the same reasons as before.

2.1.2   Set operators

We turn now to consider the basic operators which may be used to combine given sets to produce new sets. These are the operators $\cup$, $\cap$ and $\setminus$, known respectively as set union, intersection and difference. The union of two sets consists of those objects which are members of either one of the given sets, or of both sets, the intersection consists of those objects which are members of both of the given sets, and the difference consists of those members of the first set which are not members of the second set. For example,

$EU \cup NATO =$
> $\{Belgium, Canada, Denmark, France, Iceland,$
> $Italy, Luxemburg, Netherlands, Norway, Portugal,$
> $United Kingdom, United States, Greece,$
> $Turkey, Spain, Germany, Ireland\}$

$EU \cap NATO =$
> $\{Belgium, Denmark, France, Italy,$
> $Luxemburg, Netherlands, Portugal, United Kingdom,$
> $Greece, Spain, Germany\}$

$NATO \setminus EU = \{United States, Canada, Iceland, Norway, Turkey\}$

$EU \setminus NATO = \{Ireland\}$

We use the symbol $=$ here rather than the $==$ symbol because we are not defining anything; we are merely saying, for example, that $NATO \setminus EU$ is an expression which describes the same set as the explicitly listed set on the right hand side of the $=$ symbol.

Imagine a situation in which those countries which belong to both the EU and to NATO decide to meet together to hold preliminary discussions of a matter which they feel could involve a conflict of loyalties. The set of countries attending that meeting would be the set $EU \cap NATO$, while the results of their deliberations would be communicated to all the countries of each of the two groups, that is to the set $EU \cup NATO$. The reader can no doubt construct a scenario in which a meeting of the countries in $NATO \setminus EU$ is called.

We saw earlier that care is to be exercised in forming statements concerning membership; similarly, the set operators $\cup$, $\cap$ and $\setminus$ may only be used when the two sets concerned have members of the same kind. Thus the expression:

$$EU \cap TextsConsulted$$

is regarded as having no meaning.

Just as in arithmetic the idea of 0 (zero) arises in answer to the question '$n - -n = ?$', where n is a counting number, so the idea of an empty set arises as the answer to questions of the form '$X \cap Y = ?$' when sets X and Y have no members in common. For example, if we form the set:

$$CentralAmerica \cap Scandinavia$$

we find that it has no members. This could be represented by braces enclosing an empty list, $\{\,\}$, but usually it is represented by the symbol $\emptyset$, so we may write:

$$CentralAmerica \cap Scandinavia = \emptyset$$

However, now that we have been so fussy about only combining sets whose members are of the same kind, the reader may well ask if we have to distinguish between the empty set of countries and the empty set of books. Indeed, do we need an empty set of each different kind? Speaking pedantically, yes we do, but in fact confusion will rarely arise if the same symbol is used for each of them, since the context of use will usually determine which empty set is meant.

2.1.3   Set comparisons

We often want to express the idea that one set is entirely contained within another set, or that the same set may be written down in different ways, perhaps by combining other sets using the set operators. In such cases we employ the symbols $\subseteq$, $\subset$, $=$ and $\neq$, known respectively as the subset symbol, the proper subset symbol, the equality symbol and the inequality symbol. We have already met the $=$ operator in passing; this may be used between two set expressions, and signifies that those expressions describe the same set or, to put it another way, that every element of the set on the left is also an element of the set on the right, and vice versa. As may be expected, the symbol $\neq$, when used to compare two sets, has the meaning that there is at least one element of one of the sets which is not a member of the other set. Frequently we want to talk about sets all of whose members belong to some larger set; such a set is said to be a subset of that larger set. So the following statements are true:

$\{Canada, USA\} \subseteq NATO$
$Benelux \subseteq EU$

while the following is false:

$EU \subseteq NATO$

because there are members of *EU* which are not members of *NATO*. The $\subseteq$ symbol admits the possibility that the subset concerned may in fact be the whole of the set, but the $\subset$ symbol rejects this possibility, whilst allowing all other subsets. Thus:

$Benelux \subset EU$

is true because all members of *Benelux* are indeed members of *EU*, but there are members of *EU* which are not members of *Benelux*, such as *France* and *Germany*. Such a subset is called a proper subset. We shall as usual insist that the use of these new symbols is restricted: they may only stand between sets of the same kind of elements. Thus:

$Benelux \subseteq TextsConsulted$

is neither true nor false, but meaningless.

We can now make some general statements about the set operators which were introduced in the previous subsection; for example, for any sets A, B and C of the same kind, we have the following rules which concern $\cup$ and $\cap$:

$A \cup B = B \cup A$
$A \cap B = B \cap A$
$(A \cup B) \cup C = A \cup (B \cup C)$
$(A \cap B) \cap C = A \cap (B \cap C)$

The first two of these follow directly from the definition of $\cup$ and $\cap$; we shall see examples of the third and fourth of these rules in the exercises which follow, and we shall see how a general argument may be put forward which establishes the truth of these rules, and of other similar rules.

With regard to the following exercises, note that it is not essential to an understanding of the following sections that Exercises 2.2 and 2.3 be done at this point; readers may be content to draw diagrams to convince themselves of the truth of the given rules (see Exercise 2.5). Exercise 2.4 may also be safely skipped on a first reading.

Exercise 2.1 Form the following sets:

(i) ◇ *Scandinavia* \ *NATO*   (ii) ◇ *EU* ∪ *Benelux*

(iii) ◇ *EU* \ *Benelux*   (iv) ◇ *Benelux* \ *EU*

(v) ◇ *NATO* ∩ *Scandinavia*   (vi) ◇ *CentralAmerica* ∩ *Benelux*

(vii) *EU* ∩ (*NATO* ∩ *Scandinavia*)   (viii) (*EU* ∩ *NATO*) ∩ *Scandinavia*

(ix) *EU* ∪ (*NATO* ∪ *Scandinavia*)   (x) (*EU* ∪ *NATO*) ∪ *Scandinavia*

Exercise 2.2 ◇ You should have found that the last two sets of the previous exercise were equal, and similarly the previous two sets were equal. They are examples of the rules:

$$(A \cup B) \cup C = A \cup (B \cup C)$$
$$(A \cap B) \cap C = A \cap (B \cap C)$$

mentioned earlier. If asked to show that two set expressions describe the same set, then it is sufficient to show that every member of the set described by the first expression is also a member of the set described by the second, and vice versa. Take the first of the two rules above:

if $x \in (A \cup B) \cup C$, then $x \in A \cup B$ or $x \in C$ (or both)
    if $x \in A \cup B$ then $x \in A$ or $x \in B$ (or both)
        if $x \in A$ then $x \in A \cup (B \cup C)$
            if $x \in B$ then $x \in B \cup C$, and so $x \in A \cup (B \cup C)$
    if $x \in C$ then $x \in B \cup C$, and so $x \in A \cup (B \cup C)$

In all cases, $x \in A \cup (B \cup C)$, and this completes one part of the argument. Supply the other part of the argument for this rule, and then go on to provide both sides of the argument for the second of the above rules.

Exercise 2.3 Supply arguments for the rules:

(i) ◇ $A \cap (B \cup C) = (A \cap B) \cup (A \cap C)$

(ii) $A \cup (B \cap C) = (A \cup B) \cap (A \cup C)$

(iii) $A \setminus (B \cap C) = (A \setminus B) \cup (A \setminus C)$

(iv) $(A \cup B) \setminus C = (A \setminus C) \cup (B \setminus C)$

(v) $(A \cap B) \cup (A \setminus B) = A$

Illustrate the rules using the sets *EU*, *NATO* and *Scandinavia*.

Exercise 2.4 ◇ To say that $A \subseteq B$ is equivalent to saying that for all objects x of the kind concerned, if $x \in A$ then $x \in B$. Use this fact to show that

(i) $A \subseteq A$ (ii) $\emptyset \subseteq A$ (iii) $A \subseteq A \cup B$

(iv) $A \cap B \subseteq A$ (v) $A \setminus B \subseteq A$

where A and B are any two sets of the same kind of objects. Also argue that if $A \subseteq B$ and $B \subseteq C$ then $A \subseteq C$.

Exercise 2.5 The diagram below is what is known as a Venn diagram:

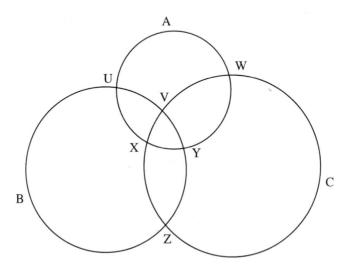

The three circles are intended to represent sets A, B and C, and there are areas corresponding to all the unions and intersections of the three sets, in pairs and all three together. Use the letters on the diagram to describe the areas corresponding to the following:

(i) $\diamond\, A \cup B$ (ii) $\diamond\, A \cap B$ (iii) $\diamond\, A \setminus B$ (iv) $\diamond\, B \setminus A$

(v) $A \cap (B \cup C)$ (vi) $(A \cap B) \cup (A \cap C)$

(vii) $(A \cup B) \setminus C$ (viii) $(A \setminus C) \cup (B \setminus C)$

As an example, the area corresponding to $B \cup (A \cap C)$ is described as $BUVWYZB$. Note that the last two areas should be the same, and likewise the previous two areas are equal; this provides a visual confirmation of the first and fourth rules of Exercise 2.3. Convince yourself of the truth of the other two rules of Exercise 2.3 in a similar way.

2.2   Propositions and predicates

So far we have only been able to specify sets by listing their elements, or by combining other sets using the set operators, $\cup$, $\cap$ and $\setminus$. To list elements explicitly is fine for sets which have only a small number of elements, but it is rather inconvenient if the set is large, and if the set concerned is infinite then clearly we cannot list all of its members.

We would like to be able to specify a set by stating a property which characterises its members. For example, we might wish to talk about the following set:

BigCountries ==
  the set of countries with more than 40 million inhabitants

In this case, the property required of a country c which is to belong to the set may be expressed as follows:

the country c has more than 40 million inhabitants

We may think of this property as a template for a whole class of statements of the form:

the country France has more than 40 million inhabitants
the country Guatemala has more than 40 million inhabitants

and so on, obtained by replacing the place marker c by particular countries. In some cases the statement yielded will be true, in other cases false, but in all cases the resulting statement makes a definite and unambiguous assertion. Such definite statements we call propositions: thus, a proposition may be true or may be false within the system we wish to talk about, but what it asserts is not simply a matter of opinion, nor is it an article of faith or declaration of intent. Of course, statements of opinion, faith and intention are of prime importance in shaping our everyday experience, but the language we are developing here will be of little help in discussing such matters. We shall of course also exclude statements like:

the country The Mill on the Floss has more than 40 million inhabitants

which we shall regard as meaningless since *The Mill on the Floss* is a novel, not a country.

What we called earlier a property or template for a class of propositions we shall in future call a predicate. Thus a predicate is like a proposition with slots to be filled by objects of particular kinds. For any such predicate there is a corresponding set which consists of exactly those objects of the appropriate kind which when used to fill the slots yield true propositions.

In this section we shall examine the ideas of propositions and predicates in more detail; in the following section we shall show how sets may be described using predicates to make precise their defining properties. In the discussion which follows, we shall use as examples of propositions statements about the physical world as we know it, some of which will be true and some of which will be false in that physical world. Whenever we make statements within a logical language, we have in mind particular 'worlds' or 'models' in which those statements are true or false. It is quite possible that a given proposition is true within one model, but false in another.

2.2.1   Combining propositions

Thus far we have only considered simple propositions, but in fact we may construct more complex propositions by combining simpler propositions using certain logical connectives. The simplest way to make a new proposition from a given proposition is to negate it, that is, to construct a proposition which says exactly the opposite. For example, if we take the proposition:

Barcelona is the capital of Spain

we may negate it thus:

Barcelona is not the capital of Spain

We prefer to write this using the negation symbol, $\neg$, as follows:

$\neg$ *Barcelona is the capital of Spain*

As we proceed we shall reduce the use of English in the propositions which we present; in the end everything will be written in a precise and formal way, using mathematical and logical notation. Thus we do not want to rely upon the grammatical structure of English in any essential way, and we prefer to use the negation symbol rather than the English word 'not', which of course serves the same function in everyday usage.

In the example above a false proposition became a true proposition when negated; as expected, a true proposition becomes a false proposition when negated, for example:

Barcelona is the largest city in Catalonia

is true whereas:

$\neg$ *Barcelona is the largest city in Catalonia*

is false. We may summarise what has been said about the $\neg$ symbol in a table as follows, where p stands for any proposition:

p	$\neg\, p$
true	false
false	true

We may also combine two given propositions in various ways to produce new propositions. The most commonly used connectives are $\wedge$, $\vee$, $\Rightarrow$ and $\Leftrightarrow$, known respectively as the 'and', 'or', 'implies' and 'if and only if' connectives. Looking at the 'and' connective first, consider the following composite propositions:

> *Paris is the capital of France*
> $\wedge$ *Brasilia is the capital of Brazil*
>
> *Paris is the capital of France*
> $\wedge$ *Brasilia is the largest city in Brazil*
>
> *Rio de Janeiro is the capital of Brazil*
> $\wedge$ *Paris is the largest city in France*
>
> *São Paolo is the capital of Brazil*
> $\wedge$ *Brasilia is the largest city in Brazil*

Only in the first case are both constituent propositions true, and only in this case do we accept the composite proposition as true. In the second, third and fourth cases the constituents are respectively true and false, false and true, false and false. In these cases we regard the composite propositions as false. Summarising in a table, where p and q stand for any two propositions:

p	q	$p \wedge q$
true	true	true
true	false	false
false	true	false
false	false	false

This definition of the $\wedge$ connective is in accordance with our intuition, but when we come to the $\vee$ connective intuition is not so helpful, because we employ the word 'or' in different and inconsistent ways in normal usage. Consider the following statements:

> *the man is crazy or I'm a monkey's uncle*
> *if you or your spouse were born before 6 April 1924*
> *you may be entitled to age allowance*
> *to be or not to be: that is the question*
> *you may take melon or soup as a starter*

In the first of these, the possibility that both constituent statements are true is not seriously entertained; in the second case, presumably the entitlement is not precluded by both you and your spouse having been born before the qualifying date; in the third case, the possibilities are mutually exclusive since you cannot be and not be; in the fourth case, taken from a notice concerning self-service conference lunch, the melon and the soup are almost certainly intended to be alternatives though this is not explicitly stated. Thus the word 'or' is sometimes used in an exclusive sense, that is to say, it means either one thing or the other but not both, sometimes it is used in an inclusive sense, allowing for both alternatives, and often the alternatives are mutually exclusive in any case, so the question does not arise.

The $\lor$ connective is in fact defined in the inclusive sense; certainly a decision must be made, and it turns out that this makes the connectives $\land$ and $\lor$ complementary in a certain sense (see Exercise 2.6). If we consider the following propositions:

> *Paris is the capital of France*
> $\lor$ *Brasilia is the capital of Brazil*
>
> *Paris is the capital of France*
> $\lor$ *Brasilia is the largest city in Brazil*
>
> *Rio de Janeiro is the capital of Brazil*
> $\lor$ *Paris is the largest city in France*
>
> *São Paolo is the capital of Brazil*
> $\lor$ *Brasilia is the largest city in Brazil*

then according to this definition, all are true except the last, since only the combination false and false makes an $\lor$ of two propositions false. The table for the $\lor$ connective is thus the following:

p	q	$p \lor q$
true	true	true
true	false	true
false	true	true
false	false	false

The 'implies' connective, $\Rightarrow$, is used where we might use the words 'if' and 'then' in ordinary language. For example:

> *if the Power On indicator is lit*
>   *then the unit is connected to the electricity supply*

becomes:

> *the Power On indicator is lit*
> $\Rightarrow$ *the unit is connected to the electricity supply*

Now when we read such a statement as the above in an Instruction Manual, what do we understand by it? Certainly if we see that the indicator is lit, we deduce that the unit is connected to the supply. On the other hand, if the indicator is not lit, we do not know whether the unit is connected to the supply or not; for example, the unit may be connected but not switched on, or the indicator light may be faulty.

The definition of the ⇒ connective is that the composite proposition is only false when the left hand proposition is true and the right hand one is false. Thus we might more precisely capture the meaning of this connective as used in the above proposition as follows:

> *the Power On indicator may not be lit*
> > *but if it is*
> > *then the unit is connected to the electricity supply*

Here is the table for ⇒:

p	q	$p \Rightarrow q$
true	true	true
true	false	false
false	true	true
false	false	true

Reiterating what was said at the beginning of the previous paragraph, $p \Rightarrow q$ is only false when p is true and q is false. An exercise will be found at the end of the section (Exercise 2.6) where the reader is asked to show that the table for $p \Rightarrow q$ is the same as that for $\neg p \lor q$; this means that the ⇒ connective can always be eliminated since it can be replaced by using the ∨ connective and negating the proposition to the left.

Propositions which are composed of simpler propositions using the ⇒ connective play an important role in proofs. If we are told that $p \Rightarrow q$ is true, and we are also told that p is true, then we can deduce that q is true. The argument goes as follows: if p were true and q were false then $p \Rightarrow q$ would be false, which contradicts what we have been told. Another similar proof rule is that if $p \Rightarrow q$ is true and q is false then p is false too. (The reader should construct the argument for this rule.) On the other hand no such deductions can be made in the case that p is false or in the case that q is true. You will find that these proof rules correspond quite precisely to our intuitions about implication.

Taking as an example the statement from the Instruction Manual, if we accept this as true, let us consider what may be deduced and what may not be deduced. Firstly, if we can see that the Power On indicator is lit, we may deduce that the unit is connected to the electricity supply. Secondly, if we know that the unit is certainly not connected to the supply (perhaps it is not plugged in), then we may deduce that the indicator is not lit; if it were this would contradict the Instruction Manual. Thirdly, if we see that the indicator is not lit, we can neither infer that the unit is connected to the supply, nor that it is not connected; either possibility is consistent with the Manual. Lastly, if we know that the unit is connected to the supply, we can neither infer that the indicator is lit, nor that it is not lit; again either is consistent with the Manual.

The $\Leftrightarrow$ connective requires that either both propositions concerned are true, or both are false. It has the table:

p	q	$p \Leftrightarrow q$
true	true	true
true	false	false
false	true	false
false	false	true

To say $p \Leftrightarrow q$ is equivalent to saying $(p \Rightarrow q) \wedge (q \Rightarrow p)$. It is left as an exercise for the reader to demonstrate that this is so. If two expressions involving propositions have the same truth value for all settings of the truth values of the atomic propositions of which they are composed, we say that the two expressions are equivalent; in such circumstances we may also write the $\Leftrightarrow$ connective between the two expressions and assert that the resulting expression is always true.

Exercise 2.6 In order to show that two expressions involving propositions are equivalent we show that they have the same truth value for all possible values of component propositions; for example, to show that $(p \wedge q) \vee r$ and $(p \vee r) \wedge (q \vee r)$ are equivalent we construct the following table, where we use T and F for true and false in order to save space:

p	q	r	$(p \wedge q)$	$\vee$	r	$(p \vee r)$	$\wedge$	$(q \vee r)$
T	T	T	T	T		T	T	T
T	T	F	T	T		T	T	T
T	F	T	F	T		T	T	T
T	F	F	F	F		T	F	F
F	T	T	F	T		T	T	T
F	T	F	F	F		F	F	T
F	F	T	F	T		T	T	T
F	F	F	F	F		F	F	F

Here we fill in the first three columns ensuring that all combinations of true and false for the three propositions p, q and r are present, we then fill in the fourth column of Ts and Fs, then the fifth column, then the sixth and eight columns, and finally the seventh column. That is to say, when we come to work out the truth values for the more complex expressions we must build up from the simpler subexpressions. The fifth and seventh columns are identical and so the formulae are equivalent, which we could also express by saying that:

$$(p \wedge q) \vee r \Leftrightarrow (p \vee r) \wedge (q \vee r)$$

since this formula is true for all settings of p, q and r. Use this method to show the following equivalences:

(i) $\diamond\, (p \Rightarrow q) \Leftrightarrow (\neg\, p \vee q)$

(ii) $\diamond\, (p \wedge q) \wedge r \Leftrightarrow p \wedge (q \wedge r)$

(iii) $\diamond\, (p \vee q) \wedge r \Leftrightarrow (p \wedge r) \vee (q \wedge r)$

(iv) $\diamond\, \neg\, p \vee (p \wedge q) \Leftrightarrow \neg\, p \vee q$

(v) $(\neg\, q \Rightarrow \neg\, p) \Leftrightarrow (p \Rightarrow q)$

(vi) $(p \Rightarrow r) \wedge (q \Rightarrow r) \Leftrightarrow (p \vee q \Rightarrow r)$

(vii) $\neg\, (p \wedge q) \Leftrightarrow \neg\, p \vee \neg\, q$

(viii) $\neg\, (p \vee q) \Leftrightarrow \neg\, p \wedge \neg\, q$

We assume here that $\wedge$ and $\vee$ bind more strongly than does $\Leftrightarrow$.

Exercise 2.7 $\diamond$ Show that $p \Leftrightarrow q$ is equivalent to $(p \Rightarrow q) \wedge (q \Rightarrow p)$.

Exercise 2.8 $\diamond$ Provide the argument for the proof rule: if $p \Rightarrow q$ is true and q is false then p is false too.

Exercise 2.9 $\diamond$ What proof rules may be associated with the $\Leftrightarrow$ connective along the lines of those discussed in connection with the $\Rightarrow$ connective?

Exercise 2.10 $\diamond$ When introducing the $\Rightarrow$ symbol we suggested that this corresponded roughly to the way we use 'if' and 'then' in everyday language. Consider examples such as:

> *if it's a sunny day then we will go for a picnic*
> *if you work hard you will pass your examinations*

(We often leave out the word 'then' in ordinary usage.) In fact we seem to use this kind of construction in different ways, so that there is some ambiguity in all the phrases of this kind that we have presented. How do you interpret the two sentences above, and how would you write them using the logical symbols introduced in this section?

2.2.2   Introducing the quantifiers

We said earlier that a predicate is a template for a class of propositions, or to put it another way, that it is like a proposition with slots to be filled by suitable objects. It often happens that a proposition if examined in more detail has internal structure which can be made explicit in mathematical notation. If we examine the proposition:

> *Beethoven was a composer of opera*

we can paraphrase this by saying:

> *there is an opera of which Beethoven was the composer*

or slightly more formally:

> *there is an opera o such that Beethoven was the composer of o*

In mathematical notation this proposition may be written:

$$\exists\, o : opera \bullet Beethoven\ was\ the\ composer\ of\ o \qquad\qquad [Op1]$$

If we separate:

> *Beethoven was the composer of o*

what we have is a predicate, which has a slot to be filled by operas. Thus:

> *Beethoven was the composer of Fidelio*
> *Beethoven was the composer of The Magic Flute*

are examples of propositions obtained by filling the slot. The symbol $\exists$ is called the 'existential quantifier', and may be read 'there is' or 'there exists'. The sequence '$\exists\, o : opera \bullet$' may be read 'there is an opera o such that'. A proposition formed from a predicate by existential quantification is true if the slot(s) in the predicate can be filled consistently by at least one object of appropriate kind so as to yield a true proposition. In our example [Op1] above, *Fidelio* fulfils this requirement, and in this case it is the only slot filler with this property. On the other hand:

> *Janacek was a composer of opera*

may be expressed:

$$\exists\, o : opera \bullet Janacek\ was\ the\ composer\ of\ o$$

and this time there are several suitable slot fillers, including *Jenufa, The Cunning Little Vixen* and *From the House of the Dead*. In the case:

$$\exists\, o : opera \bullet Brahms\ was\ the\ composer\ of\ o$$

there are no slot fillers which make the predicate yield a true proposition, since *Brahms* never composed an opera. In such cases, a proposition formed by existential quantification is false.

Now let us consider the proposition:

> *São Paolo is bigger than any city in Europe*

We can paraphrase this as follows:

> *for every city c,*
> > *if c is in Europe then São Paolo is bigger than c*

or more formally we write:

> $\forall\, c : city \bullet$
> > *c is in Europe* $\Rightarrow$ *São Paolo is bigger than c*   [SP1]

The symbol $\forall$ is called the universal quantifier, and may be read 'for every'. The sequence '$\forall\, c : city \bullet$' may be read as 'for every city c'. Again if we separate the part which follows the $\bullet$ we have a predicate:

> *c in Europe* $\Rightarrow$ *São Paolo is bigger than c*   [SP2]

which has slots to be filled by cities. The slots may be filled as follows, for example:

> *Paris in Europe* $\Rightarrow$ *São Paolo bigger than Paris*   [SP2a]
> *New York in Europe* $\Rightarrow$ *São Paolo bigger than New York*   [SP2b]
> *São Paolo in Europe* $\Rightarrow$ *São Paolo bigger than São Paolo*   [SP2c]

and in all of these cases the propositions yielded are true, as we shall now show. As far as we can ascertain, *São* Paolo is indeed bigger than any European city so that if such a city is used as a slot filler, as in [SP2a] above, the $\Rightarrow$ connective stands between two true propositions. On the other hand if a non-European city is chosen as a slot filler, as in [SP2b, c], then the proposition to the left of $\Rightarrow$ is false, in which case the composite proposition is true regardless of the truth or falsity of the proposition to the right. Thus there is no way of filling the slots so as to yield a false proposition, and in these circumstances the universally quantified proposition is true. To put it another way, a universally quantified predicate will be false only when there is a slot filler for the predicate which makes the resulting proposition false.

Taking up this last point, if we say that:

> $\forall\, c : city \bullet$
> > *c is in Europe* $\Rightarrow$ *São Paolo is bigger than c*

then this is the same as saying:

> $\neg\, \exists\, c : city \bullet$
> > $\neg\, (c$ *is in Europe* $\Rightarrow$ *São Paolo is bigger than c*)

and similarly, to say that:

> $\exists\, o : opera \bullet$ *Beethoven was the composer of o*

is to say that:

$\neg \; \forall \, o : opera \; \bullet \; \neg \; Beethoven \; was \; the \; composer \; of \; o$

If we try to paraphrase this last proposition in ordinary language we might say:

it is not the case that Beethoven was not the composer of any opera

Clearly this is a much more clumsy way to express the same idea, so although theoretically we need only one of the quantifiers, we shall use whichever seems the most natural in each context.

As a further example of propositions constructed by quantification, we shall express the proposition:

São Paolo is bigger than any other city in the same country

In this sentence we can see both the vagueness of natural language and its conciseness. On the one hand, we could ask 'in the same country as what?' but we do really know what it means; on the other hand, the fact that we say 'the same country' tells us that there is only one such country. Before trying to write the sentence with quantifiers, we try to make it a little more precise:

there is a certain country to which São Paolo belongs,
and São Paolo is bigger than any other city in that country

We can now translate into the form:

$\exists \, co : country \; \bullet$
    São Paolo is in co $\land$
    $\forall \, ci : city \; \bullet$
        ci is in co $\land \; \neg \; ci$ *is São Paolo*
            $\Rightarrow$ *São Paolo is bigger than ci*   [SP3]

We have used indentation here to indicate the structure of the composite proposition. Let us now take it apart, in order to see how it is that this proposition is true according to our definitions of the logical symbols used, referring to the physical world for each atomic fact concerned. Firstly, we remove the outer quantifier:

    São Paolo is in co $\land$
    $\forall \, ci : city \; \bullet$
        ci is in co $\land \; \neg \; ci$ *is São Paolo*
            $\Rightarrow$ *São Paolo is bigger than ci*   [SP4]

This is a composite proposition with slots to be filled, namely those represented by the name *co*. Thus we may fill those slots, first by *Paraguay*, then by *Brazil*, for example:

    São Paolo is in Paraguay $\land$

$\forall\ ci : city \bullet$
    ci is in Paraguay $\wedge \neg\ ci$ *is São Paolo*
        $\Rightarrow$ *São Paolo is bigger than ci*   [*SP4a*]

São Paolo is in Brazil $\wedge$
$\forall\ ci : city \bullet$
    ci is in Brazil $\wedge \neg\ ci$ *is São Paolo*
        $\Rightarrow$ *São Paolo is bigger than ci*   [*SP4b*]

(Note that every time we fill the *co* slots, the universally quantified part of the predicate becomes a proposition; the $\forall$ in effect hides, or we may say 'binds', the *ci* slots.) We can see straight away that the first of these propositions, [*SP4a*], is false since:

São Paolo is in Paraguay

is false, and an $\wedge$ of two propositions is only true when both of those propositions are true. We shall find that [*SP4b*] is true, since it has within it the proposition:

São Paolo is in Brazil

which is true, and the proposition:

$\forall\ ci : city \bullet$
    ci is in Brazil $\wedge \neg\ ci$ *is São Paolo*
        $\Rightarrow$ *São Paolo is bigger than ci*   [*SP5*]

which we shall find is also true. (We assume that $\wedge$ and $\vee$ bind more strongly than does $\Rightarrow$.) If we separate out the predicate:

ci is in Brazil $\wedge \neg\ ci$ *is São Paolo*
    $\Rightarrow$ *São Paolo is bigger than ci*   [*SP6*]

it has slots *ci* which may be filled, for example, by *Brasilia*, by *São Paolo* and by *Montevideo*:

Brasilia is in Brazil $\wedge \neg$ *Brasilia is São Paolo*
    $\Rightarrow$ *São Paolo is bigger than Brasilia*   [*SP6a*]
São Paolo is in Brazil $\wedge \neg$ *São Paolo is São Paolo*
    $\Rightarrow$ *São Paolo is bigger than São Paolo*   [*SP6b*]
Montevideo is in Brazil $\wedge \neg$ *Montevideo is São Paolo*
    $\Rightarrow$ *São Paolo is bigger than Montevideo*   [*SP6c*]

All of these propositions are true. Since Brasilia is in fact in Brazil and *São* Paolo is indeed the biggest city in Brazil, [*SP6a*] is true because the $\Rightarrow$ connective stands between two propositions which are themselves both true. The same would happen for any substitution of a city in Brazil other than *São* Paolo itself. Since in [*SP6b*]:

> ¬ *São Paolo is São Paolo*

is clearly false and since in [*SP6c*]:

> *Montevideo is in Brazil*

is false, what stands to the left of the $\Rightarrow$ connective in [*SP6b, c*] is false in each case; but when the left side proposition of an $\Rightarrow$ is false the composite proposition is always true regardless of the truth or falsity of the right side proposition. [*SP6c*] is an example of what happens if we substitute for *ci* a city which is not in Brazil. Thus we see that a true proposition is yielded for every slot filling city in [*SP6*], and thus the universal quantification yields a true proposition, [*SP5*]; thus, in turn, [*SP4b*] is also true, and so [*SP4*] is true when we put *Brazil* for *co*, and thus, finally, [*SP3*] is true, since one such case is enough.

Exercise 2.11 $\diamond$ Express each of the following in English in a way which sounds as natural as you can make it:

(i) $\exists\, p : person \bullet$
$\qquad \forall\, n : person \bullet$
$\qquad\qquad n$ is a neighbour of $p \Rightarrow p$ never speaks to n

(ii) $\forall\, p : person \bullet$
$\qquad \exists\, n : person \bullet$
$\qquad\qquad \forall\, t : person \bullet$
$\qquad\qquad\qquad \neg\, n = t \Rightarrow \neg\, n$ lives with t
$\qquad\qquad \wedge\, p$ knows n

(iii) $\exists\, co : country \bullet$
$\qquad \exists\, ci : city \bullet$
$\qquad\qquad ci$ in $co \wedge$
$\qquad\qquad$ the population of ci is greater than that of the capital of co

Exercise 2.12 Express each of the following using quantifiers and logical connectives wherever appropriate:

(i) $\diamond$ all the nice girls love a sailor

(ii) $\diamond$ all that glisters is not gold

(iii) ◇ Paris is the most romantic of European capitals

(iv) ◇ there are regions in Asia where the average rainfall is more than five times that of any European country

(v) in all the countries of South America, the annual rate of inflation for 1995 exceeds that of any member country of the EU

(vi) in my Spanish evening class, the oldest student is more than four times as old as the youngest student

2.2.3   Quantifiers applied to lists of variables

Consider a proposition such as:

$$\forall\, x : X \bullet (\forall\, y : Y \bullet x \text{ and } y \text{ are related})$$

where X and Y are kinds of objects, possibly the same kind in each case. The proposition is only true if:

$$\forall\, y : Y \bullet x \text{ and } y \text{ are related}$$

is true for all values of x, and this is only true for a particular value of x if:

$$x \text{ and } y \text{ are related}$$

is true for all values of y. All of this amounts to saying that *x and y are related* must be true for all values of x and of y. The same would be so if we reversed the order of quantification:

$$\forall\, y : Y \bullet (\forall\, x : X \bullet x \text{ and } y \text{ are related})$$

It helps to reduce the number of brackets if we contract double or multiple quantifications of the same kind, and thus we abbreviate to:

$$\forall\, x : X; y : Y \bullet x \text{ and } y \text{ are related}$$

Of course, this could be done whether or not the order of quantification were important, but we have also discovered that in fact the order of universal quantification does not affect the meaning. In the exercises which follow we invite the reader to consider other similar contractions and re-orderings.

Exercise 2.13 ◇ Argue that:

$$\exists\, x : X \bullet (\exists\, y : Y \bullet x \text{ and } y \text{ are related})$$

has the same meaning if the order of the quantifiers is reversed.

Exercise 2.14 ◇ Express the following two propositions in English as naturally as you can:

$$\forall\, ch : person \bullet (\exists\, par : person \bullet par\ is\ a\ parent\ of\ ch)$$
$$\exists\, par : person \bullet (\forall\, ch : person \bullet par\ is\ a\ parent\ of\ ch)$$

You should discover that they mean quite different things, so that it is not in general possible to reverse the order of a ∀ quantification and an ∃ quantification. However, one of the two propositions above is in fact stronger than the other, or to put it another way, if one of them is true then so is the other. Which is the stronger? Can you make a general statement about reversing the order of two different quantifications?

2.3   More about sets

In this section we look at further aspects of the use of sets within the kind of mathematical language upon which Z is based. We look in more detail at the idea of sets defined by properties of their members; we look at the notion of a tuple, and how we can combine sets and tuples in various ways to build a rich collection of types from given basic types; we see that sets can themselves be members of other sets.

2.3.1   Defining sets using predicates

Now we shall show how we may define sets by giving properties which characterise their members. The definition for *BigCountries*, introduced in the previous section, is quite simple:

$$BigCountries == \{c : country \mid c\ has\ more\ than\ 40\ million\ inhabitants\}$$

where we may read the sequence '*c : country* |' as 'those countries c such that'. Notice that what follows the '|' is a predicate, and the set being defined consists of exactly those slot fillers which yield a true proposition. We may define the set of novels by George Eliot using a slightly more complex predicate:

$$EliotNovels ==$$
$$\{b : book \mid b\ was\ written\ by\ George\ Eliot \wedge b\ is\ a\ novel\}$$

The next two sets have predicates involving existential quantification:

$$Sixes == \{n : integer \mid \exists\, m : integer \bullet n = 6 \times m\}$$
$$Capitals ==$$
$$\{ci : city \mid \exists\, co : country \bullet ci\ is\ the\ seat\ of\ government\ of\ co\}$$

Sixes is the set of multiples of 6, and *Capitals* is the set of capital cities. For our final example:

> *the set of cities with more inhabitants*
> *than any other city in the same country*

the appropriate predicate is a generalisation of a proposition which we encountered in the previous section, namely:

> *São Paolo is bigger than any other city in the same country*

Thus we define:

$$BiggestCities ==$$
$$\{macropolis : city \mid$$
$$\exists\, co : country \bullet$$
$$macropolis \text{ is in } co \land$$
$$\forall\, ci : city \bullet$$
$$ci \text{ is in } co \land \neg\ ci \text{ is macropolis}$$
$$\Rightarrow macropolis \text{ is bigger than } ci\}$$

Exercise 2.15 Define the following sets by expressing their characteristic properties in the notation discussed in this section:

(i) ⋄ *PrimeNumbers* ==
> the set of positive integers which are not divisible
> by any positive integer other than 1 or themselves

(ii) ⋄ *ShakespeareHistorical* ==
> the set of plays by Shakespeare based on historical events

(iii) ⋄ *ToryEnclaves* ==
> the set of parliamentary constituencies which elected
> a Conservative member of parliament, but are surrounded
> by constituencies which elected members from parties
> other than the Conservative party

(iv) ⋄ *Biographies* ==
> the set of biographies published as books in English

(v) ⋄ *PostWarAutobiographies* ==
> the set of autobiographies published in English since 1945

(vi) ⋄ *Misanthropists* ==
> the set of people who do not speak to any of their neighbours

(vii) *SciFiAddicts* ==
>> the set of people who read no books other than
>> science fiction novels

(viii) *UniLinguists* ==
>> the set of people who speak only their native language

(ix) *LawrenceFans* ==
>> the set of people who have read all the published
>> novels of D H Lawrence

2.3.2   Tuples and sets of tuples

In ordinary usage, the word 'pair' sometimes means just a set of two objects of the same kind, such as a pair of candlesticks or a pair of hinges, but more often the two objects concerned are similar but complementary in some respect, as for example a pair of gloves or a pair of shoes, where each pair consists of a left and a right, or a pair of rabbits or ballroom dancing partners, where each pair consists of a male and a female.

For the purposes of writing specifications, we shall often want to consider pairs where the objects concerned are not necessarily of the same kind, though the elements will each play a distinctive role within the pairs. A pair will not be regarded as a set at all; indeed it could not be a set if the elements are of different kinds. We also extend the notion of a pair in the obvious way to triples, quadruples, and so on. (The general word is 'tuple'.) To be more precise we should speak of 'ordered pairs' (or more generally of ordered tuples), for we shall always think of a pair as having a first component and a second component. Again notice that a pair cannot be just a set, since there is in general no notion of ordering amongst the members of a set. We may form sets of ordered pairs; in such a set, the first components of the pairs will all be of the same kind, and play the same role, and similarly the second components of the pairs will all be of another kind, and will play a different role.

A set of ordered pairs is rather like a table which we might find in a book, displayed in two columns. For example, an encyclopaedia might contain a table of countries and their capital cities; the information contained in such a table could be captured in a definition such as:

> *CountriesAndCapitals* ==
>> {(*UK*, *London*), (*USA*, *Washington*), (*USSR*, *Moscow*), ...}

where the dots, ..., indicate a missing list of pairs for all the other countries of the world. Recall that the elements of a set must all be of the same kind. So, what kind of elements does this set contain? We say that this is a set of (*country*, *city*) pairs; we use the brackets here to group together the names of the kinds which make up the pairs, just as we did earlier to group together the pairs of objects. Also note that though the table in the encyclopaedia would be set out in order according to some criterion, perhaps alphabetically by country, this information is not preserved in the definition; such ordering is after all only a matter of convenience in accessing the information in the table. If we wanted to define the same set by its characteristic property, we should write:

$CountriesAndCapitals$ ==
　　　$\{co : country;\ ca : city \mid ca\ is\ the\ seat\ of\ government\ of\ co\}$

This definition does not of course contain the explicit information which the previous definition would provide if it were complete. Here are some further examples of sets of ordered pairs:

$MixedDoubles$ ==
　　　$\{m, f : person \mid$
　　　　　　$m\ is\ male \wedge f\ is\ female \wedge$
　　　　　　$m\ and\ f\ have\ played\ as\ a\ mixed\ double\ in\ a$
　　　　　　　　$professional\ tennis\ tournament\}$

which is a set of $(person, person)$ pairs (note that $m, f : person$ is an abbreviation for $m : person;\ f : person$),

$ProfessionalInstrumentalists$ ==
　　　$\{p : person;\ inst : musical\ instrument \mid$
　　　　　　$p\ earns\ a\ living\ as\ a\ player\ of\ inst\}$

which is a set of $(person, musical\ instrument)$ pairs, and:

$Ensembles$ ==
　　　$\{n : group\ name;\ m : set\ of\ (person, musical\ instrument) \mid$
　　　　　$\forall i : (person, musical\ instrument) \bullet$
　　　　　　$i \in m \Rightarrow i \in ProfessionalInstrumentalists$
　　　　$\wedge m\ is\ the\ set\ of\ members\ of\ the\ ensemble\ known\ as\ n\}$

which is a set of:

$(group\ name, set\ of\ (person, musical\ instrument))$

pairs, where we see that a set can be used as a component of a pair, or more generally, of a tuple. Finally we give an example of a set of triples:

$Papacy$ == $\{p : person;\ ds, df : year \mid p\ was\ Pope\ from\ ds\ to\ df\}$

in this case a set of $(person, year, year)$ triples.

Exercise 2.16 ⬦ Give definitions by predicate for the following sets:

(i) *CoPrimes* ==
> *the set of (number,number) pairs having no proper factors*
> *in common, the first of the pair being greater than*
> *the second of the pair*

(ii) *TopOfThePops* ==
> *the set of (group name,title,date) triples corresponding to*
> *the best selling singles since 1950, where the date is the Saturday*
> *of the week when the record concerned sold most copies*

(iii) *GrandNationalWinners* ==
> *the set of (horse,rider,trainer,year) quadruples for horses*
> *winning the Grand National since 1950*

2.3.3   Sets of sets

We have seen that a set can be a component of a tuple, and we have defined various sets of tuples. Another frequently useful kind of set has sets as its members; that is to say, it is a set of sets. For example, suppose a darts tournament is to be arranged, and that *Competitors* is the set of those taking part. There is to be a first round in which each player must play one match against each of the other players, and the results of this round will select four players to go through to the second round. We shall assume that *Competitors* has more than four members. Now, the matches to be played in the first round correspond to all the subsets of two members of *Competitors*.

> *FirstRoundMatches* ==
> > $\{m : set\ of\ players\ |$
> > > $m\ has\ two\ members \land m \subset Competitors\}$

Note that we do not want a set of pairs, since there are no distinctive roles to be played by the two competitors in a match; they take part in a match as equals. Contrast this with the arrangement of the fixtures for a division of the Football League; in this case we do want all pairs of different member clubs, the first member being the home team and the second being the team to play away, assuming that each team must play every other team both at home and away during the season.

We can perhaps now begin to see that a hierarchy of different kinds is developing; we have had sets of pairs and sets of sets, and we could also have pairs of sets, sets of pairs of sets and so on. We shall not pursue this any further at this point because it will be much easier to discuss when we have more of the Z notation. However, we now have sufficient notation to make a first attempt at specification, as we shall see in the following chapter.

Exercise 2.17 ◇ Define the set:

> *PremierLeagueFixtures* ==
> > *the set of all pairs of different member clubs of the Premier League*

assuming that the *Premier League* is a *set of clubs*.

Exercise 2.18 ◇ Define the sets of sets:

(i) *CoPrimeSets*1 ==
> *those subsets of the positive numbers such that there is no*
> *proper factor common to all their members*

(ii) *CoPrimeSets*2 ==
> *those subsets of the positive numbers such that no two distinct*
> *members have a proper common factor*

Exercise 2.19 Define the set:

> *FactorPairs* ==
> > *the set of pairs for each of which*
> > > *the first component is a positive number and*
> > > *the second component is*
> > > > *the set of pairs of positive numbers*
> > > > *whose product is equal to the first component*

2.4   Further reading

For the reader who would like to read more about logic and set theory there are a great many textbooks which cover this material from a mathematical standpoint. Some titles of a suitably introductory nature are [NS85] and [Lem90].

Chapter 3

A first specification

In this chapter we introduce many of the important concepts of specification in the Z style; of course we have met only a small subset of the notation at this stage so that what we shall describe here conforms more to the spirit than to the letter of that style[1]. We shall first give a presentation of the specification for the chosen application which concentrates on explaining how we say what needs to be said using the notation so far introduced. We shall then re-run the specification in a style much closer to a proper specification, where it would normally be assumed that the reader already understood the notation and the way it was used.

3.1   An explanatory presentation

Suppose you want to learn a foreign language, and you would like to keep a list of words and their translations as an aid to revising and extending your vocabulary in the new language. We shall adopt a very simple view of the problem: we shall assume that it is sufficient to record a set of pairs of words, each pair comprising a word in your native language and a corresponding word in the foreign language. This is the kind of information provided by a very simple pocket bilingual dictionary. Using such a dictionary, it is possible to look up a word in the native language section to find which word or words can be used as translations of that native word, and similarly a foreign word can be looked up to discover possible native translations. In a pocket dictionary, space will usually preclude any hints about which words amongst the possible translations are the most appropriate in any given circumstances; in reality, such explanation is essential if you are to avoid making a fool of yourself, or at least raising a smile or an eyebrow when you visit a country where the foreign language is spoken. Another gross simplification we

---

[1]The departures from the usual Z style can only be explained when we have introduced schemas (see Chapter 6). Also see the Preface, where we discuss the rationale for the order of presentation which we have adopted.

are making here is to assume that it is always possible to translate a word in one language by a word in another language; it is often the case that a whole phrase will have to be recast so that it can be translated, because there is no word for word translation.

One feature common to all bilingual dictionaries, whatever their size, is that the words are arranged in two alphabetical listings, one for the native words, and one for the foreign words. This is just a matter of convenience, so that we have easy access to the information held between the covers of the dictionary. If we use a computer to hold this same information, it is not essential that there should be such alphabetical listings of the words, and indeed if we want access to the information to be as fast as possible this is probably not the best way to organise things. Thus, at this stage we are not going to concern ourselves with how the information is to be organised, but only with the content of that information. Of course if we want a printed version of our expanding vocabulary at some stage we may well want an alphabetical listing of words, but this can be produced when requested, and need not correspond to the organisation of the information as recorded by the computer system.

As we said earlier, we shall simply record a set of word pairs. When a word pair is recorded this signifies that:

- the native word of the pair may sometimes be translated by the foreign word of the pair, and

- the foreign word may sometimes be translated by the native word.

In order to make our example slightly more realistic, we shall impose a constraint upon the words which may be entered into the vocabulary. Most languages have rules of some kind concerning the way words may be built from individual characters. There are languages where whole words are represented by ideograms, as in Japanese for example; in this case the rules would be particularly simple. In languages where words are made from quite a small set of characters which correspond to the sounds which we make when we utter the words, there are usually some combinations of letters which would not be possible in any existing words of that language. For example, in English the combinations 'qz', 'xk' and 'jf' never occur, and no word ever has more than two consecutive identical characters. We are going to require that any words entered into our vocabulary must satisfy the rules (they are known as orthographic rules) of the language to which they belong.

Since we are thinking about the specification of a general system which we hope will be applicable to any pair of languages, we are not going to try to say anything at this stage about the particular form of the orthographic rules. We take as given two sets, *Native* and *Foreign*, from which the words of the two languages are drawn. These sets include all sequences of characters which belong to the alphabet of the languages concerned, even those sequences which fail to satisfy the orthographic rules. In general the two alphabets concerned will be different. We may need the Roman and Cyrillic alphabets, for example, if we want an English-Russian vocabulary. Even if both languages are based on the Roman alphabet, different accented characters may be employed in the two languages; if we need an English-French vocabulary, then the alphabet for English consists of the twenty-six letters of our alphabet, in upper and lower case, whilst in French we need in addition various accented characters such as 'é' and 'ç'. Again, since we want our system to be independent of any particular languages at this stage, we shall not give any details about the given sets *Native* and *Foreign*. This is the normal situation for given sets; we assume nothing about the structure of the individual members of such sets. The constraints imposed by the orthographic rules will be represented by requiring that words of the languages belong to two subsets *OrthoNative* and *OrthoForeign*. Note that this embraces the possibility that the subset for a language may consist of the words in a given single language dictionary; nowadays this is quite realistic since most word processing packages provide a spelling checker which in fact includes such a standard dictionary in machine accessible form. If such dictionaries are not available, then ultimately these sets would be described by the properties which distinguish correctly formed words. The reader may wonder why we do not simply take *OrthoNative* and *OrthoForeign* as the two given sets; the point here is that the system will have to deal with non-words too, even if only to report that they fail to satisfy the orthographic rules.

We are ready to make a more precise statement about what is a properly formed vocabulary. First, we state that *Native* and *Foreign* are the given sets, which is written as follows:

$$[Native, Foreign]$$

we then go on to declare the subsets of properly formed words:

$$OrthoNative : set\ of\ Native$$
$$OrthoForeign : set\ of\ Foreign$$

and then we describe well-formed vocabularies:

$$WellFormedVocabs ==$$
$$\{\, V : set\ of\ (Native, Foreign)\ |$$
$$\forall\, n : Native;\ f : Foreign \bullet$$
$$(n, f) \in V \Rightarrow$$
$$n \in OrthoNative \wedge f \in OrthoForeign\}$$

The subsets *OrthoNative* and *OrthoForeign* have to be known throughout the specification, so we introduce them at the head of the specification, stating what kinds of objects they are, just as we introduce the names of objects in a set description. In the case of *WellFormedVocabs* we give a set description in terms of the given sets, and of the subsets *OrthoNative* and *OrthoForeign*.

Now what kinds of operations do we want to be able to perform on a well-formed vocabulary? Obviously we shall want to be able to add new pairs of words to expand our vocabulary, and we shall want to be able to ask for the translations of a given native word into the foreign language and, conversely, for the translations of a foreign word into the native language. We shall call these operations *AddPair*, *ToForeign* and *ToNative*. But what is an operation? And how are we to describe an operation in the notation which we have been developing? In full generality we say that an operation may receive certain objects as inputs, may yield certain objects as outputs, and may change certain objects.

Here we digress for a moment, because we have never before suggested that an object might change. We have thought of objects as fixed entities; we have not devoted our attention to the passage of time, so the question of whether objects might change as time progressed has not arisen. Consider for a moment the object known as the River Thames. Is there anything fixed about the Thames? Certainly not the body of water which flows to the sea between its banks. Nor is it the course of the river; this changes too, though usually more slowly. And then, where is the course when we reach the estuary? Is it something to do with high water? Is this fixed? Again, think of the object known as London. Is a city the people who live there? Is it to do with geographical position, with buildings and roads, or with administrative structures set up to ensure the well being of its inhabitants? All these are changing, just as the river which flows through it. So what is it that persists about London, or the Thames? There are no simple answers here, and it seems that we shall have to admit that everything changes in the real world and that the objects to which we give names are not fixed but in a perpetual state of flux. We might think of an object such as London or the Thames as a succession of snapshots of a process of some kind. We may identify certain attributes of that process, and then at each snapshot these attributes have fixed objects as their values. If we want to use mathematical notation to describe such process objects we must select a set of attributes which are sufficient for the purposes we have in mind, ignoring irrelevant details, and we shall have to be content to discuss the values of those attributes and the relationships amongst those attribute values whenever a snapshot is taken.

To give names to process objects does not accord with the normal usage of names in mathematics. In mathematical notation, a name is thought of as standing for a fixed object from amongst a set of objects; mathematical formulæ express relationships between fixed objects, possibly of different kinds. In contrast, in the older computer programming languages names are used quite differently. Readers familiar with languages such as Basic, Fortran or Pascal will know that it is quite normal for different objects to be associated with the same name at different points of the computation. Thus in traditional programming languages names are used rather as they are used when we refer to process objects in the physical world. We can think of a programming language name as standing for the succession of values with which it is associated during the course of the computation. Here it is much easier to answer the question 'what is it that persists?' since we may imagine that a name is associated with a box, usually known as a location, into which new values are put at various moments during execution of the program.

When we write specifications we use names only in the mathematical way, never in the programming language way. In the application we have been considering in this section, the expanding vocabulary is a process-object, because we think of it as persisting whilst various operations are performed upon it, and questions are asked of it. The persistence of such objects will only be recognised by the use of naming conventions which will be described as we show how to define the required vocabulary operations. When we think of an operation as changing an object we shall need to refer to the object as it was before the operation and as it is after the operation. We shall give different names to the before and after objects, so that it may seem that there is no real distinction between a before object and an input object, or between an after object and an output object. The distinction is only made as we interpret the notation as a statement about the real world, or that part of the world which we are trying to describe formally. Though no formal distinctions are made, it will be easier to understand the statements we write if the names we use give hints about the roles which the objects so named are to play in the system described, and in particular if it is made clear which objects are to be thought of as before objects, which as after objects, which as inputs and which as outputs. The Z notation adopts certain conventions in order to make these distinctions, and since these are sufficiently suggestive and concise we shall adopt them immediately. We should emphasise that we choose to use only a subset of the facilities of Z at this stage so that we do not have to introduce too many new forms of notation before we can write even our first specification; there are many points at which, with all the facilities of Z at our disposal, more succinct forms of expression would be possible.

Now let us look in detail at the operations we need to describe. For the *AddPair* operation:

- the input objects are the two words concerned, a native and a foreign word

- there are no output objects

- the vocabulary is changed

We define the operation formally by describing the relationship which must exist between all the objects involved, the inputs, the outputs, the before and after objects; that is to say, we shall define the operation as a set of tuples whose members are appropriately related, in accordance with the intended meaning of

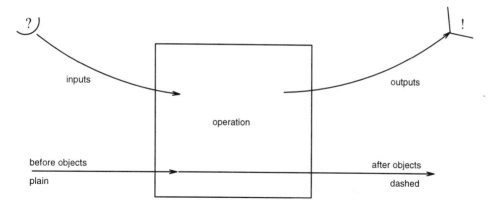

Figure 3.1: Naming conventions for operations

the operation. In this case:

> $AddPair ==$
> > $\{\,Vocab,\ Vocab' : set\ of\ (Native, Foreign);$
> > $n? : Native;\ f? : Foreign\ |$
> > > $Vocab \in WellFormedVocabs \wedge$
> > > $n? \in OrthoNative \wedge f? \in OrthoForeign \wedge$
> > > $Vocab' = Vocab \cup \{(n?, f?)\}\ \}$

where the defining predicate requires:

- that the current vocabulary be well-formed

- that the input words satisfy the orthographic rules

- that the new vocabulary be formed by taking the union of the old vocabulary and the set with just one member formed by making a pair from the two input words

The notational conventions we spoke of earlier (see Figure 3.1) are as follows:

- that input objects have names ending in '?'

- that output objects have names ending in '!' (no examples here)

- that an after object has the same name as the corresponding before object, but with a dash added

The reader may feel that the above description of the *AddPair* operation simply states the obvious; if this is so, all well and good. We set out to do no more than state the obvious precisely and unambiguously. Moving on to the operation *ToForeign*,

- it has a native word as input

- it has a set of foreign words as output

- it leaves the vocabulary unchanged

and is defined as follows:

$$ToForeign ==$$
$$\{\,Vocab,\ Vocab' : set\ of\ (Native,\ Foreign);$$
$$n? : Native;\ ftrans! : set\ of\ Foreign \mid$$
$$Vocab \in WellFormedVocabs \wedge$$
$$Vocab' = Vocab \wedge$$
$$n? \in OrthoNative \wedge$$
$$ftrans! = \{f : Foreign \mid (n?, f) \in Vocab\}\,\}$$

which is to say that:

- the vocabulary should be well-formed

- the vocabulary is unchanged

- the input word must satisfy the orthographic rules

- the output is the set of foreign words which occur as second elements in pairs belonging to the vocabulary whose first elements are the input word

It may seem odd to use two names, *Vocab* and *Vocab'*, for the before and after vocabularies when they are in fact equal. This is just a matter of convenience: we could divide operations into two classes, those which really do change the persistent objects, and those which merely enquire of them without making any changes. We take the view that potentially an operation may change the persistent objects, but sometimes it happens that they do not; this latter state of affairs can always be described in the defining predicate by setting equal the corresponding before and after objects.

The operation *ToNative* is of course very similar to *ToForeign* and will be left as an exercise for the reader.

As we have described the operations *AddPair* and *ToForeign*, the inputs must satisfy certain constraints, and the specifications say nothing about what might happen if these constraints are violated. We shall have more to say about this later. Similarly, the vocabularies are also required to be well-formed, but we do not want to consider what might happen if they are not. Rather we have in mind that there is an initialisation operation which creates a first well-formed vocabulary, and then all further operations, though they may change the vocabulary, are required to preserve this property of well-formedness.

It is easy to supply an initial well-formed vocabulary, since:

$$\emptyset \in \textit{WellFormedVocabs}$$

In general we describe the initialisation of a system by defining a set of acceptable starting configurations. For our present vocabulary system we define *InitVocab* as follows:

$$\textit{InitVocab} == \{\, \textit{Vocab}' : \textit{set of } (\textit{Native}, \textit{Foreign}) \mid \textit{Vocab}' = \emptyset \,\}$$

Here we use *Vocab'* as the variable to suggest that initialisation is like an operation which produces after objects which are acceptable as starting values for the persistent objects of the system. Admittedly, in this very simple case, this seems a complicated way of saying that the system should start with an empty vocabulary.

Do the operations we have defined preserve the well-formedness of the vocabulary? Since the operations *ToForeign* and *ToNative* do not change the vocabulary they clearly present no problem on this score. Now consider the *AddPair* operation. We have the relationship:

$$\textit{Vocab}' = \textit{Vocab} \cup \{(n?, f?)\}$$

In this case, we know that *Vocab* is well-formed, and we know that $n?$ and $f?$ satisfy the orthographic rules, so that the set $\{(n?, f?)\}$ is also a very small but well-formed vocabulary with only one pair of words. Now, if we take the union of two well-formed vocabularies, is the result well-formed? Clearly the answer is yes, since all the member pairs of such a union are members of one or other of the two given vocabularies, all of whose members satisfy the rules. This argument is of course rather informal; later on we shall discuss how we may make such arguments more formal. For the moment, we just want to make the point that there will be properties of the persistent objects which we want to be always true, at every stage of the execution of the system as operations are performed, and thus there will be obligations upon the specifier to demonstrate that these properties are indeed preserved by each of the defined operations.

We have so far only specified a few very basic operations which might be required for our vocabulary system. There are other useful operations which come to mind, such as a provision for random testing of the user's knowledge of the existing vocabulary, and the printing of alphabetical listings of the words in the vocabulary. Using the simple specification tools we have so far assembled it would be difficult to describe such operations adequately, so we shall defer their description until we come to respecify the whole system having previously introduced much more of the Z notation. For the present, we shall address the simpler problem of how the system is to handle words which do not satisfy the orthographic rules.

The operation *AddPair* as defined earlier made no provision for the possibility that one or other of the input words might be faulty. Perhaps we need another operation such as *AddPairError* defined as follows:

> *AddPairError* ==
> {*Vocab*, *Vocab'* : *set of* (*Native*, *Foreign*);
> *n*? : *Native*; *f*? : *Foreign* |
> *Vocab* ∈ *WellFormedVocabs*
> ∧ (*n*? ∉ *OrthoNative* ∨ *f*? ∉ *OrthoForeign*)
> ∧ *Vocab'* = *Vocab*}

where the predicate specifies that one of the words is faulty, and that the vocabulary is unchanged. Up to a point this is fine; the problem is that the user is not made aware that the pair of words has been discarded. Probably a spelling error was made, or a typing error; the user should be informed in this case. The attentive reader has no doubt realised that there will be many words which, though they do not violate the orthographic rules, are nevertheless not words of the language concerned. There is very little to be done about this. If we want to inform the user that an error has been detected and consequently the word pair rejected, we must output a message of some kind. Let us suppose that there is a new set *Message* and that there are two distinct elements in the set:

> *Message* == {*Ok*, *ErrorInInput*}

Then we can define:

> *AddPairError$_1$* ==
> {*Vocab*, *Vocab'* : *set of* (*Native*, *Foreign*);
> *n*? : *Native*; *f*? : *Foreign*; *rep*! : *Message* |
> *Vocab* ∈ *WellFormedVocabs*
> ∧ (*n*? ∉ *OrthoNative* ∨ *f*? ∉ *OrthoForeign*)
> ∧ *Vocab'* = *Vocab*
> ∧ *rep*! = *ErrorInInput*}

Now that the system responds to erroneous input it would be more consistent if there were also a response to valid input; thus we modify the *AddPair* operation:

> *AddPair$_1$* ==
> {*Vocab*, *Vocab'* : *set of* (*Native*, *Foreign*);
> *n*? : *Native*; *f*? : *Foreign*; *rep*! : *Message* |
> *Vocab* ∈ *WellFormedVocabs*
> ∧ *n*? ∈ *OrthoNative* ∧ *f*? ∈ *OrthoForeign*
> ∧ *Vocab'* = *Vocab* ∪ {(*n*?, *f*?)}
> ∧ *rep*! = *Ok*}

and then we can define an operation which will accept all (*Native, Foreign*) pairs, though only adding valid pairs to the vocabulary, in all cases informing the user of success or failure. Note that an operation which responds in all cases, producing suitable error messages when appropriate, is said to be a total operation; here is a definition of the total operation corresponding to *AddPair*:

$TotalAddPair ==$
           $\{ Vocab, Vocab' : set\ of\ (Native, Foreign);$
             $n? : Native;\ f? : Foreign;\ rep! : Message\ |$
                $(Vocab \in WellFormedVocabs$
                   $\wedge\ n? \in OrthoNative \wedge f? \in OrthoForeign$
                   $\wedge\ Vocab' = Vocab \cup \{(n?, f?)\}$
                   $\wedge\ rep! = Ok)\ \vee$
                $(Vocab \in WellFormedVocabs$
                   $\wedge\ (n? \notin OrthoNative \vee f? \notin OrthoForeign)$
                   $\wedge\ Vocab' = Vocab$
                   $\wedge\ rep! = ErrorInInput)\}$

or equivalently, and more succinctly, we may define:

$TotalAddPair == AddPair_1 \cup AddPairError_1$

The latter definition is a very simple example of how an operation may be defined not by giving an explicit set of tuples but by combining already defined operations. In this case we have been able to define *TotalAddPair* as the union of two other operations. This was possible because those two operations are represented by sets of the same kind of tuples; we could not take the union if this were not so. Even the names of the slots used in the definition of the operations were identical in the present case. Theoretically this would not be necessary because it is only the sequence of kinds which make up the tuples which is important. In practice it would be highly confusing to combine operations where the names were quite different, because the names have significance when we interpret the operations in terms of the real world system we wish to create.

     We shall find that this idea of combining already defined operations is an extremely powerful and useful means of expression, and one which can be generalised to cases where the kinds of tuples do not necessarily match exactly. The main benefit which accrues from this ability to combine operations is to do with separation of the concerns of largely independent parts of the system to be defined. For example, we can separate the concerns of defining normal behaviour of a system from those of the behaviour of the system under exceptional circumstances. We shall have much more to say about all of this later.

     In this section we have attempted to achieve two related but distinct ends simultaneously; the first has been to specify a very simple vocabulary system, the second to discuss and explain how such specifications are expressed using the tools we have assembled. Usually a specifier works from the assumption that the specification language to be used is already well understood, be it English or be it a formal mathematical language. Presumably the reader of the specification can consult a manual about the specification language if clarification is needed. Thus a real specification would not take quite the form of the material of this section, for it would concern itself only with description of the system required.

However, it is not proposed that a formal specification should consist of nothing more than a series of definitions in a formal language. Remember that a formal specification has to serve as a document which the customer who requires the system can agree upon with the potential supplier of the implemented system. It is important that the formal language should form a part of such a document for then there is a precise and unambiguous definition from which the implementor can work, but we do not expect that the customer is well versed in formal languages, and so it is necessary to provide a parallel natural language description of the system. This also serves to interpret the statements of the formal language as statements about the physical world which is to be modelled and the environment in which it is to operate, relating the names of objects and operations formally defined to a mental picture of the working system, its components and its operational characteristics. It is the responsibility of the specifier to ensure that the natural language description and its formal counterpart do indeed tally.

3.2   A more concise presentation

We now re-run the Word-For-Word specification, this time presenting it in the form we would normally expect of a document which might serve as part of a contract between customer and supplier. The order of presentation is intended to make the whole specification more easily comprehensible rather than to correspond to the order in which the parts of the specification might be developed. Some small changes and additions are incorporated.

3.2.1   Word-For-Word: a vocabulary system

The Word-For-Word system is intended to help in the acquisition of vocabulary by a student learning a foreign language. The system is to record pairs of words, where one word is a native language word and the other is a foreign language word, where each word of a pair may serve as a translation of the other, at least in some circumstances. Words to be added to the vocabulary must satisfy rules, known as the orthographic rules, which are concerned with spelling conventions in the two languages; the purpose of these rules is to eliminate as far as possible the addition to the vocabulary of words which could not possibly belong to the respective languages. The facilities to be provided are as follows:

- Valid pairs of words may be added to the vocabulary.

- All translations of a native word into the foreign language may be requested.

- All translations of a foreign word into the native language may be requested.

In all cases, the system will report any detected errors in words submitted for entry into the vocabulary.

Given sets and global definitions

Three sets are assumed:

$$[Native, Foreign, Message]$$

The sets *Native* and *Foreign* represent the set of all possible sequences of characters over the alphabets of the native and foreign languages respectively; the set *Message* provides responses to the user which comment on the success or failure of operations performed. The orthographic rules are represented by subsets of *Native* and *Foreign*:

> *OrthoNative* : *set of Native*
> *OrthoForeign* : *set of Foreign*

We shall require that at all times the vocabulary contains only words which satisfy the orthographic rules: we define the set of well-formed vocabularies:

> *WellFormedVocabs* ==
> $\quad$ { *V* : *set of* (*Native*, *Foreign*) |
> $\quad\quad$ ∀ *n* : *Native*; *f* : *Foreign* •
> $\quad\quad\quad$ (*n*, *f*) ∈ *V* ⇒
> $\quad\quad\quad\quad$ *n* ∈ *OrthoNative* ∧ *f* ∈ *OrthoForeign* }

We define three messages, assumed to be distinct:

> *Ok*, *ErrorInInput*, *WordNotKnown* : *Message*

Initialisation

The system is initialised by taking an empty vocabulary:

> *InitVocab* == { *Vocab'* : *set of* (*Native*, *Foreign*) | *Vocab'* = ∅ }

Definition of operations

Now we define the facilities available. Firstly, a word pair may be submitted for entry into the vocabulary:

$AddValidPair ==$
  $\{Vocab, Vocab' : set\ of\ (Native, Foreign);$
   $n? : Native;\ f? : Foreign;\ rep! : Message\ |$
    $Vocab \in WellFormedVocabs$
    $\wedge\ n? \in OrthoNative \wedge f? \in OrthoForeign$
    $\wedge\ Vocab' = Vocab \cup \{(n?, f?)\}$
    $\wedge\ rep! = Ok\}$

A pair is only added to the vocabulary if the words concerned conform to the orthographic rules of their respective languages.

 Secondly, all translations of a given native word may be requested, distinguishing the case of a word which satisfies the orthographic rules but does not occur in the current vocabulary:

$ToForeign == KnownToForeign \cup UnknownToForeign$

$KnownToForeign ==$
  $\{Vocab, Vocab' : set\ of\ (Native, Foreign);$
   $n? : Native;\ ftrans! : set\ of\ Foreign;\ rep! : Message\ |$
    $Vocab \in WellFormedVocabs$
    $\wedge\ Vocab' = Vocab$
    $\wedge\ n? \in OrthoNative$
    $\wedge\ ftrans! = \{f : Foreign\ |\ (n?, f) \in Vocab\}$
    $\wedge\ ftrans! \neq \emptyset \wedge rep! = Ok\}$

$UnknownToForeign ==$
  $\{Vocab, Vocab' : set\ of\ (Native, Foreign);$
   $n? : Native;\ ftrans! : set\ of\ Foreign;\ rep! : Message\ |$
    $Vocab \in WellFormedVocabs$
    $\wedge\ Vocab' = Vocab$
    $\wedge\ n? \in OrthoNative$
    $\wedge\ ftrans! = \{f : Foreign\ |\ (n?, f) \in Vocab\}$
    $\wedge\ ftrans! = \emptyset \wedge rep! = WordNotKnown\}$

The given word must satisfy the orthographic rules of the native language. The output consists of all those foreign words which occur in the vocabulary paired with the given native word. This set of words will be empty if the native word is unknown to the vocabulary.

 Thirdly, all translations of a given foreign word may be requested, distinguishing the case of a word which satisfies the orthographic rules but does not occur in the current vocabulary. (We shall leave this as an exercise for the reader.)

We now give a summary of the operations, showing their inputs and outputs amd the conditions which must prevail for normal operation (we call these the preconditions):

Operation	Inputs/Outputs	Preconditions
AddValidPair	$n? : Native$	$n? \in OrthoNative$
	$f? : Foreign$	$f? \in OrthoForeign$
	$rep! : Message$	
ToForeign	$n? : Native$	$n? \in OrthoNative$
	$ftrans! : set\ of\ Foreign$	
	$rep! : Message$	
ToNative	$f? : Foreign$	$f? \in OrthoForeign$
	$ntrans! : set\ of\ Native$	
	$rep! : Message$	

Note that we have not included the requirement that:

$$Vocab \in WellFormedVocabs$$

amongst the preconditions of each operation; this is because each operation is defined so as to preserve this property, and thus we can safely assume this to be so whenever an operation is called upon to act.

Total operations

We now define operations which will work in all circumstances, informing the user when errors occur. Firstly we make the *AddPair* operation total in the following way:

$$TotalAddPair == AddPair \cup AddPairError$$

where:

$$\begin{aligned}
&AddPairError == \\
&\quad \{ Vocab, Vocab' : set\ of\ (Native, Foreign); \\
&\quad\quad n? : Native;\ f? : Foreign;\ rep! : Message\ | \\
&\quad\quad\quad Vocab \in WellFormedVocabs \\
&\quad\quad\quad \wedge (n? \notin OrthoNative \vee f? \notin OrthoForeign) \\
&\quad\quad\quad \wedge Vocab' = Vocab \\
&\quad\quad\quad \wedge rep! = ErrorInInput \}
\end{aligned}$$

which reports an error when one of the words of the pair fails to conform to the appropriate orthographic rules. Secondly, the total operation corresponding to *ToForeign* is defined:

$$ToForeignTotal == ToForeign \cup ToForeignError$$

where:

> $ToForeignError ==$
> $\qquad \{\,Vocab, Vocab' : set\ of\ (Native, Foreign);$
> $\qquad\qquad n? : Native;\ ftrans! : set\ of\ Foreign;\ rep! : Message\ |$
> $\qquad\qquad Vocab \in WellFormedVocabs$
> $\qquad\qquad \wedge\ Vocab' = Vocab$
> $\qquad\qquad \wedge\ n? \notin OrthoNative$
> $\qquad\qquad \wedge\ rep! = ErrorInInput \wedge ftrans! = \emptyset\}$

which reports an error if the given word fails to satisfy the orthographic rules of the native language. The total operation *ToNativeTotal* is defined similarly, reversing the roles of the two languages.

Exercise 3.1 ⋄ Complete the specification of Word-For-Word by supplying definitions for *ToNative* and *TotalToNative*.

Exercise 3.2 ⋄ When a foreign language is studied which shares common linguistic parentage with the native language the concept of 'false friends' arises. It often happens that there are words in the two languages whose written forms are either identical or very similar, allowing for different notions of orthography. For example, if the languages are English and Spanish there are word pairs such as:

English	Spanish	true/false friend
action	acción	true
deception	decepción	false
final	final	true
possibility	posibilidad	true
tender	tender	false

True friends are very similar words which do indeed have the same meaning, while false friends look very similar but mean something quite different. Now suppose that we want to add a new facility to our vocabulary system: using predicates such as *n very similar to f* where necessary, give a definition of an operation *FalseFriends* which outputs the set of false friends in the vocabulary.

Exercise 3.3 ⋄ An Engagement Diary system is to be specified: the purpose of the system is to record future engagements and their dates. The system is aware of the current date, and dates may be compared: for instance, a predicate might include the text *d1 before d2*. The operations to be defined are as follows:

(i) A new engagement is entered for a future date.

(ii) A list of the engagements recorded for a given future date may be requested.

(iii) A new day dawns, and all the engagements of the old day are forgotten.

Take *Date* and *Event* as given sets, define the operations for valid input, say how the system is to be initialised, summarise the normal operations, and then give total operations which report on errors.

Exercise 3.4 Suppose we want to extend the Engagement Diary system described in the previous exercise. We want to be able to record appointments which happen on the same day of the week every week until further notice. Let us take as given sets *CalendarDate*, *Weekday* and *Event*, where elements of *CalendarDate* would tell us the day of the month, the month of the year and the year itself, and elements of *Weekday* just tell us the day of the week. The system will now record events associated with particular calendar dates and also events associated with days of the week. Modify the system as necessary:

(i) adding an operation which adds a new event associated with a day of the week,

(ii) and changing the operation which lists engagements for a future date so that it also includes events which occur on the day of the week which corresponds to that future date.

Assume that you can refer to *the corresponding weekday* of a given *CalendarDate*.

Now consider further extending the system so that a future event can be deleted, perhaps because it has been cancelled or rescheduled, or in the case of an event associated with a weekday, the regular weekly pattern has changed.

Chapter 4

The Z notation:
the mathematical language

In this and the two following chapters we shall give an overview of the Z notation. It will be seen that Z includes all of the familiar mathematical and logical notation already encountered, but we shall be more precise about how this is to be used. We will show how definitions are made in Z, allowing the introduction of mathematical tools which form the basis of a powerful specification language. These are so useful that we think of them as forming a basic library of definitions and laws relating them, which may be freely used in our specifications. This basic library is the subject of Chapter 5. Also provided (in Chapter 6) is notation expressly designed to assist in the structuring and presentation of specifications.

In the present chapter, we first examine in more detail the idea, introduced in Chapter 2, that all the members of a set must be the same kind of object. We have already seen that certain expressions involving sets are only regarded as meaningful if the sets are of suitable kinds. For example, the union operator only makes sense between two sets of the same kind, since otherwise the set created by the union would contain elements of two different kinds, which is forbidden.

In Z the informal notion of kinds is made formal by introducing a system of types, and from here onwards we shall speak of types, rather than kinds. We shall look at the reasons for introducing types, and explain in more detail how the type system works.

We then go on to describe various extensions of the basic notation, and we introduce some of the important construction units which make up the formal part of Z specifications.

4.1 Why types are used

There are several advantages to be gained by introducing the restrictions of the Z type system. Most obvious to the writer of specifications is that the system admits a useful checking procedure which can detect certain errors in our specifications. Sometimes these errors are just typographical, but they can also reveal deeper problems in a specification brought about by muddled thinking or a lack of understanding. Checking that a specification is correct in this respect is a simple matter and can be performed by a machine. Chapter 12 reports on systems currently available to do this.

Secondly, the restrictions enforce a structure on the specification and demand discipline in the way it is written. This is particularly useful if the programming language we intend to use is itself typed.

There is also a more theoretical reason for introducing a type system. We have seen how a set can be formed by giving a predicate which describes its members. This is very expressive, but it can also prove to be dangerous. If we allow sets to be defined by predicates but do not demand a restriction on the kind of objects in a set then paradoxes may arise.

The word 'paradox' comes from the Greek meaning 'beyond belief'. In logic it refers to a situation where apparently valid reasoning leads to a contradiction. Russell's famous paradox concerns sets which are members of themselves. This is different from the sets we have met so far: the set, EU, of European Union countries is not itself a European Union country just as a pack of wolves is not itself a wolf. However, suppose we were to drop the requirement that when we describe a set we must state the kind of objects from which the members of the set must be drawn. We may now define sets such as the set of sets with at least a million elements:

$$Numerous == \{x \mid \exists y \bullet y \subseteq x \wedge y \ has \ a \ million \ elements\}$$

or even the set containing all sets:

$$Universal == \{x \mid x = \emptyset \vee \exists y \bullet y \in x\}$$

These sets would then qualify as members of themselves:

- *Numerous* certainly has a subset with a million elements, namely:

$$\{s : set \ of \ numbers \mid$$
$$\exists n : number \bullet$$
$$1 \leq n \leq 1000000 \wedge s = \{i : number \mid n \leq i < n + 1000000\}\}$$

- *Universal* satisfies $\exists y \bullet y \in Universal$ since $\emptyset \in Universal$.

Russell's paradox arises from consideration of the set, S say, of all sets which are not members of themselves:

$$S == \{x \mid x \notin x\}$$

So the sets EU and $PrimeNumbers$ belong to S since they are not members of themselves. On the other hand, we have just seen that $Numerous$ and $Universal$ are members of themselves and so cannot be members of S. But here is the tricky question: is S a member of S?

Let us first suppose that S is a member of itself, that is, $S \in S$.

By the definition of S we know that for any x, if $x \in S$ then $x \notin x$.

But we have assumed that S itself belongs to S, and so we deduce that $S \notin S$.

So the assumption that $S \in S$ has led to the contradictory conclusion that $S \notin S$.

Perhaps our original assumption (that $S \in S$) was wrong, so now let us suppose that $S \notin S$.

Then S is an example of a set which is not a member of itself, and so by definition it must belong to S, that is $S \in S$.

So the assumption that $S \notin S$ leads to the conclusion that $S \in S$.

Starting from a seemingly innocent definition of S this reasoning has led to the self-contradictory conclusion that S is a member of itself if and only if it is not a member of itself! Such paradoxes cannot be dismissed as mere tricks or word games because they have very serious consequences for any system in which they can be derived. In such a system you could prove that black is white or that day is night; in fact anything at all would be provable.

Adopting a type system is one way to avoid these perils. A set such as S cannot be defined in Z. We know that the expression $\{x \mid x \notin x\}$ is not a correct Z expression because x has not been given a type, but if we try to assign it a type, T say, we run into further problems. The symbol $\notin$ can only be used between an element of some type (in this case T) on the left and a set of elements of T on the right. Since $\notin$ cannot occur between elements of the same type, a type checker would immediately reject a statement such as $x \notin x$; it is regarded as meaningless, just as an expression in which the syntax is incorrect is meaningless.

4.2   The Z type system

We have introduced the informal idea of members of a set being 'of the same kind'. These 'kinds' are the types of the Z type system. The type system requires that when any new variable is introduced it must be declared along with information about its type. The type determines a set over which the variable ranges. Not just variables, but each Z expression, such as the sets defined earlier, must belong to one and only one type.

A variable is introduced by a declaration which gives the name of the variable and its type. For instance, if *BOOK* is a type, the declaration:

$x : BOOK$

introduces a variable x of type *BOOK*. Declarations occur in many positions in a Z document. We have already seen their use when writing predicates:

$\exists o : opera \bullet Beethoven\ was\ the\ composer\ of\ o$

and when defining sets:

$BigCountries == \{c : country \mid c\ has\ more\ than\ 40\ million\ inhabitants\}$

In these examples we used the types *opera* and *country* and chose the variables o and c respectively to range over them.

Given any Z expression, for example, a set construction, the type rules provide a means of determining the type of that expression from the types of its sub-expressions. This task, which may be done automatically, ensures that any meaningless expressions are detected. So if a specification has the types *BOOK* and *CAR* and the declarations:

$x : BOOK$
$y : CAR$

followed at some later point by the predicate:

$x = y$

a type checker, human or otherwise, can discover that the types of the two objects are different, and therefore it makes no sense to say that the objects are equal.

We now take a first look at the range of types and type constructors which are used in Z.

4.2.1   Given sets

Every Z specification introduces and uses a number of basic types over which variables may range. These basic types are also known as given sets since they are introduced in a specification simply by giving their names enclosed in square brackets. So the type declaration:

$[BOOK, CAR]$

makes known the basic types *BOOK* and *CAR*. We are not really interested in the internal structure of these sets; we care only that introducing them in a specification makes them available as valid types and that variables of these types can now be declared. We do however make the restriction that different basic types of a specification are assumed to have no element in common. So, for instance, if a variable x is declared to be of type *BOOK* it cannot also be a member of *CAR*.

One useful type we shall take as basic is that of the integers[1] which includes all whole numbers, both positive and negative:

$$\ldots, -3, -2, -1, 0, 1, 2, 3, \ldots$$

This is denoted by $\mathbb{Z}$. Given the declaration:

$$x : \mathbb{Z}$$

then expressions such as $x = 100$, $2*x > x$, $x^2 - 2*x + 1 = 0$ will all be correctly typed. (The symbol $*$ is used in Z, as it is in many programming languages, to represent the multiplication operator. The usual precedences amongst arithmetic operators apply in Z. These are listed on page 413.) Notice that, for example, $x = x + 1$ and $x \neq x$ are also type correct even though there is no value of x for which these statements are true. A specification placing such restrictions on x would not be satisfiable, but there are no type errors involved; this demonstrates that type checking, whilst extremely useful, is limited in the sorts of errors it can detect.

The given sets are the building blocks of the Z type system. From them, other types can be made by repeated application of the type constructors described below.

4.2.2 Powersets

We want to be able to find the type of any Z expression. Looking first at sets, let us consider some examples:

$$single == \{-1\}$$
$$smalleven == \{2, 4, 6, 8\}$$
$$\mathbb{N} == \{n : \mathbb{Z} \mid n \geq 0\}$$
$$\mathbb{N}_1 == \{n : \mathbb{Z} \mid n > 0\}$$

---

[1] In fact, a more general approach is to take a basic type of *NUMBER*. Using this we can derive as subsets all the other frequently used sets of natural, integer, rational, real and complex numbers. We will not have cause to use anything beyond integers and so, for simplicity, take them as our given set.

Each member of each of these sets has type $\mathbb{Z}$, so *single, smalleven*, N and N_1 are all subsets of $\mathbb{Z}$. What is the type of the whole set in each case? Obviously, the sets themselves are not numbers and so cannot have type $\mathbb{Z}$.

In such cases we use the powerset constructor, written $\mathbb{P}$. If X is a set, then $\mathbb{P} X$ is also a set and contains all subsets of X. We could say informally that $\mathbb{P} X = \{Y \mid Y \subseteq X\}$, but notice that this is not a proper Z definition since Y has not been given a type. Some examples will make the idea of sets and their powersets clearer. Given the definition:

$$X == \{1, 2\}$$

then:

$$\mathbb{P} X = \{\emptyset, \{1\}, \{2\}, \{1, 2\}\}$$

Notice that $\mathbb{P} X$ contains both the empty set and X itself. In fact, for any type X, the powerset type $\mathbb{P} X$ is what we previously referred to informally as *set of X*. Remember the example:

> *FirstRoundMatches* ==
> $\quad \{m : set\ of\ players \mid m\ has\ two\ members \wedge m \subset Competitors\}$

We are now able to give the correct type information in this definition:

> *FirstRoundMatches* ==
> $\quad \{m : \mathbb{P}\ players \mid m\ has\ two\ members \wedge m \subset Competitors\}$

As another example, for the set *smalleven* we have:

$$\mathbb{P}\ smalleven = \{\ \emptyset, \{2\}, \{4\}, \{6\}, \{8\}, \{2, 4\}, \{2, 6\},$$
$$\{2, 8\}, \{4, 6\}, \{4, 8\}, \{6, 8\}, \{2, 4, 6\},$$
$$\{2, 4, 8\}, \{2, 6, 8\}, \{4, 6, 8\}, \{2, 4, 6, 8\}\ \}$$

The powerset $\mathbb{P}\mathbb{Z}$ is the set of all subsets of $\mathbb{Z}$, a set which is obviously too large to list. However, it is easy to see whether a set is a member of $\mathbb{P}\mathbb{Z}$ or not because from our definition of powerset it follows that:

$$Y \in \mathbb{P}\mathbb{Z} \Leftrightarrow Y \subseteq \mathbb{Z}$$

That is, a set is a member of $\mathbb{P}\mathbb{Z}$ if and only if it is a subset of $\mathbb{Z}$. So any set whose members are all integers is itself a member of $\mathbb{P}\mathbb{Z}$. We have:

$$single \in \mathbb{P}\mathbb{Z}$$
$$smalleven \in \mathbb{P}\mathbb{Z}$$
$$\{1, 3, 5, 7, ...\} \in \mathbb{P}\mathbb{Z}$$
$$N \in \mathbb{P}\mathbb{Z}$$
$$\mathbb{Z} \in \mathbb{P}\mathbb{Z}$$

Recall that whenever a variable is introduced we have to give a declaration which states the name of the variable and its type. Whenever we want to declare a variable whose value is intended to be a set of objects the powerset constructor is used to form the type for that variable, so that:

$library : \mathbb{P}\, BOOK$

says that *library* is a set of books, and:

$primes : \mathbb{P}\, \mathbb{Z}$

declares *primes* to be a set of integers.

Using the basic types of a specification and the powerset constructor a whole new range of types becomes available. If a specification has basic types X and Y, then $\mathbb{P}\, X$ and $\mathbb{P}\, Y$ are also legitimate types, as are $\mathbb{P}\mathbb{P}\, X$, $\mathbb{P}\mathbb{P}\, Y$, and so on.

Notice that the powerset constructor can be applied to any set to form another set; it is only when it is applied to a type that another type results. This perhaps leads us to question what the relationship between sets and types is. Firstly, every type is a set. If we introduce a basic type or construct a type using $\mathbb{P}$ we know that we can treat it as a set, referring to its members and using set operations on it. On the other hand, whilst a single element can be a member of many sets, it only belongs to one type. For instance, the integer 1 is a member of $\{1\}$, $\{-1, 1\}$, $\mathbb{N}$, $\mathbb{N}_1$, $\mathbb{Z}$ and many more sets. However, only one of these is a type, and in this case it is $\mathbb{Z}$. Thus the types are a special sort of set. They are sometimes referred to as 'maximal sets' since they represent the largest possible set to which an element can belong.

To see what happens when the powerset constructor is used repeatedly, consider the set X, with the single element 1:

$$
\begin{aligned}
X &== \{1\} \\
\mathbb{P}\, X &= \{\emptyset, \{1\}\} \\
\mathbb{P}\mathbb{P}\, X &= \{\emptyset, \{\emptyset\}, \{\{1\}\}, \{\emptyset, \{1\}\}\} \\
\mathbb{P}\mathbb{P}\mathbb{P}\, X &= \{\emptyset, \{\emptyset\}, \{\{\emptyset\}\}, \{\{\{1\}\}\}, \{\{\emptyset, \{1\}\}\}, \{\emptyset, \{\{1\}\}\}, \ldots\}
\end{aligned}
$$

Even though we started with a singleton set, the size of the resulting powersets soon becomes quite large. Note that $\emptyset$ is different from $\{\emptyset\}$. $\emptyset$ is the empty set and has no members whereas $\{\emptyset\}$ has exactly one member, the empty set itself.

Since every Z expression must have a type, the empty set must have a type. In $\{\emptyset, \{1\}\}$, clearly the empty set concerned is the empty set of integers; but in $\{\emptyset, \{\emptyset\}, \{\{1\}\}, \{\emptyset, \{1\}\}\}$, the first and second occurrences of $\emptyset$ are of different types. We are not saying that there is a unique empty set which belongs to many different types, for that would contradict the basic principles of the type system; we are saying that there is an empty set of elements corresponding to each type, but we do not need to distinguish between them notationally because (usually) we can deduce from the context the type concerned. Here it is clear that we are talking about sets of numbers, but we might wish to use $\emptyset$ in lots of situations. In fact, this is not a problem in Z, and we will see later in the chapter how and why $\emptyset$ and other constructs like it can be used in different contexts and how any possible ambiguity can be prevented.

With basic types and powerset types we can begin to determine whether statements about sets make sense. In the role of human type checker we can examine an expression such as:

$$\{2\} \subseteq smalleven$$

The subset symbol only makes sense if it appears between two sets of the same type. That is, the term on the left and the term on the right of the symbol must both be of type $\mathbb{P}\,X$ for some X. In the above example, $\{2\}$ is a set of integers and therefore has type $\mathbb{P}\,\mathbb{Z}$. The set *smalleven* also has type $\mathbb{P}\,\mathbb{Z}$ and therefore the expression is correctly typed.

Exercise 4.1 $\diamond$ Give the powerset of each of the following:

(i) $\{0,1\}$ (ii) $\emptyset$ (iii) $\{\emptyset\}$ (iv) $\mathbb{P}\{1\}$

Exercise 4.2 What is $\mathbb{P}\,\mathbb{P}\{-1,1\}$?

Exercise 4.3 $\diamond$ If a set X has n members how many members does $\mathbb{P}\,X$ have?

Exercise 4.4 Define the set *SetsOfPrimes*, the set of all sets of prime numbers. What is the type of *SetsOfPrimes*?

Exercise 4.5 $\diamond$ Let *shape* be the set $\{round, square\}$. List the elements of the following sets:

(i) $(\mathbb{P}\,shape) \setminus \{square\}$ (ii) $(\mathbb{P}\{round\}) \cup (\mathbb{P}\{square\})$

(iii) $\mathbb{P}((\mathbb{P}\{round\}) \setminus \{\emptyset\})$ (iv) $\mathbb{P}((\mathbb{P}\{round\}) \setminus \emptyset)$

Exercise 4.6 What is the type of each of the following?

(i) $\{0,1\}$ (ii) 37 (iii) $\{\{1,2\},\{2,3\}\}$ (iv) $\{1,\{1\}\}$

Exercise 4.7 $\diamond$ Are the following expressions correctly typed? If not, what is wrong with them?

(i) $\{\{\emptyset\},\{1,2\}\}$

(ii) $\forall x : \mathbb{Z} \bullet \exists y : \mathbb{Z} \bullet x < y$

(iii) $[OUTPUT]$

$error : OUTPUT$

$\forall x : \mathbb{Z} \bullet \exists y : OUTPUT \bullet (x \neq 0 \Rightarrow y = x - 1 \wedge x = 0 \Rightarrow y = error)$

Exercise 4.8 Using the basic type $\mathbb{Z}$ write a declaration for integers *maxval* and *minval* and a set of integers called *values*. Write predicates to express that:

(i) *maxval* must be at least as great as *minval*

(ii) no element of *values* is greater than *maxval* or less than *minval*

Exercise 4.9 Suppose that *Committee* is a subset of *STAFF*, which is a basic type. A meeting of the committee is quorate if the chairperson and at least two other members are present. Give suitable declarations for *Committee* and *chairperson* and express the fact that the chairperson is a member of the committee. Define *Quorum* as the set of subsets of *Committee* which can hold quorate meetings, expressing the defining property entirely in Z notation.

4.2.3   Cartesian product

In Chapter 2, the concept of ordered tuples was introduced. In Z we use the already familiar notation for such tuples, for example we may write:

$(1, 1)$
$(\{12, 5\}, France, blue)$

Earlier we would have described these informally as:

a *(number, number) pair*
a *(set of number, country, colour) triple*

respectively. We now give the precise notation for describing tuple types in Z. Given any two sets, T and U, their Cartesian product (written $T \times U$) is the set of all ordered pairs whose first element is a member of T and whose second element is a member of U. For example, defining $X == \{1, 2\}$ and $Y == \{p, q, r\}$, then:

$$X \times X = \{(1,1), (1,2), (2,1), (2,2)\}$$
$$X \times Y = \{(1,p), (1,q), (1,r), (2,p), (2,q), (2,r)\}$$
$$X \times \mathbb{N} = \{(1,0), (1,1), (1,2), (1,3), (1,4), \ldots,$$
$$(2,0), (2,1), (2,2), (2,3), (2,4), \ldots\}$$

Again, defining *shape* == {*round*, *square*} and *colour* == {*red*, *blue*, *green*}, we have:

$$shape \times colour = \{(round, red), (round, blue), (round, green)$$
$$(square, red), (square, blue), (square, green)\}$$
$$colour \times shape = \{(red, round), (blue, round), (green, round)$$
$$(red, square), (blue, square), (green, square)\}$$

Cartesian products may also be defined for three or more sets; for example, the Cartesian product $T \times U \times V$ of the three sets T, U and V contains all ordered triples with first element from T, second from U, and third from V. It is important to note that a Cartesian product with three sets is different from a Cartesian product with two sets, one of which happens itself to be a Cartesian product. Each of the three products:

$$T \times U \times V$$
$$(T \times U) \times V$$
$$T \times (U \times V)$$

represents a completely different set. For example, consider the set X as defined above. The following are typical members of various Cartesian products involving X:

$$(1, 1, 1) \in X \times X \times X$$
$$((1, 1), 1) \in (X \times X) \times X$$
$$(1, (1, 1)) \in X \times (X \times X)$$

The first element is a triple in which each element is the number 1. The second is a pair whose first element is itself a pair with each element 1 and whose second element is 1. The third is a pair with first element 1 and second element $(1, 1)$. None is equivalent to either of the others.

When we take Cartesian products of sets which are types we get new types. Given an ordered tuple we can determine which product type it belongs to by looking at the types of its elements. For example:

$$(1, 1) \in \mathbb{Z} \times \mathbb{Z}$$
$$(\{1\}, 1) \in (\mathbb{P}\,\mathbb{Z}) \times \mathbb{Z}$$

In Z notation, the types of the ordered tuples at the beginning of this subsection would be respectively:

$$\mathbb{Z} \times \mathbb{Z}$$
$$(\mathbb{P}\,\mathbb{Z}) \times country \times colour$$

The Cartesian product and powerset type constructors may be used together to form new types from the basic types of a specification. For instance, if a specification has basic types X and Y, we have already seen that $\mathbb{P}\,X$, $\mathbb{P}\,Y$, $\mathbb{P}\mathbb{P}\,X$, $\mathbb{P}\mathbb{P}\,Y$, ... are also types. Now we know that $X \times X$, $X \times Y$, $Y \times Y$ and $Y \times X$ are types too. If we use the two constructors together we obtain such types as $(\mathbb{P}\,X) \times (\mathbb{P}\,X)$, $\mathbb{P}(X \times X)$, $(\mathbb{P}\,X) \times Y$ and many more.

We can now use all these types when making declarations. Suppose that in a library system each copy of a book is identified by (a) what the book is and (b) a number showing which copy it is. If we want to write a specification of the system we may choose to represent each copy as an ordered pair of type $BOOK \times \mathbb{Z}$. So, for instance, if we want a particular variable to represent the latest book entering the library we could declare:

$$newestbook : BOOK \times \mathbb{Z}$$

A library could be seen as just a set of copies of books, and then we would say:

$$library : \mathbb{P}(BOOK \times \mathbb{Z})$$

Exercise 4.10 If $X == \{red, blue\}$ and $Y == \{\{round\}\}$, write out each of the following as a list:

(i) $X \times X$ (ii) $Y \times Y$ (iii) $X \times Y$ (iv) $Y \times X$

(v) $(\mathbb{P}\,X) \times (\mathbb{P}\,Y)$ (vi) $\mathbb{P}(X \times Y)$ (vii) $(\mathbb{P}\mathbb{P}\,Y) \times X$

(viii) $X \times Y \times X$ (ix) $(X \times Y) \times X$ (x) $X \times (Y \times X)$

Exercise 4.11 ◇ If a set X has n members and a set Y has m members, how many members does $X \times Y$ have?

Exercise 4.12 What are the types of the following?

(i) $(1, \{1\})$ (ii) $((1,1), 1)$ (iii) $(\{1\}, (1,1))$ (iv) $\{(\emptyset, \{3\}), (\{(0,0)\}, \emptyset)\}$

(v) $(\{1\}, 1, \{1\})$ (vi) $(\{0\}, (1,2,3))$ (vii) $((0,0), (1,1), (2,2))$

Exercise 4.13 ◇

(i) Our library has some copies which are on loan and some copies which are not. Declare the variables *onloan* and *notonloan* and write a predicate to describe the relationship between *library*, *onloan* and *notonloan*.

(ii) The librarian wants to keep track of who has borrowed which book, so we introduce a new basic set:

[*USERS*]

which is the set of all valid borrowers. A record is kept, with each entry consisting of the borrower's name and the copy that has been borrowed. Using integers to represent copy numbers, make a declaration for the variable *issued* to represent this record. What is the relationship between *issued* and *onloan*? Write a predicate to express the fact that a copy can be on loan to at most one person.

4.2.4 Declaration abbreviations

It has been noted earlier that an object may be a member of many sets, but will be a member of exactly one unique type. Until now the declarations in this chapter have been of the form $x : T$, where T is a type, but suppose we have defined a set:

$$PosEven == \{x : \mathbb{Z} \mid \exists y : \mathbb{Z} \bullet y > 0 \wedge x = 2 * y\}$$

and we wish to introduce a number, *SomeEven*, which is intended to be an even number. To do this we could declare:

$$SomeEven : \mathbb{Z}$$

and then write out a predicate which expresses the requirement that *SomeEven* is even:

$$\exists y : \mathbb{Z} \bullet y > 0 \wedge SomeEven = 2 * y$$

As a shorthand for this we can instead simply write our declaration as:

$$SomeEven : PosEven$$

which captures in one line the two requirements stated above. How can we be sure from this single declaration that *SomeEven* has type $\mathbb{Z}$? Well, it says that *SomeEven* is a member of *PosEven* and the declaration of *PosEven* tells us that everything belonging to it is of type $\mathbb{Z}$. Hence, *SomeEven* must have type $\mathbb{Z}$. The fact that *SomeEven* belongs to *PosEven* also says that it must obey the defining predicate of *PosEven*, and so it follows that *SomeEven* really is a multiple of 2.

This sort of declaration helps to make specifications shorter and more readable by allowing us to use definitions of sets that have already been introduced. Given such a declaration, of the form $y : S$ it is worth remembering that:

- It is always possible to discover what the type of y is by looking at the definition of S and seeing what type its members must be.

- y is constrained to satisfy the defining properties of S.

A useful example of declaration abbreviation arises when we want to declare a set to be a finite subset of some other, usually infinite, type or set. There is a notation $\mathbb{F}\,S$ for the set of all finite subsets of a given set S. Since $\mathbb{P}\,S$ is the set of all subsets of the set S, we have:

$$\mathbb{F}\,S \subseteq \mathbb{P}\,S$$

It should be noted that, though for any type T the powerset $\mathbb{P}\,T$ is again a type, in general $\mathbb{F}\,T$ is not a type (see Exercise 4.16). Thus if we declare:

$$finset : \mathbb{F}\,\mathbb{Z}$$

this is an abbreviation, since the type of $finset$ is $\mathbb{P}\,\mathbb{Z}$.

Exercise 4.14 Suppose the following declarations are given:

$$x : \mathbb{P}\,PosEven$$
$$y : PosEven \times \mathbb{Z}$$
$$z : \mathbb{P}(\{0,1\} \times \mathbb{N})$$

(i) What are the types of x, y and z?

(ii) Give equivalent definitions for x, y and z where each variable is declared with its type and then further described by a predicate.

(iii) Give possible values for x, y and z.

(iv) Say which of the following statements are correctly typed:

    (a) $2 \in x$

    (b) $y \in z$

    (c) $(0, x) \in z$

    (d) $\{1, 3, 5\} \subseteq x$

    (e) $\forall t : \mathbb{N} \bullet (\exists u : PosEven \bullet (t, u) \in z)$

    (f) $(1, 3, 2) \in z \times x$

Exercise 4.15 ⋄ Declare and define the variable *numpair* which is a pair of positive odd numbers, the first of which is at least as great as the second.

Exercise 4.16 If *Fin* is a finite set and *Inf* is an infinite set, for each of the following say whether the expression is true, false or incorrectly typed, and justify your answers:

(i) $\mathbb{F}\,Inf \subset \mathbb{P}\,Inf$ (ii) $\mathbb{F}\,Fin \in \mathbb{F}\,\mathbb{F}\,Fin$

(iii) $\mathbb{P}\,Fin \not\subseteq \mathbb{F}\,Fin$ (iv) $\mathbb{P}\,Fin = \mathbb{F}\,Fin$

4.2.5   Simple data types

Before leaving the subject of types for a while we introduce a convenient way of defining types with a small number of named elements. As an example, suppose we wish to describe a switch which has exactly two positions, *on* and *off*. Using the notation developed so far we might introduce a basic type for the possible positions of the switch:

[*POSITION*]

and then declare *on* and *off* to be of that type:

on, *off* : *POSITION*

This would certainly make available the positions we wanted, but it does not quite capture what was intended. Firstly, *on* and *off* are supposed to be two distinct positions. To be sure of achieving this we would need to add explicitly the statement:

off $\neq$ *on*

Secondly, *on* and *off* are meant to be the *only* possible positions, so we must add the constraint:

$\forall x : POSITION \bullet x = on \lor x = off$

Since it is rather inconvenient to add these extra statements, especially if there are more possible values than the two in our example, Z allows a shorthand form of definition called a data type definition. In its simplest form we simply list the elements we wish the type to have:

POSITION ::= *on* | *off*

The symbol '::=' indicates that this is a data type definition and elements of the list are separated by '|'. It incorporates the information that the named elements are all distinct and that there are no other elements in the type.

4.2.6   Free type definitions

The simple data type definitions used in the previous section are a special case of a very useful type introduction mechanism known as free type definition (you may also find these referred to in other texts as structured set definitions, user-defined types or data type definitions). Using a structured set definition we can introduce a new type together with constructor functions which show how elements of the new type can be viewed as being built up from existing types.

To illustrate this, suppose we have a specification which includes the basic types *EMPLOYEE* and *CLIENT*, referring to the people employed by a company and the people who are its customers. It is certainly reasonable to suppose that there could be many uses for these two types, such as specifying which employees serve which clients. Now suppose that the company also wants to consider both groups of people together for some purpose: perhaps it wants to make money by selling all the addresses to a mailing company. We may be tempted to try to create the union of *EMPLOYEE* and *CLIENT*, but this would cause a type error. It would be possible to go back and rework the specification in terms of a new type *PERSON*, with *EMPLOYEE* and *CLIENT* now relegated to being subsets of this type. However, this may well make the existing specification more complicated. Another option is to stick with the original types and use a free type definition:

$$PERSON ::= emp \langle\!\langle EMPLOYEE \rangle\!\rangle$$
$$| \ client \langle\!\langle CLIENT \rangle\!\rangle$$

This does several things at once. It introduces a new type *PERSON*. It says that *PERSON* is made up of elements corresponding to those in *EMPLOYEE* and *CLIENT*. It also imposes the condition that *PERSON* can contain no other members. So for every employee *e*, and client *c*, there are corresponding elements *emp e* and *client c*, of *PERSON*. Conversely, any element of *PERSON* must be related to exactly one employee or client. This means that we have made a new type *PERSON*, in which each person is either an employee or a client, but not both. Note that elements of *PERSON* cannot be compared directly with members of *EMPLOYEE* or *CLIENT*. This is because they are different types. If *Jones* is of type *EMPLOYEE* then *emp Jones* is the corresponding *PERSON*. Although there is more that can be said about free type definitions and how they may be defined within the Z language, we will not pursue the matter further here. More details and examples can be found in [Spi92].

This approach is also useful for creating different structures such as trees. Suppose we wish to store information about our ancestors. This can be done pictorially with a binary tree (in which no node can have more than two ancestors). Figure 4.1 pictures one showing two generations back for Helen.

Here all the labels in the boxes are of the same type *NAME*, say. A free type definition can be given for this:

$$FAMTREE ::= node \langle\!\langle NAME \times FAMTREE \times FAMTREE \rangle\!\rangle$$
$$| \ unk$$

At each level, either there is a name and two subtrees, or we have reached a point where the ancestors are unknown (represented by the *unk* tree). As an element of *FAMTREE* the example depicted in Figure 4.1 could be written:

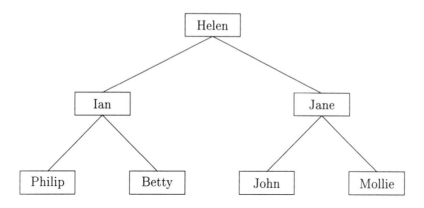

Figure 4.1: Helen's ancestral family tree

node(*Helen*,
    node(*Ian, node*(*Philip, unk, unk*), *node*(*Betty, unk, unk*)),
    node(*Jane, node*(*John, unk, unk*), *node*(*Mollie, unk, unk*))
)

Exercise 4.17 ⋄ Represent each of the following trees as an element of the type *FAMTREE*:

(i)

(ii)

(iii)

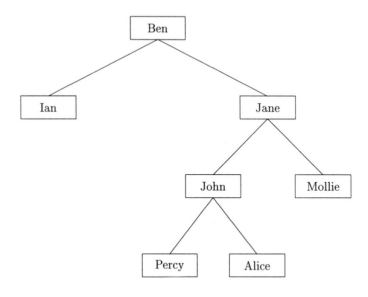

Exercise 4.18 Draw pictures of:

(i) $node(Ben, node(Ian, node(Philip, unk, unk), unk), unk)$

(ii) $node(Helen,$
$\qquad node(Ian, unk, unk),$
$\qquad node(Jane, node(John, unk, unk),$
$\qquad\qquad node(Mollie, node(Alfred, unk, unk), node(Ellen, unk, unk)))$
$\qquad)$

Exercise 4.19 An operation to write data to a file may be successful or it may fail. Possible reasons for failure are because the file does not exist, because it has already reached some maximum size limit, or because the user does not have the correct access permission. Create a free type definition, *REPORT*, to represent suitable responses to the user for each case.

Exercise 4.20 ⋄ Write a free type definition for binary trees in which integers may be stored, but at the end nodes only, for example:

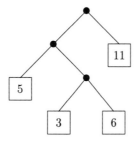

How would the given tree be represented as an element of this type?

4.2.7   Other type construction mechanisms

There is a further type construction mechanism, namely the schema type. Since these can best be understood after schemas themselves have been encountered, we defer explanation of schema types until Chapter 6.

4.3   Extending the notation

In Chapters 2 and 3 we introduced many of the concepts which are used in Z, but in some cases we used an informal notation and in some cases we gave only examples of more general ideas. In this section we introduce more of the Z notation: sometimes this is just Z shorthand, sometimes it is a matter of giving names to generally useful objects, for example, certain sets.

4.3.1   From the basic Z library

It has been mentioned that, apart from all the definitions we make in particular specifications, there is a body of Z constructs which are so useful that they are regarded as a basic library which can be used as required in our specifications without explicit declarations. These can all be defined in Z, and many of them are introduced in the next chapter. For now we note that the basic type $\mathbb{Z}$ of integers, the sets $\mathbb{N}$ of non-negative numbers and $\mathbb{N}_1$ of strictly positive numbers, are all part of the basic library, along with the usual arithmetic operations and relations such as $+, -, *, /, <, \leq, >, \geq$, etc.

As an example of useful shorthand in Z, if we want to define the set of all integers from a to b (inclusive) we use the notation $a \mathinner{\ldotp\ldotp} b$. Thus:

$$2 \mathinner{\ldotp\ldotp} 5 = \{2, 3, 4, 5\}$$
$$8 \mathinner{\ldotp\ldotp} 8 = \{8\}$$
$$5 \mathinner{\ldotp\ldotp} 2 = \emptyset$$
$$-1 \mathinner{\ldotp\ldotp} 1 = \{-1, 0, 1\}$$

When dealing with finite sets we often want to speak of 'the number of items in set S': in Z the operator # is used, so that, for example:

$$\#\{1,2\} = 2$$
$$\#smalleven = 4$$
$$\#(5 \mathbin{..} 2) = 0$$

Exercise 4.21 ◇ Referring to the definitions on page 63, give the values of:

(i) $\#shape$ (ii) $\#(\mathbb{N} \setminus \mathbb{N}_1)$ (iii) $(\#shape) - (\#colour)$ (iv) $\#(n \mathbin{..} (n+1))$

Exercise 4.22 Use # to give a simplified definition of the set *Quorum* of Exercise 4.9.

Exercise 4.23 ◇ Suppose m and n are declared elsewhere to be integers. Give an expression for the set $m \mathbin{..} n$ in the form $\{Decs \mid Pred\}$, for suitable *Decs* and *Pred*.

4.3.2   Extending the quantification notation

We have already seen how a predicate can be written with a list of declarations and a property relating them, as in:

$$\forall x : \mathbb{Z}; y : \mathbb{Z} \bullet x - y \in \mathbb{Z}$$
$$\exists z : \mathbb{Z} \bullet z < 0$$

If we wish to declare more than one variable of the same type we can list them together without repeating the type name: the first of the two propositions above may thus be written:

$$\forall x, y : \mathbb{Z} \bullet x - y \in \mathbb{Z}$$

The variable names are separated by a comma, and the semicolon is no longer needed.

When writing Z predicates we are allowed to give an extra property along with the declarations which further constrains the declared variables. For instance, suppose we wish to say that for any two integers x,y with x greater than y, $x - y$ is a positive number. We can write:

$$\forall x, y : \mathbb{Z} \mid x > y \bullet x - y \in \mathbb{N}_1$$

and this might be read: 'for all integers x,y satisfying $x > y$, $x - y$ is in $\mathbb{N}_1$'. The extra constraint, $x > y$, is added as another condition that x and y must satisfy. The same can be done with existential quantification; for example:

$$\exists x : \mathbb{Z}; s : \mathbb{P}\mathbb{Z} \mid x \in s \bullet x = \#s$$

which might be read: 'there exists an integer x, and a set s of integers, with $x \in s$, such that $x = \#s$'. Notice that simply constraining the type as in:

$$\forall x : \mathbb{Z} \mid x \in \mathbb{N}_1 \bullet x - 1 \in \mathbb{N}$$

is equivalent to just using the more restricted set in the declaration:

$$\forall x : \mathbb{N}_1 \bullet x - 1 \in \mathbb{N}$$

In fact, although the notation has been extended to allow more convenient expressions we have not added anything to the power of the language; the same thing could always be written in another way. The expression:

$$\forall \textit{Decs} \mid \textit{Constr} \bullet \textit{Pred}$$

says that for all *Decs*, if *Constr* is satisfied then *Pred* must be satisfied too. It is equivalent to the more conventional form:

$$\forall \textit{Decs} \bullet \textit{Constr} \Rightarrow \textit{Pred}$$

The expression:

$$\exists \textit{Decs} \mid \textit{Constr} \bullet \textit{Pred}$$

says that there exists some *Decs* which satisfies *Constr*, and which also satisfies *Pred*. It is equivalent to:

$$\exists \textit{Decs} \bullet \textit{Constr} \wedge \textit{Pred}$$

As an example of the use of the extended notation, recall the following proposition from Chapter 2:

São Paolo is bigger than any other city in the same country

which was captured more formally as follows:

$\exists \, co : country \, \bullet$
    São Paolo is in co $\wedge$
    $\forall \, ci : city \, \bullet$
        ci is in co $\wedge \neg$ *ci is São Paolo*
            $\Rightarrow$ *São Paolo is bigger than ci*

We can rewrite this now as follows:

$\exists \, co : country \mid$ *São Paolo is in co* $\bullet$
    $\forall \, ci : city \, \bullet$
        ci is in co $\wedge \neg$ *ci is São Paolo*
            $\Rightarrow$ *São Paolo is bigger than ci*

Similarly we can go further and write:

$$\exists\, co : country \mid S\tilde{a}o\,Paolo\;is\;in\;co \bullet$$
$$\forall\, ci : city \mid ci\;is\;in\;co \wedge \neg\; ci\;is\;S\tilde{a}o\,Paolo \bullet$$
$$S\tilde{a}o\,Paolo\;is\;bigger\;than\;ci$$

Once this notation is familiar it can make long expressions much clearer and allows the removal of logical connectives such as $\wedge$ and $\Rightarrow$.

Exercise 4.24 Write the following statements in Z notation, firstly without using the extended notation discussed in the present section, and secondly using the extended notation where appropriate:

(i) ⋄ For integers x, y, with x greater than y, the difference $x - y$ is positive.

(ii) For every member of $\mathbb{N}$ other than 0, there are members of $\mathbb{N}$ which are smaller.

(iii) There is a set of integers which contains 1 but not -1.

(iv) ⋄ Every interval $a\mathbin{..} b$ with $a < b$ contains an even number.

(v) There is no greatest prime number.

(vi) There are positive integers a, b and c, with no common factors, for which the equation $a * x^2 + b * x + c = 0$ has no integer solutions.

4.3.3   Extending the notation of set expressions

We have already seen the declarations-plus-constraint pattern when constructing sets, as in:

$$\{n : \mathbb{Z} \mid n > 0\}$$
$$\{i : \mathbb{Z} \mid \exists\, j : \mathbb{Z} \bullet i = (j + j) - 1\}$$

In each of these examples there is only one declaration, but in fact we are allowed a list of declarations. If a list is present, the elements of the set will be the ordered tuples (according to the order of the declarations) of all values satisfying the set predicate. For example:

$$\{i : \mathbb{N};\; s : \mathbb{P}\,\mathbb{N} \mid s = \{i\} \wedge i < 4\}$$

is the set:

$$\{(0, \{0\}), \ (1, \{1\}), \ (2, \{2\}), \ (3, \{3\})\}$$

and:

$$\{x, y, z : \mathbb{Z} \mid z = x - y\}$$

is an infinite set of triples including such triples as:

$$(0, 0, 0), \ (2, 1, 1), \ (1, -1, 2), \ etc$$

Sometimes we do not want the elements of the set to be tuples according to the declaration list and would like the freedom to choose something else. This freedom is provided in Z set expressions by allowing a term to be added which specifies the shape of the set element. So instead of just:

$$\{Decls \mid Pred\}$$

we are allowed:

$$\{Decls \mid Pred \bullet Expr\}$$

Here are some examples:

- $\{n : \mathbb{N} \mid n < 4 \bullet n^2\}$

  This set is formed by considering $n : \mathbb{N}$ satisfying $n < 4$ and for each such n, taking its square. We can enumerate the set:

  $$\{0, 1, 4, 9\}$$

  Notice that the type of the elements in the set is the type of the expression in the set definition.

- $\{i, j : \mathbb{Z} \bullet i + j\}$

  Here we consider integers i and j. There is no constraining predicate. The elements of the set are formed by adding i and j and are therefore themselves integers. Since by varying i and j we can make $i + j$ equal to any integer we please, this set is in fact the whole of $\mathbb{Z}$.

- $diagonal \ = \ \{i : \mathbb{Z} \mid 1 \leq i \leq 8 \bullet (i, i)\}$

  Thinking of positions on a chessboard as pairs of numbers from 1 to 8, we can represent one of the diagonals by this set. As i ranges from 1 up to 8 we take the pair (i, i) for each possible value.

Again, although this new form of set expression allows convenient and concise definitions, we are not adding any new power to the language. It is always possible to write any set expression using just the declarations plus predicate format.

Exercise 4.25 Argue that:

$$\{ Decs \mid Pred \bullet Expr \}$$

can always be rewritten as:

$$\{ t : T \mid (\exists\, Decs \mid Pred \bullet t = Expr) \}$$

where T is the type of $Expr$ and t is a variable name not otherwise in use.

Exercise 4.26 ◇ Define *diagonal* as given above in two further ways:

   (i) using the form $\{ Decs \mid Pred \}$

   (ii) using the form $\{ Decs \bullet Expr \}$

Note that if no constraint is required then the '$\mid Pred$' part can be omitted from a set expression.

Exercise 4.27 Give set expressions for the following, making use of the extended notation where appropriate in order to make those expressions as simple as possible:

   (i) the set containing the singleton sets of each of the numbers 1 to 5 inclusive

   (ii) the set of pairs of distinct elements of a set S

   (iii) the other diagonal of the chessboard

   (iv) the set of all members of $\mathbb{N}$ which are multiples of 3

4.3.4 Definite descriptions

Another way of defining an expression is by writing a description which says what type of expression is required and gives an exact value for it. This is known as a definite description and its general form is:

$$\mu\, Decs \mid Pred \bullet Expr$$

If the $Expr$ part is omitted, a term of the type of $Decs$ results. For example:

$$\mu\, x : \mathbb{N} \mid x + 5 = 12$$

introduces the number x with value 7, and:

$$\mu\, y : \mathbb{N};\ s : \mathbb{P}\,\mathbb{N} \mid y = 1 \wedge s = \{ y, y + 1 \}$$

makes a pair with values $(1, \{1, 2\})$. Using the *Expr* part we could define:

$$\mu\, x : \mathbb{N} \mid x * x = 81 \bullet \{x\}$$

which evaluates to $\{9\}$.

For a definite description there must be one and only one possible way of assigning a value. For example:

$$\mu\, x : \mathbb{N} \bullet x > 10$$

is not a meaningful definite description since there are many possible values for x.

In practice, this notation is not often seen in Z specifications, but there is one situation where it can be extremely useful. We shall make use of definite descriptions for this purpose later when dealing with objects of schema type.

4.4   Some specification construction units

We have now introduced some of the essential ingredients of the mathematical language: how to make declarations, how to write predicates and how to construct sets. In the remainder of this chapter we will begin to combine these basic ingredients as the first step towards producing a formal specification.

A Z specification consists of sections of formal text usually separated by a good deal of explanatory informal prose; these formal sections are known as paragraphs. We have already met two of the varieties of formal paragraph. Firstly, there are the basic types of the specification. These very often appear together at the top of a specification since it is sensible to sort out at an early stage what types will be needed. The second sort of paragraph we have seen is the data type definition.

We now introduce another example to illustrate the Z approach to specification. We shall not attempt to give a fully developed specification here, since to do this would need schemas which are not introduced until Chapter 6; rather, we look at fragments of formal text which might form part of such a specification. Suppose we wish to describe a simple stock control system to record the quantity of each item stocked by a shop. Eventually we will want to specify operations to model how the stock can change, but we start by simply defining the basic types needed and by using a data type definition to describe possible reports that can be used to inform the user whether an operation is successful or whether an error has occurred. We introduce the type corresponding to the different items stocked in the shop as follows:

[*ITEM*]

Suppose that the report *Ok* is sent when an operation has been successfully accomplished, and that when a requested item is not in stock the report is *NotInStock*.

We make the definition:

$$REPORT ::= Ok \mid NotInStock$$

We saw similar definitions in the earlier Word-For-Word specification; we now see that such fragments of formal text are properly formed paragraphs in Z.

4.4.1   Axiomatic descriptions

Suppose we are told that there is a limit to the number of different lines a shop can hold. This limit is not the same for all possible shops, so we wish to introduce it as a variable which will be known throughout the specification. We know how to declare a number:

$$maxlines : \mathbb{Z}$$

and we might also want a constraint to say that it is strictly positive:

$$maxlines > 0$$

But how should this appear in the specification?

The sort of formal paragraph used for this purpose is known as an axiomatic description. It is used to introduce variables along with predicates giving further information. These variables will then be known throughout the rest of the specification; we say they are global variables. An axiomatic description is written by presenting the declaration and predicate in a box as follows:

$$
\begin{array}{|l}
maxlines : \mathbb{Z} \\
\hline
maxlines > 0
\end{array}
$$

If a declaration only is required we can omit the predicate part. For example, earlier in the chapter $\mathbb{N}_1$ is defined to be the set $\{n : \mathbb{N} \mid n > 0\}$. We could therefore introduce *maxlines* simply by:

$$
\begin{array}{|l}
maxlines : \mathbb{N}_1
\end{array}
$$

Similarly, if at some stage we want to add a predicate describing some further property of global variables that have already been introduced we can do that by simply writing down the predicate. For example:

$$maxlines > 100$$

4.4.2 Abbreviation definitions

Suppose we wish to introduce into our specification a constant, *initialstock*, to represent the stock initially held in our shop. What sort of an object will this be? For each sort of item the shop wishes to stock we need to know how many are currently being held. So we need to keep information relating items to numbers. This can be done by keeping (*ITEM*, $\mathbb{N}$) pairs. Thus a stock record might be described using a set of pairs, for example the initial stock might be:

$$\{(widget1, 62), (widget2, 12), (thingummy, 0), (whatsit, 8)\}$$

where a stock level of 0 indicates a line which we intend to stock but have currently run out of. The type of this set of pairs is $\mathbb{P}(ITEM \times \mathbb{Z})$. In fact, since the stock levels can never be negative we can state that our stock record belongs to $\mathbb{P}(ITEM \times \mathbb{N})$.

There is another restriction that should be made. It would not make sense for the same item to be associated with two different stock levels. To capture this we can construct the subset of $\mathbb{P}(ITEM \times \mathbb{N})$ which disallows this possibility:

$$\{s : \mathbb{P}(ITEM \times \mathbb{N}) \mid \forall i : ITEM; \, m, n : \mathbb{N} \bullet$$
$$(i, m) \in s \wedge (i, n) \in s \Rightarrow n = m\}$$

This set includes all the possibilities for valid stock records, and so *initialstock* must belong to it. The definition of the set is quite cumbersome so it would be useful to give it a name (let us call it *Stock*) by which it will be known throughout the specification. (We shall see later that there are, fortunately, simpler ways to express this in Z.) We could do this by giving an axiomatic description as described above, but since we know the exact value we wish *Stock* to take we can use another, shorter, way to introduce it, known as the abbreviation definition.

The abbreviation definition is used to introduce global constants, that is, objects with a determined value to be known throughout the specification. This kind of Z paragraph is written using the $==$ symbol:

$$Stock == \{s : \mathbb{P}(ITEM \times \mathbb{N}) \mid \forall i : ITEM; \, m, n : \mathbb{N} \bullet$$
$$(i, m) \in s \wedge (i, n) \in s \Rightarrow n = m\}$$

The constant *Stock* is not explicitly given a type in this form of declaration, but its type can immediately be determined since it is the same as that of the expression on the right. We have of course used the $==$ symbol from the beginning of the book to mean 'is defined as', being careful to use the symbol in ways consistent with its usage in Z.

Notice that it would not have been possible to define *maxlines* in this way because there is no one particular value to which it is equal. All we could do for *maxlines* was to describe the range of possible values it might take.

Having defined *Stock* we can now introduce *initialstock*. We know it is a member of *Stock* since it must be a valid stock record, but we do not know precisely which one it is. This suggests that an axiomatic description is appropriate:

$$
\begin{array}{|l}
initialstock : Stock \\
\hline
\# \, initialstock \leq maxlines
\end{array}
$$

The predicate part says that the number of pairs in *initialstock* cannot be greater than *maxlines*. Since for each line we intend to stock there is exactly one pair in *initialstock*, this expresses the restriction that the number of different product lines in our stock record cannot exceed *maxlines*.

Exercise 4.28 What basic types were used in the Word-For-Word specification?

Exercise 4.29 Give axiomatic descriptions for:

  (i) ⋄ *evensize*, a set containing an even number of integers

 (ii) *notgreen*, a colour other than green

(iii) *relatedpair*, a pair whose first element is a positive number and whose second is a set of integers containing that number

Exercise 4.30 Give abbreviation definitions for:

  (i) ⋄ *origin*, a pair of zeros

 (ii) *bignumbers*, the set of all numbers greater than a million

(iii) *incpair*, the set of all pairs of integers whose second elements are exactly one greater than their first elements

 (iv) *notwidget*, the set of all items except for *widget1* and *widget2*

Exercise 4.31 Suppose the stock control specification must impose the further constraint on *initialstock* that there should be no more than 1000 of any item held in the shop. Write an axiomatic description to reflect this.

Exercise 4.32 Give an axiomatic description for *initiallowlines*, the set of all product lines from *initialstock* whose stock level is less than 10.

4.4.3   Generic definitions

We have already seen that it can be useful to have constants such as $\emptyset$, the empty set, which can be used in contexts where objects of differing types are expected. For example:

$$1 \mathbin{.\,.} 0 = \emptyset$$
$$\mathbb{P}\,\mathbb{N} \setminus \mathbb{P}\,\mathbb{N} = \emptyset$$

In the first case the expression on the left has type $\mathbb{P}\,\mathbb{Z}$ and in the second, $\mathbb{P}\,\mathbb{P}\,\mathbb{Z}$. So what is the type of $\emptyset$?

The answer is that $\emptyset$ and many other constants are defined generically; that is to say, they have a definition which uses type parameters. When such a constant is used at any later stage in the specification, actual sets must be provided to replace the type parameters. Replacing the generic parameters with actual sets is known as instantiation. Sometimes (as in the example involving $\emptyset$ above) it can be inferred from the context which instantiation is intended. In some circumstances we must state explicitly what the instantiation should be. In either case, it must be completely clear precisely which values the generic parameters should take.

The generic definition is another in the series of formal paragraphs of a Z document. In the case of $\emptyset$ the definition might look like this:

$$
\begin{array}{l}
\underline{\!= [X] \!=\!=\!=\!=\!=\!=\!=\!=\!=\!=\!=\!=\!=\!=\!=\!=\!=} \\
\quad \emptyset : \mathbb{P}\,X \\
\hline
\quad \emptyset = \{x : X \mid x \neq x\} \\
\end{array}
$$

The box used for this has a top and a bottom, the top being a double line. In square brackets along the top line we write the generic parameters that are to be used in the definition, in this case only X. Inside the box a familiar pattern is seen. Above the line the new generic constant is declared. It is a set of elements of X and therefore has type $\mathbb{P}\,X$. Below the line we write the predicate defining $\emptyset$. Since there can be no x which satisfies $x \neq x$ the set is always empty.

When we use $\emptyset$ it may be possible to infer the appropriate value for X from the context. In the case of:

$$1 \mathbin{.\,.} 0 = \emptyset$$

it is clear that $\emptyset$ must be of the same type as $1 \mathbin{.\,.} 0$ and is therefore a set of integers. Hence X has been implicitly instantiated with $\mathbb{Z}$.

Where it is not possible to infer the type or where we wish to make absolutely clear to the reader of our specification what instantiation is being made we can instantiate the generic parameters explicitly as in:

$$1 \mathbin{.\,.} 0 = \emptyset[\mathbb{Z}]$$

The sets concerned are given in square brackets next to the name of the constant. If there is more than one parameter to instantiate the order of the sets provided should match the order of the generic parameters in the definition.

As another example of generic definition, we consider the definition of the symbol $\subseteq$. This symbol relates subsets of the same type, so that it is in fact a set of $(set\ of\ X, set\ of\ X)$ pairs, which is to say that its type is $\mathbb{P}(\mathbb{P}\,X \times \mathbb{P}\,X)$, where X is the underlying type of the members of the subsets concerned. Thus we may define:

$$
\begin{array}{|l}
\hline
= [X] \overline{} \\
\quad \_ \subseteq \_ : \mathbb{P}(\mathbb{P}\,X \times \mathbb{P}\,X) \\
\hline
\quad \forall S, T : \mathbb{P}\,X \bullet S \subseteq T \Leftrightarrow (\forall x : X \bullet x \in S \Rightarrow x \in T) \\
\hline
\end{array}
$$

The notation $\_ \subseteq \_$ indicates that the symbol is to be placed between the two sets which it relates. So we see now that $\subseteq$ is in fact a constant of a particular kind (in fact it is a relation, but we come to that in Chapter 5), and there is such a constant for every type X.

As with abbreviation definitions, generic definitions must be uniquely defined for each possible instantiation of the generic parameters. In fact, the abbreviation definition as described earlier is also allowed to take generic parameters. As an example, we could define $\emptyset$ in an alternative but equivalent manner by:

$$\emptyset[X] == \{x : X \mid x \neq x\}$$

It is often a matter of taste and convenience as to which style of definition is chosen.

Finally we remark that generic abbreviation definitions may sometimes be expressed in a slightly different format. Instead of the generic parameters being enclosed in square brackets they are used as place holders in the definition; for instance, we might say:

$$\mathbb{P}_1\,X == \mathbb{P}\,X \setminus \{\emptyset\}$$

which defines $\mathbb{P}_1\,X$ to be the powerset of X except that the empty set is excluded. When this is used, an actual set is given in place of X, as in:

$$\mathbb{P}_1\{0, 1\} = \{\{0\}, \{1\}, \{0, 1\}\}$$

Exercise 4.33 Suppose that Z had the notation SX for the set of all singleton sets whose single elements are drawn from the set X; give an abbreviation definition with X as a place holder, that is to say:

$$SX == \{...\}$$

Note that Z does not in fact have such a notation.

Exercise 4.34 ⋄ Give a definition for the symbol $\subset$ similar to that for $\subseteq$ given above. Give a definition from first principles, rather than making use of the earlier definition; that is to say, express the fact that if S is a proper subset of T then any element of S is also an element of T, but there must exist at least one of element of T which is not an element of S.

Exercise 4.35 Give a generic definition of *zeropair*, the set of pairs whose first elements are all the members of the set X and whose second elements are all zero. Give examples of members of *zeropair* when X is instantiated with:

(i) $\mathbb{Z}$ (ii) $\mathbb{P}\,\mathbb{Z}$ (iii) $\mathbb{Z} \times \mathbb{Z}$

Exercise 4.36 ⋄ Describe what is wrong with the following attempt to define a generic *singleton*:

$$
\begin{array}{|l}
\hline
[X] \\
\hline
singleton : \mathbb{P}\,X \\
\hline
\#singleton = 1 \\
\hline
\end{array}
$$

4.5   Summary of notation introduced

We now give a summary of the new notation introduced in this chapter, giving examples which for the most part have already been encountered in the main body of the chapter.

- The *basic types* of a specification are declared by enclosing them in square brackets; For example:

  $[BOOK, CAR]$
  $[ITEM]$

- A *declaration* may take the form $x : T$, where T is a type or $x : S$, where S is a subset of a type. Constraints may be added by following the declaration(s) by a $|$ *Pred* part which expresses some relationship amongst the declared variables. If the declaration is global, then an axiomatic description is needed (see below). Examples showing how a collection of variables may be declared, some of the same type, some of different types:

  $m, n : \mathbb{N}$
  $i, j : 1..8 \mid i \neq j$
  $e1, e2 : S; \; s : \mathbb{P}\,S \mid e1 \in s \wedge e2 \notin s$

- *Free type definitions* allow us to define types with a small number of distinct elements; for example:

$$POSITION ::= \mathit{off} \mid \mathit{on}$$
$$REPORT ::= \mathit{Ok} \mid \mathit{NotInStock}$$

and to construct new types from existing ones:

$$PROPERTY ::= \mathit{col}\langle\!\langle COLOUR \rangle\!\rangle$$
$$\mid \mathit{sha}\langle\!\langle SHAPE \rangle\!\rangle$$

- New sets can be created from old by use of the powerset and Cartesian product operators, $\mathbb{P}$ and $\times$. If $\mathbb{P}$ and $\times$ are applied to types, new types result. Every Z variable and expression belongs to one and only one type, although it may belong to many different sets.

- *Axiomatic descriptions* introduce global variables with constraints on their values. They take the form:

$$\begin{array}{|l}
\hline
Decls \\
\hline
Pred
\end{array}$$

Examples are:

$$\begin{array}{|l}
\hline
initlowstock : \mathbb{P}\,ITEM \\
\hline
initlowstock = \\
\quad \{i : ITEM;\ n : \mathbb{N} \mid (i, n) \in initialstock \wedge n < 10 \bullet i\}
\end{array}$$

$$\begin{array}{|l}
\hline
initialstock : Stock \\
\hline
\#initialstock \leq maxlines \\
\forall i : item;\ n : \mathbb{N} \mid (i, n) \in initialstock \bullet n \leq 1000
\end{array}$$

$$\begin{array}{|l}
maxlines : \mathbb{N}_1
\end{array}$$

where the third example is a degenerate case which requires no predicate.

- An *abbreviation definition* introduces a global constant:

$$Name == Expr$$

for example:

$$Stock == \{s : \mathbb{P}(ITEM \times \mathbb{N}) \mid$$
$$\forall i : ITEM;\ m, n : \mathbb{N} \bullet (i, m) \in s \wedge (i, n) \in s \Rightarrow m = n\}$$

They may also have generic parameters:

$$\emptyset[X] == \{x : X \mid x \neq x\}$$

or:

$$\mathbb{P}_1 X == \mathbb{P} X \setminus \{\emptyset\}$$

- *Generic definitions* can also be written using generic boxes:

$$
\begin{array}{|l}
\!\![X, Y, \ldots]\!\!\rule{3cm}{0pt} \\
\hline
Decls \\
\hline
Pred \\
\hline
\end{array}
$$

for example:

$$
\begin{array}{|l}
\!\![X]\!\!\rule{3cm}{0pt} \\
\hline
\emptyset : \mathbb{P} X \\
\hline
\emptyset = \{x : X \mid x \neq x\} \\
\hline
\end{array}
$$

4.6   Further reading

For those readers interested in the paradoxes of set theory, we would suggest [Qui76, Qui69]. Details of the Z basic library and other aspects of Z notation will be found in [Spi92]; this work is of course a reference manual, and in general gives only brief explanations. The Z Standard [BN92] contains this material and much more. It is intended that a revised version of [BN92] will shortly become the internationally accepted standard for Z. There is little difference between [BN92] and [Spi92] with respect to the basic mathematical definitions.

Chapter 5

The Z notation: relations and functions

In preceding chapters we have introduced the ideas of sets, propositions and predicates, and in Chapter 4 we gave more rigorous definitions of the basic building blocks of the Z notation. Now we can go on to explore some ways of standing on the shoulders of these basic concepts, with the aim of equipping ourselves with further powerful techniques. These will allow us to write more concisely concerning quite complicated ideas without losing any of the precision already achieved.

5.1 Relations

We have shown how sets and logic may be used to describe systems such as the bilingual dictionary of Chapter 3. There will be occasions when we wish to describe ways in which elements of sets are related. This is commonly done in everyday language; for instance, we might wish to make some observations concerning people and musical instruments as in:

> *Ashkenazy plays piano*
> *Williams plays guitar*

Here, the first element is taken from the set of people and the second from the set of instruments. A person is related to an instrument if he or she plays that instrument. Again, we might record relationships between people such as:

> *Huw is brother of Alice*
> *Kate is mother of Huw*
> *Kate is mother of Alice*

In this case, pairs of people are related so the two sets concerned are in fact the same. We borrow the familiar term 'relation', used to describe kinship of people, to refer to any interesting connection between the elements of sets.

It is sometimes helpful when thinking about relations to use pictures to gain an intuition about the ideas before making a formal expression of them using mathematical notation. This can be done in the form shown below. We could capture some information about modes of transport of the Potter family from the following:

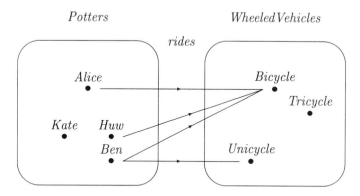

This describes the relation between the Potters and the subset of wheeled vehicles upon which they ride. Elements related by the *rides* relation are shown by the arrowed lines. The diagram draws our attention to two noteworthy points. Firstly, each element in each of the sets may be related to any number of elements in the other set. For this reason relations are sometimes called many-to-many or just many-many mappings. Here, *Ben* rides both a bicycle and a unicycle and so is related to both. Three members of the family ride a bicycle, so there are three arrows pointing to *bicycle*. We can see that not every element in the sets needs to be related. In this example *Kate* and *Tricycle* have no connecting arrows, which means that Kate does not ride any of the wheeled vehicles and that none of the Potters rides a tricycle. Relations between two sets such as *rides* are known as binary relations.

Secondly, the relation itself is completely defined by the connections between the elements of the sets. Another way of recording the information contained in the picture would be to write down all the pairs of related elements. For the *rides* relation these are:

(*Alice, Bicycle*) (*Huw, Bicycle*) (*Ben, Unicycle*) (*Ben, Bicycle*)

Each pair in the list corresponds to a pair in the diagram. Using this approach we can represent any binary relation in Z as a set of ordered pairs. So to define the *rides* relation we could write:

$$rides == \{(Alice, Bicycle), (Huw, Bicycle),$$
$$(Ben, Unicycle), (Ben, Bicycle)\}$$

Since a relation is just a set of ordered pairs, two elements are related if and only if they form a pair in the set. From the above example we know that:

$$(Alice, Bicycle) \in rides$$

but:

$$(Huw, Tricycle) \notin rides$$

Also, from our knowledge of sets we can deduce that the type of *rides* is:

$$\mathbb{P}(Potters \times WheeledVehicles)$$

since this is the type of such a set of ordered pairs.

Exercise 5.1 Give examples (other than the empty relation) of:

(i) a relation which is a subset of *rides*

(ii) a relation between $\mathbb{Z}$ and $\mathbb{Z}$

(iii) a relation between $1 .. 10$ and $\mathbb{N}$

Exercise 5.2 ⋄ Using *rides'* to represent the new relation in each case, write expressions to describe how *rides* changes when:

(i) Kate learns to ride a bicycle

(ii) Ben forgets how to ride the unicycle

(iii) all the Potters decide to stop riding bicycles

5.1.1   Notation for relations

Since the idea of a relation is so useful and occurs so often in Z specifications we introduce some special notation. A relation between sets X and Y is a member of:

$$\mathbb{P}(X \times Y)$$

As a shorthand for this, and to emphasise the relational nature of a set of ordered pairs, we introduce the double-headed arrow notation:

$$X \leftrightarrow Y == \mathbb{P}(X \times Y)$$

This notation can be used when declaring relations, for instance:

> *rides : Potters ↔ WheeledVehicles*
> *plays : People ↔ Instruments*

A special notation may also be used for the pairs which make up a relation. Instead of writing (x, y) for a related pair we sometimes use the maplet notation:

> $x \mapsto y$

which is read '*x* maps to *y*'. Using maplet notation the *rides* relation may be written:

> $\{Alice \mapsto Bicycle, Huw \mapsto Bicycle, Ben \mapsto Unicycle, Ben \mapsto Bicycle\}$

and as before we can make statements about maplets:

> $Alice \mapsto Bicycle \in rides$

and:

> $\{Huw \mapsto Bicycle, Ben \mapsto Bicycle\} \subseteq rides$

Yet another way of saying that two objects are related was seen earlier, as in:

> *Ashkenazy plays piano*
> *Huw is brother of Alice*

Again, these are really just a shorter, more expressive form of:

> $(Ashkenazy, piano) \in plays$
> $(Huw, Alice) \in is\ brother\ of$

Relations such as these which we expect to see used between the names of two objects are known as infix relations. When we first declare a relation we can indicate that it is intended to be infix by using underscores as place markers to show that the relation may appear between two related objects:

> *_plays_ : People ↔ Instruments*
> *_is brother of_ : People ↔ People*

Definitions using ordered pairs or the maplet notation are convenient for small relations but impractical for larger ones and impossible for infinite ones. For instance, consider the 'less than' relation between integers:

> $\_ < \_ : \mathbb{Z} \leftrightarrow \mathbb{Z}$

(notice that this is declared as an infix relation, since we expect to see the $<$ symbol used between two integers, as in $1 < 2$). We could never write down every pair of integers which stand in this relation. There is no problem in defining such relations however, because relations are just sets of ordered pairs and we have already seen how an infinite set may be defined by giving a predicate which its members must satisfy. So a definition of the 'less than' relation would give its declaration plus a defining predicate:

$$
\begin{array}{|l}
\_ < \_ : \mathbb{Z} \leftrightarrow \mathbb{Z} \\
\hline
\forall x, y : \mathbb{Z} \bullet (x < y \Leftrightarrow \exists z : \mathbb{N}_1 \bullet y = x + z)
\end{array}
$$

Exercise 5.3 ⬦ You will encounter a number of different arrows during the course of this chapter. It is advisable to become confident about the meanings of $\leftrightarrow$ and $\mapsto$ before proceeding.

  (i) If A, B are the sets $\{0,1\}, \{blue, green\}$ respectively, write out the set for which $A \leftrightarrow B$ is a shorthand.

  (ii) What is $\emptyset[A] \leftrightarrow \emptyset[A]$?

  (iii) What is the type of $\{1 \mapsto (1,1), 2 \mapsto (2,2)\}$?

Exercise 5.4 The set *WellFormedVocabs* from Chapter 3 is in fact a set of relations. Use the new notation to rewrite its definition.

5.1.2   Domains and ranges

The two sets used in the declaration of a relation are sometimes referred to as the source and target respectively. The *rides* relation is an example of a relation between *Potters* and *WheeledVehicles*: in this case, *Potters* is the source set and *WheeledVehicles* is the target. Of course, a relation need not relate every member of the source or of the target; in either set, only a subset might be used in the description of the relation. In the *rides* example *Kate* is a member of the source but is not related to anything, and in the target set *Tricycle* is an element not ridden by anyone.

   It can be useful to give names to the subsets of the source and target whose elements really are involved in the description of the relation. The subset of elements of the source which are related to at least one element of the target is known as the domain of the relation. The domain of *rides* is:

$\{Alice, Huw, Ben\}$

Similarly, the range consists of all elements of the target set which are related to some element of the source. The range of *rides* is:

{*Bicycle, Unicycle*}

If R is any relation of type $X \leftrightarrow Y$ we generally refer to its domain as dom R and its range as ran R. The informal descriptions of domain and range already given can be stated more clearly using set expressions: for any relation R:

$$\text{dom } R = \{x : X \mid (\exists y : Y \bullet x \mapsto y \in R)\}$$
$$\text{ran } R = \{y : Y \mid (\exists x : X \bullet x \mapsto y \in R)\}$$

Note that these would ordinarily be given as full generic definitions, but we shall defer this until sufficient notation has been introduced.

Exercise 5.5 ⋄ Assume the definition of two relations involving the sets *People*, *Instruments* and *Actions* as follows:

$$plays == \{Ashkenazy \mapsto piano, Williams \mapsto guitar, David \mapsto violin,$$
$$Huw \mapsto trumpet, Alice \mapsto flute, Alice \mapsto piano, Kate \mapsto piano\}$$

$$worksby == \{piano \mapsto hammering, guitar \mapsto plucking,$$
$$harpsichord \mapsto plucking, trumpet \mapsto blowing,$$
$$flute \mapsto blowing, violin \mapsto bowing, violin \mapsto scraping\}$$

(i) What are the domain and range of *plays* and of *worksby*?

(ii) What are the types of the domain and range of *plays* and of *worksby*?

Exercise 5.6 Let S be the set of numbers from 1 to 12 inclusive. Let R be an infix relation of type $S \leftrightarrow S$ such that x is related to y exactly when y is greater than the square of x but less than the square of $x + 1$.

(i) Write down a definition of R using declaration and predicate.

(ii) Draw a diagram of this relation and write down the set of pairs representing it.

Exercise 5.7 Give the domain and range of:

(i) ⋄ $\{n, m : \mathbb{N} \mid n = 2 * m\}$

(ii) $\{x : X \bullet (x, x)\}$ for any set X

(iii) ⋄ $\{x : X \mid x \neq x \bullet (x, x)\}$ for any set X

(iv) $\{s : \mathbb{P} \, Potters; \, w : WheeledVehicles \mid (\forall p : Potters \bullet p \in s \Leftrightarrow p \; rides \; w)\}$

Exercise 5.8 ⋄ The relation *pairsum* relates pairs of integers to their sum. What is the type of *pairsum*? Give a definition for *pairsum*.

Exercise 5.9 Use a generic definition to define the relation *contains* where x contains y whenever x is a set of which y is a member. What are dom *contains* and ran *contains*?

5.1.3   Example

We can use the new vocabulary of relation, domain and range to continue our stock control specification of the previous chapter.

Firstly, remember that the stock is represented by a set of ordered pairs; we now know that we can view this as a relation between *ITEM* and $\mathbb{N}$. We could therefore rewrite the definition of *Stock* using $ITEM \leftrightarrow \mathbb{N}$ instead of $\mathbb{P}(ITEM \times \mathbb{N})$.

Further, suppose we wish to find the set *stockitems*, of lines that the shop initially intends to stock, mindful of the fact that this will include lines with an original stock level of zero. Recall that we defined:

$$
\begin{array}{|l}
initialstock : Stock \\
\hline
\#initialstock \leq maxlines \\
\forall i : ITEM;\, n : \mathbb{N} \mid (i, n) \in initialstock \bullet n \leq 1000
\end{array}
$$

so *initialstock* is a valid stock record, and is therefore a relation from *ITEM* to $\mathbb{N}$. To obtain *stockitems* all we need to do is to find the domain of *initialstock*:

$$
\begin{array}{|l}
stockitems : \mathbb{P}\, ITEM \\
\hline
stockitems = \mathrm{dom}\, initialstock
\end{array}
$$

So if *initialstock* happens to be:

$$\{ widget1 \mapsto 62, widget2 \mapsto 12, thingummy \mapsto 0, whatsit \mapsto 8 \}$$

then *stockitems* is just the set:

$$\{ widget1, widget2, thingummy, whatsit \}$$

5.2   Operations on relations

We have already seen many useful operations on sets, such as union, intersection and subtraction. When writing specifications it will often be convenient to use operations on relations as part of the description. Since relations are really just sets of pairs, all the set operations met so far can immediately be applied to relations. For example:

$$
\begin{aligned}
rides &\setminus \{(Ben, Unicycle), (Ben, Bicycle)\} \\
&= \{(Alice, Bicycle), (Huw, Bicycle)\}
\end{aligned}
$$

and if Kate starts to ride the tricycle, one way to describe the new relation would be:

$$rides \cup \{(Kate, Tricycle)\}$$

Besides the ordinary set operations, the nature of relations makes it desirable to provide some more specialised operations. Some of these are introduced below.

5.2.1 Relational inverse

Sometimes it may be useful to look at relations the other way round. For example, having defined the *rides* relation it may be found desirable to know what is ridden by whom rather than who rides what. We might call this the *isriddenby* relation. To obtain the new relation we would have to reverse the order of each pair in the original. For instance, since:

> *Ben rides Unicycle*

is part of the *rides* relation, we would expect to see:

> *Unicycle isriddenby Ben*

Reversing all the pairs defines the new relation:

> *isriddenby* ==
> $\{(Unicycle, Ben), (Bicycle, Ben), (Bicycle, Alice), (Bicycle, Huw)\}$

This process of reversing a relation gives a new relation which is known as the inverse. We denote the inverse operation by the superscript, $\sim$. So for example:

> *isriddenby* = *rides*$^\sim$

Notice that it is also true that:

> *rides* = *isriddenby*$^\sim$

In general, for any relation R of type $X \leftrightarrow Y$ the inverse relation is given by:

> $R^\sim = \{x : X; y : Y \mid x \mapsto y \in R \bullet y \mapsto x\}$

For every maplet appearing in R, the reversed maplet appears in $R^\sim$. An alternative notation for $R^\sim$ is R^{-1}.

Exercise 5.10 ◇ Given the *plays* and *worksby* relations of the previous exercises what are *plays*$^\sim$ and *worksby*$^\sim$? What are the domain and range in each case?

Exercise 5.11 What are the inverses of the relations in Exercise 5.2?

Exercise 5.12 Use the definition of inverse to argue that for any relation R:

(i) $(R^\sim)^\sim = R$

(ii) ◇ dom R = ran$(R^\sim)$

(iii) ran R = dom$(R^\sim)$

5.2.2   Restriction and subtraction

Suppose that, given the *rides* relation, the modes of transport of Alice and Kate are found to be of special interest, perhaps as part of a survey to see which cycles women ride. We might want to make a smaller relation by considering only the pairs which relate Alice and Kate to some wheeled vehicle. Restricting *rides* in this way would produce the relation:

$$wrides = \{Alice \mapsto Bicycle\}$$

Creating a smaller relation like this, by considering only a part of the original domain, is known as domain restriction. The following notation is used:

$$wrides == \{Alice, Kate\} \lhd rides$$

The domain restriction operator, $\lhd$, appears between the set that we wish to restrict the domain to and the name of the relation being restricted. Notice that the restricting set appears on the left with one point of the triangle facing towards it.

There is a complementary range restriction operation which creates a smaller relation by considering only a part of the original range. For instance, suppose we are interested in a relation which tells us who rides a bicycle. This can be obtained by restricting the range of *rides* to the singleton set $\{Bicycle\}$. For this we would write:

$$rides \rhd \{Bicycle\}$$

For range restriction the restricting set appears to the right of the range restriction symbol, $\rhd$. Again, the triangle points towards the restricting set.

As before, we can give precise expressions for domain and range restrictions for any relation R of type $X \leftrightarrow Y$. Suppose S is a set of elements of the domain type, X, then:

$$S \lhd R = \{x : X; y : Y \mid x \in S \land x \mapsto y \in R \bullet x \mapsto y\}$$

Bearing in mind the short form, which allows us to omit the defining term where it may be inferred directly, we can write this more tersely as:

$$S \lhd R = \{x : X; y : Y \mid x \in S \land x \mapsto y \in R\}$$

This says that a pair (x, y) is in the restricted relation if and only if it was in the original relation and x is a member of the restricting set S. Similarly, for range restriction, if T is a set of elements of the range type Y then:

$$R \rhd T = \{x : X; y : Y \mid y \in T \land x \mapsto y \in R\}$$

Suppose that instead of restricting the domain (or range) to a certain set we have a particular set of elements which we would like to remove from the domain (or range). This can be done in a similar way by using domain (or range) subtraction. For instance:

$$\{Ben\} \lhd rides$$

is the relation which no longer contains any pairs relating Ben to anything. So:

$$\{Ben\} \lhd rides = \{Alice \mapsto Bicycle, Huw \mapsto Bicycle\}$$

The set $\{Ben\}$ has been subtracted from the domain, and the result no longer contains any information about the things to which Ben was related in the original. An example of range subtraction is:

$$rides \rhd \{Bicycle, Tricycle\}$$

Removing all pairs which relate someone to a bicycle or a tricycle leaves just $\{Ben \mapsto Unicycle\}$.

Notice that the pattern is the same as for domain and range restriction: a set to be subtracted from the domain appears to the left of the pointing triangle symbol, whereas in range subtraction the set is on the right. The symbols for subtraction have a subtraction sign inside the triangle as a reminder:

$$S \lhd R = \{x : X; y : Y \mid x \notin S \wedge x \mapsto y \in R\}$$
$$R \rhd T = \{x : X; y : Y \mid y \notin T \wedge x \mapsto y \in R\}$$

Exercise 5.13 Using the *plays* and *worksby* relations of previous exercises write out the contents of each of the relations defined below:

(i) $\{piano, harpsichord\} \lhd worksby$

(ii) $plays \rhd \{piano, violin\}$

(iii) $plays \rhd \{piano\}$

(iv) $worksby \rhd \{bowing, scraping\}$

Exercise 5.14 ◇ Use the operators on relations introduced so far to write down expressions for:

(i) the subset of *WheeledVehicles* ridden by Kate

(ii) the Potters who ride either a bicycle or a tricycle

(iii) the relation of male Potters riding *WheeledVehicles* other than the bicycle

Exercise 5.15 Use the definitions to argue that for $R : X \leftrightarrow Y$; $S : \mathbb{P} X$; $T : \mathbb{P} Y$:

(i) $\diamond \operatorname{dom}(S \triangleleft R) = S \cap (\operatorname{dom} R)$

(ii) $\operatorname{ran}(R \triangleright T) = (\operatorname{ran} R) \cap T$

(iii) $(S \triangleleft R) \triangleright T = S \triangleleft (R \triangleright T)$

(iv) $S \triangleleft R = (X \setminus S) \triangleleft R$

(v) $R \triangleright T = R \triangleright (Y \setminus T)$

(vi) $(S \triangleleft R) \cup (S \triangleleft R) = R$

5.2.3   Composition of relations

Given two relations such that the range type of the first is the same as the domain type of the second, it is useful to be able to put the relations 'end to end' and form a single relation containing all pairs joined by some common element. To see how this works, let us define a new relation *haswheels* which relates wheeled vehicles to the number of wheels they possess:

$$haswheels == \{ Unicycle \mapsto 1, Bicycle \mapsto 2, Tricycle \mapsto 3 \}$$

We now have two relations:

$$rides : Potters \leftrightarrow WheeledVehicles$$
$$haswheels : WheeledVehicles \leftrightarrow \mathbb{N}_1$$

The range type of *rides* and the domain type of *haswheels* are the same so we can compose *rides* with *haswheels* to produce a new relation *ridesonwheels* of type $Potters \leftrightarrow \mathbb{N}_1$ which records how many wheels each of the Potters can ride on. A picture shows how this composition is achieved:

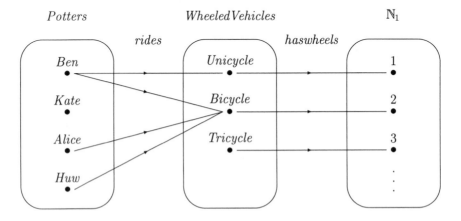

To find which Potters are related to which numbers we must include all possible paths through this diagram from Potters to N_1. This shows that:

$$ridesonwheels == \{Ben \mapsto 1, Ben \mapsto 2, Alice \mapsto 2, Huw \mapsto 2\}$$

The composition operation is denoted by $\S$ and we write:

$$ridesonwheels = rides \mathbin{\S} haswheels$$

As another example, suppose we have two relations, $R_1, R_2 : N \leftrightarrow N$ with:

$$R_1 = \{0 \mapsto 1, 2 \mapsto 0, 2 \mapsto 1\}$$
$$R_2 = \{1 \mapsto 0, 1 \mapsto 2, 2 \mapsto 1\}$$

As before we draw a diagram to represent their composition:

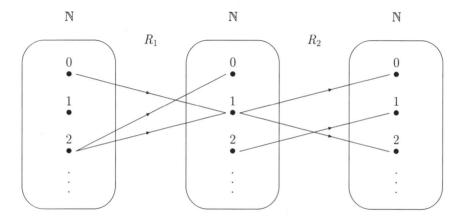

To obtain $R_1 \mathbin{\S} R_2$ we must find all pairs of numbers where the first is in dom R_1, the second is in ran R_2 and they are connected to some common intermediate number by both R_1 and R_2. This time there are more branching paths so we must be careful to include all the possibilities. We see that R_1 connects 0 to 1 and that R_2 connects 1 to both 0 and 2. So the composed relation must contain both $(0, 0)$ and $(0, 2)$. R_1 does not connect 1 to anything, so there can be no pairs with first element 1 in the composition. Finally, 2 is related to both 0 and 1 by R_1. R_2 does not connect 0 to anything so that path comes to an end. But again, 1 is connected to both 0 and 2 so the pairs $(2, 0)$ and $(2, 2)$ are both present in the composition. Putting this together gives:

$$R_1 \mathbin{\S} R_2 = \{0 \mapsto 0, 0 \mapsto 2, 2 \mapsto 0, 2 \mapsto 2\}$$

Suppose we have two relations:

$$Q : X \leftrightarrow Y; R : Y \leftrightarrow Z$$

then:

$$Q \,\S\, R = \{x : X; y : Y; z : Z \mid x \mapsto y \in Q \wedge y \mapsto z \in R \bullet x \mapsto z\}$$

This gives all pairs (x, z) for which there is some $y : Y$ with (x, y) related in Q and (y, z) related in R.

Exercise 5.16 What are the relations defined by:

(i) $\{Alice\} \lhd (rides \,\S\, haswheels)$

(ii) $(\{Alice\} \lhd rides) \,\S\, haswheels$

Exercise 5.17 ⋄ If $R_1, R_2 : \mathbb{N} \leftrightarrow \mathbb{N}$ are the relations:

$$R_1 = \{1 \mapsto 4, 2 \mapsto 3, 3 \mapsto 2, 3 \mapsto 3, 4 \mapsto 1\}$$
$$R_2 = \{1 \mapsto 2, 2 \mapsto 3, 3 \mapsto 4\}$$

write out:

(i) $R_1 \,\S\, R_2$ (ii) $R_2 \,\S\, R_1$ (iii) $R_1 \,\S\, R_1$ (iv) $R_1 \,\S\, R_1 \,\S\, R_1$

Exercise 5.18 The identity relation on any given set maps each element of the set to itself. Give a generic definition of this relation, known as id.

Exercise 5.19 Argue from the definitions that for relations $Q : X \leftrightarrow Y; R : Y \leftrightarrow Z$ and sets $S : \mathbb{P} X; T : \mathbb{P} Y$ the following equalities hold:

(i) $\mathrm{id}[X] \,\S\, Q = Q \,\S\, \mathrm{id}[Y] = Q$

(ii) ⋄ $Q \,\S\, Q^\sim = \mathrm{id}[\mathrm{dom}\, Q]$

(iii) $S \lhd Q = \mathrm{id}[S] \,\S\, Q$

(iv) $Q \rhd T = Q \,\S\, \mathrm{id}[T]$

(v) $S \lhd (Q \,\S\, R) = (S \lhd Q) \,\S\, R$

Exercise 5.20 Show that composition of relations is associative, that is, for $P : W \leftrightarrow X; Q : X \leftrightarrow Y; R : Y \leftrightarrow Z$ the following holds:

$$(P \,\S\, Q) \,\S\, R = P \,\S\, (Q \,\S\, R)$$

5.2.4   Relational image

The final operation we shall introduce for relations is one which, given any set of domain-type elements of a relation, will give the subset of range elements to which they are related. For example, suppose we wish to find the set of all vehicles ridden by either Ben or Alice. We know that:

$$(Ben, Unicycle), (Ben, Bicycle), (Alice, Bicycle)$$

are all the relevant pairs from *rides*, and to find the required set we must take all the wheeled vehicles to which either person is related, giving:

$$\{Unicycle, Bicycle\}$$

The set formed by looking through the relation in this way to find just those elements of the range which are related to one of the domain elements we are interested in is called the relational image. For the above example we would write:

$$rides(\!|\ \{Ben, Alice\}\ |\!)$$

giving the name of the relation followed, in fat brackets, by the set whose image under the relation is to be found.

To define relational image for any relation $R : X \leftrightarrow Y$ and set $S : \mathbb{P}X$ we could write:

$$R(\!|\ S\ |\!) = \{x : X; y : Y \mid x \in S \land x \mapsto y \in R \bullet y\}$$

In fact, there is a strong connection between relational image and domain restriction. If we restrict the domain of R to elements of some set S using:

$$S \lhd R$$

we obtain those maplets of R which relate elements of S to something. The range of this is exactly the set required for relational image. Hence:

$$R(\!|\ S\ |\!) = \mathrm{ran}(S \lhd R)$$

Exercise 5.21 ◇ Write out:

   (i) $rides(\!|\ \{Kate, Alice\}\ |\!)$

   (ii) $rides\!\sim\!(\!|\ \{Unicycle\}\ |\!)$

Exercise 5.22 With R_1 and R_2 defined as in Exercise 5.17, write out the elements of:

(i) $R_1(\{2,3\})$ (ii) $R_2(\{0\})$

(iii) $R_1^{\sim}((0 .. 10))$ (iv) $(R_1 \,_9^9\, R_2)(\{3\})$

(v) $((\{2\} \lhd R_1) \,_9^9\, (R_2^{\sim}))(\{2\})$ (vi) $(R_1(\{2\})) \setminus (R_2(\{2\}))$

(vii) $(R_1 \setminus R_2)(\{2\})$

Exercise 5.23 Use the operations on relations introduced so far to write expressions for:

(i) $\diamond$ the subset of *WheeledVehicles* ridden by Ben and Huw

(ii) the subset of *WheeledVehicles* ridden by any of the Potters

(iii) the subset of *WheeledVehicles* ridden by all of the Potters

(iv) the subset of Potters who ride the unicycle

Exercise 5.24 Argue that for any $R : X \leftrightarrow Y$; $Q : Y \leftrightarrow Z$; $S : \mathbb{P}\,X$, we have:

(i) $R(\operatorname{dom} R) = \operatorname{ran} R$

(ii) $(Q \cup R)(S) = Q(S) \cup R(S)$

Exercise 5.25 $\diamond$ The following are proposed as laws for any $R : X \leftrightarrow Y$; $S : \mathbb{P}\,X$; $T : \mathbb{P}\,X$. In each case give either a justification to show that the law follows from the definitions or a counter example to show that it is false.

(i) $R(S \cup T) = R(S) \cup R(T)$

(ii) $R(S \cap T) = R(S) \cap R(T)$

5.3   Functions

We have seen that a relation may relate any number of domain elements to any number of range elements and that they are sometimes referred to as many-to-many mappings. In the *rides* relation for example, *Ben* is related to both *bicycle* and *unicycle*, and *Ben*, *Alice* and *Huw* are all related to *bicycle*. Consider another example of a relation *IsIn* of type *Cities* $\leftrightarrow$ *Countries* which relates certain cities to the countries in which they are located:

$$IsIn == \{London \mapsto England, Oxford \mapsto England, Bonn \mapsto Germany$$
$$Paris \mapsto France, Nice \mapsto France, Barcelona \mapsto Spain\}$$

We view the sets *Cities* and *Countries* as containing all recognised cities and countries respectively. Obviously, in reality all cities will belong to a country, but the relation *IsIn* only records certain instances. Figure 5.1 shows that only six

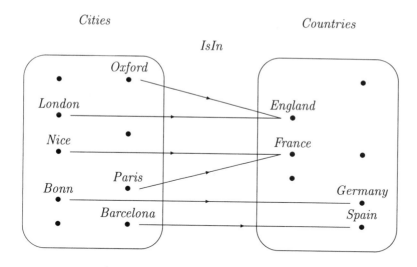

Figure 5.1: The *IsIn* function

cities are in the domain of *IsIn*. Perhaps *IsIn* records the relationships between cities and countries which a class of geography pupils have encountered during lessons to date.

Each city is related to just one country by the *IsIn* relation (we will leave aside any issues of disputed or multiple nationalities). This property, namely that any element of the source is related to no more than one element of the target, is extremely useful in specification. For any element in the domain of such a relation we can ask what range element it is related to and get a unique answer. It contrasts with the general case of relations where a single domain element can be related to many range elements.

We single out the class of relations which have this special property. They are known as functions. Figure 5.1 is a picture of the *IsIn* function, although only a small number of the possible related pairs are shown. This illustrates what the property of functionality means in terms of the arrows of the diagram.

If we look at any element of the domain we see that as it can only be in one country there is only one arrow connecting it in the picture. Being a function does not require any restriction on the range, so many arrows can still point to a single range element. In the example, this is the same as saying that although a city can be in only one country, a country may contain many cities.

The requirement for functionality can be captured formally by the following property:

$$(x \mapsto y) \in R \land (x \mapsto z) \in R \Rightarrow y = z$$

which says that if x is related to both y and z then y and z must in fact be the same element (this is exactly the same as saying that two different arrows cannot start from the same domain element).

5.3.1   Partial and total functions

Just as the symbol $\leftrightarrow$ is used to denote a relation, we introduce some new arrows to represent the special case of functions. The most general sort of function as described above is known as a partial function. It is called partial since the domain of the function need not be the whole of the source. In the *IsIn* function for example, the source is the set *Cities*, but the domain of *IsIn* is only a small subset of *Cities*. Partial functions are represented by a single headed arrow with a bar across:

$$IsIn : Cities \nrightarrow Countries$$

The partial function arrow can be formally defined with a generic definition, making use of the functionality property given above:

$$X \nrightarrow Y ==$$
$$\{R : X \leftrightarrow Y \mid (\forall x : X; \, y, z : Y \bullet x \mapsto y \in R \wedge x \mapsto z \in R \Rightarrow y = z)\}$$

For any sets X and Y, the partial functions from X to Y are all those relations which map elements of the domain uniquely.

One special case of functions is that for which the domain is the whole of the source set. These are known as total functions since the domain completely covers the source. Suppose we define a new relation relating each Potter to their age in years:

$$ageofPotter : Potters \leftrightarrow \mathbb{N}$$

Firstly, this is really a function since each Potter is related to only one number. Secondly, every Potter has an age, so the domain of this function is the whole of the source set, *Potters*. This means the function is total.

To indicate that a function is total we use a different arrow, $\rightarrow$. It is like the partial function arrow but without the bar across. Using this we could declare:

$$ageofPotter : Potters \rightarrow \mathbb{N}$$

To define this new arrow all that needs to be said is that total functions are functions whose domain is the whole of their source:

$$X \rightarrow Y == \{f : X \nrightarrow Y \mid \mathrm{dom}\, f = X\}$$

Since a function maps each element of its domain to one range element we use the notation:

$f\ x$

to denote for any x in the domain of f the unique range element to which f maps x. For instance:

ageofPotter Huw

would give Huw's age and:

IsIn Bonn = Germany

5.3.2   Examples

In our introduction to the notion of a function as a special kind of relation we used the example of:

IsIn : *Cities* $\twoheadrightarrow$ *Countries*

to illustrate a simple function. Consider for a moment the requirements of a system used by geographers to record this information in a computer, perhaps to facilitate the construction of the gazetteer sections of a range of atlases being prepared for publication.

In a budget priced atlas aimed at the schools market our geographers might decide to include only those cities whose population is greater than some chosen value, and to represent this by a separate function, *BudgetIsIn*. In this case the domain will be a subset of the set *Cities*, and the function *BudgetIsIn* will be defined for this subset only. So *BudgetIsIn* is partial.

In the largest and most expensive atlas we might expect to be able to find the location of every city in the world, according to some useful definition of city. In other words we would expect the domain of the function to be equal to the set *Cities*. This indicates that a total function is necessary:

FullIsIn : *Cities* $\rightarrow$ *Countries*

As another example, remember that in the stock control specification we defined:

$$Stock == \{s : ITEM \leftrightarrow \mathbb{N} \mid \forall i : ITEM;\ n, m : \mathbb{N} \bullet$$
$$(i, n) \in s \wedge (i, m) \in s \Rightarrow n = m\}$$

so *Stock* is the set of all relations from *ITEM* to $\mathbb{N}$ in which no item is related to more than one stock level. We can now see that this is really saying that stock records must be functions, and in fact *Stock* is simply the set of all functions from *ITEM* to N. We can therefore greatly simplify the definition of *Stock* using:

$$Stock == ITEM \nrightarrow \mathbb{N}$$

There is no requirement that the functions be total since many members of *ITEM* might not be on our shop's stock list; hence the arrow used is that for partial functions.

Exercise 5.26 Which of the following relations defined in the previous section are also functions?

(i) *plays*   (ii) *worksby*   (iii) *haswheels*   (iv) *haswheels*~

Exercise 5.27 ⋄ Assume the existence of two sets *LET* and *NUM*, defined as follows:

$$LET == \{a, b, c, d, e\}$$
$$NUM == \{1, 2, 3, 4, 5\}$$

Give examples of functions whose declarations are:

(i) $LET \rightarrow NUM$

(ii) $LET \nrightarrow NUM$

Exercise 5.28 Give two examples of relations belonging to $\mathbb{N} \leftrightarrow \mathbb{N}$ which are also functions.

Exercise 5.29 ⋄ If we define the subset of relations for which:

$$(x \mapsto z) \in R \wedge (y \mapsto z) \in R \Rightarrow x = y$$

what would such relations be like? (This is an important property which is introduced and named later in the chapter.)

Exercise 5.30 If the function square is defined:

$$square : \mathbb{Z} \rightarrow \mathbb{N}$$
$$\forall x : \mathbb{Z} \bullet square\ x = x * x$$

which sort of arrow has been used and why is it appropriate? Give the values of:

(i) *square* 0   (ii) *square* 2   (iii) *square*(−2)

Exercise 5.31 Define the following functions using $\mathbb{Z}$ as the source and target, using partial or total arrows in the declaration as appropriate:

(i) ◦ the function *plus2*, which adds 2 to any integer

(ii) the constant function *tozero*, which maps each integer to 0

(iii) ◦ the function *squareroot*, which maps integers which are perfect squares to their non-negative root

(iv) the empty function *emp*

(v) the function *temp*, which maps an integer to the nearest multiple of ten greater than or equal to it

(vi) the function *flip*, which changes the sign of all strictly positive integers to negative

What is the domain and range in each case?

Exercise 5.32 ◦ For the functions in Exercise 5.31 which are partial on $\mathbb{Z}$, define the sets representing the domain and use these to give a definition where the declaration uses a total function arrow.

Exercise 5.33 Use the definitions to argue that for any sets X, Y:

$$X \rightarrow Y \subseteq X \nrightarrow Y \qquad \text{and} \qquad X \nrightarrow Y \subseteq X \leftrightarrow Y$$

For what values of X and Y do equalities (rather than strict subsets) hold?

5.3.3   Injective functions

There are several other special cases of functions which have been deemed deserving of their own distinctive arrows. We introduce these with reference to the atlas example.

Firstly, suppose the geographers wish to provide a mapping which would record the capital city of each country. Now each country has exactly one capital, so this is definitely a function. Further, no city is the capital of more than one country, so no two elements of the domain are ever mapped to the same element of the range. We refer to such a function as being one-to-one or injective.

To mark the rise in importance of the EU the geographers wish to produce a special section in their latest atlas to cover this topic. They wish to produce a table listing the capitals of the EU countries, based on information drawn from the main body of the text; this will require a partial injective function to allow it to be accurately specified. To indicate that a function is injective we add a tail to the function arrow. This can be done for both partial and total functions, so in the atlas examples we have:

$FullCapitals : Countries \rightarrowtail Cities$
$EUCapitals : Countries \rightarrowtail\!\!\!\!\!\cdot Cities$

If we were to draw a picture of an injective function we would see that no two arrows can converge on the same range element. Any element of the range is related to only one domain element. For example, remember the relation *haswheels* with diagram:

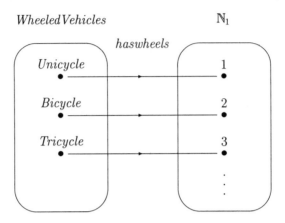

This is a function since no two arrows start from the same domain element. Also we see that no two arrows point to the same range element. This means that it is injective. Finally, since every element of the set *WheeledVehicles* is in the domain of the function, it is also total. We could therefore use the total injective function arrow to declare:

$$haswheels : WheeledVehicles \rightarrowtail \mathbb{N}_1$$

For the definition of injectivity we use a property which looks quite similar to the way that functionality was defined:

$$X \nrightarrowtail Y == \{f : X \nrightarrow Y \mid (\forall x_1, x_2 : \mathrm{dom}\, f \bullet f\, x_1 = f\, x_2 \Rightarrow x_1 = x_2)\}$$

This says that injective functions are those functions with the property that if x_1 and x_2 are mapped to the same value then x_1 and x_2 must in fact be the same element. Total injective functions can be defined in the same way, except that they form a subset of the total functions:

$$X \rightarrowtail Y == \{f : X \rightarrow Y \mid (\forall x_1, x_2 : \mathrm{dom}\, f \bullet f\, x_1 = f\, x_2 \Rightarrow x_1 = x_2)\}$$

Exercise 5.34 Give examples of partial and total injections from *LET* to *NUM* as defined in Exercise 5.27. Is it possible to give examples of partial and total injections from *LET* to $1..4$?

Exercise 5.35 ⋄ An injective function could be defined in terms of the fact that its inverse is also a function, since the requirement that both a function and its inverse be single valued can only be satisfied by the function being one to one. Try to write this down as a definition, and compare it with the one given in the preceding section.

Exercise 5.36 Which of the functions in Exercise 5.31 are injective?

Exercise 5.37 ⋄ Describe the set defined by:

$$(X \nrightarrow Y) \cap (X \rightarrow Y)$$

Exercise 5.38 Given *ITEM*, the set of all possible items from the shop example, give appropriate declarations for:

(i) *supplycost*, to record the cost of each item from the supplier

(ii) *shopprice*, to record the price to be charged by the shop for the items it stocks

(iii) *spares*, the supplier's record of which items might be required as spare parts for other items

5.3.4 Surjections and bijections

Yet another arrow is used to describe the following situation. The atlas must show which continent each country belongs to. Since each country belongs to just one continent we can represent this information as a function *BelongsTo*, from *Countries* to the set of continents, *Continents*. There are some other important facts that we might observe about this function. One is that every continent has one or more countries belonging to it and so each element of *Continents* will be a range element of *BelongsTo*. That is, the range covers the whole of the target set. Again, another example of information to be recorded about countries might be to relate each country to its reigning monarch (if it has one). Not every country has a monarch, but every reigning monarch must have a country to reign over.

Both these functions share the property that the range is the whole of the target set. Such functions are called surjective or onto. As with injectivity, we add a distinguishing mark to the basic partial and total function arrows to indicate the special case of surjective functions. In this case the new arrow is formed by adding another head, giving ⇻ for the partial injective functions and ↠ for total ones.

In the atlas example, the function recording continents would be declared:

$$BelongsTo : Countries \twoheadrightarrow Continents$$

It is total since we required the means to find the continent containing any country in the world. It is surjective since every continent contains at least one country. We could also declare:

$$Monarch : Countries \twoheadrightarrow ReigningMonarchs$$

which is surjective but partial. As before the arrows can be defined formally. We have:

$$X \twoheadrightarrow Y == \{f : X \nrightarrow Y \mid \operatorname{ran} f = Y\}$$
$$X \twoheadrightarrow Y == \{f : X \rightarrow Y \mid \operatorname{ran} f = Y\}$$

Finally, a function which is both injective and surjective is known as a bijection. The bijection arrow has both a tail and an extra head. As an example, suppose the geographers have accumulated pictures of all the national flags and wish to provide a few colourful pages where these are laid out. Since they wish to be sure that the information base contains exactly one flag for each and every country they specify that this information is to be modelled by a bijective function which relates each member of the source to just one member of the target. They write this as follows:

$$FlagDisplay : NationalFlags \rightarrowtail\!\!\!\twoheadrightarrow Countries$$

5.3.5   Finite functions

For many specification tasks it is useful to be able to ignore the issue of whether the sets being used to model a system are finite or otherwise. Infinite sets avoid the need to address problems such as the exhaustion of sets and similar trivial issues which distract from the main task of capturing the essential features of the problem in hand.

However, there are occasions, particularly when more detailed models of possible implementations of systems are being given, when finite sets are required. In such cases it may become desirable to use functions whose domains are also finite to model aspects of the system, and special notations are provided for finite partial functions $\nrightarrow\!\!\!\rightarrow$ and finite partial injections $\rightarrowtail\!\!\!\rightarrow$.

Exercise 5.39 ⋄ Give examples of partial and total surjections from *LET* to *NUM*, using the definitions of Exercise 5.27.

Exercise 5.40 Are *FullCapitals* and *EUCapitals* surjective? Also, are *Monarch* and *BelongsTo* injective?

Exercise 5.41 ⋄ Give examples of functions (other than the identity function) with source and target $\mathbb{Z}$ which are:

(i) a partial surjection

(ii) a total surjection which is not injective

(iii) a bijection

Exercise 5.42 Which of the functions in Exercise 5.31 are surjections?

Exercise 5.43 ◇ Give a definition for $\rightarrowtail\!\!\!\rightarrow$, the total bijection arrow.

Exercise 5.44 Are *FullCapitals* and *EUCapitals* finite functions?

5.3.6   Summary of properties of functions

In the previous sections we have introduced notations for many differing and useful sub-classes of functions. The variety and subtlety of these are summarised in the table of Figure 5.2, which assumes that a function f has source X and target Y. The property *OneOne* shows when a function is required to be injective (see the definition of injectivity above). For functions which must have the property a *Yes* appears in the appropriate position. Where a row is left blank it is an indication that being one-to-one is not a specific requirement. Of course, the finite functions must also satisfy the constraint of finiteness.

Function		Constraints		
Name	Symbol	dom f	*OneOne*	ran f
Total function	$\rightarrow$	$= X$		$\subseteq Y$
Partial function	$\nrightarrow$	$\subseteq X$		$\subseteq Y$
Total injection	$\rightarrowtail$	$= X$	*Yes*	$\subseteq Y$
Partial injection	$\rightarrowtail\!\!\!\!\!\!\!\!\!$	$\subseteq X$	*Yes*	$\subseteq Y$
Total surjection	$\twoheadrightarrow$	$= X$		$= Y$
Partial surjection	$\nrightarrow\!\!\!\!\!$	$\subseteq X$		$= Y$
Bijection	$\rightarrowtail\!\!\!\rightarrow$	$= X$	*Yes*	$= Y$
Partial bijection	no symbol defined	$\subseteq X$	*Yes*	$= Y$
Finite partial function	$\nrightarrow\!\!\!\!$	$\subseteq X$		$\subseteq Y$
Finite partial injection	$\rightarrowtail\!\!\!\!$	$\subseteq X$	*Yes*	$\subseteq Y$

Figure 5.2: The varieties of functions

When declaring a function in a specification the important questions to consider are as follows:

- Is it total or partial?

- Is it injective?

- Is it surjective?

- Is the source a finite set?

The appropriate arrow can then be selected. As familiarity with the notation is achieved this process becomes much simpler. However, the task of memorising the arrows and their meanings can be quite daunting on first acquaintance. For this reason, and at risk of labouring the point, we offer a further presentation of the family of functions in Figure 5.3. Since all functions are subsets of relations, it is possible to draw a Venn diagram which illustrates this and also shows the classification of the members of the function family.

Exercise 5.45 The examples below have been declared to have source and target $\{0,1,2\}$. Which of the following properties do they possess: functionality, totality, injectivity, surjectivity?

    (i) $\{0 \mapsto 1, 1 \mapsto 2\}$ (ii) $\{0 \mapsto 1, 1 \mapsto 1, 2 \mapsto 1\}$

    (iii) $\emptyset$ (iv) $\{0 \mapsto 0, 0 \mapsto 1, 0 \mapsto 2\}$ (v) $\{0 \mapsto 1, 1 \mapsto 2, 2 \mapsto 0\}$

Exercise 5.46 Give examples of functions, having source and target $\mathbb{Z}$, belonging to each of the classes defined by the arrows in the above table. What is the domain and range in each case?

5.4   Operations on functions

Since functions are just a special sort of relation, all the operations which were defined earlier for relations can also be applied to functions. Composition, domain and range restriction and subtraction, inverse, relational image and so on can all be used with functions. For example, the function *Capitals* could be created from the old *IsIn* relation by removing certain cities from the domain:

$$Capitals == \{Oxford, Nice, Barcelona\} \lhd IsIn$$

Care must be taken however since the operations do not always produce a function. For instance, if we take the union of two relations of the same type we obtain another relation of that type. But the union of two functions does not necessarily give a function (see exercises). Again, the inverse of a function need not itself be functional.

We introduce one further operator which is used specifically to update a function with new information and which guarantees that a function will result. Suppose that a mistake is found in the expensive atlas. The *FullIsIn* function records the city of Brussels as being in France. To remedy the situation we must remove the incorrect pair from the function and add the correct maplet. The step of

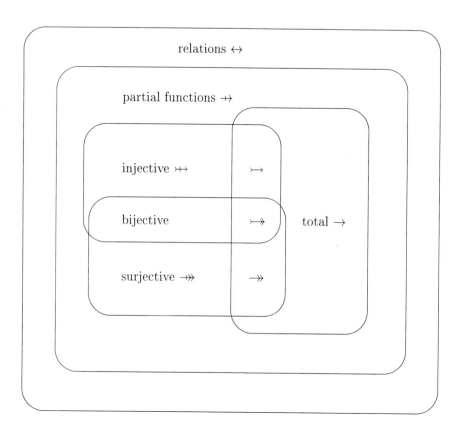

Figure 5.3: The varieties of functions, again

removing the original pair is vital; simply adding in the new pair would give a relation which maps Brussels to two values. That is not what we want. One way to describe the updating using existing operations is:

$$CorrectIsIn == (\{Brussels\} \lhd IsIn) \cup \{Brussels \mapsto Belgium\}$$

Firstly, domain subtraction is used to remove all existing information concerning the city in question. This allows the new information to be added safely using set union.

This operation is known as functional overriding and is used frequently. Instead of writing out an expression to remove and replace elements each time, we introduce a new symbol, $\oplus$. With this we can write for example:

$$CorrectIsIn == IsIn \oplus \{Brussels \mapsto Belgium\}$$

thus allowing updating to be modelled using one simple operation. Suppose that f and g are both functions of type $X \nrightarrow Y$ for some source X and target Y. Then:

$$f \oplus g = ((\text{dom } g) \lhd f) \cup g$$

This removes from f all pairs whose first elements are in the domain of g. Once this has been done, all the new pairs from function g can be added.

Notice that as well as altering the values of existing components, functional overriding can add completely new pairs. The definition of domain subtraction ensures that trying to subtract a non-existent element leaves f unchanged, and the new pair is simply added. Given the following functions:

$$f = \{0 \mapsto 1, 1 \mapsto 1\}$$
$$g = \{0 \mapsto 2, 2 \mapsto 1\}$$

we can override f with g to obtain:

$$f \oplus g = \{0 \mapsto 2, 1 \mapsto 1, 2 \mapsto 1\}$$

The resulting function contains the updated mapping for 0, the old mapping for 1 and a completely new mapping for 2. This can be summarised by saying that the new function agrees with g everywhere on the domain of g and with f elsewhere.

Exercise 5.47 With f and g defined as above write out in full the elements of:

(i) $f \cup g$ (ii) $f^{\sim}$ (iii) $g^{\sim}$

(iv) $(f^{\sim}) \,{}^{\circ}_{9}\, g$ (v) $f \rhd (\text{dom } g)$ (vi) $g \oplus f$

Which of these are functions?

Exercise 5.48 ◇ Consider each of the function arrows in turn. What can you say about the inverse of elements of each class of function?

Exercise 5.49 If $f_1, f_2 : X \nrightarrow Y$ and $f_3 : Y \nrightarrow Z$ which of the following are also necessarily functions?

(i) $f_1 \cup f_2$ (ii) $f_1 \cap f_2$ (iii) $f_1^{\sim}$ (iv) $f_1 \,\mathring{\,}\, f_3$ (v) $f_1 \,\mathring{\,}\, (f_2^{\sim})$

Justify your answers, giving counter examples where appropriate.

Exercise 5.50 If $shopprice : ITEM \nrightarrow \mathbb{N}$ records the prices charged for items stocked in the shop, write expressions (using $shopprice'$ for the changed state) to show how $shopprice$ changes when the following occur:

(i) ◇ Item i has its price altered to p.

(ii) ◇ Item i has its price doubled.

(iii) Items i and j have inadvertently been recorded with each other's price, which must be rectified.

(iv) A number of items are to be given new prices and the information is given in:

$$priceupdate : ITEM \nrightarrow \mathbb{N}$$

(v) Items in the set $S : \mathbb{P}\,ITEM$ are no longer to be stocked by the shop and their price information is to be removed from the price records.

5.4.1   Generic definitions of operations

Definitions of operations such as overriding have so far been given by saying something like 'for all functions $f, g : X \nrightarrow Y$ and sets X, Y ...'. Now that functions have been described these definitions can be made completely formal in Z by using the generic boxes introduced earlier. For example, in the case of functional overriding we would have:

$$
\begin{array}{l}
\underline{} [X, Y] \underline{} \\
\quad \underline{} \oplus \underline{} : (X \nrightarrow Y) \times (X \nrightarrow Y) \rightarrow (X \nrightarrow Y) \\
\hline
\quad \forall f, g : X \nrightarrow Y \bullet f \oplus g = ((\operatorname{dom} g) \lhd f) \cup g
\end{array}
$$

Here there are two generic parameters, X and Y. The arrow, $\rightarrow$, in the declaration indicates that we are declaring a total function. The predicate is the same as before but now the generic parameters and the declaration part give the information which was previously given in words. From the declaration we know that $\oplus$ is an infix function which takes two functions (both of type $X \nrightarrow Y$) and produces another function of the same type. The overriding function is a total function since it works for any two given functions of matching types. It is worth noting that a function whose arguments are themselves functions is known as a higher-order function.

The function arrows are also used in the formal Z definitions of operations on sets and relations. For example, it would be very useful to be able to project out the first element (or the second) of an ordered pair. Functions to do this can be generically defined and they can then be applied to pairs of any type.

$$
\begin{array}{l}
\hline
[X, Y] \\
\hline
first : (X \times Y) \to X \\
second : (X \times Y) \to Y \\
\hline
\forall x : X; y : Y \bullet \\
\quad first(x, y) = x \land \\
\quad second(x, y) = y \\
\hline
\end{array}
$$

Both *first* and *second* are functions which may be applied to any pair (using the generic parameters we say the pair is of type $X \times Y$). The function *first* gives an element of type X, and *second* an element of type Y. The predicate below the line tells us that, as expected, these elements are the first and the second of the pair respectively. These functions can now be applied to pairs of all types. For example:

$$
first(4, blue) = 4 \\
second(1, \{1\}) = \{1\}
$$

As noted earlier, whenever a generic constant is used all generic parameters must be instantiated. So, for example:

$$
first(\emptyset, red) = \emptyset
$$

may seem fair enough, but unless it is in a wider context which tells us what type the empty set is, we should instantiate explicitly. This could be perhaps:

$$
first(\emptyset, red) = \emptyset[\mathbb{Z}]
$$

Exercise 5.51 ⋄ In the following examples what types have the generic parameters of *first* and *second* been instantiated with?

(i) $first(1, (0, 0))$ (ii) $first(second(\{0\}, (1, 1)))$

(iii) $first(1, \emptyset)$ (iv) $first(first((1, \{1\}), -1))$

Exercise 5.52 Write a generic definition for *revpair* which reverses the order of elements in a pair.

Exercise 5.53 Write a generic definition for *singleset* which relates each element to the set containing just that element.

Exercise 5.54 ◇ Consider the operations defined earlier for relations (dom, ran, $\sim$, $\lhd$, $\rhd$, $\lhd\!\!\!-$, $\rhd\!\!\!-$, $\S$ and ($|\!|$)). Give completely formal versions of the definitions using generic boxes with appropriate declaration parts. Try to work out the predicate parts yourself before referring back.

5.4.2 Example

Now that we have the full range of functions available we can use the various arrows to define some useful functions in the stock control specification.

Earlier we defined a set *initlowstock* of items of *initialstock* for which stocks were low. We will now define a function *checkstock* which examines a stock record and returns the set of items low in stock. What will the type of this function be? We wish to apply it to a stock record so the source must be *Stock*. The result is a set of items, so the target is $\mathbb{P}\,ITEM$. Next we need to consider what sort of function it will be. Whatever stock record we apply the function to, we would like to get a valid set returned (even if it is empty). That means that the function should be total. There are no other special properties it can claim, so the declaration is:

$$checkstock : Stock \rightarrow \mathbb{P}\,ITEM$$

Now for the predicate, which looks quite similar to the way *lowstock* was defined:

$$\forall\, s : Stock \bullet checkstock\ s = \mathrm{dom}(s \rhd 0 \ldots 9)$$

Putting the complete definition together we have:

$$checkstock : Stock \rightarrow \mathbb{P}\,ITEM$$
$$\forall\, s : Stock \bullet checkstock\ s = \mathrm{dom}(s \rhd 0 \ldots 9)$$

We now have a function to check the stock of any stock record. In particular:

$$initlowstock = checkstock\ initialstock$$

Functions are also useful to describe stock management operations. For example, if an item is sold, we wish to record the fact. We could do this by recording a function which takes a stock record and the item which has been sold and modifies the stock record appropriately. For instance:

$$sellitem : (Stock \times ITEM) \nrightarrow Stock$$
$$\forall\, s : Stock;\ i : ITEM\ |\ s\ i > 0 \bullet sellitem\ (s, i) = s \oplus \{i \mapsto (s\ i) - 1\}$$

In this definition the function can only be partial since we do not specify what happens if the stock level for the item in question is 0. The stock record is modified by overwriting at position i with the old value minus 1.

This definition is unsatisfactory in a number of ways. The fact that it is partial may give cause for concern. We could of course make it total by specifying, for instance, that if $s\ i = 0$ then s is unchanged. Maybe we would want to give error reports too, using the data type *REPORT* defined earlier. At this stage we are dealing only with the mathematical notation of Z. We will see later that there are more convenient ways of structuring specifications, allowing operations to be written in a modular way with error reports added as appropriate.

5.5   Lambda notation

Another way of writing functions is to use the lambda (written λ) notation. This way of recording a function often proves to be more convenient and shorter than the forms of definition we have met so far. A lambda expression adopts the familiar form of declarations plus predicate followed by a term:

$$\lambda\ decls\ |\ pred \bullet term$$

Such an expression takes arguments of the shape $decls\ |\ pred$ and maps them to a value defined by *term*. So the lambda expression:

$$\lambda\,x\,:\,T\ |\ pred \bullet term$$

is equivalent to the function described by the set expression:

$$\{x\,:\,T\ |\ pred \bullet x \mapsto term\}$$

The predicate part is optional. Here is an example of a lambda expression:

$$\lambda\,n\,:\,\mathrm{N}\ |\ n < 5 \bullet n^2$$

This is the function which maps any number which is less than 5 to its square. It could also be written:

$$\{n\,:\,\mathrm{N}\ |\ n < 5 \bullet n \mapsto n^2\}$$

or, equivalently, it can be written down as the set of pairs:

$$\{0 \mapsto 0, 1 \mapsto 1, 2 \mapsto 4, 3 \mapsto 9, 4 \mapsto 16\}$$

In the next example there are two declarations in the list:

$$\lambda\,m, n\,:\,\mathrm{N}\ |\ m \geq n \bullet m - n$$

This function takes a pair of numbers whose first element is at least as great as the second and returns the difference. It is equal to:

$$\{m, n : \mathbb{N} \mid m \geq n \bullet (m, n) \mapsto m - n\}$$

As an example of a simple lambda expression with the predicate part omitted note that:

$$\lambda\, n : \mathbb{N} \bullet n$$

is just the function which maps n to itself; this is in fact the identity function on $\mathbb{N}$.

Exercise 5.55 ⋄ Write in more familiar set notation the following functions:

  (i) $\lambda\, i : \mathbb{N} \bullet i + 1$

  (ii) $\lambda\, i, j : \mathbb{N} \mid i + j = 6 \bullet (i + 1, j)$

  (iii) $\lambda\, i : \mathbb{N};\ S : \mathbb{PN} \mid i \in S \bullet S \setminus \{i\}$

  (iv) $\lambda\, i : \mathbb{N};\ S : \mathbb{PN} \bullet S \setminus \{i\}$

Exercise 5.56 Write lambda notation for the functions of Exercise 5.31.

Exercise 5.57 ⋄ If n is some positive number what does $f == \lambda\, x : 1 .. n \bullet (n + 1) - x$ do? If g is a function with domain $1 .. n$ what is the effect of $f \, \S \, g$?

5.6 Sequences

There will be occasions when the properties of sets render them inadequate for the particular facet of the modelling task in hand. For instance, consider the modelling of some of the Potters in a queue for service at their local café. This could be modelled thus:

$$queue == \{Kate, Alice, Huw\}$$

As we have already noted, the ordering of elements within a set makes no difference to its equality (or otherwise) with other sets, so:

$$queue = \{Alice, Huw, Kate\} = \{Huw, Alice, Kate\}$$

Desirable as this may be from a set theoretical viewpoint, it clearly has limitations in terms of modelling queues of people in particular, and ordered collections of objects in general.

There is another reason why a simple set is inadequate to model a structure such as a queue or a list. Suppose the Potters decide to keep a list recording who has done the washing up on each night of a week. By the third night the list records that Huw did the washing up on the first night and that Alice did it on the second and third nights. If we try writing the set:

$\{Huw, Alice, Alice\}$

we see the additional shortcoming that repeating elements in a set definition is simply redundant and the above set is equivalent to:

$\{Huw, Alice\}$

and also to:

$\{Alice, Huw\}$

Thus the important information that Alice has done the washing up twice is lost.

In Z, sequences are used to allow the modelling of ordered collections of objects. In a sequence the order of elements is significant and elements may appear more than once. We do not have to add a completely new structure to Z to capture this idea since it is possible to describe the desired properties using a particular class of functions. Before introducing this formal definition we introduce the notation that will be used for sequences and give some examples. Sequences are written using pointed brackets, for example:

$\langle Kate, Alice, Huw \rangle$
$\langle Huw, Alice, Alice \rangle$
$\langle Ben \rangle$
$\langle \rangle$

The first sequence has three elements, the first being *Kate*, the second *Alice* and the third *Huw*. This models the Potters in the café queue; unlike sets:

$\langle Kate, Alice, Huw \rangle \neq \langle Alice, Huw, Kate \rangle$

The second example models the washing up list. Again it has three elements, it just so happens that two are the same. Again, unlike sets:

$\langle Huw, Alice, Alice \rangle \neq \langle Huw, Alice \rangle$

The third example is a sequence with only one element, *Ben*. The fourth example of pointed brackets only is an empty sequence. One similarity with sets is that the elements of any one sequence must all be of the same type.

5.6.1   Representing sequences

As noted above, the important features of a sequence are not just the elements that it contains, but also the positions in which they occur. The sequence:

$$\langle Huw, Alice, Alice \rangle$$

contains information about positions and elements as follows:

Position	Element
1	*Huw*
2	*Alice*
3	*Alice*

Another way to record this is by writing it as a function with domain $\{1, 2, 3\}$ mapping positions to elements:

$$\{1 \mapsto Huw, 2 \mapsto Alice, 3 \mapsto Alice\}$$

This gives the clue to how a sequence is represented in Z. It is viewed as a function from some initial segment, $1 \,..\, n$, of $\mathbb{N}$ to the elements of the sequence. Each maplet in such a function maps a number (the position) to the element occurring at that position in the sequence. The pointed bracket notation generally used for sequences is just a shorthand for this. So:

$$\begin{aligned}
\langle Kate, Alice, Huw \rangle &= \{1 \mapsto Kate, 2 \mapsto Alice, 3 \mapsto Huw\} \\
\langle Huw, Alice, Alice \rangle &= \{1 \mapsto Huw, 2 \mapsto Alice, 3 \mapsto Alice\} \\
\langle Ben \rangle &= \{1 \mapsto Ben\} \\
\langle\,\rangle &= \emptyset
\end{aligned}$$

From this underlying representation it is clear that sequences are equal exactly when they have the same elements in the same order. For example:

$$\langle Kate, Alice, Huw \rangle \neq \langle Alice, Huw, Kate \rangle$$

because:

$$\{1 \mapsto Kate, 2 \mapsto Alice, 3 \mapsto Huw\} \neq \{1 \mapsto Alice, 2 \mapsto Huw, 3 \mapsto Kate\}$$

Just as special arrows were introduced to denote special cases of functions we introduce the notation seq X for the type of all sequences with elements from the set X. For instance:

$$cafequeue : \text{seq}\, Potters$$

with:

$$cafequeue = \langle Kate, Alice, Huw \rangle$$

Since sequences are just functions of the sort described above we can give the following formal definition for sequences of any set X:

$$\operatorname{seq} X == \{f : \mathbb{N} \nrightarrow X \mid \operatorname{dom} f = 1 \mathinner{\ldotp\ldotp} \#f\}$$

There are several points to note about this definition. Firstly, with $\operatorname{seq} X$ we choose to model sequences of X with a finite number of elements. That is why the finite partial function arrow is used. Sequences must therefore be finite functions from $\mathbb{N}$ to X. The constraint tells us that they must also have a domain which is some continuous interval of $\mathbb{N}$, starting at 1 and continuing up to the number of elements in the sequence.

Exercise 5.58 ⋄ Write out the sets which are represented in the sequence notation thus:

    (i) $\langle 1, 1, 1 \rangle$ (ii) $\langle 3, 2, 1 \rangle$ (iii) $\langle \{Ben, Kate\}, \{Alice, Huw\} \rangle$

Exercise 5.59 Write as sequences:

    (i) $\{1 \mapsto Kate, 2 \mapsto Kate\}$

    (ii) $\{3 \mapsto Alice, 1 \mapsto Alice, 4 \mapsto Huw, 2 \mapsto Huw\}$

    (iii) $\{x : \mathbb{N} \mid 0 < x < 5 \bullet (x, x^2)\}$

Exercise 5.60 State which of the following are sequences:

    (i) ⋄ $\{1 \mapsto 1\}$ (ii) ⋄ $\{0 \mapsto Huw, 1 \mapsto Alice\}$ (iii) $\{x : 1 \mathinner{\ldotp\ldotp} 10 \bullet (x, x + 1)\}$

    (iv) $cafequeue \setminus \langle \rangle$ (v) $cafequeue \cup \langle \rangle$

    (vi) $cafequeue \cup \{1 \mapsto Huw\}$ (vii) $cafequeue \oplus \{1 \mapsto Huw\}$

Exercise 5.61 ⋄ Give a definition for $\operatorname{seq}_1 X$, the non-empty sequences with elements from X.

Exercise 5.62 Cars are queueing to get on to a cross channel ferry. They are queued in lanes by the traffic controllers. It is decided to model the embarkation system representing the queues as a sequence of sequences.

    (i) Define *Embarkation*, the set of all possible embarkation situations, using the given set CAR. The points you will need to consider include:

        (a) finding a suitable type abbreviation for the declaration

        (b) ensuring that no car is in the same queue more than once

        (c) no car is in more than one queue

(ii) If the car queueing area can take no more than 15 queues what extra constraint should be added to *Embarkation*?

(iii) The traffic controllers want to signal their control when none of the 15 queues is empty. Give an axiomatic description for *Flag* which is on when this situation is reached, but is switched off otherwise. (You could use a simple data type definition first to describe the possible values of *Flag*.)

Exercise 5.63 ◇ In the previous exercise it was required that no car should occur in more than one position in a queue. This property is often needed when modelling physical queues. By analogy with functions, we call such sequences injective. Give a definition for iseq X, the set of all injective sequences of X.

Sequences are modelled by functions, which in turn are modelled by sets, so in theory all the operations for sets, relations and functions can be applied to sequences. In practice however this is not particularly useful because we need operations which preserve the special properties of being a sequence. For example, consider the sequences $\langle Ben \rangle$ and $\langle Kate \rangle$. We could combine them using various set or function operations, for example:

$$\langle Ben \rangle \cup \langle Kate \rangle$$

by considering their representation as sets:

$$\{1 \mapsto Ben\} \cup \{1 \mapsto Kate\} = \{1 \mapsto Ben, 1 \mapsto Kate\}$$

but the result is certainly not a sequence. It is not even a function. In general we will need special-purpose operations for sequences.

There is, however, one operation which is derived immediately from the functional representation of sequences. Suppose we wish to find out which element occurs in a particular position of a given sequence. Because a sequence is just a function from $1 \mathinner{.\,.} n$ (for some n) we can simply apply the function at position i $(1 \leq i \leq n)$ to obtain the value at that position. For example, to obtain the second element of *cafequeue*:

$$cafequeue\ 2 = Alice$$

We now introduce some of the operations peculiar to sequences.

Head, tail, front and last

The head of a non-empty sequence is its first element and its tail is everything but the first element. So:

$$head\ cafequeue = Kate$$
$$tail\ cafequeue = \langle Alice, Huw \rangle$$

Similarly, the last of a non-empty sequence is its final element, and the front is the sequence made by removing the last element.

$$front\ cafequeue = \langle Kate, Alice \rangle$$
$$last\ cafequeue = Huw$$

Consider *head* and *tail* to see how formal definitions can be given for sequence operations. Firstly, since these particular operations work only for non-empty sequences we introduce the notation:

$$\text{seq}_1\ X == \text{seq}\ X \setminus \{\langle\rangle\}$$

The definitions can then be given as follows:

$$
\begin{array}{l}
\hline
[X] \\
\hline
head : \text{seq}_1\ X \rightarrow X \\
tail : \text{seq}_1\ X \rightarrow \text{seq}\ X \\
\hline
\forall\, s : \text{seq}_1\ X\ \bullet \\
\quad head\ s = s\ 1\ \wedge \\
\quad tail\ s = \lambda\, n : 1 .. \#s - 1 \bullet s\,(n+1) \\
\hline
\end{array}
$$

A generic definition is used since we wish the operations to work for a sequence of any type. Both operations are guaranteed to work for any non-empty sequence and hence are declared as total functions on $\text{seq}_1\ X$. The operation *head* returns a single element of type X while *tail* returns a sequence (this can be empty if the original sequence had only one element). This explains the declarations. The predicate part for *head* is quite simple: we merely need to find the first element of the sequence. For *tail*, the predicate has to be a little more complicated because the result has to be a sequence. Consider the example of:

$$cafequeue == \langle Kate, Alice, Huw \rangle = \{1 \mapsto Kate, 2 \mapsto Alice, 3 \mapsto Huw\}$$

If we remove the first pair concerning Kate, this leaves:

$$\{2 \mapsto Alice, 3 \mapsto Huw\}$$

which is not a sequence, since sequences must start at position 1. What is needed is to slide all the positions down one to give:

$$\{1 \mapsto Alice, 2 \mapsto Huw\} = \langle Alice, Huw \rangle$$

The predicate part of the definition of *tail* achieves this using the lambda notation for a function which maps each i (up to one less than the length of the original sequence) to the $(i+1)$th position of the original sequence. So in the case of *cafequeue*:

$$1 \mapsto cafequeue \ (1+1) = cafequeue \ 2 = Alice$$
$$2 \mapsto cafequeue \ (2+1) = cafequeue \ 3 = Huw$$

Putting this together gives:

$$\{1 \mapsto Alice, 2 \mapsto Huw\}$$

as required.

Another way of describing *tail* in terms of the set which it constructs may be of interest, and perhaps simpler to grasp:

$$tail \ s = \{n : \mathbb{N} \mid n \in 2 \mathinner{.\,.} \#s \bullet n - 1 \mapsto s \ n\}$$

This captures the notions that the *tail* consists of $n - 1$ being mapped to the nth element of the original sequence, beginning with the second element. It also ensures that the result is indeed a sequence by constraining the domain of it to $1 \mathinner{.\,.} \#s - 1$. Formal definitions of *front* and *last* are left as an exercise.

Concatenation

It is often necessary to join two sequences together by placing one in front of the other to form a new sequence. For instance, if the washing up record is continued for the second half of the week on a separate piece of paper, we would need to join the two together to obtain a full week's list.

We have already seen that an operation as simple as union is not sufficient to join two sequences in this way. We introduce the new operation of sequence concatenation, written $\frown$. Given the two parts of the washing up record:

$$wuplist1 == \langle Huw, Alice, Alice \rangle$$
$$wuplist2 == \langle Alice, Huw, Huw, Ben \rangle$$

concatenation can be used to join them:

$$wuplist1 \frown wuplist2 = \langle Huw, Alice, Alice, Alice, Huw, Huw, Ben \rangle$$

Similarly, if Ben alone is at a separate service queue in the café, his queue could be represented as:

$$shortqueue = \langle Ben \rangle$$

If the first service point now closes and all the other Potters join Ben's queue in their original order, the new queue could be represented by:

$$shortqueue \frown cafequeue = \langle Ben, Kate, Alice, Huw \rangle$$

If it is Ben's service point which closes and he joins the back of *cafequeue* we now have:

$$cafequeue \frown shortqueue = \langle Kate, Alice, Huw, Ben \rangle$$

To see how a formal definition of concatenation might be given consider the positions of the elements in the resulting sequence, for instance:

$$shortqueue \frown cafequeue = \langle Ben, Kate, Alice, Huw \rangle$$
$$= \{1 \mapsto Ben, 2 \mapsto Kate, 3 \mapsto Alice, 4 \mapsto Huw\}$$

The first sequence to be joined appears unchanged as the first part of the new sequence. The second sequence is added by adding the appropriate number (the length of the first sequence) to each position to reflect the position in the new sequence. This prompts the following definition:

$$
\begin{array}{l}
\underline{\quad} \frown \underline{\quad} : \text{seq } X \times \text{seq } X \to \text{seq } X \\
\hline
\forall s, t : \text{seq } X \bullet \\
\quad s \frown t = s \cup \{n : 1 .. \#t \bullet (n + \#s) \mapsto t\,n\}
\end{array}
$$

with signature $[X]$.

Exercise 5.64 Which of the following are sequences?

(i)   *cafequeue* $\cup$ *cafequeue*

(ii) *cafequeue* $\oplus$ $\{1 \mapsto Ben, 2 \mapsto Kate\}$

(iii) *cafequeue* $\cup$ $\{1 \mapsto Ben, 2 \mapsto Kate\}$

(iv) *cafequeue* $\frown$ $\{1 \mapsto Ben, 2 \mapsto Kate\}$

(v)   *head shortqueue*

(vi) *tail shortqueue*

(vii) *front shortqueue*

(viii) *last shortqueue*

Exercise 5.65 $\diamond$ Write out the following in full:

(i)   *(tail cafequeue)* $\frown$ *shortqueue*

(ii) $\langle last\ cafequeue \rangle \frown \langle front\ cafequeue \rangle$

(iii) *cafequeue* $\setminus \{3 \mapsto Huw\}$

(iv) *cafequeue* \ {1 ↦ *Kate*}

Exercise 5.66 Give generic definitions for *front* and *last* as described above.

Exercise 5.67 ◇ Define a function *rev* which reverses a sequence. For example:

$$rev \langle 2, 4, 6 \rangle = \langle 6, 4, 2 \rangle$$
$$rev \ cafequeue = \langle Huw, Alice, Kate \rangle$$
$$rev \langle \rangle = \langle \rangle$$

You should be able to argue from your definition that for any sequence *S*:

$$rev \ (rev \ S) = S$$

Exercise 5.68 Given the ferry embarkation system of the previous exercises, suppose that *ferryqueue* : *Embarkation*, *c* : *CAR* and *i, j* : 1 .. 15. Write expressions:

(i) stating that *c* is not currently in *ferryqueue*

(ii) to describe the effect of *c* joining the end of the *i*th queue (using *ferryqueue'* to represent the new situation)

(iii) to describe the effect of the *j*th queue being closed and all the cars joining the *i*th queue in their current order

(iv) as for (iii), but this time cars from the back of queue *j* join first

(v) to describe the whole of queue *i* boarding the ferry and thus leaving the embarkation system

5.6.2 Distributed operations

As we have seen, the elements of a sequence may themselves be sequences. For example, in Exercise 5.62 the queueing system for a ferry was described as a sequence of sequences. It is often convenient in such cases to apply operations across the whole range of sequences occurring as elements of the overall sequence. For example, to join all the individual car queues of the above example we could concatenate all the individual queues. So, given:

$$ferryport = \langle\langle q1car1, q1car2 \rangle, \langle \rangle, \langle q3car1 \rangle\rangle$$

forming this, in order, into one queue gives:

$$\langle q1car1, q1car2, q3car1 \rangle$$

In doing this we say we have distributed the concatenation operation across the sequence of sequences. Concatenation is defined between two sequences. Distributed concatenation, written $^\frown\!/$, allows it to be extended across a whole sequence of sequences. The distributed operation may be defined as follows:

$$
\begin{array}{l}
\underline{[X]}\\
\hline
^\frown\!/ : \mathrm{seq}(\mathrm{seq}\,X) \to \mathrm{seq}\,X\\
\hline
^\frown\!/\langle\rangle = \langle\rangle\\
\forall\, s : \mathrm{seq}\,X \bullet {}^\frown\!/\langle s\rangle = s\\
\forall\, s1, s2 : \mathrm{seq}(\mathrm{seq}\,X) \bullet {}^\frown\!/(s1 \frown s2) = (^\frown\!/\, s1) \frown (^\frown\!/\, s2)
\end{array}
$$

The definition follows the possible structure of the sequence over which distributed concatenation is to be performed. If it is empty, the result is also empty. If it contains one element, the result consists of just that element. If it has more than one element, then it can itself be thought of as a concatenation of two sequences. The distributed concatenation is then defined recursively as the concatenation of the distributed concatenations of these two parts.

Other useful distributed operations may be defined in the same way. For example, given a sequence of relations, each of type $X \leftrightarrow X$, we could perform distributed relational composition, $\S/$. This results in a single sequence of type $X \leftrightarrow X$. For a sequence of functions of similar types we may need distributed overriding , $\oplus/$.

Exercise 5.69 Give definitions for $\S/$ and $\oplus/$.

Exercise 5.70 ◇ An idea closely related to the distributed operations of this section is the generalisation of the set union and intersection operations to allow them to be applied to a set of sets. Generalised union of a set of sets S results in a set of elements each of which belongs to at least one of the sets in S. Generalised intersection of S produces a set whose members each belong to all of the sets in S. The declaration part of the definition for these operators is:

$$
\begin{array}{l}
\underline{[X]}\\
\hline
\cap, \cup : \mathbb{P}(\mathbb{P}\,X) \to \mathbb{P}\,X\\
\hline
\ldots
\end{array}
$$

Complete this definition by supplying a suitable predicate.

5.7   Bags

Earlier we met sets, in which the order of members is irrelevant and where adding an element which is already a member has no effect. We have also encountered sequences, in which the order of the elements is very important and there can be many positions with the same value. A third possibility is a structure in which multiple elements are allowed, but the order is unimportant. We can think of all the elements of such a structure being jumbled together in a bag: there is no particular ordering, but different occurrences of the similar items are distinguished. Such a structure is known as a bag.

An example of an everyday situation which could be modelled as a bag is an inventory of the contents of a cupboard. We want to record how many of each item is in there but it would be artificial to impose any particular order on the contents. Suppose that in one kitchen cupboard we find:

- 12 dinner plates

- 8 soup bowls

- 6 wine glasses

- 1 chipped egg cup

To represent the kitchen cupboard as a bag we introduce a notation of double square brackets:

$$cupboard = [\![dinnerplate, soupbowl, wineglass, eggcup]\!]$$

This tells us that the four named items are to be found in the cupboard. To discover how many times each item occurs we use a function, *count*, which, for a particular bag and item of the correct type, records how many times that item appears in the bag. So, for example:

$$count\ cupboard\ soupbowl = 8$$
$$count\ cupboard\ eggcup = 1$$
$$count\ cupboard\ sideplate = 0$$

The empty bag is written $[\![]\!]$ with *count* being 0 for each item of source type.

5.7.1 Representing bags

As was the case with sequences, we can use existing Z constructs to define bags. For each item in the bag we need to record its name and how many times it occurs. We could do this by using a function, such as:

$$\{dinnerplate \mapsto 12, soupbowl \mapsto 8, wineglass \mapsto 6, eggcup \mapsto 1\}$$

This prompts the following definition:

$$bag\ X == X \nrightarrow \mathbb{N}_1$$

For any set X, a bag of type X is simply a partial function from X to $\mathbb{N}_1$. The items in the bag are the domain of the function, and the positive number that each item is mapped to represents the number of times it occurs.

Bag notation such as:

$$cupboard = [\![dinnerplate, soupbowl, wineglass, eggcup]\!]$$

shows graphically what items are in the bag, but to get a full picture of how many times each occurs we must use the count function described above. This can be defined:

$$
\begin{array}{l}
\underline{\quad[X]\quad} \\
\hline
count : bag\ X \rightarrowtail (X \rightarrow \mathbb{N}) \\
\hline
\forall x : X;\ B : bag\ \bullet \\
\qquad count\ B = (\lambda x : X \bullet 0) \oplus B
\end{array}
$$

The function, *count*, is constructed by taking the function $\lambda x : X \bullet 0$ which maps all x to 0, and then overriding this with the bag function. So, for $i : X$, *count i* returns the number of occurrences if i is in the bag, and 0 otherwise.

Exercise 5.71 ◇ Define a relation _ *in* _ between a bag and an element of appropriate type which holds exactly when the element is a member of the bag.

Exercise 5.72 How is the empty bag $[\![\,]\!]$ different from the empty set $\{\}$ and the empty sequence $\langle\rangle$?

Using the basic definition, operations on bags may be defined as required. Here is a useful example.

Bag union

Suppose that we wish to reorganise our kitchen and the contents of the cupboard are to be amalgamated with the contents of a drawer and placed in a new unit. The bag representing the drawer is:

$$drawer = [\![eggcup, mug]\!]$$

with:

$$count\ drawer\ eggcup = 3$$
$$count\ drawer\ mug = 7$$

The new unit will contain all the items from both the cupboard and the drawer. The total number of occurrences of each item in the unit will be the sum of its occurrences in the cupboard and the drawer. The operation which joins two bags in this way is called bag union, written ⊎. For the kitchen example:

$$unit = cupboard \uplus drawer$$

Bag union may be defined:

$$
\begin{array}{l}
\underline{\quad\quad}[X]\underline{\quad\quad} \\
\quad \_\ \uplus\ \_ : (bag\ X \times bag\ X) \rightarrow bag\ X \\
\quad \forall\ B1, B2 : bag\ X;\ x : X\ \bullet \\
\qquad count\ (B1 \uplus B2)\ x = count\ B1\ x\ +\ count\ B2\ x
\end{array}
$$

Exercise 5.73 ⋄ Use bag notation and the count function to describe *unit*, the contents of the new kitchen unit. What is the equivalent set notation?

Exercise 5.74 Suppose that the Potters want to record how many times each has done the washing up, but they do not care on which nights each performed the task.

(i) Suggest a suitable way of representing this.

(ii) Define a function *YourTurn* which, using this representation of the washing up situation, returns the name(s) of the person(s) who have done the washing up the least number of times.

Exercise 5.75 Sometimes it is useful to create a bag from a given sequence by recording how many times each item occurs. Write a formal definition for a total function *items* which when applied to a sequence produces the corresponding bag.

Chapter 6

The Z notation: schemas and specification structure

We have now met all of the main features of the mathematical component of the Z language. We go on to show how the mathematical notation is used in order to write formal specifications of systems.

In Chapter 3 we had a foretaste of the Z style of presentation. There we defined sets which described the admissible states or configurations of the system to be specified, and we also defined sets whose properties described the relationship amongst the inputs, the outputs and the before and after values of the persistent objects of the system for the various operations required. We also saw that it was useful to be able to combine units of specification in certain ways, allowing us to divide and rule when faced with a major specification task. When we pursue this idea of being able to create units of specification by combining other units we find that using set descriptions is rather too restrictive; in particular, we do not want the type system to impose restrictions here, nor do we want the order of declarations within units to be significant.

So it is that, instead of set descriptions, a new construct known as the schema is taken as a basic unit of formal specification, to be accompanied by corresponding and complementary informal description. Schemas will be used to describe the admissible states and the operations of a system just as set descriptions were used in the Word-For-Word specification; in the present chapter we shall show how this is done. Later we shall see that schemas may also be used to capture the relationship between the states of the system at different levels of abstraction as we move from specification to executable program.

The concept of declaration-and-constraint, already encountered in the contexts of set descriptions, quantification and λ-definitions of functions, forms the basis of the schema. Since the schema is intended to be an important structural device for the creation of specifications, a new form of notation is provided which ensures that it stands out from surrounding informal text.

As expected, a variety of ways of combining schemas are provided; this aspect of the Z notation, known as the schema calculus, makes a significant contribution, both notational and conceptual, to our ability to separate concerns within Z specifications. It is perhaps worth remarking that the separation of concerns at specification level will not always be reflected in an implementation; it is important that we should be able to separate conceptually distinct issues at the abstract level, but when we come to develop a concrete system we may need to recombine at some stage, perhaps in the interests of efficiency, for example.

6.1 Schema notation

Within specifications whenever we use a schema to describe some aspect of a system, it is also very useful to be able to give a name to that schema. The new notation which we mentioned earlier can be used to introduce the text of a schema and at the same time to give it a name. Thus, using the facilities of the Z language which are now familiar, we might define:

$$
\begin{array}{l}
\rule{3cm}{0pt} WellFormedVocab \rule{6cm}{0pt} \\
\hline
Vocab : OrthoNative \leftrightarrow OrthoForeign \\
NativeKnown : \mathbb{F}\ OrthoNative \\
ForeignKnown : \mathbb{F}\ OrthoForeign \\
\hline
NativeKnown = \mathrm{dom}\ Vocab \\
ForeignKnown = \mathrm{ran}\ Vocab \\
\end{array}
$$

Here we declare:

- a vocabulary *Vocab* which is a relation between the sets *OrthoNative* and *OrthoForeign*

- a set *NativeKnown*, which is a subset of *OrthoNative*

- a set *ForeignKnown*, which is a subset of *OrthoForeign*

and then the predicate insists that the sets *NativeKnown* and *ForeignKnown* should be the domain and range of the vocabulary. The schema could form part of a proper Z specification for the Word-For-Word system; we shall revisit Word-For-Word in the next chapter. Points to note about the notation are the following:

- The name of the schema is introduced into the top line of the box.

- The central horizontal line separates the declaration part from the predicate part of the schema.

- If the predicate is of the form $P_1 \wedge P_2$ then P_1 and P_2 may be written on separate lines and the $\wedge$ symbol elided; this may of course be extended to any number of conjuncts making up the predicate part.

- Similarly declarations D_1; D_2 may be written on separate lines and the semicolon omitted.

- By analogy with the declaration part, a predicate $P_1 \wedge P_2$ may also be written P_1; P_2, and similarly for any number of conjuncts.

- The order of declarations makes no difference to the meaning of a schema, nor does the order of the conjuncts in the predicate.

There are in fact two equivalent notations for schema definitions. We have seen the form which is normally used when we are defining a schema which represents an important component of a specification and we want it to stand out from surrounding informal text; there is also a linear form which is sometimes useful for subsidiary definitions or when we want to save space. Thus the above schema could also be expressed in the form:

$WellFormedVocab \mathrel{\widehat{=}}$
    $[\,Vocab : OrthoNative \leftrightarrow OrthoForeign;$
    $NativeKnown : \mathbb{F}\, OrthoNative;\ ForeignKnown : \mathbb{F}\, OrthoForeign \mid$
    $NativeKnown = \mathrm{dom}\ Vocab \wedge ForeignKnown = \mathrm{ran}\ Vocab]$

For a non-trivial schema definition, this will not save much space on the page and clarity is lost, as our example illustrates. For a very simple schema, for example:

$Success \mathrel{\widehat{=}} [rep! : Report \mid rep! = Ok]$

it can be worthwhile, but the reason for choosing one style of presentation rather than the other will usually depend on the importance of the schema as part of the whole specification. In the linear form, the enclosing square brackets distinguish a schema from a set expression which would require curly brackets.

When a new schema is to be defined in terms of other schemas already defined, using the facilities of the schema calculus, we are usually obliged to use a linear form of notation: thus, assuming suitable definitions of *WellFormedVocab* and *RecordOfProgress* are given elsewhere, we might define:

$WordForWord \mathrel{\widehat{=}} WellFormedVocab \wedge RecordOfProgress$

where $\wedge$ is an operator of the schema calculus which we shall meet later. Note that the symbol $\widehat{=}$ is used when a new schema name is defined, either by giving an explicit schema text or by an expression involving other schemas and schema operators.

6.2   An example application: LibSys

In the following sections of the present chapter we shall take as a running example a simple library system, which will be known as LibSys. (Such systems have often been used as examples of specification; see Section 6.7 for references.) First we describe informally the system we have in mind:

- The library comprises a stock of books and a community of registered readers.

- Each copy of a book is assigned a unique copy identifier.

- At any time a certain number of copies of books are on loan to readers; the remainder of the stock is on the shelves of the library and available for loan.

- There is a maximum number of books which any reader may have on loan at any one time.

The operations to be defined include the following:

- Issue a copy of a book to a registered reader.

- A reader returns a book to the library.

- Add a copy of a book to the stock.

- Remove a copy of a book from the stock.

- Enquire which books are on loan to a given reader.

- Enquire which reader has a particular copy of a book.

- Register a new reader.

- Cancel a reader's registration.

In the sections which follow we will show how the states of the LibSys system can be defined, and we will also use some of its operations as specification fodder, while others will be left as exercises for the reader. We shall not attempt to provide a proper formal specification for LibSys here; the purpose of the present section is to discuss how the Z notation may be used to describe formally the properties of a required system; the focus will be on that notation and the facilities it provides. In the next chapter we shall give an example of a full specification using the techniques presented in the current chapter. We shall defer discussion of a general method for the production of complete specifications until we have been through all the motions once.

6.3   Schemas describing abstract states

One of the first things we have to think about when we come to write a formal specification concerns level of detail. When we write a specification we are attempting to construct a mathematical model of the essential features of some real world system. Choices have to be made, so that all the necessary properties of the system are represented, but without imposing any unnecessary constraints or making any assumptions which are not implied by the informal specification. In the case of LibSys, for the purposes of formally describing the operations listed above, we do not need to consider exactly what kind of information is kept on the library records about the registered readers. In a realistic library system, of course, there would probably be a requirement to keep information such as name, address and expiry date of registration. Similarly, we do not need to consider details such as title, author(s), date of publication and so on, for the books of which there are copies in stock, though obviously a more comprehensive system would certainly need such information. At some point decisions would be made about the form of the copy identifiers to be used, but it is not necessary to worry about such detail at this level of formal description. All we require is that we can assume it is possible to recognise when identifiers are the same, and when they are different. Thus we shall take the following as given sets:

$$[Copy, Book, Reader]$$

Notice that even though we assume nothing about what a *Book* might be, it is necessary to distinguish the sets *Copy* and *Book*, since the library may have several copies of the same book. Clearly, a *Book* is not an artefact of paper, cardboard, glue, thread and ink, but rather a collection of data relating to title, author(s), subject matter and so on; as far as a reader is concerned it makes no difference which copy of a book is issued to him or her.

The informal specification given earlier also tells us that there is a maximum number of books which a reader may have on loan at any given time. Actually there is a whiff of ambiguity here: it is not absolutely clear whether it means that:

$$\forall r : Reader \bullet (\exists max : \mathbb{N} \bullet r \text{ may borrow no more than } max \text{ books})$$

or that:

$$\exists max : \mathbb{N} \bullet (\forall r : Reader \bullet r \text{ may borrow no more than } max \text{ books})$$

We opt for the second of these interpretations, and thus we declare a global constant:

$$\mid maxloans : \mathbb{N}$$

We will now give a schema which describes the admissible states of such a system; we usually refer to the admissible states of a system as the abstract states. The word 'abstract' is used here in contrast to the word 'concrete'; this latter word is used to describe the states of the system when we come to consider more implementation details on the way to providing a computer program which realises the abstract system. Here is the schema for the abstract states:

$$
\begin{array}{l}
\underline{\text{Library}} \\
\hline
stock : Copy \nrightarrow Book \\
issued : Copy \nrightarrow Reader \\
shelved : \mathbb{F}\ Copy \\
readers : \mathbb{F}\ Reader \\
\hline
shelved \cup \text{dom}\ issued = \text{dom}\ stock \\
shelved \cap \text{dom}\ issued = \emptyset \\
\text{ran}\ issued \subseteq readers \\
\forall\, r : readers \bullet \#(issued \rhd \{r\}) \leq maxloans
\end{array}
$$

The declaration part may be explained informally as follows:

- *stock* records which book is associated with each copy identifier currently in use.

- *issued* records which copies are on loan, and to whom.

- *shelved* is the subset of copies on the shelves and available for issue.

- *readers* is the set of registered readers.

Note that *stock* is a partial function because each copy identifier can correspond to at most one book, but normally there will be many copy identifiers which are unused. Similarly, *issued* is declared to be a partial function because not all copies are on loan at any given moment; again, its domain is a subset of that of *stock*. The predicate part of the schema *Library* may be explained thus:

- The first two conjuncts state that all copies in stock are either on loan or on the shelves, but not both.

- The third conjunct says that loans are only made to registered readers.

- The final conjunct says that the number of loans to any registered reader must be no greater than the maximum number of loans allowed.

The reader will probably have noticed that it would be possible to express the *Library* schema using fewer components. To be more precise, we could do without the *shelved* component since this can be expressed in terms of the other three components. The strictest economy with regard to the number of components of the abstract state is not necessarily the best approach. A more important consideration is the overall clarity of the whole specification: it may be easier to express the operations of the specification if we have names for conceptually significant aspects of the abstract state, even where some of these aspects are interdependent. The predicate part of the schema for the abstract states must of course specify any constraints upon the components of that state. We call these constraints the state invariant. Where there are interdependent components then the relationships involved must form part of the state invariant: if there are more components than the minimal number then the state invariant is going to be more complex, but this should be compensated by the fact that we can express the system operations more succinctly.

Exercise 6.1 ◇ Write a schema for the abstract states of a slightly modified LibSys in which each registered reader is assigned to a category and the number of books which a reader may borrow is determined by the reader's category. In all other respects the system is as before.

Exercise 6.2 ◇ In order to use the facilities of a shared computer system each user must be registered and must have a password which is to be supplied when requested by the system. The system LogSys is to be specified: this system will administer the process of gaining access to the computer system. LogSys must maintain information about registered users and their passwords, and must also keep track of which users are currently active on the system. Write a schema *LogSys* which describes the states of the system, not necessarily using the minimum number of components, bearing in mind that many of the operations to be defined for the system will want to check that a given user is registered. (Note: a possible *LogSys* is given in Exercise 6.6, but the reader is invited to carry out the present exercise before comparing with the schema given there.)

6.4   Schemas describing operations

The *Library* schema given above describes all the possible states of the persistent objects of the system. Of course, we want to be able to describe the operations of the system too. In the earlier Word-For-Word specification, we found that we needed some conventions in order to distinguish inputs, outputs, before and after objects. The conventions we adopted were those used within the Z notation, namely:

- inputs have '?' as final character

- outputs have '!' as final character

- before objects are represented by plain variables and corresponding after objects by corresponding dashed variables

In order to describe an operation we need to declare any inputs and outputs of the operation together with a full set of before components of the global state and a set of after components, and we must express the required relationships amongst all of these. As an example, the operation of issuing a book to a registered reader requires:

- as inputs, a copy identifier, say $c?$, and a reader, say $r?$

- that the copy to be issued must be on the shelves initially, which may be expressed formally as:

  $c? \in shelved$

- that the reader must be registered:

  $r? \in readers$

- that the reader must have less than the maximum number of books allowed before this copy may be issued:

  $\#(issued \rhd \{r?\}) < maxloans$

- that the copy now be recorded as issued to the reader:

  $issued' = issued \oplus \{c? \mapsto r?\}$

- that neither the stock nor the set of registered readers should be changed:

  $stock' = stock;\ readers' = readers$

Putting this together with declarations and constraints for the before and after components of the state we define:

$$
\begin{array}{|l}
\hline
\textit{Issue} \\\hline
stock, stock' : Copy \twoheadrightarrow Book \\
issued, issued' : Copy \twoheadrightarrow Reader \\
shelved, shelved' : \mathbb{F}\, Copy \\
readers, readers' : \mathbb{F}\, Reader \\
c? : Copy;\ r? : Reader \\\hline
shelved \cup \mathrm{dom}\ issued = \mathrm{dom}\ stock \\
shelved' \cup \mathrm{dom}\ issued' = \mathrm{dom}\ stock' \\
shelved \cap \mathrm{dom}\ issued = \emptyset;\ shelved' \cap \mathrm{dom}\ issued' = \emptyset \\
\mathrm{ran}\ issued \subseteq readers;\ \mathrm{ran}\ issued' \subseteq readers' \\
\forall\, r : readers \bullet \#(issued \rhd \{r\}) \leq maxloans \\
\forall\, r : readers' \bullet \#(issued' \rhd \{r\}) \leq maxloans \\
c? \in shelved;\ r? \in readers;\ \#(issued \rhd \{r?\}) < maxloans \\
issued' = issued \oplus \{c? \mapsto r?\};\ stock' = stock;\ readers' = readers \\\hline
\end{array}
$$

This schema looks rather formidable, but we have expressed it in this form so that the reader may appreciate the desirability of descriptive devices which allow us to say what needs to be said more succinctly. As given here, the first eight conjuncts express the invariants for the before and after states: we must start from a valid state and the operation must give rise to another valid state. These would be required for any operation of the system. The remaining conjuncts characterise the specific operation of issuing a book to a registered reader.

The reader may well feel that, in spite of the length of the *Issue* schema given here, there are things which could be said about the operation which have not been said. We mentioned earlier in the Word-For-Word specification of Chapter 3 that the specifier might be required to prove rigorously certain properties of any operations defined. In that earlier specification, we did not explicitly assert that for each operation the resulting vocabulary must also be well-formed, which is to say:

$$Vocab' \in WellFormedVocabs$$

though we could have done so, at the expense of making all the predicates for those operations that much longer. In fact it was unnecessary to do so, because we could easily prove that this is true in each case. Similarly, in the LibSys application, we might also have stated within the predicate for the operation *Issue* that:

$$shelved' = shelved \setminus \{c?\} \quad .$$

but in fact this property can be deduced from the information already included in the *Issue* schema. Thus, we could argue informally as follows:

- *shelved* and dom *issued* partition the domain of *stock*

- but so do *shelved'* and dom *issued'*, since *stock* = *stock'*

- since dom *issued'* has acquired a new element, namely *c?*, then *shelved'* must have lost that same element

We defer any more detailed discussion of these ideas: our first priority at present is to look at ways of defining schemas, using the facilities of the schema calculus, which allow us to express those schemas more compactly. We hope to demonstrate that greater clarity can also be achieved, because the notation allows us to focus on just those properties which are characteristic of the particular operations being defined.

Exercise 6.3 ⋄ Give a schema *Issue* for the modified LibSys system described in Exercise 6.1.

Exercise 6.4 ⋄ Argue informally that the conjunct $\#(issued \triangleright \{r?\}) < maxloans$ could have been omitted from the *Issue* schema as given in the text, since this can be deduced from the other conjuncts.

Exercise 6.5 ⋄ Suppose we had added a further declaration to the *Library* schema, namely:

$$readerloans : Reader \nrightarrow \mathbb{N}$$

which is intended to record the number of current loans to each registered reader. Write the predicate for the new schema, say *LibraryXtra*, ensuring that the partial function *readerloans* tallies with the information recorded by the *issued* function.

Exercise 6.6 The following schema would serve as the definition of the abstract states for the system LogSys (see Exercise 6.2):

```
┌─ LogSys ─────────────────────────────────────
│ password : User ⇸ Word
│ regd, active : 𝔽 User
├──────────────────────────────────────────────
│ active ⊆ regd = dom password
└──────────────────────────────────────────────
```

assuming given sets *Word* and *User*. An example LogSys operation might be to register a new user and password:

```
┌─ RegisterUser ───────────────────────────────
│ password, password' : User ⇸ Word
│ regd, active, regd', active' : 𝔽 User
│ u? : User; p? : Word
├──────────────────────────────────────────────
│ active ⊆ regd = dom password; u? ∉ regd
│ password' = password ⊕ {u? ↦ p?}
│ regd' = regd ∪ {u?}; active' = active
└──────────────────────────────────────────────
```

Give schemas for the following operations:

(i) ⋄ deregister a user, password to be supplied

(ii) a registered user becomes active on the system (logs on)

You might use *LogSysOpDecs* to stand for the first two lines of the declarations of *RegisterUser*; these declarations will be needed for any LogSys operation. Also argue that we can deduce *active'* ⊆ *regd'* = dom *password'* from the conjuncts included in the *RegisterUser* schema.

6.5   The schema calculus

The concept of the schema occupies a central place in the Z notation, being one of the most important building blocks for the construction of specifications. A variety of operators are defined for schemas which allow us to express a schema by making reference to other already defined schemas, thus making it possible to divide up the information content of a specification into manageable pieces. Ideally each fragment of specification should be not too large a piece of text, nor contain too much detailed information, so that they are largely self-explanatory without the need to consult other parts of the specification. They should correspond to a conceptual unit of specification, describing some aspect of the system which has a certain independence from other aspects, though of course at some level all aspects will be interrelated. We speak of the separation of concerns, a notion which is of paramount importance for any descriptive enterprise, be it a computer program, an instruction manual for a washing machine or a railway timetable. In this section we shall review the most significant of the features of Z which enable us to achieve this separation in formal specifications.

6.5.1   Schema inclusion

One of the simplest and most useful ideas of the schema calculus is that the name of a schema may be included amongst the declarations of another schema. As an example of schema inclusion used in the description of abstract states we give an alternative way of describing the LibSys state. We begin by defining two subsidiary schemas: the first of these is concerned with the details of the stock and the registered readers:

```
┌─ LibDB ──────────────────────────────────────
│  stock : Copy ⇸ Book
│  readers : 𝔽 Reader
└──────────────────────────────────────────────
```

(note that there is no explicit constraining predicate here), and the second is concerned with information about the current loans:

LibLoans
─────────────────────────────
$issued : Copy \nrightarrow Reader$
$shelved : \mathbb{F}\ Copy$
─────────────────────────────
$\forall\, r : Reader \bullet \#(issued \rhd \{r\}) \leqslant maxloans$
$shelved \cap \mathrm{dom}\ issued = \emptyset$

We can now go on to redefine the schema *Library* by including these two schemas and imposing further constraints:

Library
─────────────────────────────
LibDB
LibLoans
─────────────────────────────
$\mathrm{dom}\ stock = shelved \cup \mathrm{dom}\ issued$
$\mathrm{ran}\ issued \subseteq readers$

The effect of inclusion of a schema R amongst the declarations of a schema S is that the declarations of R are included in those of S and the predicate of R is appended to the predicate of S, forming one or more further conjuncts. When a schema is fully expanded there must be no type clashes; the same variable name may arrive by two or more different routes but in this case the declared type must be the same on each occasion.

Exercise 6.7 ◇ Expand the *Library* schema as given above in order to check that it is in fact the same schema as the earlier *Library* schema.

Exercise 6.8 ◇ Consider a redefinition of *LibraryXtra* (see Exercise 6.5), combining by inclusion two further schemas, *LibStock* which declares *stock*, *issued* and *shelved*, and *LibReaders* which declares *readers* and *readerloans*. Distribute the necessary constraints amongst the three schemas in the most appropriate way.

6.5.2   Schema decoration

We saw earlier that we can add characters such as '?', '!' and the prime character to the names of variables: this is known as decoration. We can also decorate schemas; in particular we shall want to add a prime to the name of a schema, the effect being that the decoration is applied to all the variables in its declaration, both within the declaration part of the schema and within the predicate part. With these notational conventions we can now define the operation *Issue* as follows:

Issue

Library
Library'
$c? : Copy; r? : Reader$

$c? \in shelved; r? \in readers; \#(issued \rhd \{r?\}) < maxloans$
$issued' = issued \oplus \{c? \mapsto r?\}$
$stock' = stock; readers' = readers$

Here we import all the variables of *Library* and the constraint upon those variables, and we import a corresponding set of dashed variables and the equivalent constraint upon those variables. This expresses the fact that we must start from a valid state of the system, and the operation must give rise to a new valid state. A further notational convention allows us to write *Issue* even more succinctly:

Issue

$\Delta Library$
$c? : Copy; r? : Reader$

$c? \in shelved; r? \in readers; \#(issued \rhd \{r?\}) < maxloans$
$issued' = issued \oplus \{c? \mapsto r?\}$
$stock' = stock; readers' = readers$

---

where the Δ is used to suggest change in the way that δ is used for small changes in the differential calculus. For any schema S, ΔS is normally defined as follows:

ΔS

S
S'

---

which is to say that we have all the declarations of S, and the predicate relating the variables declared therein, together with another set of declarations for a corresponding set of dashed variables, and the equivalent predicate relating those variables. (The reader should check that *Issue* as defined here is equivalent to the earlier *Issue* schema.)

It frequently happens that some of the operations to be defined for a system do not cause any change of state. In the case of LibSys the operation to enquire which reader has a certain copy is such an operation. We use another convention for operations of this kind; for example, we may define:

WhoHasCopy

$\Xi Library$
$c? : Copy; r! : Reader$

$c? \in dom\ issued; r! = issued\ c?$

We may think of the Ξ notation as an extension of the Δ notation since for any schema S, ΞS is defined as follows:

$$
\begin{array}{|l}
\underline{\quad \Xi S } \\
\quad \Delta S \\
\quad \overline{} \\
\quad NoChange \\
\hline
\end{array}
$$

where for any given S we would have to supply the appropriate predicate in place of *NoChange* which would state the requirement that corresponding dashed and undashed variables are to be equal. (The constraint *NoChange* can in fact be written $\theta S = \theta S'$; see Section 6.6 for more detail.) It should be noted that the use of Δ and Ξ is only a convention rather than a formal part of the Z notation, albeit a convention recognised by the Reference Manual ([Spi92], see page 131). It is quite in order to use Δ slightly differently, though it is always used to suggest a change of state. Sometimes it is useful to include a constraint, over and above the declarations for the before and after states; when it is used in a non-standard way then it must of course be properly defined.

It is now possible to see that the ability to import other schemas allows us to write definitions for operations which focus on the relationship amongst the variables concerned which are peculiar to those operations, leaving implicit the invariant properties of the system which are described in the schema for the abstract states of the system. Those other properties can be made explicit by expanding the schemas, but we can be rather selective about how much we want to spell out in each of the schemas as they appear in the specification.

It could be seen as a slight disadvantage that the details of the declarations of a schema can be hidden away in other schemas, for then all the salient information is not gathered together in one place in the specification. Certainly judicious choices have to be made, with the over-riding consideration being that of clarity. One of the tools which any Z specifier would want is a schema expander which, upon demand, could display more details of a chosen schema.

Exercise 6.9 ◇ Given the schema:

$$
\begin{array}{|l}
\underline{\quad S } \\
\quad x, y : \mathbb{N} \\
\quad \overline{} \\
\quad x < y \\
\hline
\end{array}
$$

write out the schema S', and then fully expand the schema:

$$
\begin{array}{|l}
\hline
T \\\\
\hline
S;\ S' \\
g? : \mathbb{N} \\
\hline
x < g? < y \\
x' > x \lor y' < y \\
\hline
\end{array}
$$

Are there any simplifications which can be made to the predicate of schema T?

Exercise 6.10 ⋄ Give schemas for the following LibSys operations, using a Δ or Ξ as appropriate:

(i) to enquire which books are currently on loan to a given reader

(ii) to deregister a given reader

Exercise 6.11 Define the following LogSys operations using the Δ and Ξ notation where appropriate:

(i) change a user's password, current password to be supplied

(ii) a registered user leaves the system (logs off)

(iii) produce a list of active users

6.5.3   Schema disjunction

In the Word-For-Word specification we gave earlier we found it was useful to be able to combine operations described by sets; in particular, we saw examples where operations were defined by taking the union of simpler operations elsewhere defined by set descriptions. For example, we made the definition:

$$ToForeign == KnownToForeign \cup UnknownToForeign$$

We describe the operation *ToForeign* in terms of *KnownToForeign*, which handles the case when a valid native word is supplied which is already known to the vocabulary, and *UnknownToForeign*, which deals with the case when the word supplied, though a valid word, is not yet known to the vocabulary.

In our earlier notation, we could only take unions of sets of objects of the same type: in the schema calculus operations upon schemas are defined which allow us to combine schemas with quite different declaration parts (always assuming no type clashes). If we turn to consider another of the LibSys operations, namely *AddCopy* which is the operation of adding a new copy of a book to the stock, we could distinguish two slightly different cases; firstly, the case when a further copy of a book is added to the stock which already has one or more copies of that same book, and secondly, the case when a copy of a new book is added, of which there are currently no copies in the stock. Let us assume that the system is going to make some comment about each operation it is called upon to perform, and that the set *Report* is a set of suitable messages. We could then define:

$$AddCopy \;\hat{=}\; AddKnownTitle \lor AddNewTitle$$

where we use the schema operator $\lor$, which suggests that schemas *AddKnownTitle* and *AddNewTitle* are alternatives. We may define these two schemas as follows:

```
__ AddKnownTitle _____
  ΔLibrary
  b? : Book
  rep! : Report
_____
  b? ∈ ran stock
  ∃ c : Copy | c ∉ dom stock •
              stock' = stock ⊕ {c ↦ b?} ∧
              shelved' = shelved ∪ {c}
  issued' = issued; readers' = readers
  rep! = FurtherCopyAdded
```

and:

```
__ AddNewTitle _____
  ΔLibrary
  b? : Book
  rep! : Report
_____
  b? ∉ ran stock
  ∃ c : Copy | c ∉ dom stock •
              stock' = stock ⊕ {c ↦ b?} ∧
              shelved' = shelved ∪ {c}
  issued' = issued; readers' = readers
  rep! = NewTitleAdded
```

An informal explanation of the *AddKnownTitle* schema goes like this:

- $b? \in$ ran *stock*: there is a copy of the book currently in stock

- $\exists\, c : Copy \mid c \notin$ dom *stock*... : an unused copy identifier is given to this new copy

- ...*stock'* = *stock* $\oplus \{c \mapsto b?\}$: it is recorded that this copy identifier refers to the book of which this is a new copy

- ...*shelved'* = *shelved* ∪ {*c*}: the new copy is put on the shelves

- *issued'* = *issued*: the loans are unchanged

- *readers'* = *readers*: the set of readers is unchanged

- *rep!* = *FurtherCopyAdded*: it is reported that a further copy has been added to stock

The schema *AddNewTitle* is explained in a very similar way, with the obvious changes.

In general, if we define schema $S \,\hat{=}\, P \vee Q$ then the declarations of S are formed by merging the declarations of P and of Q, and the predicate of S is formed by taking the predicate of P and that of Q and placing between them the logical operator ∨. There must be no type clashes when the schemas are combined[1]. Since the logical operator ∨ is associative and commutative, then so is the schema operator ∨. No confusion will arise from this double use of the symbol ∨, since it will always be clear from the context which meaning is intended.

We give now the expansion of the schema *AddCopy*, taking literally the instructions set out above:

$\quad$ *AddCopy* _____
$\quad$ Δ*Library*
$\quad$ *b?* : *Book*
$\quad$ *rep!* : *Report*
$\quad$ _____
$\quad$ (*b?* ∈ ran *stock*
$\quad\quad$ ∧ (∃ *c* : *Copy* | *c* ∉ dom *stock* •
$\quad\quad\quad\quad$ *stock'* = *stock* ⊕ {*c* ↦ *b?*} ∧
$\quad\quad\quad\quad$ *shelved'* = *shelved* ∪ {*c*})
$\quad\quad$ ∧ *issued'* = *issued* ∧ *readers'* = *readers*
$\quad\quad$ ∧ *rep!* = *FurtherCopyAdded*)
$\quad$ ∨
$\quad$ (*b?* ∉ ran *stock*
$\quad\quad$ ∧ (∃ *c* : *Copy* | *c* ∉ dom *stock* •
$\quad\quad\quad\quad$ *stock'* = *stock* ⊕ {*c* ↦ *b?*} ∧
$\quad\quad\quad\quad$ *shelved'* = *shelved* ∪ {*c*})
$\quad\quad$ ∧ *issued'* = *issued* ∧ *readers'* = *readers*
$\quad\quad$ ∧ *rep!* = *NewTitleAdded*)

Here we have had to make explicit the ∧ operators which were implicit in the predicates of the two schemas to be combined. Fortunately, the predicate of this

---
[1]There are some subtleties here which arise from the fact that declarations can include constraints on the variables declared; see Exercise 6.14 at the end of this subsection and also Section 6.5.5 on schema negation.

expansion can be considerably simplified. Firstly, we can factor out the common parts of the original predicates: this is valid (see Exercise 2.6) because for all propositions p, q and r:

$$(p \wedge q) \vee (p \wedge r) \Leftrightarrow p \wedge (q \vee r)$$

This yields the following:

```
__AddCopy_____
 ΔLibrary
 b? : Book
 rep! : Report
_____
 ∃ c : Copy | c ∉ dom stock •
              stock' = stock ⊕ {c ↦ b?} ∧
              shelved' = shelved ∪ {c}
 issued' = issued; readers' = readers
 ((b? ∈ ran stock ∧ rep! = FurtherCopyAdded)
     ∨ (b? ∉ ran stock ∧ rep! = NewTitleAdded))
```

We can go further, simplifying the last conjunct using the equivalence:

$$(p \wedge q) \vee (\neg p \wedge r) \Leftrightarrow (p \Rightarrow q) \wedge (\neg p \Rightarrow r)$$

We then derive the following schema:

```
__AddCopy_____
 ΔLibrary
 b? : Book
 rep! : Report
_____
 ∃ c : Copy | c ∉ dom stock •
              stock' = stock ⊕ {c ↦ b?} ∧
              shelved' = shelved ∪ {c}
 issued' = issued; readers' = readers
 b? ∈ ran stock ⇒ rep! = FurtherCopyAdded
 b? ∉ ran stock ⇒ rep! = NewTitleAdded
```

which is a slightly more convenient form since the disjunction has been replaced by a conjunction.

Exercise 6.12 ⋄ Using the schema disjunction operator we can separate the normal cases from the error conditions for an operation; for example, in the case of the *AddCopy* operation, we could define an operation which will work in all circumstances:

$$FailSafeAddCopy \;\widehat{=}\; AddCopy \vee AddCopyError$$

where *AddCopyError* causes no change of state but reports that an error has occurred. Note that an error can only occur when there are no unused copy identifiers. Define a suitable *AddCopyError*.

Exercise 6.13 ⋄ Check the equivalence given above:

$$(p \wedge q) \vee (\neg p \wedge r) \Leftrightarrow (p \Rightarrow q) \wedge (\neg p \Rightarrow r)$$

using the truth table method. Argue that, given the predicate of *AddCopy* in its most recent form (see page 147) and assuming that *FurtherCopyAdded* ≠ *NewTitleAdded*:

(i) when *b*? ∈ ran *stock* then *rep!* = *FurtherCopyAdded* and *rep!* ≠ *NewTitleAdded*

(ii) when *b*? ∉ ran *stock* then *rep!* = *NewTitleAdded* and *rep!* ≠ *FurtherCopyAdded*

Exercise 6.14 ⋄ Expanding a schema disjunction is not always straightforward when the schemas involved include declarations which contain constraints on the variables in addition to declaring their types. Recall that we can make declarations such as $x : X$, where X may be a proper subset of some type T.

Suppose we take the two schemas:

$$S \;\widehat{=}\; [x, y : \mathbb{N} \mid x < y]$$
$$T \;\widehat{=}\; [y, z : \mathbb{N} \mid y < z]$$

Consider $S \vee T$. We might expect the expansion to be as follows:

$$SorT \;\widehat{=}\; [x, y, z : \mathbb{N} \mid x < y \vee y < z]$$

but this is not in fact correct. To investigate further, we first define:

$$ExpandS \;\widehat{=}\; [x, y : \mathbb{Z} \mid 0 \le x \wedge 0 \le y \wedge x < y]$$
$$ExpandT \;\widehat{=}\; [y, z : \mathbb{Z} \mid 0 \le y \wedge 0 \le z \wedge y < z]$$

These schemas can be simplified to:

$$ExpandS \;\widehat{=}\; [x, y : \mathbb{Z} \mid 0 \le x < y]$$
$$ExpandT \;\widehat{=}\; [y, z : \mathbb{Z} \mid 0 \le y < z]$$

Since these are equivalent to S and T respectively, we would expect their disjunction *ExpandS* ∨ *ExpandT* to be equivalent to the disjunction $S \vee T$. The following exercises should clarify the situation:

(i) Write out the expansion of *ExpandS* ∨ *ExpandT*.

(ii) Show that this is not equivalent to *SorT* as given above. (Hint: find values of x, y, z which satisfy the predicate of one but not the other.)

(iii) Try to discover what has gone wrong.

6.5.4 Schema conjunction

The two schemas *AddKnownTitle* and *AddNewTitle*, which were combined to define the operation *AddCopy*, declare the same variables. If we look at the details of the schemas we see that they are indeed almost identical, and this prompts a reformulation of the definition of *AddCopy* which recognises that a copy is going to be added in either case, the only differences being concerned with whether or not $b?$ is an existing title, and with the appropriate message to be output. This is also reflected in the simplification which we performed in order to derive the expansion given above. Thus, using the schema operator $\wedge$, we may say:

$$AddCopy \triangleq EnterNewCopy \wedge AddCopyReport$$

where we define:

$$
\begin{array}{|l}
\hline
\ EnterNewCopy \underline{\hspace{6cm}} \\
\ \Delta Library \\
\ b? : Book \\
\hline
\ \exists\, c : Copy \mid c \notin \mathrm{dom}\, stock \;\bullet \\
\qquad\qquad stock' = stock \oplus \{c \mapsto b?\} \wedge \\
\qquad\qquad shelved' = shelved \cup \{c\} \\
\ issued' = issued;\ readers = readers' \\
\hline
\end{array}
$$

and:

$$
\begin{array}{|l}
\hline
\ AddCopyReport \underline{\hspace{5cm}} \\
\ stock : Copy \nrightarrow Book \\
\ b? : Book;\ rep! : Report \\
\hline
\ b? \in \mathrm{ran}\, stock \Rightarrow rep! = FurtherCopyAdded \\
\ b? \notin \mathrm{ran}\, stock \Rightarrow rep! = NewTitleAdded \\
\hline
\end{array}
$$

This time the declarations of the two schemas are quite different. It may at first seem a strange idea to combine schemas with different declarations, but we can see now that the schema operators are defined this way so that schemas may contribute information relating to distinct issues or distinct parts of the abstract state. This is an example of what we mean by the separation of concerns; we can address different aspects of specification in separate schemas and then combine them using $\wedge$ (and similarly $\vee$).

The $\wedge$ operator for schemas is defined so that if $S \triangleq P \wedge Q$ then the declarations of S are the merger of those of P and of Q and the predicate of S is the logical $\wedge$ of those of P and Q.

Notice that we have chosen here to define *AddCopyReport* so that it mentions only the component *stock* of *Library*. We could extract a general principle here, namely that schemas should declare only those variables about which they need to make a statement in the predicate part. On the other hand, the reader may have noted that *AddCopyReport* taken in isolation is not a schema which describes an operation, since it does not declare a full set of before and after components of the abstract state. Rather, it is a schema which imposes a constraint upon certain components of an operation, and also chooses an appropriate message. (If it is felt that schemas using the decorations '?' and '!', normally associated with operations, should indeed be operations then we could include $\Delta Library$ amongst the declarations instead of *stock* : *Copy* $\nrightarrow$ *Book*, and this same principle could be applied throughout the present section where we have adopted the minimalist philosophy.)

A further reformulation could be proposed which recognises that certain kinds of operation affect only certain parts of the state of the system, while other operations affect other parts of the state. For example we might identify a class of operations:

$$
\begin{array}{|l}
\_StockTransaction_____ \\
\Delta Library \\
\hline
readers' = readers;\ issued' = issued \\
\end{array}
$$

These operations can affect neither the registered readers nor the record of loans to readers. Similarly we could define *LoanTransaction* and *Registration* which respectively describe operations concerned with loans or with the registration of readers. (These definitions will be left as an exercise.) We could now redefine *EnterNewCopy* as follows:

$$
\begin{array}{|l}
\_EnterNewCopy_____ \\
StockTransaction \\
b? : Book \\
\hline
\exists\,c : Copy \mid c \notin \mathrm{dom}\ stock \bullet \\
\qquad stock' = stock \oplus \{c \mapsto b?\} \wedge \\
\qquad shelved' = shelved \cup \{c\} \\
\end{array}
$$

As a further example of the separation of concerns, we now want to consider an aspect of specification which we have so far ignored, namely what to do about errors in the inputs to operations. Earlier we gave a schema for the operation *Issue*, but this only specified what was to happen in the normal case. However, various irregularities could occur: the reader may not be registered, the reader may already have the maximum number of books on loan, or the copy could be already on loan according to the library records. We may deal with the normal case of issue and the cases where some irregularity occurs, producing a suitable message in each case, by making the definitions:

$TotalIssue \;\hat{=}\; NormalIssue \lor IssueError$
$NormalIssue \;\hat{=}\; Issue \land Success$
$IssueError \;\hat{=}\;$
$\qquad \Xi Library \land (AlreadyIssued \lor NotRegistered \lor HasMaxLoans)$

The name *TotalIssue* is meant to convey the idea that the operation forms part of a total system interface; we may imagine that the choice about which operation is to be executed next is made outside the system which our specification describes, so that every operation must be prepared to respond in all circumstances, even if only to say that the operation is not applicable. We go on to define:

Issue

$LoanTransaction$
$c? : Copy; \; r? : Reader$

$c? \in shelved; \; r? \in readers; \; \#(issued \rhd \{r?\}) < maxloans$
$issued' = issued \oplus \{c? \mapsto r?\}$

NotRegistered

$readers : \mathbb{F}\, Reader$
$r? : Reader; \; rep! : Report$

$r? \notin readers; \; rep! = ReaderNotRegistered$

AlreadyIssued

$issued : Copy \twoheadrightarrow Reader$
$c? : Copy; \; rep! : Report$

$c? \in \mathrm{dom}\; issued; \; rep! = CopyAlreadyIssued$

HasMaxLoans

$issued : Copy \twoheadrightarrow Reader; \; readers : \mathbb{F}\, Reader$
$r? : Reader; \; rep! : Report$

$r? \in readers; \; \#(issued \rhd \{r?\}) = maxloans$
$rep! = ReaderHasMaxLoans$

Success

$rep! : Report$

$rep! = Ok$

All these schemas are, we hope, self-explanatory. It is worth noting again here that there are dangers associated with disjunction of schemas when they have different declaration parts. As we saw in Exercise 6.14, if one schema of a pair of schemas to be disjoined makes no mention of a variable declared in the other, when they are combined that variable will be entirely unconstrained in the case which corresponds to the first schema part of the disjunction. The use of disjunction in the definition of *IssueError* is made safe against these dangers by the fact that it includes $\Xi Library$ as a conjunct.

Exercise 6.15 ◇ Define the schemas *LoanTransaction* and *Registration*, mentioned in the text of this subsection.

Exercise 6.16 ◇ Expand and simplify the schemas *NormalIssue* and *IssueError* given above.

Exercise 6.17 ◇ For the operation *IssueError* defined above, what happens when the reader has the maximum number of loans allowed and the copy is already issued? You should find that there is more than one possibility; redefine one or both of the schemas *HasMaxLoans* and *AlreadyIssued* in order to remove any uncertainty about what happens in such cases.

6.5.5   Schema negation

There is a negation operator for schemas, in addition to the $\wedge$ and $\vee$ operators which we have already introduced. This is defined as might be expected; that is to say, for any schema S, we may obtain the schema $\neg\ S$ by keeping the same declaration and negating the predicate. However, this definition forces us to confront an issue which we have so far skated over, though in reality it has a bearing on the definitions of the $\wedge$ and $\vee$ operators too. We have seen that it is permissible to use abbreviated forms of declaration within the declaration parts of schemas; for example we may write $f : A \nrightarrow B$ which is equivalent to the declaration $f : \mathbb{P}(A \times B)$ together with the requirement that:

$$\forall\, x : A;\, y, z : B \bullet x \mapsto y \in f \wedge x \mapsto z \in f \Rightarrow y = z$$

which expresses the functionality of f. When we use such abbreviated declarations we are in fact contributing to both the declaration and predicate parts of the schema. When we negate the predicate part of a schema then it is the complete predicate, obtained by eliminating all abbreviations from the declaration part, which is to be negated. This could well have effects which are not expected or required: for example, if we negate a schema which has a function as one of its declared components, then the negated predicate will contain a disjunction which allows the possibility that the corresponding component may not be functional. This is probably not what the specifier wanted to say, but it is not possible to dispose of this difficulty by decreeing that when a schema is negated then only the explicit predicate is negated. If this definition were adopted we could have two equivalent schemas which only differed in the way they were written but nevertheless had different negations: this would be unacceptable.

As we said above, this issue has some bearing on the other logical schema operators, and indeed on schema inclusion too. We said that when we combine schemas there must be no name clashes; however, it is possible for a variable to have different declarations without giving rise to conflict when one of the declarations is an abbreviated form of the other. All these difficulties can be overcome by introducing the concept of normalisation of schemas: a schema is normalised when all its declarations are given in their full form, and any consequent additions to the predicate have been made. When schemas are combined, strictly speaking it is their normalised forms which are combined.

We give here a very simple example of schema negation. We define:

$$OneToFortyNine \mathrel{\widehat{=}} [n : 1..100 \mid n < 50]$$

In this case the normalised form would be:

$$OneToFortyNine \mathrel{\widehat{=}} [n : \mathbb{Z} \mid 1 \leqslant n \wedge n \leqslant 100 \wedge n < 50]$$

and then the negation $\neg\ OneToFortyNine$ is:

$$notOneToFortyNine \mathrel{\widehat{=}} [n : \mathbb{Z} \mid 1 > n \vee n > 100 \vee n \geqslant 50]$$

which is not the same as:

$$FiftyToHundred \mathrel{\widehat{=}} [n : 1..100 \mid n \geqslant 50]$$

Figure 6.1 illustrates the difference. The negation operator for schemas is of rather limited utility, but it can sometimes be used in combination with other operators of the schema calculus. Whereas the schema conjunction and disjunction operators correspond to important specification decomposition mechanisms, namely the presentation of alternatives in the case of disjunction and the superposition of constraints in the case of conjunction, negation has no such structural counterpart. There are in fact some further logical schema operators, namely the operators $\Rightarrow$ and $\Leftrightarrow$. As far as specification construction is concerned, the important schema operators are $\wedge$ and $\vee$; since as logical operators $\Rightarrow$ and $\Leftrightarrow$ may be expressed in terms of $\wedge$ and $\vee$ only if we also employ negation, these operators are not very useful either.

The remainder of this subsection illustrates a possible use for the negation operator. This could well be omitted on a first reading, but readers might find it

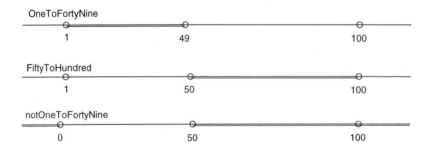

Figure 6.1: Negation of schemas

useful as a way of reinforcing their understanding of schema notation and operators. It is only fair to point out that amongst experienced users of the Z notation
opinion would be divided as to whether this is a good way to write specifications
because of the dangers associated with the schema disjunction operator.

In order to give examples of the use of schema negation in specifications we are
going to look at the possibility of a finer-grained approach to specification. We
shall define a repertoire of tests and atomic operations which can be combined,
using the operators of the schema calculus, to define the operations to be specified
for the system LibSys. The tests (we shall refer to them as LibSysTests) are the
following, using the linear form to save space:

$$InStock \cong [stock : Copy \nrightarrow Book; c? : Copy \mid c? \in \text{dom } stock]$$
$$OnLoan \cong [issued : Copy \nrightarrow Reader; c? : Copy \mid c? \in \text{dom } issued]$$
$$Registered \cong [readers : \mathbb{F} Reader; r? : Reader \mid r? \in readers]$$
$$MaxLoans \cong [issued : Copy \nrightarrow Reader; r? : Reader \mid$$
$$\#(issued \rhd \{r?\}) = maxloans]$$

and here are the atomic operations (LibSysAtoms):

$$ToStock \cong [StockTransaction; c? : Copy; b? : Book \mid$$
$$stock' = stock \oplus \{c? \mapsto b?\} \wedge shelved' = shelved \cup \{c?\}]$$
$$FromStock \cong [StockTransaction; c? : Copy \mid stock' = \{c?\} \lhd stock]$$
$$ToReader \cong [Registration; r? : Reader \mid readers' = readers \cup \{r?\}]$$
$$FromReader \cong [Registration; r? : Reader \mid readers' = readers \setminus \{r?\}]$$
$$Loan \cong [LoanTransaction; c? : Copy; r? : Reader \mid$$
$$issued' = issued \oplus \{c? \mapsto r?\}]$$
$$Return \cong [LoanTransaction; c? : Copy \mid issued' = \{c?\} \lhd issued]$$

Having made these definitions we may go on to define, for example:

$TotalRemoveCopy \;\widehat{=}$
$\qquad (RemoveCopy \wedge Success)$
$\qquad \vee \; RemoveErrors$
$RemoveCopy \;\widehat{=}$
$\qquad InStock \wedge \neg \; OnLoan \wedge FromStock$
$RemoveErrors \;\widehat{=}$
$\qquad \Xi Library \wedge$
$\qquad (OnLoanError \vee NotInStockError)$
$OnLoanError \;\widehat{=}$
$\qquad OnLoan \wedge [rep! : Report \mid rep! = CopyOnLoan]$
$NotInStockError \;\widehat{=}$
$\qquad \neg \; InStock \wedge [rep! : Report \mid rep! = CopyNotInStock]$

Here we have employed the negation operator on two occasions. Let us look in detail at the process of negation as applied to *OnLoan*. Now the normalised form of *OnLoan* is as follows:

```
┌─ NormalisedOnLoan ──────────────────────────
│ issued : ℙ(Copy × Reader)
│ c? : Copy
├─────────────────────────────────────────────
│ c? ∈ dom issued; issued ∈ Copy ⇸ Reader
└─────────────────────────────────────────────
```

Thus the schema *NotOnLoan* corresponding to $\neg \; OnLoan$ is as follows:

```
┌─ NotOnLoan ─────────────────────────────────
│ issued : ℙ(Copy × Reader)
│ c? : Copy
├─────────────────────────────────────────────
│ c? ∉ dom issued ∨ issued ∉ Copy ⇸ Reader
└─────────────────────────────────────────────
```

where we have negated the predicate of *NormalisedOnLoan* using the fact that:

$$\neg \; (p \wedge q) \Leftrightarrow \neg \, p \vee \neg \, q$$

for any p and q. Now when we wrote $\neg \; OnLoan$ as part of the definition of *RemoveCopy* we did not entertain the possibility that *issued* might not be a function, but this is allowed by the schema *NotOnLoan*. However, in combination with *FromStock*, this possibility is eliminated, since this latter schema includes all the requirements of the *Library* schema, one of which is that *issued* should indeed be functional.

Exercise 6.18 Define *RegisterNewReader* and *AddCopyToStock*, dealing with any irregularities which could occur, making use of LibSysTests and LibSysAtoms as given above.

6.5.6   Schema hiding operators

When we earlier specified the operation *EnterNewCopy* we assumed that the operation is given a *Book* as input, but that the *Copy* identifier to be assigned is to be determined by the system. We could have defined this operation in terms of another operation which is given both the *Book* and the *Copy* as inputs, namely:

```
┌─ AssignNewCopy ──────────────────────────────
│ StockTransaction
│ b? : Book; c? : Copy
├──────────────────────────────────────────────
│ c? ∉ dom stock
│ stock' = stock ⊕ {c? ↦ b?}
│ shelved' = shelved ∪ {c?}
└──────────────────────────────────────────────
```

Now we can express *EnterNewCopy* in the following way:

$$EnterNewCopy \mathrel{\widehat{=}} AssignNewCopy \setminus (c?)$$

The hiding operator $\setminus$ is applied to a schema given as its left argument and a list of variables as its right argument; the variables are hidden by existentially quantifying them in the predicate part of the schema and removing them from the declaration part. Thus:

$$[Decs \mid Pred] \setminus Hidden\,Vars$$

is equivalent to:

$$[ReducedDecs \mid \exists\, HiddenDecs \bullet Pred]$$

where *ReducedDecs* is just *Decs* after removal of the declarations corresponding to *HiddenVars*, and *HiddenDecs* is the set of declarations which corresponds to *HiddenVars*. In our case, we obtain for *EnterNewCopy* the following schema:

```
┌─ EnterNewCopy ───────────────────────────────
│ StockTransaction
│ b? : Book
├──────────────────────────────────────────────
│ ∃ c? : Copy • c? ∉ dom stock
│           ∧ stock' = stock ⊕ {c? ↦ b?}
│           ∧ shelved' = shelved ∪ {c?}
└──────────────────────────────────────────────
```

which is equivalent to our earlier specification (see page 150) since a change of existentially quantified variable name does not change the meaning.

We can go one step further: using the explicit existential quantification operator, we may define:

$$EnterNewCopy \;\hat{=}\; \exists\, c? : Copy \mid c? \notin \mathrm{dom}\; stock \bullet ToStock$$

where *ToStock* is one of the LibSysAtoms defined earlier. The meaning of this quantification operator is, as expected, that the quantification should be applied to the predicate of the schema, whilst the variables thus quantified are removed from the declaration part of the schema. Clearly this requires that there should be no type clashes between variables declared in the schema and those under quantification. This schema quantification operator has the effect of hiding the quantified variables, but may also add constraints on the values of those variables. In the case given here, $c?$ is not only hidden, but also constrained to be outside the domain of the *stock* function.

There are two further hiding operators, but we do not give examples of their use here since they seem to be less generally applicable:

- There is a universal quantification operator, so that it is possible to write:

  $$\forall\, Decs \mid Pred \bullet Schema$$

  which has the effect to be expected by analogy with existential quantification.

- There is a projection operator, $\upharpoonright$, so that it is possible to write:

  $$Schema_1 \upharpoonright Schema_2$$

  where the two schemas are type-compatible, which hides all the variables of $Schema_1$ except those which are declared in $Schema_2$.

The hiding operators $\backslash$ and $\exists$ are useful in themselves, as we have seen, when we want to define operations in which the system makes choices with regard to the values of some variables; we shall see that they are also useful concepts in terms of which other schema operators may be defined, in particular the composition and pre-condition operators.

Exercise 6.19 ⋄ Suppose it is decided to reduce the stock of the library by discarding copies of books of which the library has more than two copies. Specify a new LibSys operation *DiscardCopy* which is applicable when the library has more than two copies of a given book, at least one of which is currently on the shelves: its effect is to remove from the stock one of the shelved copies of the book concerned. Use a hiding operator in the definition of *DiscardCopy*, and also give an operation *TotalDiscardCopy* which reports success or failure, with suitable error messages when necessary.

Exercise 6.20 ⋄ Suppose we want to add an operation to *LibSys* where a reader *r*?
takes out of the library any available copy of a particular book *b*?. It is perhaps worth
thinking about the system as we have described it so far: what we have had in mind is
that a reader arrives at the issue counter with a particular copy of a book in his or her
hands, and that copy bears its copy identifier, so the system sees only the copy identifier
and the reader; now we are envisaging a more automated library where the reader can
request a book and the library system locates and delivers to the counter an available
copy of that book and issues it to the reader, so as far as the proposed new operation
is concerned the inputs are the requested book and the reader. This new operation
BookIssue can now be described as follows:

$$BookIssue \mathrel{\hat=} [Issue[c/c?]; \; b? : Book \mid FurtherConstraint] \setminus (c)$$

where the notation *Issue*[*c*/*c*?] means *Issue* with *c* replacing *c*? throughout. Now express the necessary *FurtherConstraint*.

6.5.7   Schema composition

It is sometimes useful to be able to specify an operation as a composition of
operations. The basic idea is that we make a definition such as:

$$A \mathrel{\hat=} B \mathbin{\mathring{,}} C$$

where operation *A* is defined to be the composition of operations *B* and *C*, in the
sense that if *B* can cause a change of state from say *S*1 to *S*2 and *C* can cause a
change of state from *S*2 to *S*3 then *A* can cause a change of state from *S*1 to *S*3.
Thus any change of state described by *A* can be thought of as a two stage process
which passes through an intermediate state which arises as a result of operation *B*
and serves as starting point for operation *C*. As a (somewhat artificial) example
of the use of the composition operator for LibSys, suppose a further operation is
defined whereby an unregistered reader may donate a book to the library and be
automatically registered as a new reader. We might define:

$$Donate \mathrel{\hat=} EnterNewCopy \mathbin{\mathring{,}} RegisterReader$$

EnterNewCopy was defined earlier (see page 149) and we shall give a definition of
RegisterReader in a little while, when we come to the details of the expansion of
the schema *Donate*. In the case of the *Donate* operation, the intermediate state
is one in which the new book has been added to the stock but no new registration
has yet been performed. Note that when the reader is already registered this
'intermediate' state is also the final state since the schema *RegisterReader* causes
no further change of state in this case.

Of course we must provide a more formal explanation of what the ⨾ operator
means: indeed we must describe how it is possible to derive an explicit description
of the schema which results from the composition of any two given schemas. For
schemas *S* and *T*, say, this is done as follows:

(a) First check that the set of dashed and plain variables declared in the schemas to be composed is exactly the same; if not then composition is undefined for these schemas – it really only makes sense if the two schemas describe operations on the same kind of abstract states.

(b) Check that there are no type clashes for any input or output variables declared; if there are, then composition is undefined.

(c) Replace all the dashed variables by corresponding doubly dashed variables throughout the first of the two schemas, giving $S[''/']$ say.

(d) Replace all plain variables by doubly dashed variables throughout the second of the two schemas, giving $T[''/\,]$ say.

(e) Form the composition as follows:

$$\exists\, State'' \bullet S[''/'] \wedge T[''/\,]$$

where $State''$ is the intermediate state of the system whose components are the doubly dashed variables.

(f) Perform any useful simplification of the predicate of the resulting schema, if possible eliminating all the doubly dashed variables.

Taking *Donate* as our example, the schemas which have to be composed are:

```
┌─ EnterNewCopy ──────────────────────────────────────
│ ΔLibrary
│ b? : Book
├─────────────────────────────────────────────────────
│ ∃ c : Copy | c ∉ dom stock •
│                 stock' = stock ⊕ {c ↦ b?} ∧
│                 shelved' = shelved ∪ {c}
│ issued' = issued; readers = readers'
└─────────────────────────────────────────────────────
```

and:

```
┌─ RegisterReader ────────────────────────────────────
│ ΔLibrary
│ b? : Book; r? : Reader
│ rep! : Report
├─────────────────────────────────────────────────────
│ r? ∉ readers ⇒ (readers' = readers ∪ {r?}
│                    ∧ rep! = Ok)
│ r? ∈ readers ⇒ (readers' = readers
│                    ∧ rep! = ReaderAlreadyRegistered)
│ stock' = stock; issued' = issued; shelved' = shelved
└─────────────────────────────────────────────────────
```

We have been careful to make manifest here the constraints on all the components of the abstract state, rather than leaving them implicit in some cases: this will make it easier to simplify the resulting predicate. Now proceeding with the steps described above:

(a) The dashed and plain variables are the same for the two schemas.

(b) There are no type clashes for input or output variables.

(c) The modified *EnterNewCopy* is:

$$
\begin{array}{|l}
\hline
\text{\textit{EnterNewCopy}}[''/'] \\\hline
\textit{Library}; \textit{Library}'' \\
b? : \textit{Book} \\\hline
\exists\, c : \textit{Copy} \mid c \notin \text{dom}\, \textit{stock} \bullet \\
\qquad \textit{stock}'' = \textit{stock} \oplus \{c \mapsto b?\} \wedge \\
\qquad \textit{shelved}'' = \textit{shelved} \cup \{c\} \\
\underline{\textit{issued}}'' = \textit{issued}; \underline{\textit{readers}}'' = \textit{readers} \\\hline
\end{array}
$$

Note we have underlined the doubly dashed variables here to make them stand out; this is merely for the present purpose of explanation.

(d) The modified *RegisterReader* is:

$$
\begin{array}{|l}
\hline
\text{\textit{RegisterReader}}[''/\,] \\\hline
\textit{Library}''; \textit{Library}' \\
r? : \textit{Reader} \\
\textit{rep}! : \textit{Report} \\\hline
r? \notin \underline{\textit{readers}}'' \Rightarrow (\textit{readers}' = \underline{\textit{readers}}'' \cup \{r?\} \\
\qquad\qquad\qquad \wedge \textit{rep}! = \textit{Ok}) \\
r? \in \underline{\textit{readers}}'' \Rightarrow (\textit{readers}' = \underline{\textit{readers}}'' \\
\qquad\qquad\qquad \wedge \textit{rep}! = \textit{ReaderAlreadyRegistered}) \\
\textit{stock}' = \underline{\textit{stock}}''; \textit{issued}' = \underline{\textit{issued}}''; \textit{shelved}' = \underline{\textit{shelved}}'' \\\hline
\end{array}
$$

(e) Now we form $\exists\, \textit{Library}'' \bullet \textit{EnterNewCopy}[''/'] \wedge \textit{RegisterReader}[''/\,]$:

$\boxed{\begin{array}{l}
\underline{\ Donate\ } \\
\Delta Library \\
b? : Book;\ r? : Reader \\
rep! : Report \\
\hline
\exists\, Library'' \bullet \\
\qquad \exists\, c : Copy \mid c \notin \operatorname{dom} stock \bullet \\
\qquad\qquad\qquad\qquad stock'' = stock \oplus \{c \mapsto b?\}\ \wedge \\
\qquad\qquad\qquad\qquad \underline{shelved''} = shelved \cup \{c\} \\
\qquad\quad \underline{issued''} = issued;\ \underline{readers''} = readers \\
\qquad\quad r? \notin \underline{readers''} \Rightarrow (readers' = \underline{readers''} \cup \{r?\} \\
\qquad\qquad\qquad\qquad \wedge\ rep! = Ok) \\
\qquad\quad r? \in \underline{readers''} \Rightarrow (readers' = \underline{readers''} \\
\qquad\qquad\qquad\qquad \wedge\ rep! = ReaderAlreadyRegistered) \\
\qquad\quad stock' = \underline{stock''};\ issued' = \underline{issued''};\ shelved' = \underline{shelved''}
\end{array}}$

(f) We now want to try to eliminate the doubly dashed variables and in the process discover the relationships between the plain and the dashed variables; using the various equalities included in the predicate we can rewrite as follows:

$\boxed{\begin{array}{l}
\underline{\ Donate\ } \\
\Delta Library \\
b? : Book;\ r? : Reader \\
rep! : Report \\
\hline
\exists\, Library'' \bullet \\
\qquad \exists\, c : Copy \mid c \notin \operatorname{dom} stock \bullet \\
\qquad\qquad\qquad\qquad stock' = stock \oplus \{c \mapsto b?\}\ \wedge \\
\qquad\qquad\qquad\qquad shelved' = shelved \cup \{c\} \\
\qquad\quad issued' = issued \\
\qquad\quad r? \notin readers \Rightarrow (readers' = readers \cup \{r?\} \\
\qquad\qquad\qquad\qquad \wedge\ rep! = Ok) \\
\qquad\quad r? \in readers \Rightarrow (readers' = readers \\
\qquad\qquad\qquad\qquad \wedge\ rep! = ReaderAlreadyRegistered) \\
\qquad\quad stock' = \underline{stock''};\ issued' = \underline{issued''} \\
\qquad\quad shelved' = \underline{shelved''};\ \underline{readers''} = readers
\end{array}}$

where we have now related all the dashed variables to the corresponding plain variables; the $\exists\, Library''$ quantification may now be eliminated since each doubly dashed variable is equal to one of the plain or dashed[2], so that this quantification conveys no further useful information (but see Exercise

---

[2] We are using the One Point Rule, which will be introduced later (see Section 9.6.3).

6.22); thus we derive:

```
┌─ Donate ─────────────────────────────────────────────────┐
│ ΔLibrary                                                  │
│ b? : Book; r? : Reader                                    │
│ rep! : Report                                            │
├──────────────────────────────────────────────────────────┤
│ ∃ c : Copy | c ∉ dom stock •                             │
│                stock' = stock ⊕ {c ↦ b?} ∧               │
│                shelved' = shelved ∪ {c}                   │
│ issued' = issued                                          │
│ r? ∉ readers ⇒ (readers' = readers ∪ {r?}                │
│                 ∧ rep! = Ok)                              │
│ r? ∈ readers ⇒ (readers' = readers                       │
│                 ∧ rep! = ReaderAlreadyRegistered)         │
└──────────────────────────────────────────────────────────┘
```

The reader may feel that we could have derived the *Donate* schema directly, and indeed this is so. Our intention here has been to give an example of how the details of a schema given as a composition may be derived. It should be noted that we have a special case here in that there are many equalities amongst the components of the three abstract states involved, enough to allow us to eliminate the intermediate state components altogether. Though theoretically this will not always happen, in many practical examples most or all of the intermediate state components may be eliminated in this way, thus allowing considerable simplification of the expansion of the composed schema.

Exercise 6.21 ⋄ It often happens that all contact is lost with a registered reader, though the reader may have books on loan according to the library records. Eventually those books have to be regarded as irretrievably lost and removed from the stock records. Define a new LibSys operation *ReaderLostContact* as a composition of two operations, one which removes any books on loan to the reader from the stock and one which removes the reader from the list of registered readers. For these operations give definitions which explicitly relate the components of the before and after states. Go through the process of deriving the expansion of the schema for the operation *ReaderLostContact*.

Exercise 6.22 In step (f) of the expansion of *Donate* given above we should really have shown that the abstract state with components:

$$stock'' = stock',$$
$$issued'' = issued',$$
$$shelved'' = shelved',$$
$$readers'' = readers$$

satisfies the predicate of *Library''* before it is safe to eliminate the existential quantifier. Confirm that this is indeed so.

6.5.8   Schema preconditions

The operator we describe in this section is somewhat different from the schema operators described so far in that it is rarely useful as part of the description of a system operation; rather it is useful as a means of computing the precise conditions under which a given operation is applicable. The operator concerned is known as schema precondition (written pre). It is only applied to schemas representing operations: an operation is said to be applicable for those combinations of before state and inputs such that there exist an after state and outputs satisfying the specified relationships amongst all the variables involved. Thus we define pre *Op* to mean:

$\exists \, State'; \; Outs! \bullet Op$

where *State* is the abstract state of the system for which *Op* is defined and *Outs!* is the set of declarations of the output variables of *Op*.

We shall have more to say about precondition calculations in subsequent chapters but we show here some simple examples of such calculations. We first do a very simple example to illustrate the mechanics of the calculation of preconditions before applying these ideas to one of the LibSys operations.

Suppose we have a system whose abstract states are described by:

$$\boxed{\begin{array}{l} \underline{\textit{Simple}\,} \\ x, y : \mathbb{N} \\ \hline x \leq y \end{array}}$$

We consider an operation:

$$\boxed{\begin{array}{l} \underline{\textit{NonEndPoint}\,} \\ \Delta \textit{Simple}; \; z! : \mathbb{N} \\ \hline x \leq x' < z! < y' \leq y \end{array}}$$

If we define $PreNEP \,\widehat{=}\, \text{pre } NonEndPoint$, then we expand $PreNEP$ as follows:

$$\boxed{\begin{array}{l} \underline{\textit{PreNEP}\,} \\ \textit{Simple} \\ \hline \exists \, x', y', z! : \mathbb{N} \bullet x \leq x' < z! < y' \leq y \end{array}}$$

Usually it is possible to simplify the predicate which arises from the existential quantification; in this case, the predicate may be written in the following equivalent form:

$\exists \, x', y', z! : \mathbb{N} \bullet$
$$x + 1 \leq x' + 1 \leq z! \leq y' - -1 \leq y - -1$$

and this in turn requires that:

$$x + 1 \leq y - - 1$$

since the relation $\leq$ is transitive, which is to say that:

$$\forall i, j, k : \mathbb{N} \bullet i \leq k \wedge k \leq j \Rightarrow i \leq j$$

Thus we can rewrite the precondition schema as:

```
┌─ PreNEP ──────────────────────────────────
│ Simple
│ ────────────
│ x + 1 ≤ y − − 1
└───────────────────────────────────────────
```

so that the predicate is now a simple relationship amongst the components of the incoming state. Note that this predicate is a stronger constraint than that imposed by the schema *Simple*. (Also, see Exercise 6.25.)

Now we examine the *Issue* operation for the library system. Earlier in this chapter we gave a definition of the operation: we give now a slightly different definition which does not explicitly include the requirement that:

$$\#(issued \rhd \{r?\}) < maxloans$$

Thus we define:

```
┌─ Issue1 ──────────────────────────────────
│ LoanTransaction
│ c? : Copy; r? : Reader
│ ──────────────────────────────────────────
│ c? ∈ shelved; r? ∈ readers
│ issued' = issued ⊕ {c? ↦ r?}
└───────────────────────────────────────────
```

If we now apply the precondition operator to this schema we obtain:

```
┌─ PreIssue1 ───────────────────────────────
│ Library
│ c? : Copy; r? : Reader
│ ──────────────────────────────────────────
│ ∃ Library' •
│         c? ∈ shelved ∧ r? ∈ readers
│         ∧ issued' = issued ⊕ {c? ↦ r?}
│         ∧ stock' = stock ∧ readers' = readers
└───────────────────────────────────────────
```

Unpacking the quantified *Library'* schema somewhat we may rewrite this:

```
┌─ PreIssue1 ─────────────────────────────────────────────────
│ Library
│ c? : Copy; r? : Reader
├─────────────────────────────────────────────────────────────
│ c? ∈ shelved; r? ∈ readers
│ ∃ stock' : Copy ↠ Book; issued' : Copy ↠ Reader;
│     shelved' : 𝔽 Copy; readers' : 𝔽 Reader | Library'Predicate •
│         stock' = stock
│         ∧ issued' = issued ⊕ {c? ↦ r?}
│         ∧ readers' = readers
└─────────────────────────────────────────────────────────────
```

where we write *Library'Predicate* to stand for the invariant which *Library'* is required to satisfy. Note that *PreIssue1* is not a schema describing a change of state: what it does is to describe the relationship which must exist between the various components of the *Library* state and the inputs $c?$ and $r?$ for the *Issue1* operation to be applicable. We want to discover the nature of this relationship in its simplest form, if possible eliminating the dashed components.

We have already separated out those conjuncts which make no mention of any of the dashed components. We can eliminate the existentially quantified variables if we can express each of those variables in terms of the *Library* components and the inputs, $c?$ and $r?$, and these values satisfy the *Library'Predicate*. Now *stock'*, *issued'* and *readers'* are already so expressed. Since *shelved'* and *issued'* must partition *stock'*, which is the same as *stock*, and since $c? \in shelved$, we have:

$$shelved' = shelved \setminus \{c?\}$$

(We encountered this argument about *shelved'* earlier in the present chapter.) So now we can derive a more explicit version of *PreIssue1*, namely:

```
┌─ PreIssue1 ─────────────────────────────────────────────────
│ Library
│ c? : Copy; r? : Reader
├─────────────────────────────────────────────────────────────
│ c? ∈ shelved; r? ∈ readers
│ ∃ stock' : Copy ↠ Book; issued' : Copy ↠ Reader;
│     shelved' : 𝔽 Copy; readers' : 𝔽 Reader | Library'Predicate •
│         stock' = stock
│         ∧ issued' = issued ⊕ {c? ↦ r?}
│         ∧ shelved' = shelved \ {c?}
│         ∧ readers' = readers
└─────────────────────────────────────────────────────────────
```

In order to satisfy the *Library'Predicate* the value of $\#(issued' \rhd \{r?\})$ must be no greater than *maxloans*, but note that a new element is to be added to $issued \rhd \{r?\}$, so that:

$$\#(issued' \rhd \{r?\}) = \#(issued \rhd \{r?\}) + 1$$

thus it is required that:

$$\#(issued' \rhd \{r?\}) = \#(issued \rhd \{r?\}) + 1 \leqslant maxloans$$

or more simply, that:

$$\#(issued \rhd \{r?\}) < maxloans$$

We can now eliminate the existential quantifier and the variables it governs so long as we retain the constraints upon the plain variables which the existence of the dashed values entails; thus we derive the simplified version:

```
┌─ PreIssue1 ──────────────────────────────────────────
│ Library
│ c? : Copy; r? : Reader
├──────────────────────────────────────────────────────
│ c? ∈ shelved; r? ∈ readers
│ #(issued ▷ {r?}) < maxloans
└──────────────────────────────────────────────────────
```

A constraint which was merely implicit in the definition of *Issue1* has been made explicit by this process of simplifying the corresponding precondition for the operation. It should be noted that in theory it will not always be possible to express all of the dashed components in terms of the plain components and the inputs for a given operation; however in practice it does frequently happen that way. Clearly if we want to extend a partial operation to a total operation which will detect and report all the various errors which could occur then we need to know where the operation is applicable and where it is inapplicable; the area of applicability may be a more restricted area than is immediately evident. It should be noted that the dashed variables must satisfy the other constraints of *Library'Predicate* too; see Exercise 6.26.

We shall say no more here about precondition calculations since this issue will be treated more fully and more formally in Chapter 9.

Exercise 6.23 ⋄ Consider the schema, given earlier:

```
┌─ EnterNewCopy ───────────────────────────────────────
│ ΔLibrary
│ b? : Book
├──────────────────────────────────────────────────────
│ ∃ c : Copy | c ∉ dom stock •
│            stock' = stock ⊕ {c ↦ b?} ∧
│            shelved' = shelved ∪ {c}
│ issued' = issued; readers' = readers
└──────────────────────────────────────────────────────
```

Argue informally that pre$EnterNewCopy$ can be simplified to:

┌─ *PreEnterNewCopy* ─────────────────────────
│ *Library*; *b*? : *Book*
├───
│ ∃ *c* : *Copy* • *c* ∉ dom *stock*
└───

Exercise 6.24 Suppose the abstract states of a simple system, ClassRecSys, for recording who is registered for a class and who has handed in the coursework is as follows:

┌─ *ClassRecord* ─────────────────────────────
│ *regd*, *done* : $\mathbb{F}$ *Student*
├───
│ #*regd* ≤ *maxclass*; *done* ⊆ *regd*
└───

where *maxclass* is a globally declared positive integer, and suppose that the operation *NewRegistration* is defined as follows:

┌─ *NewRegistration* ─────────────────────────
│ Δ *ClassRecord*; *s*? : *Student*
├───
│ *s*? ∉ *regd*; *regd*′ = *regd* ∪ {*s*?}; *done*′ = *done*
└───

Derive a simplified expansion of pre *NewRegistration*.

Exercise 6.25 ◇ Refer to the calculation of pre *NonEndPoint* near the beginning of Section 6.5.8. Argue that if $x + 1 \leq y - -1$ then there are indeed integers x', y' and $z!$ such that:

$$x + 1 \leq x' + 1 \leq z! \leq y' - -1 \leq y - -1$$

giving examples of possible values for x', y' and $z!$. (Taken together with the transitivity of the ≤ relation, this justifies our replacement of:

$$\exists\, x', y', z! : \mathbb{N} \bullet$$
$$x + 1 \leq x' + 1 \leq z! \leq y' - -1 \leq y - -1$$

by $x + 1 \leq y - -1$ in the predicate of *PreNEP*.)

Exercise 6.26 Refer to the discussion of *PreIssue*1; see page 165. Check that the components *stock*′, *issued*′, *shelved*′ and *readers*′, taken together, where:

$$stock' = stock$$
$$issued' = issued \oplus \{c? \mapsto r?\}$$
$$shelved' = shelved \setminus \{c?\}$$
$$readers' = readers$$

satisfy each of the conjuncts of the *Library*′ *Predicate*, provided that:

$$\#(issued \rhd \{r?\}) < maxloans$$

and that the plain components satisfy the *Library* constraints.

6.6   Further uses of schemas

It is not our intention in this book to cover every feature of the Z notation just for the sake of completeness, but we do want to illustrate those features which we feel are of real importance in the context of specification construction. In the present section we look at some of the aspects of the usage of schemas which are less centrally important for a basic understanding. The reader can safely skip the remainder of this section on a first reading, but may need to come back to it in order to understand some aspects of case studies later in the book.

6.6.1   Schema types

The reader may well have surmised that schemas could be used rather as record types are used in programming languages, that is to say, as a way of binding together associated pieces of data. On one level, of course this is what all uses of the schema do, but the point here is that we can create data types with interesting and useful structures based on the schema idea.

In the LibSys example, we declared *Book* to be a given set. We had in mind that each member of the set would correspond to some aggregate of detailed information about a particular published work. Such information might well include the name of the author or editor, the date of publication, the title, the number of pages, and so on. However, we have never looked at this detail formally because it was not important to do so at the level of system description we have so far adopted, though we were always aware that an implementation of a LibSys system would have to consider such details at some stage.

Now we could in fact specify this kind of detail in a schema such as the following:

$$
\begin{array}{|l}
\hline
\_\,Book _____ \\
title, author, publisher, isbn : String \\
pubdate, pp : \mathbb{Z} \\
\hline
slength\ title \leqslant 80;\ slength\ author \leqslant 40 \\
slength\ publisher \leqslant 40;\ slength\ isbn = 13 \\
(checksum\ isbn)\ \mathsf{mod}\ 11 = 0 \\
0 < pp;\ 1800 \leqslant pubdate \leqslant 2050 \\
\hline
\end{array}
$$

Here we illustrate the fact that besides declaring the names of components and their types – they would be called fields of a record type in programming language terms – we can also impose constraints on the values of those components. (We assume here that *String* is a given set, and that appropriate definitions of function $slength, checksum : String \to \mathbb{N}$ are given elsewhere.)

However, once we allow schemas as the types of objects in specifications, we have to ask what these objects are and what operations we can perform upon them. If we declare $b : Book$, then we envisage that it makes sense to ask, for example: 'What is the *isbn* for *b*?' We can in fact select the *isbn* component of *b* using the notation *b.isbn*. The type corresponding to *Book* as it is defined above can be written:

$$\langle author : String, \ title : String, \ publisher : String,$$
$$isbn : String, \ pubdate : \mathbb{N}, \ pp : \mathbb{N} \rangle$$

We can think of this type as one for which there are at least the six functions defined corresponding to the names of the components, and that these functions deliver values of the types declared in the schema definition. When we want to apply one of these selection functions to an object of schema type we use the dot notation, as in *b.isbn*. Two objects of a given schema type are only equal if the pairs of corresponding components are each equal. However, it is important to note that the type given above makes no mention of the constraints imposed in the predicate of the *Book* schema. When we declare $b : Book$ we are using an abbreviated declaration: this declaration specifies the type of *b* to be that which corresponds to the schema *Book*, as given above, but the components of *b* are also required to satisfy the constraints expressed in the predicate of schema *Book*.

As a very simple example using these ideas, suppose we use the new schema definition of *Book* type in place of the given set definition in the original LibSys, and we want an operation which outputs the titles of books in stock by a given author. Here is a definition of such an operation:

$$\begin{array}{|l}
\hline
\underline{\ WorksOfAuthorByTitle\ }\rule{3cm}{0.4pt} \\
\ \Xi LibSys \\
\ auth? : String \\
\ titles! : \mathbb{F}\ String \\
\hline
\ titles! = \{b : \mathrm{ran}\ stock \mid b.author = auth? \bullet b.title\} \\
\hline
\end{array}$$

6.6.2   The theta operator: binding formation

We mentioned earlier that we could express the *NoChange* constraint needed in the definition of ΞS in the form $\theta S = \theta S'$. The θ operator is useful in other contexts too, so we shall now explain in some detail how it may be used. Here are the main points to be understood:

- θ may only be applied to a schema name, which may be plain or decorated; all the variables declared in the schema must be in scope at the point in the text where the θ operator is used.

- When the name is plain, as in θS, then it produces an element of schema type $\langle x_1 : t_1, ..., x_n : t_n \rangle$ where $x_1, ..., x_n$ are the names of the variables declared in S and $t_1, ..., t_n$ are the types of these variables in the current scope[3]; the value of the x_i component of the element is of course the value of the variable x_i which is in scope.

- When the name is decorated, as in $\theta S'$, then it produces an element whose schema type is $\langle x_1 : t_1, ..., x_n : t_n \rangle$ where $x'_1, ..., x'_n$ are the names of the variables declared in S' and $t_1, ..., t_n$ are the types of these variables in the current scope; thus the decoration of the variables is ignored in the names of the components of the binding; the value of the x_i component is the value of the variable x'_i which is in scope.

Now when we write $\theta S = \theta S'$ this is equivalent to saying that the values of corresponding variables must be equal, which is exactly what we want to say in order to define the notation ΞS. The reader may well ask if it would not have been easier to say that ΞS means just this anyway, thus treating Ξ itself as an operator which may be applied to schema names. However, neither Δ nor Ξ are regarded as operators; they are no more than characters which can be introduced into the names of schemas, albeit with the convention for their usage described earlier in the present chapter.

The θ operator is useful in other contexts too. One of the most important of these is when we want to promote an operation defined for an abstract state which at some later stage in the development of a specification will form a part of the abstract state for a larger system. We shall devote the next subsection to the exploration of this idea.

6.6.3   Operation promotion

When we come to construct specifications for large systems it is useful to be able to write specifications for smaller parts of a system and then to promote those operations, in a more or less mechanical way, to become operations for the larger system. We shall see good examples of such promotion of operations in the case study of Chapter 8. As a simple example for present purposes, suppose we wish to describe a library of musical recordings on tape or compact disc. We shall call this system AudioLib to distinguish it from LibSys, though it is in fact quite similar. One way in which it differs is that we wish to associate some information with each recording copy over and above the details of works and artists on the recordings. Specifically, suppose that we want to attach a loan category to each

---

[3]There is a subtle point here, which can be ignored for the purposes of the example to follow. Suppose the expression θS occurs in the predicate part of a schema X, but that S itself is not included by name in the declaration part of X; suppose, further, that in the declaration part of X the variables of S are all declared individually; now the types for the binding θS are those defined in X which could be different from those of S. It should be said that it would be very confusing to do such a thing in a specification, however.

recording copy and that we also want to maintain a record of the dates on which the copy was loaned out, for the purposes of stock management.

For this system the set *Recording* is defined by a schema, rather than being a given set, since we want the members of this set to have a particular structure.

```
┌─ Recording ─────────────────────────────────
│ cat : Category
│ loans : seq Date
│ rec : RecordingDetails
└─────────────────────────────────────────────
```

Assume here that *Date* is a given set and that *RecordingDetails* is either a given set or a schema type defined elsewhere, along the lines of *Book* in the section on schema types. For the purposes of this illustration we need only two different loan categories:

$$Category ::= Loanable \mid Restricted$$

We also need a given set of identifiers which will be used to identify uniquely each distinct physical tape or compact disc in the AudioLib stock:

$$[RecId]$$

Next we define the abstract state for the AudioLib system:

```
┌─ AudioLib ──────────────────────────────────
│ stock : RecId ↦ Recording
│ out : RecId ↦ Listener
│ listeners : 𝔽 Listener
│ ────────────────────────────────────────────
│ dom out ⊆ dom stock
│ ran out ⊆ listeners
│ ∀ r : dom out • (stock r).cat = Loanable
└─────────────────────────────────────────────
```

The predicate part of this schema says that:

- only items of stock can be out on loan

- loans can only be made to registered listeners

- items out on loan must be loanable and not restricted to the library

Now we could define an operation to change the loan category of a *Recording*, as follows:

ChangeCategory
$\Delta Recording$
$newcat? : Category$
$report! : Report$

$cat \neq newcat? \Rightarrow (report! = Ok \wedge cat' = newcat?)$
$cat = newcat? \Rightarrow (report! = NoChange \wedge cat' = cat)$
$loans' = loans; rec' = rec$

In order to be able to promote operations on individual *Recordings* to be operations on the AudioLib abstract state we can define a framing schema; remember we wanted to be able to perform promotions more or less mechanically. Here is a suitable schema in the present case:

$\Phi Recording$
$\Delta AudioLib$
$\Delta Recording$
$rcid? : RecId$

$rcid? \in \operatorname{dom} stock$
$\theta Recording = stock\ rcid?$
$stock' = stock \oplus \{rcid? \mapsto \theta Recording'\}$

Note that the Greek letter Φ is often used to indicate that a schema is a framing schema. Looking at this schema in some detail:

- the constraint $\theta Recording = stock\ rcid?$ ensures that the *Recording* concerned is the one corresponding to *stock rcid?*

- the constraint $stock' = stock \oplus \{rcid? \mapsto \theta Recording'\}$ ensures that *stock* is unchanged except that *rcid?* is now associated with the modified *Recording*

- note that we do not constrain other parts of the abstract state to be unchanged because we assume that if $\Phi Recording$ is used as part of the description of an operation on the whole abstract state, such constraints on other components will be expressed elsewhere if and when necessary.

We could now define an operation *ChangeRecordingCateg$_0$* thus:

$ChangeRecordingCateg_0 \mathrel{\widehat{=}}$
$\qquad [\Delta AudioLib; rcid? : RecId\ |$
$\qquad\qquad\qquad out' = out; listeners' = listeners; rcid? \notin out]$
$\qquad\quad \Phi Recording \wedge ChangeCategory$

This says that:

- *ChangeRecordingCateg$_0$* is an AudioLib operation which changes neither the items on loan, nor the listeners, and which has a recording identifier as input corresponding to an item not currently on loan.

- It is a promoted *Recording* operation.

- Its effect on the recording copy concerned is described by *ChangeCategory*.

But note that there is something not quite as it should be about this schema. It is intended to be an AudioLib operation, but it has too many variables. In particular, we would not expect to see the components of the recording copy concerned amongst the declarations for a system-level operation, which they do here because they are declared in *ChangeRecordingCateg*. We need to hide these variables as follows:

$$ChangeRecordingCateg \mathrel{\hat{=}} \exists\, \Delta Recording \bullet ChangeRecordingCateg_0$$

Now *ChangeRecordingCategory* is a proper AudioLib operation.

Exercise 6.27 ◇ Consider a further small change to the AudioLib system. Just as copies of recordings may have attributes which we may need to change from time to time, so also listeners will have associated information which may change. For example a listener may move house, so that the address associated with that listener will have to be updated. Suppose the AudioLib system abstract state is now described in the following schema:

```
__ AudioLib _____
  stock : RecId ↛ Recording
  out : RecId ↛ ListenerId
  listeners : ListenerId ↛ ListenerDetails
 _____
  dom out ⊆ dom stock
  ran out ⊆ dom listeners
```

Now, by analogy with the operations defined above:

(i) Define a schema for *ListenerDetails* which includes an *Address* component.

(ii) Define a *ChangeAddress* operation.

(iii) Then define a *ListenerPromote* operation, which promotes any operation on a *ListenerDetails* record into an *AudioLib* operation.

(iv) Finally, define an operation *ChangeListenerAddress* which has as input

$$listenerid? : dom\ listeners$$

and which changes the information associated with the *ListenerDetails* record to which *listenerid?* refers.

6.7   Further reading

In this chapter we introduced the Z schema and illustrated its usage, in combination with the operators of the schema calculus. We have used a very simple application as a source of examples. Of course, ideally the reader would like to see a wide range of applications demonstrating the general utility of the ideas presented here. Unfortunately this would occupy more space than could reasonably be devoted to it in a book of this nature; however, there are many more examples in the Z literature, and a particularly valuable and readily accessible source is [Hay93]. See also [Bow95]. Other work which may be consulted, where the features of the schema calculus are presented in sequence, include [Woo90] and [Inc88]; in [KS89] will be found the description of a more comprehensive system for a library.

Chapter 7

A first specification revisited

In this chapter we are going to revisit the Word-For-Word system described in Chapter 3, this time using the facilities of the full Z language. Since we now have greater powers of expression as a result of familiarity with those facilities, we also take the opportunity to add new capabilities to the system; for example, we shall add a feature which allows the user to ask for a test of his or her vocabulary on the basis of the current stock of words which has been built up, and it will also be possible to ask for a printed list of all those words, ordered by native words and by foreign words according to the alphabetical ordering used for those languages.

In Chapter 3 we began with a section which mixed the description of the system itself with explanation of the means at our disposal for writing the specification. This time we shall not pursue this course: since in any case a Z specification should contain within it a natural language description of the system being specified, we shall let the specification tell its own story, both in Z and in English. There will necessarily be some duplication of what was given in the earlier specification, but we feel it is worthwhile giving the complete enhanced system here. The section on printing lists of words (see Section 7.1.5), and the theory of alphabetical orders upon which it depends (see Section 7.1.2), may be found quite tricky and can safely be skipped on a first reading. We end the present chapter with a section where we suggest an overall structure for specification documents; by that stage the proposed format will in fact be quite familiar since we shall present the new Word-For-Word specification accordingly.

7.1 The expanded vocabulary system

The Word-For-Word system is intended to help in the acquisition of vocabulary by a student learning a foreign language. The system is to record pairs of words, where one word is a native language word and the other is a foreign language word, where each word of a pair may serve as a translation of the other at least in some circumstances. Words to be added to the vocabulary must satisfy rules, known as the orthographic rules, which are concerned with spelling conventions in the two languages; the purpose of these rules is to eliminate as far as possible the addition to the vocabulary of words which could not possibly belong to the respective languages. The system will also maintain a record of progress for the student, based on vocabulary tests. The facilities to be provided are as follows:

- Valid pairs of words may be added to the vocabulary.

- All translations of a native word into the foreign language may be requested.

- All translations of a foreign word into the native language may be requested.

- The student may be tested on the current vocabulary; native to foreign or foreign to native translation may be tested; in the native to foreign case, the system chooses a native word, and the student must supply as many as possible of the known foreign translations, scoring a mark for each correct response; in the foreign to native case, the roles of the languages are reversed.

- The student can request an alphabetical list of all the native words in the vocabulary, together with all the known foreign translations of those words; similarly the student can request a list of the foreign words and their native translations.

The system will comment on each operation performed, reporting any error conditions.

7.1.1   Given sets and global variables

Two sets are assumed:

$$[Native, Foreign]$$

representing the sets of all possible sequences of characters over the alphabets of the native and foreign languages respectively. Note that, at least in the case when the languages concerned are represented by sound signs rather than ideograms, if the interword spacing character is regarded as part of the alphabet then it is possible to enter phrases into the vocabulary as well as words.

The orthographic rules are characterised by subsets of *Native* and *Foreign*:

$$OrthoNative : \mathbb{P}\ Native$$
$$OrthoForeign : \mathbb{P}\ Foreign$$

For any particular pair of languages, definitions of these subsets would have to be supplied at some stage during the implementation process. We shall require that at all times the vocabulary contains only words which satisfy the orthographic rules; that is to say, each native or foreign word in the vocabulary must be an element of the appropriate one of these subsets.

The set *Message* consists of various messages used to tell the user about the results of operations carried out:

> *Message* ::=
>> *Ok* | *AlreadyKnownPair* | *NewPairEntered*
>> | *ErrorInForeignWord* | *ErrorInNativeWord* | *ErrorInBothWords*
>> | *UnknownNativeWord* | *UnknownForeignWord*
>> | *VocabIsEmpty* | *NoCorrectResponses*

We shall need the function *percent*, defined for all pairs of non-negative integers; this function converts a fraction x/y, represented by the pair (x, y), to the nearest whole number percentage, half a per cent rounding upwards.

$$\begin{array}{|l}
percent : \mathbb{N} \times \mathbb{N} \to \mathbb{N} \\
\hline
percent = \\
\quad \{x, y, p : \mathbb{N} \mid \\
\qquad (y = 0 \land p = 0) \lor \\
\qquad (y > 0 \land y * (2 * p - - 1) \le 200 * x < y * (2 * p + 1)) \\
\qquad \bullet (x, y) \mapsto p\}
\end{array}$$

When $y = 0$ the function delivers value 0 (this is needed for the case when no tests have been done); for $y > 0$ the constraint on the value delivered, say p, is equivalent to:

$$(100x/y) - - \tfrac{1}{2} < p \le (100x/y) + \tfrac{1}{2}$$

There is only one such p for given x and y. The function will be used to calculate an average mark over vocabulary tests.

7.1.2   Some general theory: alphabetical orders

When we come to describe the operation of printing alphabetical lists of words and their translations, we shall need to assume that alphabetical orderings are defined for the types *Native* and *Foreign*. Thus we need to say what it means for a set to have an alphabetical ordering upon it:

$$\begin{array}{|l}
= [X] = \\
\hline
alphorder : \mathbb{P}(X \leftrightarrow X) \\
\hline
alphorder = \{\_rel\_ : X \leftrightarrow X \mid \\
\qquad \forall x, y, z : X \bullet \\
\qquad\quad (x \ rel \ y \land y \ rel \ z \Rightarrow x \ rel \ z) \\
\qquad\quad \land (x \ rel \ y \land y \ rel \ x \Rightarrow x = y) \\
\qquad\quad \land (x \ne y \Rightarrow x \ rel \ y \lor y \ rel \ x)\}
\end{array}$$

Thus we require an alphabetical order to have the following properties:

- If an element x comes earlier in the ordering than an element y, and y is earlier than z, then x is earlier than z (this property of a relation is known as transitivity).

- For distinct elements x and y then either x is earlier than y in the ordering or y is earlier than x, but not both.

We do not mind whether an element x is related to itself or not; we shall not want to compare an element with itself. For a given type X, the set $alphorder[X]$ is the set of all alphabetically ordered relations of type $X \leftrightarrow X$.

The function $putinorder$ takes a finite set and converts it into a sequence whose length is the size of the set, and which contains all the elements of the set, ordered according to a given alphabetical order.

$$
\begin{array}{l}
\hline
[X] \\
\hline
putinorder : (\mathbb{F}\, X \times alphorder[X]) \rightarrow \text{seq}\, X \\
\hline
putinorder = \\
\quad \{nset : \mathbb{F}\, X;\ order : alphorder[X];\ nseq : \text{seq}\, X \mid \\
\quad\quad \#nseq = \#nset \wedge nset = \text{ran}\, nseq \\
\quad\quad \wedge\, (\forall\, i, j \in 1..\#nset \mid i < j \bullet (nseq\, i, nseq\, j) \in order) \\
\quad\quad\quad \bullet (nset, order) \mapsto nseq\} \\
\hline
\end{array}
$$

We now declare the alphabetical orderings corresponding to the two languages:

$$
\begin{array}{l}
\_Native\,WordOrder\_ : alphorder[Native] \\
\_Foreign\,WordOrder\_ : alphorder[Foreign]
\end{array}
$$

and we go on to define functions which convert sets of native and of foreign words into corresponding alphabetically ordered sequences:

$$
\begin{array}{l}
\hline
SetInNative\,WordOrder : \mathbb{F}\, Native \rightarrow \text{seq}\, Native \\
SetInForeign\,WordOrder : \mathbb{F}\, Foreign \rightarrow \text{seq}\, Foreign \\
\hline
SetInNative\,WordOrder = \\
\quad \lambda\, nset : \mathbb{F}\, Native \bullet putinorder(nset, Native\,WordOrder) \\
SetInForeign\,WordOrder = \\
\quad \lambda\, fset : \mathbb{F}\, Foreign \bullet putinorder(fset, Foreign\,WordOrder)
\end{array}
$$

Now a list of native words and their foreign translations is going to be an alphabetical ordering of a set of pairs of type $Native \times \text{seq}\, Foreign$, where the sequences of foreign words are themselves alphabetically ordered. Such sets of pairs are in fact functions of type $Native \rightarrow\!\!\!\!\!\rightarrow \text{seq}\, Foreign$. Similarly, a list of foreign words and their native translations is an alphabetical ordering of a function of type *Foreign* $\twoheadrightarrow$ seq *Native*.

Thus, we also need to define an alphabetical ordering on these functions, and clearly we need an ordering which respects that of the native or foreign words which form the first components. Thus we declare the orderings:

$\_NativeDictOrder\_$: *alphorder*[*Native* × seq *Foreign*]
$\_ForeignDictOrder\_$: *alphorder*[*Foreign* × seq *Native*]

$\forall n1, n2 : Native;\ fseq1, fseq2 : $ seq *Foreign* •
$\quad n1 \neq n2 \Rightarrow$
$\quad\quad\quad (n1, fseq1)\ NativeDictOrder\ (n2, fseq2)$
$\quad\quad\quad\quad \Leftrightarrow n1\ NativeWordOrder\ n2$
$\forall f1, f2 : Foreign : nseq1, nseq2 : $ seq *Native* •
$\quad f1 \neq f2 \Rightarrow$
$\quad\quad\quad (f1, nseq1)\ ForeignDictOrder\ (f2, nseq2)$
$\quad\quad\quad\quad \Leftrightarrow f1\ ForeignWordOrder\ f2$

---

and then we go on to define the functions which will set the lists of words in their correct orders:

$SetInNativeDictOrder$:
$\quad\quad\quad (Native \twoheadrightarrow$ seq $Foreign) \rightarrow$ seq$(Native \times$ seq $Foreign)$
$SetInForeignDictOrder$:
$\quad\quad\quad (Foreign \twoheadrightarrow$ seq $Native) \rightarrow$ seq$(Foreign \times$ seq $Native)$

$SetInNativeDictOrder =$
$\quad \lambda\ tset : (Native \twoheadrightarrow$ seq $Foreign)$ •
$\quad\quad\quad putinorder(tset, NativeDictOrder)$
$SetInForeignDictOrder =$
$\quad \lambda\ tset : (Foreign \twoheadrightarrow$ seq $Native)$ •
$\quad\quad\quad putinorder(tset, ForeignDictOrder)$

Note that for the alphabetical order *NativeDictOrder* we do not say what is to be the relationship for pairs $(n, fseq1)$ and $(n, fseq2)$ when $fseq1 \neq fseq2$; the definition of an alphabetical order requires that such pairs be related by the order; however, we shall find that it is not important which way the order relates such pairs, because we want to impose the alphabetical ordering upon sets which would not in any case contain such pairs of pairs.

7.1.3 Abstract state definition

In the following schema we define the vocabulary as a relation between pairs of correctly formed words; we also give names to its domain and range, which are the sets of native and foreign words known to the vocabulary.

```
┌─ WellFormedVocab ──────────────────────────────────────
│ Vocab : OrthoNative ↔ OrthoForeign
│ NativeWordsKnown : F OrthoNative
│ ForeignWordsKnown : F OrthoForeign
├────────────────────────────────────────────────────────
│ NativeWordsKnown = dom Vocab
│ ForeignWordsKnown = ran Vocab
└────────────────────────────────────────────────────────
```

We define a schema *RecordOfProgress* which will be used to record the progress of the student, based on the results of vocabulary tests:

```
┌─ RecordOfProgress ─────────────────────────────────────
│ CumuMaxMarks, CumuMarksScored, AveragePercent : N
├────────────────────────────────────────────────────────
│ 0 ≤ AveragePercent ≤ 100
│ CumuMarksScored ⩽ CumuMaxMarks
│ AveragePercent = percent(CumuMarksScored, CumuMaxMarks)
└────────────────────────────────────────────────────────
```

A record is kept of how many words have been tested to date, of how many correct responses were given and of the average number of correct responses to the nearest percentage point. The complete abstract state of the system is described in the schema:

```
┌─ WordForWord ──────────────────────────────────────────
│ WellFormedVocab
│ RecordOfProgress
└────────────────────────────────────────────────────────
```

7.1.4   Initialisation

We assume that the system starts with an empty vocabulary, and that no vocabulary tests have been performed.

```
┌─ InitWord − For − Word ────────────────────────────────
│ WordForWord'
├────────────────────────────────────────────────────────
│ Vocab' = ∅
│ CumuMaxMarks' = CumuMarksScored' = 0
└────────────────────────────────────────────────────────
```

All of the components of the unique initial state may be deduced from this definition.

7.1.5 Definition of partial operations

Adding new pairs to the vocabulary

A word-pair consisting of a native and a foreign word satisfying the orthographic rules of their respective languages may be added to the vocabulary; the user will be informed whether or not the pair was already known to the vocabulary:

$$AddPair \mathrel{\hat=} EnterPair \wedge ReportIfAlreadyKnown$$

The schema *EnterPair* adds a given pair of valid words to the vocabulary:

```
┌─ EnterPair ──────────────────────────────────────────
│ Δ WellFormedVocab
│ Ξ RecordOfProgress
│ n? : OrthoNative; f? : OrthoForeign
│ ────────────────────────────────────────
│ Vocab' = Vocab ∪ {n? ↦ f?}
└──────────────────────────────────────────────────────
```

This operation can never affect the record of progress. If the given pair of words is already entered, the vocabulary is unchanged. Appropriate messages to the user are specified as follows:

```
┌─ ReportIfAlreadyKnown ───────────────────────────────
│ Vocab : OrthoNative ↔ OrthoForeign
│ n? : OrthoNative; f? : OrthoForeign; rep! : Message
│ ────────────────────────────────────────
│ n? ↦ f? ∈ Vocab ⇒ rep! = AlreadyKnownPair
│ n? ↦ f? ∉ Vocab ⇒ rep! = NewPairEntered
└──────────────────────────────────────────────────────
```

This schema needs to refer only to the *Vocab* component of the abstract state.

Asking for translations of given words

All translations of a given native word may be requested, distinguishing the case of a word which satisfies the orthographic rules but does not occur in the current vocabulary:

$$ToForeign \mathrel{\hat=} ForeignTranslations \wedge ReportIfKnownNative$$

Now defining *ForeignTranslations* for the case when the native word submitted satisfies the orthographic rules:

```
┌─ ForeignTranslations ────────────────────────────────
│ Ξ WordForWord
│ n? : OrthoNative; ftrans! : 𝔽 OrthoForeign
│ ────────────────────────────────────────
│ ftrans! = Vocab⦇ {n?} ⦈
└──────────────────────────────────────────────────────
```

The set of foreign translations will of course be empty if the native word is unknown to the vocabulary. *ReportIfKnownNative* specifies appropriate messages:

$$
\begin{array}{l}
\_\_ReportIfKnownNative _____ \\
NativeWordsKnown : \mathbb{F}\ OrthoNative \\
n? : OrthoNative;\ rep! : Message \\
_____ \\
n? \in NativeWordsKnown \Rightarrow rep! = Ok \\
n? \notin NativeWordsKnown \Rightarrow rep! = UnknownNativeWord
\end{array}
$$

In a similar way, all translations of a given foreign word may be requested. Clearly the necessary definitions for this facility are exactly analogous to those which relate to asking for translations of a given native word, with the rôles of native and foreign words exchanged. We shall not give them here in the interests of brevity.

Vocabulary tests

We shall consider only tests of native to foreign words, since the other test is again exactly the same apart from reversal of the rôles of the two languages. A native to foreign test may be described as follows:

- The system selects a native test word; this is output, together with a count of the number of known translations.

- The user provides a sequence of foreign words, of any desired length.

- The record of progress is updated in accordance with the number of distinct correct responses in that sequence.

- The set of correct responses is output.

- A new average over all tests to date is output.

Formal description of the operation can be achieved by the combination of three sets of constraints:

$$
\begin{array}{l}
VocabTestNtoF \ \widehat{=} \\
\qquad SelectTestWordN \wedge CheckResponsesF \wedge UpdateScoreNtoF \\
\qquad\quad \setminus (Translations)
\end{array}
$$

where we hide the set of foreign translations of the native test word. We define each of the conjoined schemas in turn:

$$\begin{array}{l}
\rule{6cm}{0pt} \\
\hline
\textit{SelectTestWordN} \\
\hline
\textit{WellFormedVocab} \\
\textit{TestWord!} : \textit{OrthoNative} \\
\textit{Translations} : \mathbb{F}\ \textit{OrthoForeign} \\
\textit{TransCount!} : \mathbb{N} \\
\hline
\textit{TestWord!} \in \textit{NativeWordsKnown} \\
\textit{Translations} = \textit{Vocab}(\!|\ \{\textit{TestWord!}\}\ |\!) \\
\textit{TransCount!} = \#\textit{Translations}
\end{array}$$

A test word is chosen from amongst the native words known to the vocabulary; this is output, together with a count of the number of translations of the test word known to the vocabulary.

$$\begin{array}{l}
\hline
\textit{CheckResponsesF} \\
\hline
\textit{Translations}, \textit{CorrectResponses!} : \mathbb{F}\ \textit{OrthoForeign} \\
\textit{Responses?} : \text{seq } \textit{Foreign}, \textit{rep!} : \textit{Message} \\
\hline
\textit{CorrectResponses!} = \textit{Translations} \cap \text{ran } \textit{Responses?} \\
\textit{CorrectResponses!} = \emptyset \Rightarrow \textit{rep!} = \textit{NoCorrectResponses} \\
\textit{CorrectResponses!} \neq \emptyset \Rightarrow \textit{rep!} = \textit{Ok}
\end{array}$$

The student supplies a sequence of foreign words, possibly including mis-spelt words; the set of correct translations of the test word given in the response sequence are identified and output as confirmation. If no correct responses are given this is commented upon.

$$\begin{array}{l}
\hline
\textit{UpdateScoreNtoF} \\
\hline
\Xi\,\textit{WellFormedVocab} \\
\Delta\,\textit{RecordOfProgress} \\
\textit{CorrectResponses!} : \mathbb{F}\ \textit{OrthoForeign} \\
\textit{TransCount!}, \textit{NewAverage!} : \mathbb{N} \\
\hline
\textit{CumuMaxMarks}' = \textit{CumuMaxMarks} + \textit{TransCount!} \\
\textit{CumuMarksScored}' = \textit{CumuMarksScored} + \#\textit{CorrectResponses!} \\
\textit{NewAverage!} = \textit{AveragePercent}'
\end{array}$$

The vocabulary is not affected by the operation. The record of progress is appropriately adjusted to take account of this latest test. The new average percentage over all tests to date is output. Notice that though we may think of this operation as a simple dialogue with the user, the formal description given here expresses no more than the logical relationship amongst the inputs, the outputs and the components of the state, and says nothing about ordering in time.

Printing lists of words

The user may request that a list of all the native words with all of their translations should be printed out. Similarly, a list of the foreign words and their native translations may be requested. The lists of words are to be alphabetically ordered according to the orderings defined for the alphabets of the two languages concerned. The user will be informed if the vocabulary is currently empty; thus we define:

$$RequestNativeDict \;\hat{=}\; NativeDict \,\wedge\, ReportIfVocabEmpty$$

where we further define:

$$
\begin{array}{|l}
\hline
\;NativeDict \underline{\hspace{7cm}} \\
\;\; \Xi\, WordForWord \\
\;\; dict! : \mathrm{seq}(Native \times \mathrm{seq}\; Foreign) \\
\hline
\;\; dict! = SetInNativeDictOrder \\
\;\;\qquad\qquad (\lambda\, n : NativeWordsKnown \;\bullet \\
\;\;\qquad\qquad\qquad SetInForeignWordOrder(\,Vocab(\!|\; \{n\}\; |\!)\,)\,) \\
\hline
\end{array}
$$

which is to say that we must set in native dictionary order the function which maps known native words to the sets of foreign words which may serve as their translations ordered according to the foreign word order. The following schema generates an appropriate message:

$$
\begin{array}{|l}
\hline
\;ReportIfVocabEmpty \underline{\hspace{5cm}} \\
\;\; Vocab : OrthoNative \leftrightarrow OrthoForeign \\
\;\; rep! : Message \\
\hline
\;\; Vocab = \emptyset \Rightarrow rep! = VocabIsEmpty \\
\;\; Vocab \neq \emptyset \Rightarrow rep! = Ok \\
\hline
\end{array}
$$

A dictionary of foreign words and their native translations is obtained similarly, reversing the roles of the languages.

7.1.6   Precondition investigation and summary

Taking each of the partial operations in turn, we consider what are the precise conditions for their successful use. We assume that when a native word is required as input then the system interface will provide a native word, though it may not satisfy the orthographic rules; similarly if a sequence of native words is required then the system interface packages up a sequence of possibly mis-spelt native words and supplies this package as the input needed. How this might be achieved on the other side of the system interface is not our concern.

- In the case of *AddPair*, it is always possible to add a new valid pair of words to the vocabulary; all we ask is that the words satisfy the orthographic rules. Thus the inputs which the operation might receive are $n?$ of type *Native* and *f?* of type *Foreign*, and the precondition is that $n? \in OrthoNative$ and $f? \in OrthoForeign$. In effect we have unpacked the declarations given in *EnterPair*, namely $n? : OrthoNative; f? : OrthoForeign$.

- For the operation *ToForeign*, the input native word must be properly formed, but then the output *ftrans!* is always well-defined even if the correctly spelled native word is unknown to the vocabulary. Thus the precondition is simply $n? \in OrthoNative$.

- For *VocabTestNtoF*, a test word has to be provided as output, and this is only possible if the vocabulary is non-empty. Any sequence of foreign words, possibly mis-spelt, is acceptable as a response, even if none of them is a correct translation. For a non-empty vocabulary the set of foreign translations for any choice of native test word is well-defined and thus so is the count of the number of distinct elements it contains; so too are the remaining outputs and the updated components of the record of progress, whatever sequence of foreign words is input.

- For *RequestNativeDict*, the output is always well defined for any current vocabulary; thus the precondition is *true*.

The preconditions for the remaining operations *ToNative*, *VocabTestFtoN* and *RequestForeignDict* may be deduced by analogy, reversing the rôles of the two languages.

We summarise the operations of the system, their inputs and outputs and their preconditions for normal operation in Table 7.1.

7.1.7   Error handling

Adding new pairs to the vocabulary
We define the following total operation:

$$TotalAddPair \;\widehat{=}\; AddPair \lor AddPairError$$

The following schema defines what is to be done in case of error in one or both of the input words:

Operation	Inputs/Outputs	Preconditions
AddPair	*n? : Native; f? : Foreign* *rep! : Message*	*n? ∈ OrthoNative* *f? ∈ OrthoForeign*
ToForeign	*n? : Native* *ftrans! : 𝔽 OrthoForeign* *rep! : Message*	*n? ∈ OrthoNative*
ToNative	*f? : Foreign* *ntrans! : 𝔽 OrthoNative* *rep! : Message*	*f? ∈ OrthoForeign*
VocabTestNtoF	*Responses? : seq Foreign* *TestWord! : OrthoNative* *CorrectResponses! : 𝔽 OrthoForeign* *TransCount!, NewAverage! : ℕ* *rep! : Message*	*Vocab ≠ ∅*
VocabTestFtoN	*Responses? : seq Native* *TestWord! : OrthoForeign* *CorrectResponses! : 𝔽 OrthoNative* *TransCount!, NewAverage! : ℕ* *rep! : Message*	*Vocab ≠ ∅*
RequestNativeDict	*dict! : seq(Native × seq Foreign)* *rep! : Message*	*true*
RequestForeignDict	*dict! : seq(Foreign × seq Native)* *rep! : Message*	*true*

Table 7.1: Summary of partial operations

```
┌─ AddPairError ─────────────────────────────────────────
│ Ξ WordForWord
│ n? : Native; f? : Foreign; rep! : Message
├────────────────────────────────────────────────────────
│ n? ∈ OrthoNative ∧ f? ∉ OrthoForeign
│           ⇒ rep! = ErrorInForeignWord
│ n? ∉ OrthoNative ∧ f? ∈ OrthoForeign
│           ⇒ rep! = ErrorInNativeWord
│ n? ∉ OrthoNative ∧ f? ∉ OrthoForeign
│           ⇒ rep! = ErrorInBothWords
└────────────────────────────────────────────────────────
```

The vocabulary is of course unchanged, and a suitable message is generated.

Asking for translations of given words

For the *ToForeign* operation, we define the corresponding total operation thus:

$$TotalToForeign \,\hat{=}\, ToForeign \lor ToForeignError$$

where the following schema applies when the submitted word is ill-formed:

```
┌─ ToForeignError ───────────────────────────────────────
│ Ξ WordForWord
│ n? : Native; rep! : Message
├────────────────────────────────────────────────────────
│ n? ∉ OrthoNative; rep! = ErrorInNativeWord
└────────────────────────────────────────────────────────
```

The operation *TotalToNative* is defined analogously.

Vocabulary tests

For native to foreign vocabulary tests, we define:

$$TotalVocabTestNtoF \,\hat{=}\, VocabTestNtoF \lor VocabTestError$$

The only error condition arises when the vocabulary is empty, for then no test word can be selected.

```
┌─ VocabTestError ───────────────────────────────────────
│ Ξ WordForWord
│ NewAverage! : ℕ; rep! : Message
├────────────────────────────────────────────────────────
│ Vocab = ∅; NewAverage! = AveragePercent
│ rep! = VocabIsEmpty
└────────────────────────────────────────────────────────
```

Note that when *VocabTestError* is combined by disjunction with *VocabTestNtoF* the values of *TestWord!*, *Responses?*, *TransCount!* and *CorrectResponses!* are unconstrained in the case that the vocabulary is empty.

Printing lists of words

For the dictionary printing operations, no errors can occur, since they have no inputs and there always is a dictionary to be printed, though an empty vocabulary would not generate useful output.

7.1.8   Summary of operations

$$AddPair \; \hat{=} \; EnterPair \wedge ReportIfAlreadyKnown$$

$$ToForeign \; \hat{=} \; ForeignTranslations \wedge ReportIfKnownNative$$

$$VocabTestNtoF \; \hat{=}$$
$$\qquad SelectTestWordN \wedge CheckResponsesF \wedge UpdateScoreNtoF$$
$$\qquad \setminus (Translations)$$

$$RequestNativeDict \; \hat{=} \; NativeDict \wedge ReportIfVocabEmpty$$

$$TotalAddPair \; \hat{=} \; AddPair \vee AddPairError$$

$$TotalToForeign \; \hat{=} \; ToForeign \vee ToForeignError$$

$$TotalVocabTestNtoF \; \hat{=} \; VocabTestNtoF \vee VocabTestError$$

In addition, the partial operations *ToNative*, *VocabTestFtoN* and their total counterparts are defined by analogy with the corresponding native-to-foreign operations given here. Similarly *RequestForeignDict* is defined by analogy with the native dictionary operation.

———————— End of Word-For-Word specification ————————

7.2   The structure of specification documents

We now offer suggestions about the overall structure of specification documents, designed to ensure that all the necessary steps are taken towards the production of a consistent and comprehensive system description. These suggestions are based on ideas developed by IBM Hursley and Oxford University Programming Research Group [Wor89] as a result of a series of collaborative projects. We have adhered to the proposed format in our presentation of the enhanced Word-For-Word specification, and indeed even in the earlier specification in Chapter 3 we followed it as closely as was possible with the limited means of expression then at our disposal. Of course there are many possible approaches, and the one we propose is not necessarily the best, but there is considerable advantage to be gained from consistency of style over different specifications, for then both the specifier and the customer will develop certain expectations about the structure of what could be rather voluminous documents for non-trivial applications. The structure envisaged consists of the following sections in order:

(a) Declaration of given sets and global variables.

(b) Presentation of any general theory needed for the specification.

(c) Description of the abstract states of the system.

(d) Definition of suitable initialisations for the system.

(e) Definition of the operations of the system under normal circumstances.

(f) Derivation of preconditions for the operations which have been defined.

(g) If required, definition of total operations corresponding to each of the partial operations handling all possible error conditions.

(h) A summary and index for the specification.

Throughout the document informal presentation will accompany each unit of formal specification with the intention of relating what is said in that unit to the real world application, as far as possible using the conventional terminology of the application field. At the head of the document, before any formality is encountered, it is helpful if a comprehensive informal statement of the purpose and scope of the system is given. Within each section the requirement that objects must be declared before they are referred to should be observed. If the formal sections of the specification are extracted from the whole document without disturbing their relative textual order, the requirements of the formal notation will then be satisfied.

It should be noted that the structure of the specification document does not necessarily reflect the order of development of its constituent parts. The logical order suggested, partly imposed by considerations of the scope rules of Z, provides a sensible starting point for a development strategy, but of course the development of any complex artefact seldom proceeds along a straight line trajectory. Discoveries of difficulties at later stages of any preconceived ordering of activities will cause rethinking of earlier stages. We now expand and comment upon each of the sections listed above.

(a) Given sets and global definitions

In a certain sense the given sets and the global variables are parameters of the whole specification. The given sets, together with a few standard types such as $\mathbb{Z}$, form the basis of the types of the specification, and represent sets of elements whose internal structure we need to know nothing about, at the level of abstraction of the specification. Global variables are used to make generally available useful definitions and to express global constraints; for example, in the LibSys system we declared *maxloans* globally, and this embodies the overall constraint that no reader can borrow more than a certain number of books at any one time; similarly, in Word-For-Word, the sets *OrthoNative* and *OrthoForeign* represent the constraints on words which will be regarded as well formed and eligible for entry to the vocabulary.

(b) Presentation of general theory

In the Word-For-Word specification we needed some theory about alphabetical orderings; though in this case this was only needed for one of the operations, it is arguably worthwhile separating out general theory from the schemas which define the operation. It often happens that a body of theory is needed throughout a specification, and this is then a natural place for it to be included in the document.

(c) Describing the abstract states

The abstract state description should identify the important components of the data structure used to model the real world application, where appropriate major components may have defining schemas of their own, so that the complete abstract state schema may be assembled by importing these major component schemas.

(d) Initialising the system

This phase will generate an obligation to demonstrate that the proposed initialisations are feasible; so far we have done this only informally, but we shall see in the next chapter how this may be made more formal. For the Word-For-Word system this obligation is trivially satisfied since the initialisation schema in effect specifies the components of a unique initial state.

(e) Describing the partial operations, normal conditions

It is part of the philosophy of separation of concerns that we should give at this point the definitions of the operations of the system when all their prerequisites are satisfied, before (and separated from) consideration of what should be done when error conditions arise.

(f) Calculating and tabulating preconditions

We want to know the precise conditions under which each operation is applicable. We could, in extreme cases, discover that an operation is never applicable, or to put it another way that such an operation cannot be performed while maintaining the system invariants. This would almost certainly cause some redesign activity. As we calculate preconditions we identify the range of error conditions which may arise. It is useful to give a summary of what is discovered in a table, showing for each operation its inputs, outputs and preconditions. In general, precondition investigation can involve simplification of large predicates; the techniques which enable this to be done will be presented in the next chapter.

(g) Describing total operations

The preconditions of the partial operations indicate when those operations may be applied successfully, and thus the negations of those preconditions indicate the range of cases which have to be treated as errors and handled accordingly, if we want to ensure that the system can respond appropriately under all circumstances. However, the concept of 'all circumstances' itself needs to be examined. In Word-For-Word we are prepared for mis-spelt native or foreign words as inputs to certain operations, but we do not expect to be given a foreign word instead of a native word. In the case of *VocabTestNtoF*, the *Responses?* input may contain mis-spelt words, but again we do not expect any foreign words in the sequence; the type of *Responses?* is in fact $\mathbb{P}(\mathbb{N} \times Native)$, but we do not have to be prepared for the possibility that this input might be something other than a sequence even though seq *Native* is a proper subset of $\mathbb{P}(\mathbb{N} \times Native)$. It could also happen that a specification describes a sub-system of a larger system, and that certain assumptions can be made about what the larger system will pass across the system interface to the sub-system; in such cases, it may not be necessary to provide total operations at all. For simple systems such as LibSys and Word-For-Word it is perhaps helpful to imagine that the choice of which operation is to be applied next is made outside the specified system, perhaps by selection from a menu. For systems of this kind, each operation must either perform successfully when called upon to do so, or demure in a controlled manner when presented with erroneous inputs or when the current state renders the operation inapplicable.

(h) Summary and index

Specification documents can grow quite large for non-trivial systems and it is essential that readers of the specification should be able to find their way around the document; a useful form of index might include lists of variable and schema names accompanied by the numbers of the pages on which references to them occur. It is also useful to provide here a summary of the total and partial operations down to the level of schemas whose texts are given explicitly.

Exercise 7.1 ◇ Construct a complete specification document, with all of the sections as described in the section above, for the LibSys system described in Chapter 6, taking the list of operations given in Section 6.2 as definitive.

Exercise 7.2 ⋄ In Exercise 3.2 we introduced the concept of 'false friends'. Add the same *FalseFriends* facility to the enhanced Word-For-Word specification, making a global definition of a relation which embodies the notion of a native and a foreign word being very similar.

Exercise 7.3 ⋄ In Section 7.1.2 where we define the alphabetical order *NativeDictOrder* we do not say what the relationship is for pairs $(n, fseq1)$ and $(n, fseq2)$, that is to say, for two pairs which have the same first component. Give two different possibilities consistent with the requirement that *NativeDictOrder* should be an alphabetical order.

Exercise 7.4 ⋄ Supply the definition of the operation *RequestForeignDict* by analogy with *RequestNativeDict*.

Exercise 7.5 ⋄ If we want to define the total operation *TotalVocabTestFtoN*, can we re-use the schema *VocabTestError* precisely as given?

7.3 Further reading

For more information about the development method described in this chapter we refer the reader to [Wor87] or [Wor89].

Chapter 8

Camp Energy: a case study

The best way to become familiar with any language is by using it yourself. Fluency in speaking or writing the language only comes with much practice and the many mistakes that the user inevitably makes reveal misunderstandings and gaps in vocabulary and grammar. The same is true for Z. To start with, the approach may seem new and the syntax unfamiliar. As we progress, use of the various constructs becomes second nature and the once-strange symbols now help with the process of encapsulating and clarifying ideas.

Throughout this book a large number of exercises are provided to help readers gain their own experience of the ideas being presented. This chapter extends that approach by introducing a case study which the reader is invited to consider and participate in. The case study is presented as a tutorial with some aspects explored in the text and others taken forward in the exercises. The exercises are thus an important part of the exposition and answers for all the exercises in this chapter are included at the end of the book. We highlight a number of places where different ways of specifying the same thing would be possible. In each case we examine the likely consequences of the various courses of action and give reasons for the one we choose to adopt.

In this chapter we work through the steps required to describe the state of this system and show how some of the operations may be specified in a clear and succinct way by using the technique of promotion introduced earlier. There are many possible operations that might be useful for such a system. We give formal definitions for just a few and encourage the reader to investigate some of the others. We follow the general approach to structuring a specification outlined in the previous chapter. However, since this is a tutorial rather than the presentation of a finished specification the reader should not be surprised to notice some deviation from the suggested format.

8.1   Camp Energy

Camp Energy[1] is a holiday playscheme for children catering for 5 to 16 year olds. For each day of the Camp, children may attend a morning session, an afternoon session or both. Before being booked into any session a child must be formally registered in the system. In practice this will involve the child's parent or guardian filling in a form with various details about the child and a telephone number in case of emergency.

During each Camp session the children are divided into groups. Children in any one group must all have ages within the same band according to:

Band	Lower limit	Upper limit
1	5	7
2	8	9
3	10	11
4	12	16

An adult leader is assigned to each group. Each leader must be registered with the scheme, following satisfactory completion of all application and acceptance procedures.

A leader can look after a maximum of 8 children from Band 1 and a maximum of 15 children in each of the other age bands. So, if 20 children of 8 or 9 years enrol for a particular session, two Band 2 groups would need to be set up. There is also an overall figure set for the maximum number of children allowed at any one session. No more than 250 children may be in the Camp per session.

The specifier's task is to model the registration and booking system of Camp Energy. There are other aspects of the system which could be investigated (for example, what activities will there be and how will these be timetabled) and many more details about this particular part of it (such as, what details should be obtained for each child and how should they be recorded). However, the information that we have here will provide a sufficient basis for an abstract description of the state of the booking system and the operations that may be performed on it.

8.2   The Camp Energy specification

Following the suggested structure for a specification given in Chapter 7 we should first consider what the basic types or given sets of the specification are. Of course, we may find out at a later stage that there are others to be added, but a first attempt at sorting out basic types makes a good start.

---

[1] Camp Energy is run by Harpenden Sports Centre and was originally formally specified by Vitoria Cunningham-Smith. We thank Vitoria for permission to adapt her original ideas to our own rather different version.

8.2.1   Basic types

Firstly, since children seem central to the whole enterprise we need to consider how a child should be represented in the system. There are many items of information which might be associated with a child, such as name, age, address and telephone number. Yet none of these is certain to identify a child uniquely, although a combination might be quite likely to. Trying to use a collection of attributes to identify a child within the system would become very cumbersome and there are still cases where confusion might arise. A very common way to get round this problem is to declare a set of identifiers. A unique identifier may then be assigned to each child entering the system. You have already seen this approach with the library system in Chapter 6 where the basic type *Copy* was in fact thought of as a set of identifiers. Following this approach we introduce a basic type:

[*CHILDID*]

Exercise 8.1 ◇ What other basic types can you identify at this stage?

8.2.2   Global definitions

There will be much more to say about children and leaders later on, but now we turn to considering which variables will be required throughout the specification and should therefore be declared with global definitions right at the start.

Exercise 8.2 ◇ From the requirements of Section 8.1 identify any suitable candidates for global definition. Give a formal definition for each.

When you have decided upon and defined the global definitions, compare your answers with the given solution. There will of course be differences: most obviously, the choice of names will vary, and the definitions themselves may also differ. However, you should have identified the same components as being suitable for global definition, and the definitions should be written in a similar format.

The approach to the global definitions taken in the solution to Exercise 8.2 is a very concrete one, with numbers given explicitly for maximum group and session sizes and for age bands. It is true that these are the values given in the requirements and we may think there can be no objection to using them.

However, a specification written in this way suffers from the need for alteration whenever any of these values changes. Also, a top-level specification with such particular detail will in general be applicable only to the one situation for which it was written. A more abstract specification might be reused in many similar circumstances.

Exercise 8.3 ◇ Give alternative global definitions which do not constrain the variables to take any particular values.

In the following specification we will, for simplicity, work with the earlier, more concrete, definitions. You might like to note as you go along where alterations would be required for the abstract versions.

8.2.3   Description of the system state

It is now time to decide upon the components of the state for the Camp Energy specification and to represent these in a state schema.

Exercise 8.4 ◇ From the requirements, write down (informally) the aspects you would expect to be represented within the state schema.

The given solution identifies three major components. You may well view the situation rather differently. Here and throughout the specification we obviously have to pick one course to follow. If your ideas are substantially different from ours, you may like to follow ours through at a first reading and come back later to develop yours and compare the results.

The components we have identified are fairly independent and self-contained and each seems to represent a major element of the state. So, instead of defining one large state schema directly, it could be useful to define the three parts of the state as separate schemas and to combine them with the schema calculus to give the full state. This helps with what is sometimes referred to as 'separation of concerns'; specification techniques which allow us to concentrate on one aspect of a system at a time. It may also help to simplify operations if we can define them on a smaller part of the state and methodically broaden them to apply to the full state.

With this in mind we turn to defining a schema to specify the register of children enrolled in the Camp Energy scheme. We already have a set of possible child identifiers, *CHILDID*. Now we need to associate the details of each registered child with a unique identifier. Once again, there are a number of ways to proceed. We investigate two possibilities here.

Firstly, we could view the child registers as a set of identifiers currently in use with functions to indicate the related details:

```
┌─ ChildReg1 ──────────────────────────────────────
│ children : ℙ CHILDID
│ c_age : CHILDID ↦ (5 .. 16)
│ c_info : CHILDID ↦ CHILDINFO
│──────────────────────────────────────────────────
│ dom c_age = dom c_info = children
└──────────────────────────────────────────────────
```

We need the predicate to ensure that exactly those children registered in the system have ages and details recorded for them. This approach gives three state components. If at this level we had needed to make use of details other than a child's age, then a separate function, and hence an additional state component, would be needed for each one. This might soon grow very cumbersome. In addition, all the components must be related in the predicate and each time a child is added, all the components must be updated.

An alternative approach is to view a child as an entity in the system and to collect together the details relating to each one:

```
┌─ Child ──────────────────────────────────────────
│ age : 5 .. 16
│ details : CHILDINFO
└──────────────────────────────────────────────────
```

As the details of each child are not necessarily unique to that child we still need the identifiers to remove possible ambiguity within the system. This leads to an alternative definition of the child register:

```
┌─ ChildReg2 ──────────────────────────────────────
│ creg : CHILDID ↦ Child
└──────────────────────────────────────────────────
```

Here, the schema *Child* is used as the type of the function's range. This definition associates each currently used child identifier with the child's age and details: known children are simply those in the domain of *creg*. It performs the same task as *ChildReg1*, but it reduces the number of functions and does away with the explicit predicate. Only one element, *creg*, will appear as a component of the system state.

The second approach appears to be neater and it recognises a child as a cohesive unit of specification. It gives a good structure to the specification: with this sort of approach we can start to think about modularity of operations and promotion. However, there may be other considerations which influence our choice. We have mentioned before that 'least is not always best' when it comes to specification. It may be better for the sake of clarity to have more components explicitly named (of course, we can always add derived elements such as the set of known children to *ChildReg2*). All the information available in *ChildReg1* can also be obtained from *ChildReg2*, but in the latter it may be more deeply buried. When it comes to proof, the neater specification may actually make life more difficult.

We must now make a choice. We define *ChildReg* to be *ChildReg2* to be used as the child register within our specification. This will allow us to investigate the use of schemas as types and to exploit the structure of the register for the promotion of operations.

Exercise 8.5 ◇ Define a schema *LeaderReg*, the register of Camp Energy leaders.

Exercise 8.6 ◇ Initially, both the children's register and the leaders' register will be empty. Give initialisation schemas for these two parts of the state. What check should you make to ensure these definitions make sense?

The remaining part of the state to consider is the booking register itself. A child will book in for a particular session or sessions. In each session, a number of groups may be running, each with a unique leader. We will tackle this in the same way as we did the first two parts of the state; we shall aim to construct a booking register where each session is indexed in a unique way.

Exercise 8.7 ◇ Is there a need for a type, *SESSIONID*, which would allow us to identify each session uniquely?

Let us first consider the definition of a session. Within each session, leaders are allocated to groups of children, so we begin with:

```
┌─ Session ────────────────────────────────
│  session : LEADERID ⇸ Group
│  ────────
│  . . .
└───────────────────────────────────────────
```

How should *Group* be defined? We could have it simply as a set of children, but there does seem to be more to a group than that. Each group is associated with one particular age band, and each child in the group must belong to that age band. If it is felt that a group is really a unit within the specification, then perhaps a schema would be appropriate:

```
┌─ Group ─────────────────────────────────────────────
│ members : ℙ CHILDID
│ band : CampAgeBands
├─────────────────────────────────────────────────────
│ #members ≤ maxgpsize band
└─────────────────────────────────────────────────────
```

This approach uses the leader of a group to index that group within a session: each group is uniquely identified by its leader and this is reflected in the use of a function to define *session*. Another possible approach would be to include the leader within *Group*, thus viewing the leader as an integral part of the group. We have chosen not to do this because the functional description of a session allows the required group to be referenced very easily and paves the way for a modular description of operations using promotion. With the alternative approach, a session would still have to be defined as some collection of groups, and the constraint that no two groups have the same leader would need to be introduced explicitly.

Exercise 8.8 ⋄ Should this schema also include the requirement that each member of the group is within the correct age band?

Exercise 8.9 ⋄ What predicates should appear in the *Session* schema? Write them down informally first, and then express them in Z for inclusion in the schema. Note that you may find some requirements concerning leaders and children in sessions which cannot be expressed at this level. Make a note of them for inclusion in the full state schema later on.

The bookings register can now be defined. As discussed in Exercise 8.7, the date and time are sufficient to identify a particular session. We do not care about the structure of the date, and so make it another given set:

[*DATE*]

Time could also be defined in this way, but since we are told that there are only two possibilities and we know what these are, we can use a free type definition:

TIME ::= *am* | *pm*

The schema for the booking register is:

$$
\begin{array}{|l}
\hline
\_BookingReg_____ \\
\hline
breg : DATE \times TIME \nrightarrow Session \\
\hline
\end{array}
$$

Again, the initial state can be described:

$$
\begin{array}{|l}
\hline
\_InitBookingReg_____ \\
BookingReg' \\
\hline
breg' = \emptyset \\
\hline
\end{array}
$$

This is an acceptable initialisation since the empty set is of the correct type to satisfy:

$$\emptyset \in DATE \times TIME \nrightarrow Session$$

Exercise 8.10 ◇ The three components of the state of the Camp Energy system have now been defined. Also, in the course of the development we have identified three constraints which are needed. Use these to define the full state of the system.

Exercise 8.11 ◇ Use the initial states of the component schemas to define the initial state of Camp Energy. What checks should be made?

8.2.4   Operations on individual registers

Part of the aim in our structuring of the state was to allow operations to be defined on a small part of the state and then to be 'enlarged' to refer to the state of the whole system. We mentioned that promotion may well be of use here. In this section we look at some of the operations in the Camp Energy system and investigate these ideas further.

When we start to look at the operations it is soon apparent that some operations are fairly simple and will require access to one register only, whereas others are more complicated and will need to refer to two or even all three registers. For example, to register a child will require an addition to the children's register only; however, when a child is deleted from the system we must also consider whether the child is currently booked into any sessions.

Exercise 8.12 ⋄ Make a list of about a dozen useful operations for Camp Energy. For each, state which registers may need to be available.

It will be useful to have a type for the possible reports and error messages that can be output from operations. At this stage we do not know all the messages that might be needed, so we give a partial definition:

$$Rep ::= Success \mid \ldots$$

As operations are defined it will become apparent which extra elements should be included in the definition of *Rep*. We take the liberty of generating and using *Rep* elements without declaring them: when presenting a completed specification, all the elements could be gathered together and given in the definition here.

8.2.5 Operations on the register of children

We start by considering some operations on the children's register (although some may also involve other parts of the state and we must be careful to incorporate these changes later on). In fact, promotion can be used here if the operations are first defined at the level of the *Child* schema. The first one defined is the operation to alter the details recorded about a child:

```
┌─ SmallAlterChildDetails ──────────────────────
│ ΔChild
│ c_info? : CHILDINFO
├──────────────────────────────────────────────
│ age' = age
│ details' = c_info?
└──────────────────────────────────────────────
```

Exercise 8.13 ⋄ Other similar operations might be to alter a child's age, to obtain a child's details, and to obtain a child's age. Define these.

Exercise 8.14 ⋄ Before promoting the operations on the small state it is usual to check that they are all total. Calculate the preconditions of the four operations defined on *Child*. For any which are not total define suitable error conditions and use the schema calculus to construct a total version.

The operation to add a child is slightly different because there is no before state; it is rather like an initialisation. This leads to the following definition:

SmallAddChild0
Child'
$c\_age? : \mathbb{N}$
$c\_info? : CHILDINFO$
$r! : Rep$

$c\_age? \in 5 .. 16$
$age' = c\_age?$
$details' = c\_info?$
$r! = Success$

There is a potential problem with this definition. We have mentioned in the solution to Exercise 8.14 that it is best to promote total operations. One reason for this is that it maintains the modularity of the specification: errors which can be detected and reported at the lower level are dealt with here making the definitions of the promoted operations simpler. The *SmallAddChild0* operation is not total since it does not specify what should happen if $c\_age? \notin 5 .. 16$. Yet we *cannot* specify that situation at this level since if the input age is incorrect there will be no *Child'* and the child register will not be altered. We will have to deal with this at the higher level. There is nothing wrong with promoting a partial operation when there is good cause for it, but it complicates the development slightly as we shall see.

The remaining operation for deleting a child will need to be done at the level of the promoted operations since deletion is indicated by freeing the identifier previously allocated to the child.

Promoting the operations on the register of children

The promotion, or *framing*, schema introduces the before and after versions of the larger state (in this case, *creg*) and makes a link between these and the smaller state referred to in the existing operations. In the following framing schema, the input identifies which child the operation is for:

$\Phi 1C$
$\Delta ChildReg$
$\Delta Child$
$c? : CHILDID$

$\theta Child = creg\ c?$
$c? \in \text{dom } creg$
$creg' = creg \oplus \{c? \mapsto \theta Child'\}$

The first predicate says that the child referred to by the before state of the small operations is the one identified by $c?$ in the child register. Recall from Section 6.6.2 that the term $\theta\,Child$ makes an object of schema type $Child$ by drawing together the variables of $Child$ which are currently in scope along with their current values. The expression is sometimes read as 'the Child', meaning, 'the Child currently in scope'. In this case, the one referred to is the one introduced by the before state of the declaration $\Delta\,Child$. The purpose of the second predicate is to ensure that the input identifier is known within the system: error cases can be added later. The third predicate says that $creg$ will be updated according to the after state of the small operation. Notice that the framing schema does not stand in its own right: by itself it does not represent any system operation. Rather, it is a specification device which can be combined with the previous definitions to produce meaningful operations at the level of the register. They are combined in the following way:

$$AlterChildDetails0 \,\hat{=}\, \exists\,\Delta\,Child \,\bullet\, \Phi1\,C \,\wedge\, SmallAlterChildDetails$$
$$AlterChildAge0 \,\hat{=}\, \exists\,\Delta\,Child \,\bullet\, \Phi1\,C \,\wedge\, SmallAlterChildAge$$
$$ObtainChildDetails0 \,\hat{=}\, \exists\,\Delta\,Child \,\bullet\, \Phi1\,C \,\wedge\, SmallObtainChildDetails$$
$$ObtainChildAge0 \,\hat{=}\, \exists\,\Delta\,Child \,\bullet\, \Phi1\,C \,\wedge\, SmallObtainChildAge$$

Let us consider the first of these. It defines the successful case of altering a child's details at the level of the child register. The schema definition joins together the framing schema $\Phi1\,C$ and the operation on the small state $SmallAlterChildDetails$. It then hides the before and after $Child$ states to remove them from the declarations. We will expand this expression step by step to see exactly what is going on. Firstly, conjunction of the $\Phi1\,C$ and $SmallAlterChildDetails$ schemas gives:

$$
\begin{array}{|l}
\hline
\Phi1\,CandSmallAlterChildDetails \\\hline
\Delta\,ChildReg \\
\Delta\,Child \\
c? : CHILDID \\
c\_info? : CHILDINFO \\
r! : Rep \\\hline
\theta\,Child = creg\ c? \\
c? \in \mathrm{dom}\ creg \\
creg' = creg \oplus \{c? \mapsto \theta\,Child'\} \\
age' = age \\
details' = c\_info? \\
r! = Success \\\hline
\end{array}
$$

Hiding, in the form of existential quantification of $\Delta\,Child$, is used because it is not necessary to refer to the smaller schema in the declarations of the promoted operation; the identifier $c?$ is sufficient to identify the required one. Hiding removes the variables from the declaration part and existentially quantifies them in the predicate part of the schema. The full operation after hiding is thus:

$$
\begin{array}{l}
\underline{\quad AlterChildDetails0 \quad\rule{6cm}{0pt}} \\
\Delta ChildReg \\
c? : CHILDID \\
c\_info? : CHILDINFO \\
r! : Success \\
\hline
\exists\, age, age' : 5\mathinner{\ldotp\ldotp}16;\ details, details' : CHILDINFO\ \bullet \\
\quad \theta Child = creg\ c?\ \wedge \\
\quad c? \in dom\ creg\ \wedge \\
\quad creg' = creg \oplus \{c? \mapsto \theta Child'\}\ \wedge \\
\quad age' = age\ \wedge \\
\quad details' = c\_info?\ \wedge \\
\quad r! = Success
\end{array}
$$

Since $\theta Child$ refers to the component names of $Child$ currently in scope, another way of writing $\theta Child = creg\ c?$ is:

$$ age = (creg\ c?).age \wedge details = (creg\ c?).details $$

We can use the One Point Rule as in the solution to Exercise 8.14 to replace all reference to age and $details$ and to remove them from the list of quantified variables. After these changes the schema becomes:

$$
\begin{array}{l}
\underline{\quad AlterChildDetails0 \quad\rule{6cm}{0pt}} \\
\Delta ChildReg \\
c? : CHILDID \\
c\_info? : CHILDINFO \\
r! : Rep \\
\hline
\exists\, age' : 5\mathinner{\ldotp\ldotp}16;\ details' : CHILDINFO\ \bullet \\
\quad c? \in dom\ creg\ \wedge \\
\quad creg' = creg \oplus \{c? \mapsto \theta Child'\}\ \wedge \\
\quad age' = (creg\ c?).age\ \wedge \\
\quad details' = c\_info?\ \wedge \\
\quad r! = Success
\end{array}
$$

The One Point Rule can also be used to eliminate the dashed variables, but care must be taken with the $\theta Child'$ since this uses age' and $details'$. We might be content to leave the predicate in its current form, but if we wish to pursue it to the most succinct version possible we arrive at:

```
┌─ AlterChildDetails0 ────────────────────────────────────
│  ΔChildReg
│  c? : CHILDID
│  c_info? : CHILDINFO
│  r! : Rep
├────────────────────────────────────────────────────────
│  c? ∈ dom creg
│  creg' = creg ⊕ {c? ↦ (μ Child' | age' = (creg c?).age ∧
│                                    details' = c_info?)}
│  r! = Success
└────────────────────────────────────────────────────────
```

The μ expression as described in Section 4.3.4 makes an object of schema type *Child'* using the supplied values for *age'* and *details'*.

It is certainly not necessary to expand every promoted schema: the whole purpose of promotion is to modularise the description and to avoid complicated expressions at the lowest level. However, it is useful to know exactly what is going on in a promotion and the expansion given above shows that there is no mystery and that the promoted operation really does work as intended. Once we have confidence in the technique it would be usual to work at the level of the schema calculus definition of the promoted operation with no need for expansions.

Exercise 8.15 ⋄ The operation to add a child to the register requires a rather different framing schema. What is this difference? Define a suitable framing schema, $\Phi 2C$. Use the schema calculus and the new framing schema to promote *SmallAddChild0*. Expand and simplify the promoted operation.

Deleting a child from the register

This operation is defined at the level of the child register only: there is no need for promotion.

Exercise 8.16 ⋄ Write a schema, *DeleteChild0*, to describe the successful case of deleting a child from the register.

Exercise 8.17 ⋄ Calculate the precondition of *DeleteChild0*.

Total operations on the register of children

The operations defined above describe what happens in the successful cases. We must also consider possible error cases and construct schemas which cover all possible outcomes. The schema calculus can then be used to produce total operations for the children's register.

For most of the operations, it appears that an error will occur if the input identifier is not known. In the case of adding a child, the opposite is true. To confirm these informed guesses we should calculate the precondition of the existing operations. One bonus of using promotion is that the preconditions of the promoted operations can be calculated very easily. The following result shows how (see also Exercise 8.18). Suppose that Φ is a framing schema which promotes the operation SOp on the small state S to the operation LOp on the larger state L, then:

$$\text{pre } LOp = (\text{pre } SOp \wedge \text{pre } \Phi) \setminus S$$

Hence, if we know the preconditions of the operations on the smaller state then we simply need to conjoin each of these with the precondition of Φ and hide S. This is particularly easy when SOp is total: another good reason for promoting total operations. For our example, the preconditions of $AlterChildDetails0$, $AlterChildAge0$, $ObtainChildDetails0$ and $ObtainChildAge0$ are all obtained from:

$$(\text{pre } SmallOp \wedge \text{pre } \Phi 1 C) \setminus Child$$

where $SmallOp$ is the unpromoted version in each case. Since each $SmallOp$ is total, the only difference between the preconditions will be any different inputs they may have.

The precondition of $\Phi 1 C$ is:

```
┌─ preΦ1C ──────────────────────────────────
│ ChildReg
│ Child
│ c? : CHILDID
│ ├───────────────────────────────────────
│ │ ∃ Child'; ChildReg' •
│ │     θChild = creg c? ∧
│ │     c? ∈ dom creg ∧
│ │     creg' = creg ⊕ {c? ↦ θChild'}
```

The quantified variables do not appear in the first two conjuncts, so the predicate may be rearranged to:

$\theta Child = creg\ c? \wedge$
$c? \in \text{dom } creg \wedge$
$\exists\ Child';\ ChildReg' \bullet creg' = creg \oplus \{c? \mapsto \theta Child'\}$

The quantified predicate is true since we can readily supply values for *creg'*, *age'* and *details'* which satisfy the requirements. This leaves a precondition of:

```
┌─ preΦ1C ─────────────────────────────────────────────
│  ChildReg
│  Child
│  c? : CHILDID
│ ┌────────────────────────────
│  θChild = creg c?
│  c? ∈ dom creg
└──────────────────────────────────────────────────────
```

With this result the preconditions of the first four promoted schemas follow immediately:

pre *AlterChildDetails*0 = [*c_info?* : *CHILDINFO*] ∧ pre Φ1*C*
pre *AlterChildAge*0 = [*c_age?* : ℕ] ∧ pre Φ1*C*
pre *ObtainChildDetails*0 = pre Φ1*C*
pre *ObtainChildAge*0 = pre Φ1*C*

Exercise 8.18 ◇ Before using the result about promotion of preconditions we should in theory show that this result is applicable. In fact, it holds when each possible update to the smaller state gives rise to a valid instance of the larger state (otherwise additional safeguards will be needed). This is equivalent to:

$$\Phi \setminus L' = (\text{pre } \Phi) \wedge S'$$

Check this is true for the situation above.

Bearing in mind the results of the precondition calculations we will need an additional error condition. For operations which rely on a known identifier, in the case of an unknown identifier being supplied the state should remain unchanged and an error report given:

```
┌─ UnknownCidErr ──────────────────────────────────────
│  ΞChildReg
│  c? : CHILDID
│  r! : Rep
│ ┌────────────────────────────
│  c? ∉ dom creg
│  r! = CidNotKnown
└──────────────────────────────────────────────────────
```

Total versions of the operations on the register of children are then given by:

$$AlterChildDetails \triangleq AlterChildDetails0 \lor UnknownCidErr$$
$$AlterChildAge \triangleq AlterChildAge0 \lor UnknownCidErr$$
$$ObtainChildDetails \triangleq ObtainChildDetails0 \lor UnknownCidErr$$
$$ObtainChildAge \triangleq ObtainChildAge0 \lor UnknownCidErr$$
$$DeleteChild \triangleq DeleteChild0 \lor UnknownCidErr$$

The one remaining operation is $AddChild0$. Its precondition will require extra work since a different framing schema was used.

Exercise 8.19 ⋄ Calculate the precondition of $AddChild0$.

Exercise 8.20 ⋄ Using the result of the previous exercise, define the total operation, $AddChild$.

These operations are all total with respect to their effect on the children's register. However, we must remember that the full state of the system involves other components and once the operations on the partial state have been defined we must consider how they may be combined to represent operations on the whole state.

8.2.6   Operations on the register of leaders

Since the register of leaders does not make use of a lower level of schemas, it is simplest to define operations directly for *LeaderReg*. So promotion will not be needed here.

Exercise 8.21 ⋄ Define the following total operations on the register of leaders:

$AddLeader$, $DeleteLeader$, $AlterLeaderDetails$, $ObtainLeaderDetails$

8.2.7   Operations on the bookings register

The operations we shall consider are: adding a session, adding a group, making a booking, deleting a booking, and two enquiries for booking information: returning the total number of children booked into a session and the number of children of a particular age band booked into a particular session. This is another chance to practice the technique of promotion, with operations defined first on the smaller state *Session*, and then promoted to the larger state *BookingReg*. In fact, looking at the specification of a session we see that there is yet another level underneath this, with a session defined as a function from *LEADERID* to the schema *Group*. Would it be possible to have two levels of promotion? Indeed it would, but we should weigh up the pros and cons. In favour of promotion is the fact that it deals with 'buried' schemas well. To define operations at the higher level can involve some tricky reasoning and complicated predicates. As we have seen, promoted operations are straightforward to define. On the negative side is the point that half the operations we aim to define do not involve one, single group: adding a session does not require reference to groups at all and the enquiries both need information from all groups in a session. This means that they are not suitable for promotion.

We take the view that defining the operations without promotion is very complicated and extremely unappealing (try it and see!) Indeed, without the use of promotion to manage the specification it would probably be better to define the state in a different way. Hence the operations on the bookings register will be specified with two levels of promotion.

Operations on groups

There are three operations which can be defined at the group level. The operations to add a new member to a group and to delete a member from a group will include Δ *Group* in their declarations, whereas adding a new group has no before state but introduces a *Group'*.

Exercise 8.22 ⋄ Define partial operations:

> *VSmallAddToGroup0, VSmallDeleteBooking0, VSmallAddNewGroup0*

Write suitable error schemas and define the total operations.

Promoting the operations on groups

As with the promotion of operations on *Child*, two separate promotion schemas are needed here. One is for operations including $\Delta Group$ and the other is for the initialisation case where just $Group'$ is needed. As before, the first framing schema includes in its declarations the changing state of both the smaller state, *Group* and the larger one to which it is promoted, *Session*. There will also be an input *LEADERID* to identify which group in the session is under consideration. The predicate part needs to make the link between small and large state explicit and to say how the larger state changes as a result of the change in the small state. This leads to the following definition of the framing schema:

$$
\begin{array}{|l}
\hline
\Phi 1G \underline{\hspace{8cm}} \\
\Delta Session \\
\Delta Group \\
l? : LEADERID \\
\hline
\theta Group = session\ l? \\
l? \in \text{dom } session \\
session' = session \oplus \{l? \mapsto \theta Group'\} \\
\hline
\end{array}
$$

Exercise 8.23 ⋄ Define $\Phi 2G$, the second framing schema needed for this promotion.

Exercise 8.24 ⋄ Using the two framing schemas write schema calculus expressions to promote the operations on *Group* to operations on *Session*.

Exercise 8.25 ⋄ One complication about this promotion is that we cannot use the result about promoting preconditions since the promotion does not satisfy the requirement that:

$$\Phi \setminus L' = (\text{pre } \Phi) \wedge S'$$

Expand the schemas on the right hand side and the left hand side of this expression for $\Phi 1G$ to confirm that they are different. Explain why the promotion of preconditions would fail for this example.

Exercise 8.26 ⋄ Define suitable error conditions for the partial operations from Exercise 8.24.

Exercise 8.27 ⋄ Define total versions of the promoted operations for *Session*.

Other operations on a session

There are three remaining operations on sessions which were not suitable for definition via promotion. Firstly, to initialise a session an empty session is added:

```
┌─ SmallInitSession ──────────────────────────
│ Session'
├─────────────────────────────────────────────
│ session' = ∅
└─────────────────────────────────────────────
```

This makes sense since the empty set satisfies the requirements for a valid session. The two enquiry schemas will each return a number. In the first case it will be the total number of children in a session and in the second it will be the number of children of a particular age band in the session:

```
┌─ SmallGetNo ────────────────────────────────
│ ΞSession
│ n! : ℕ
│ r! : Rep
├─────────────────────────────────────────────
│ n! = #(⋃{l : dom session • (session l).members})
│ r! = Success
└─────────────────────────────────────────────
```

```
┌─ SmallGetAgeBandNo ─────────────────────────
│ ΞSession
│ b? : CampAgeBands
│ n! : ℕ
│ r! : Rep
├─────────────────────────────────────────────
│ n! = #(⋃{l : dom session | (session l).band = b?
│                      • (session l).members})
│ r! = Success
└─────────────────────────────────────────────
```

These are both total since the enquiry can always be satisfied and no change is made to the state.

Exercise 8.28 ⋄ Define an operation which returns the names of all children currently booked into a session.

Promoting the operations on sessions

Amongst the many possible operations at the session level we have defined:

SmallInitSession
SmallAddNewGroup
SmallAddToGroup
SmallDeleteBooking
SmallGetNo
SmallGetAgeBandNo

It is time to promote these to operations on the booking register. Much of this work is routine and follows the same pattern as the two promotions carried out so far in this chapter.

Exercise 8.29 ⋄ Define the two framing schemas needed for the promotion and use these to promote the six listed operations to operations on *BookingReg*.

Exercise 8.30 ⋄ Does the condition for simplified precondition calculations hold?

Exercise 8.31 ⋄ Give suitable error schemas and construct total operations on the booking register.

Exercise 8.32 ⋄ Suppose that a further operation is required to delete a session. Define this, assuming that a session can only be deleted if there are no children booked on it.

8.2.8   Operations on the full state

In this final section of the specification we give some examples to show what must be done to produce operations on the full Camp Energy state containing all three registers.

Operations involving only one register

For operations involving one state only there is no additional complication, for example:

```
┌─ FullAddChild ──────────────────────────────────
│ ΔCampEnergy
│ ΞLeaderReg
│ ΞBookingReg
│ AddChild
└──────────────────────────────────────────────────
```

The first line, $\Delta CampEnergy$, includes not only the declarations of the full state (indeed, it would not be necessary for these alone since they are all introduced by succeeding lines) but also the constraints introduced by the predicate part of the full Camp Energy state. The next two lines ensure that the two registers not involved in adding a child do not change, and the final line states how the register of children changes.

However, even with a definition like this it is necessary to check that the full after state really does satisfy the predicate of $CampEnergy$, that is:

$$\forall\, sess : \operatorname{ran} breg' \bullet \forall\, grp : \operatorname{ran} sess \bullet$$
$$\operatorname{dom} sess \subseteq \operatorname{dom} lreg' \wedge$$
$$grp.members \subseteq \operatorname{dom} creg' \wedge$$
$$\forall\, cid : (grp.members) \bullet (creg'\, cid).age \in grp.ageband$$

Since $breg$ and $lreg$ are unchanged, the dashes may be removed from these variables in the above predicate and:

$$\operatorname{dom} sess \subseteq \operatorname{dom} lreg$$

then follows because the before states are required to satisfy $CampEnergy$. Also:

$$grp.members \subseteq \operatorname{dom} creg'$$

holds since:

$$grp.members \subseteq \operatorname{dom} creg$$

and the $AddChild$ operation ensures that $\operatorname{dom} creg \subseteq \operatorname{dom} creg'$. Finally, the last part holds because $creg'$ does not change the recorded ages of any children previously known in the system.

Exercise 8.33 ⋄ Define $FullAddLeader$ and check that the definition is consistent.

Operations involving more than one register

For some operations, although their definition involves one principal register, cross-checks necessitating access to other registers may be required. For instance, the operation to add a new group is defined on the booking register, but it will have to refer to the leader's register to ensure that the input leader identifier really is known to the system. This leads to the following definition of the partial definition on the full state:

```
┌─ FullAddNewGroup0 ─────────────────────────────────────
│ ΔCampEnergy
│ ΞLeaderReg
│ ΞChildReg
│ AddNewGroup
├────────────────────────
│ l? ∈ dom lreg
└─────────────────────────────────────────────────────────
```

The extra predicate is of use when showing that this definition is consistent with maintaining the *CampEnergy* constraint. The operation *AddNewGroup* ensures that no sessions are altered and that just one new empty group is added. So it is still the case that all group members are registered and are in correct groups for their age. All leaders who were previously in charge of groups are still registered, and the predicate added to *FullAddNewGroup0* ensures that the new group leader is also registered. Hence the definition does ensure a valid after state satisfying *CampEnergy'*.

The above schema defines the partial operation on the full state. If the identifier is unknown the whole state should remain unchanged:

```
┌─ UnknownLErr ─────────────────────────────────────────
│ ΞCampEnergy
│ l? : LEADERID
│ r! : Rep
├────────────────────────
│ l? ∉ dom lreg
│ r! = LeaderUnknown
└─────────────────────────────────────────────────────────
```

The total operation on the full state is then:

$$FullAddNewGroup \mathrel{\widehat{=}} FullAddNewGroup0 \vee UnknownLErr$$

As another example, consider the operation to make a booking. This is defined on the booking register, but it will also need access to the register of children to ensure that the child is known and of the correct age for the group. So we define:

```
┌─ FullAddToGroup0 ──────────────────────────────────────
│ ΔCampEnergy
│ ΞLeaderReg
│ ΞChildReg
│ AddToGroup
├────────────────────────
│ c? ∈ dom creg
│ (creg c?).age ∈ (((breg (d?, t?)).session) l?).band
└─────────────────────────────────────────────────────────
```

Again, this can be seen to maintain the *CampEnergy* state constraint since the leaders do not change and the predicates added to *FullAddToGroup0* ensure that the additional booked child is registered and of the correct age. We can then use the added predicates to guide the definition of error schemas:

```
┌─ UnknownCErr ──────────────────────────────────────
│ ΞCampEnergy
│ c? : CHILDID
│ r! : Rep
├────────────────────────────────────────────────────
│ c? ∉ dom creg
│ r! = ChildUnknown
└────────────────────────────────────────────────────
```

```
┌─ AgeBandErr ───────────────────────────────────────
│ ΞCampEnergy
│ c? : CHILDID
│ d? : DATE
│ t? : TIME
│ l? : LEADERID
│ r! : Rep
├────────────────────────────────────────────────────
│ (creg c?).age ∉ (((breg (d?, t?)).session) l?).band
│ r! = WrongAgeBand
└────────────────────────────────────────────────────
```

The total operation is:

$$FullAddToGroup \; \widehat{=} \; FullAddToGroup0 \lor UnknownCErr$$
$$\lor \; AgeBandErr$$

Exercise 8.34 ⋄ Define the following total operations on the full state:

FullDeleteChild, FullDeleteLeader, FullAlterAge

Assume that a child may only be deleted from the register if no bookings exist for that child and a leader can only be deleted if not currently timetabled to lead any sessions. A child's age can only be altered if it does not result in existing bookings becoming invalid.

8.3   Summary and discussion

In this chapter we have taken a real life situation and produced an abstract Z specification for it. We have followed the steps of the development method outlined in Chapter 7 and have attempted to explore various possible routes and to justify the decisions made. We have made use of promotion, showing how it can simplify specifications by structuring both definitions and proofs. There are a number of other operations which could be defined for this system, with and without promotion. The eager reader might like to tackle some of these. There are also various preconditions and initialisation theorems which could be proved, perhaps after reading the next chapter on reasoning in Z.

Throughout this chapter, readers have been encouraged to participate in the specification and to investigate their own ideas as far as possible. Although at each step we have to make a choice for our continued presentation, there are many possible alternatives which might be just as good. The important thing is to gain a feel for writing specifications and to be aware of the possible options. Each choice that is made will have implications for the future course of the development in terms of both specification and proof. There can often be a trade-off between the neat, concise specification of one part of the system and additional complexity for another aspect. For example, the use of nested layers of schemas as in the booking register makes a pleasing specification at that level, but trying to define operations for the booking register as a whole would become very complicated because of the need to refer down through the layers (it is not simply the use of schemas which has this effect: the very approach of layering the specification has this consequence). In this case, the use of promotion to structure the specification has made our approach manageable.

8.4   Further reading

Further case studies can be found in [Hay93] and [Bow95]. [Hay93] includes an example of a specification using promotion, as does [Wor93]. The result about promotion of preconditions was published in [Woo89].

Chapter 9

Formal reasoning

So far we have concentrated on presenting a formal language for specifying programs and giving examples to show how it may be used. Even at this early stage in learning to write specifications, we hope that the reader has begun to appreciate some of the benefits to be gained for the effort spent in producing a specification. The discipline of concentrating on a problem and setting down precisely what is required is more likely to lead to a well-thought-out, well-structured program. The specification itself provides an unambiguous statement of intent which can be discussed with customers and colleagues. It will also act as documentation for the finished program, helping those who have to maintain and update the program in the future.

When a formal notation such as Z is first used for specification these are the sorts of gains that will be apparent. Many users of Z have found that this is justification enough for investing in formal methods. The huge cost and inconvenience of correcting errors in a system once it has been released mean that prevention is much preferable to cure. However, there are still questions that might reasonably be asked, such as: 'How can I be sure that my specification really does have the properties I require?' The engineer designing a bridge would be expected not just to draw plans of a suitable-looking construction, but to demonstrate that it can carry the designated maximum load, withstand gale-force winds, and so on. Another question that might be asked is: 'How do I know that my final program accords with my specification?' A specification may express exactly what is wanted, but if the program produced does not capture the intentions of the specification it will be as prone to flaws as a bridge which does not quite meet its design.

In this and the following chapters we discuss how such questions may be answered. Just as learning to specify requires an investment of time and effort and improves with practice, so this next step of starting to prove things about specifications demands knowledge of the mathematical language of proof. The compensation for this mental exertion is that the potential rewards are great.

The idea of producing software which is provably correct with respect to a formal specification is very attractive, particularly where safety or security is critical.

9.1   A first example

In the Z notation we may write theorems to record important facts which are consequences of a specification. As an example, consider the case study of the library system. Recall that the state of the library was defined:

```
┌─ Library ──────────────────────────────────────────────
│  stock : Copy ⇸ Book
│  issued : Copy ⇸ Reader
│  shelved : 𝔽 Copy
│  readers : 𝔽 Reader
├────────────────────────────────────────────────────────
│  shelved ∪ dom issued = dom stock
│  shelved ∩ dom issued = ∅
│  ran issued ⊆ readers
│  ∀ r : readers • #(issued ▷ {r}) ≤ maxloans
└────────────────────────────────────────────────────────
```

The first two lines of the predicate relate the component *shelved* to other components of the schema. In Chapter 6 it was claimed that *shelved* can be defined completely in terms of the other components by:

$$shelved = \text{dom } stock \setminus \text{dom } issued$$

To demonstrate that this really is so we need to use both the particular properties about *shelved* given in the schema and some laws about sets in general. We could write down a proof as follows (do not worry about the details of the proof for now – we will consider how to construct proofs and what laws are available later in the chapter):

$$\text{dom } stock \setminus \text{dom } issued$$

$$= (shelved \cup \text{dom } issued) \setminus \text{dom } issued \quad [\text{first line of } Library \text{ predicate}]$$

$$= (shelved \setminus \text{dom } issued) \cup (\text{dom } issued \setminus \text{dom } issued)$$

$$[\text{property of } \cup \text{ and } \setminus]$$

$$= (shelved \setminus \text{dom } issued) \cup \emptyset \quad\quad\quad\quad\quad [\text{property of } \setminus]$$

$$= shelved \setminus \text{dom } issued \quad\quad\quad\quad\quad\quad [\text{property of } \cup]$$

$$= shelved \quad\quad\quad\quad [\text{from line 2 of } Library \text{ predicate}]$$

At each stage of the proof we use some known fact to write down an equivalent expression. For instance, in the very first step we use the fact recorded in the

Library schema that *shelved* ∪ dom *issued* = dom *stock*. This allows us to re-write our original expression with *shelved* ∪ dom *issued* replacing dom *stock*. The comments record a brief justification for each step.

When a property is found to be true of a specification we can record the knowledge by stating it as a theorem in the specification. The fact just proved can be recorded:

Library ⊢ *shelved* = dom *stock* \ dom *issued*

Notice the use of the 'turnstile' symbol, ⊢, to express a theorem. Its meaning is as follows: given the definitions of the specification so far, if we assume the statements on the left hand side of the turnstile then we can prove the statement on the right hand side. We refer to the definitions and predicates up to the point where the theorem is stated, including definitions in the standard library, as the current environment. On the left of the turnstile there may be a list of declarations, predicates or schema names. These statements are known as the hypotheses of the theorem. On the right of the turnstile is the conclusion we wish to prove. This is a single predicate. To prove the conclusion we may use any of the information in the current environment or in the hypotheses.

Just as schemas are used to structure specifications they are also used to structure the statement of theorems. In the above example a schema name, *Library*, is used as a hypothesis. This is just a shorthand for writing down all the declarations and constraints appearing in that schema. We can expand the schema to give the equivalent statement of the theorem:

$stock : Copy \nrightarrow Book$; $issued : Copy \nrightarrow Reader$;
$shelved : \mathbb{F}\ Copy$; $readers : \mathbb{F}\ Reader$ |
    $shelved \cup \text{dom } issued = \text{dom } stock$
    $shelved \cap \text{dom } issued = \emptyset$
    $\text{ran } issued \subseteq readers$
    $\forall r : readers \bullet \#(issued \rhd \{r\}) \leq maxloans$
⊢
    $shelved = \text{dom } stock \setminus \text{dom } issued$

where stacking is used to mean conjunction just as it is within the predicate part of a boxed schema. The bar symbol | is used as in a horizontal schema to separate the declarations from the predicates on the left of the turnstile. Without the use of the schema name the statement of the theorem has grown considerably in length. This can have the effect of obscuring the real import of the theorem, making it seem harder to prove because our intuition for the direction of the proof is lost. When schemas are referred to in the statement of a theorem they can be unwrapped as required during the course of a proof to reveal the information they contain. We will see examples of this later.

The above example shows how theorems may be used to state consequences of a specification. In the remainder of this section we concentrate on the form of a theorem and how to capture the facts we wish to record by expressing them as theorems. (Strictly speaking a theorem must have a proof; when we write $H \vdash C$ we are merely asserting that C may be proved assuming H, and of course it is possible to make assertions of this form which could not be backed up by a proof, or indeed for which counter-examples could be provided, as is the case for the 'theorem' $x : N \vdash \exists y : N \bullet y < x$. We often use the word 'theorem' where it might be more honest to say 'conjecture'.) Here is a first example:

$$\vdash \exists x : N \bullet \forall y : N \bullet x \leq y$$

In this case the theorem has no statements on the left of the turnstile. The conclusion, that there exists a number at least as small as any number you can think of, stands on its own as a theorem; no hypotheses are needed. A second example:

$$x, y : N \vdash (x \leq y) \vee (y \leq x)$$

This theorem says that given numbers x and y, either $x \leq y$ or $y \leq x$. The x and y are declared in the hypothesis and can then be referred to in the predicates of the hypothesis (although in this case there are none) and in the conclusion of the theorem. Since the theorem is true for any x and y it is rather like a universally quantified statement. In fact, another way of stating it is:

$$\vdash \forall x, y : N \bullet (x \leq y) \vee (y \leq x)$$

Just as there are many different ways of writing the same predicate, so can a theorem be expressed in a number of possible ways. This is also seen in the next example:

$$x : N \vdash \exists q, r : N \mid r < 10 \bullet x = 10 * q + r$$

which says that for any non-negative number x there exist numbers q and r, with $r < 10$, such that x is ten times q plus r, which is to say that q and r are the quotient and remainder when x is divided by 10. We could also write this:

$$\vdash \forall x : N \bullet (\exists q, r : N \mid r < 10 \bullet x = 10 * q + r)$$

Notice that while both declarations and predicates are allowed on the left of the turnstile, the conclusion must be a predicate. The following is therefore not a meaningful theorem:

$$\vdash x : N; \ y : N \mid (x \leq y) \vee (y \leq x)$$

It is syntactically incorrect since to the right of the turnstile appear a declaration list, a separating bar and then a predicate.

Exercise 9.1 Write the following theorems in our formal notation with numbers ranging over the set $\mathbb{N}$:

(i) $\diamond$ Given any number we can prove that there is a greater number.

(ii) Given a set of numbers which is not empty, we can prove that there is a non-empty subset.

(iii) There exists a number which is greater than zero.

Exercise 9.2 A specification includes the definitions:

$$\begin{array}{|l}
max : \mathbb{N} \\
f : \mathbb{N} \to \mathbb{N} \\
\hline
\forall x : \mathbb{N} \bullet f\, x \leq max
\end{array}$$

Decide which of the following are syntactically correct theorems and for those which are, give an informal expression of their meaning:

(i) $\diamond y : \mathbb{N} \mid y > max \vdash y \notin \operatorname{ran} f$

(ii) $\vdash \operatorname{ran} f \in \mathbb{F}\mathbb{N}$

(iii) $\operatorname{ran} f \vdash x : \mathbb{N} \mid x \leq max$

(iv) $\operatorname{dom} f \subseteq \operatorname{ran} f \vdash f \subseteq \{x, y : \mathbb{N} \mid x < max \wedge y < max\}$

9.2   Schemas as predicates

In the last section it was stressed that the conclusion in a theorem statement must be a predicate. If a reference to a schema appears on the right of a turnstile then the schema will be interpreted as a predicate. That is, the conclusion of the theorem is just the predicate of the schema. For the statement to make sense, all the variables declared in the schema must be in scope, that is, they must have been introduced either in the hypotheses or globally. For instance, returning to the *Library* example, suppose we wish to consider a subsystem of the library defined:

$$\begin{array}{|l}
\underline{\ \textit{ShelfRecord}\ } \\
shelved : \mathbb{F}\ Copy \\
stock : Copy \nrightarrow Book \\
issued : Copy \nrightarrow Reader \\
\hline
shelved = \operatorname{dom} stock \setminus \operatorname{dom} issued
\end{array}$$

We could then state the following theorem:

$Library \vdash ShelfRecord$

That is to say, if we assume the conditions described in *Library* are met we could prove that the relationship described in *ShelfRecord* also holds. Since *ShelfRecord* is a schema occurring as the conclusion of a theorem we must interpret it as a predicate. Firstly, we must check that the variables it declares are all in scope with the correct types. In this case it is easy to check that *shelved*, *stock* and *issued* all occur in the declaration part of *Library* (which is our hypothesis) and all have the correct types. It is therefore safe to peel away the declarations of *ShelfRecord* leaving the predicate:

$shelved = \text{dom } stock \setminus \text{dom } issued$

In fact, what we are left with is the equivalent statement of the theorem:

$Library \vdash shelved = \text{dom } stock \setminus \text{dom } issued$

which is exactly the theorem already proved above.

9.3 Reasoning about specifications

To introduce the syntax of theorems we have used a number of rather contrived examples. In practice, there are certain standard theorems that would be stated in a specification. We have seen that it is usual for a specification to describe the state of a system along with operations on the state. If S is the name of the schema describing the state, the possible initial states of the system might be described by another schema, *InitS*. It would then be useful to show that there really is a state satisfying the requirements of *InitS*. A system with no possible initial states would be of little use! As an example, consider the following specification. A government proposes to introduce a national identity card scheme for football fans. Each fan will be allocated a single, unique identity code. The system will keep track of who has been allocated which identity code. It will also keep a list of the codes of troublemakers who have been banned from attending matches. The specification introduces the basic types, *PERSON*, the set of people, and *ID*, the set of all possible identity codes. The state of the system is recorded by the schema *Fid*. Thus we declare given sets:

$[PERSON, ID]$

and we define the states of the system:

$$
\begin{array}{|l}
\hline
\text{\_\_} Fid \text{_____} \\
\quad members : ID \rightarrowtail PERSON \\
\quad banned : \mathbb{P}\, ID \\
\hline
\quad banned \subseteq \text{dom } members \\
\hline
\end{array}
$$

The schema tells us the following:

- The function recording membership information, *members*, is a partial injection; being a function means that no identity code is shared by more than one person; being an injection says that a person can have no more than one identity code; the function is partial since not all identity codes need be allocated.

- The set *banned* contains the identity codes of some subset of the registered members.

9.3.1 The Initialisation Theorem

We now define the initial state of the system, *InitFid*, where no members have yet been registered, and no-one has been banned:

$$
\begin{array}{|l}
\_\_ InitFid _____ \\
\; Fid' \\
\hline
\; members' = \emptyset \\
\; banned' = \emptyset \\
\end{array}
$$

The initial state is just *Fid'* with the additional requirement that *members'* and *banned'* are both empty.

We are now in a position to state for this system a theorem of the kind mentioned above concerning the existence of at least one suitable initial state. It is called the Initialisation Theorem, and takes the form:

$$\vdash \exists\, Fid' \bullet InitFid$$

This theorem states that there really is a *Fid'* system which also satisfies the requirements of *InitFid*. That this should be true is no surprise because *InitFid* actually tells us the values of the components of such a system; it is the one with an empty membership relation and an empty set of banned members. The statement of the theorem can be expanded to give:

$$
\vdash \exists\, members' : ID \rightarrowtail PERSON;\ banned' : \mathbb{P}\, ID\ |
$$
$$
banned' \subseteq \mathrm{dom}\ members' \bullet
$$
$$
members' = \emptyset \land banned' = \emptyset
$$

The requirement of *Fid'* that *banned'* $\subseteq$ dom *members'* is certainly met when both *banned'* and *members'* (and thus dom *members'*) are empty.

An Initialisation Theorem of this form may be written down for any specification where schemas are used to describe the state and initial state of the system. As with the current example, it may be a simple, even trivial, theorem, but it is still a useful check to make. It is often the case that the initialisation schema gives explicit values for the components of the state; it is then usually a simple matter to confirm that these components jointly satisfy the state invariant. In the present case, during the course of the proof it would become necessary to expand the reference to the schema *Fid'* to show the declarations and predicates it contains, and to interpret *InitFid* as a predicate as described in the previous section. When simply stating the theorem, however, the use of schemas makes a much clearer, more concise expression which can be included in the specification to record the fact that initial states do indeed exist for our system.

9.3.2   Precondition simplification

Having described the states of the system, there are a number of operations that may be required, for instance, registering a new member in the scheme and allocating an identity code. Suppose this is specified as follows:

$$
\begin{array}{|l}
\hline
\_AddMember _____ \\
\Delta Fid \\
applicant? : PERSON \\
id! : ID \\
\hline
applicant? \notin \text{ran } members \\
id! \notin \text{dom } members \\
members' = members \cup \{id! \mapsto applicant?\} \\
banned' = banned \\
\hline
\end{array}
$$

AddMember is an operation on *Fid* with the following features:

- Its input is the name of a person applying for membership.
- An identity code is issued.
- The applicant must not already be a member.
- The identity code should not already be in use.
- The function *members* is updated with the new information.
- The set *banned* remains unchanged.

One of the important things to know about an operation is in which states it can be successfully applied. Other cases could then be identified and error messages supplied as appropriate to create a robust interface. As we have seen, the set of starting states from which the operation could successfully be carried out is given by the precondition of that operation. It looks as though the operation

AddMember will be successful as long as the applicant is not already registered and the identity codes are not all in use. To check that this really is the case we need a way of calculating the precondition of the operation.

Chapter 6 describes how a precondition can be found by removing the after-state variables and outputs from the declaration part of the schema and existentially quantifying them in the predicate. If we apply this process to the *AddMember* operation we obtain:

```
┌─ PreAddMember ─────────────────────────────────────────
│ Fid
│ applicant? : PERSON
│ ─────────────────────────────────────────
│ ∃ Fid'; id! : ID •
│     applicant? ∉ ran members ∧
│     id! ∉ dom members ∧
│     members' = members ∪ {id! ↦ applicant?} ∧
│     banned' = banned
└────────────────────────────────────────────────────────
```

This schema describes the precondition, but it looks very different from the fairly simple condition which intuition suggests will guarantee successful completion of *AddMember*. The problem is that introducing the existential quantification often leaves an over-complicated predicate. In many cases the predicate part of the schema can be simplified to give a much neater, but logically equivalent, statement. To do this we will need laws which tell us how predicates can be rewritten in different ways without changing their meaning. By applying such laws we could move from the complicated quantified expression and arrive at a statement of the precondition which should look more like the one we expected.

Later in the chapter when we have introduced the necessary laws we will be able to return to this example and carry out the simplification. It will then be clear in exactly which circumstances the operation will work, and we can go on to identify the cases outside the precondition for which there is no guarantee of success. If error cases are added to cover these situations we can construct a total interface for the operation.

9.3.3 Properties of a specification

Proof of the Initialisation Theorem and simplification of preconditions are standard checks that may be carried out for any state-based specification. For a particular specification there may be certain other properties which are desired consequences (the very first theorem of this chapter is an example). These properties may be demanded in the informal requirements for the specification, or they may be identified by the specifier as key points about the specification. Also, if a specification is going through a review process, the specifiers might be challenged to demonstrate certain properties of the specification.

Suppose the operation to ban a member is defined:

```
┌─ BanMember ─────────────────────────────────────
│ ΔFid
│ ban? : ID
├─────────────────────────────────────────────────
│ ban? ∈ dom members
│ banned' = banned ∪ {ban?}
│ members' = members
└─────────────────────────────────────────────────
```

To show that banning a member who is already banned leaves the state of the system unchanged, the theorem we need to state and prove is:

$$BanMember \mid ban? \in banned \vdash \Xi Fid$$

That is, given the declarations and constraint of the *BanMember* operation, together with the requirement that the person to be banned is already banned, we can show that *Fid* does not change. The schema references may be expanded to give the next level of detail. Expanding *BanMember* we get:

$$\Delta Fid; \; ban? : ID \mid$$
$$\qquad ban? \in \mathrm{dom}\; members$$
$$\qquad banned' = banned \cup \{ban?\}$$
$$\qquad members' = members \wedge ban? \in banned$$
$$\vdash$$
$$\qquad \Xi Fid$$

Since the declaration part of ΞFid (that is, ΔFid) occurs in the hypotheses it is safe to interpret ΞFid as a predicate. This gives:

$$\Delta Fid; \; ban? : ID \mid$$
$$\qquad ban? \in \mathrm{dom}\; members$$
$$\qquad banned' = banned \cup \{ban?\}$$
$$\qquad members' = members \wedge ban? \in banned$$
$$\vdash$$
$$\qquad members' = members \wedge banned' = banned$$

To prove this it is easy to see that $members' = members$ follows immediately from the hypotheses, and:

$$banned'$$
$$\quad = banned \cup \{ban?\} \qquad\qquad\qquad\qquad\qquad \text{[hypothesis]}$$
$$\quad = banned \qquad\qquad\qquad\qquad\qquad\qquad \text{[since } ban? \in banned]$$

As another example, suppose that someone reviewing the specification is worried that our successful *AddMember* operation might allow a banned person to apply and be enrolled with another identity code. To show that their fears are groundless we might prove the following theorem:

$$AddMember \vdash applicant? \notin members (\!| \ banned \ |\!)$$

9.3.4   Refinement

This section has concentrated on stating theorems about a specification. Proving theorems such as these begins to answer the question posed earlier about how we can be sure that specifications have the properties we require. The second question concerned the problem of deciding whether a program really does what the specification demands. The process of taking an abstract specification and moving towards an executable program is known as refinement. This is the subject of the next chapter. For now we merely note that to be sure that a program really is a refinement of a specification we have to prove that it correctly implements that specification. The refinement procedure is a major source of theorems since each step must satisfy a number of standard conditions. Proving that these conditions are met is the only way to guarantee that the program meets its specification.

Exercise 9.3 Write a suitable initial state schema for the library system discussed in Chapter 6. State the Initialisation Theorem for the system.

Exercise 9.4 ◇ Write a schema *DeleteMember* which takes a member's identity code as input and deletes reference to that member.

Exercise 9.5 What do you think the precondition of *DeleteMember* is? Write down the precondition, *PreDeleteMember*, in its unsimplified form.

Exercise 9.6 If a member were added to a *Fid* system, and then that same user removed without any other intervening operations we would expect our system to be unaltered. Write down formally what you would need to prove if this is to be so.

Exercise 9.7 ◇ Explain why we cannot express the predicate of the schema *InitFid* as:

$$members' = banned' = \emptyset$$

9.4   What is a proof?

The examples of the previous section show where mathematical reasoning might be of use in a specification. Looking at this we can see that there are two different styles of reasoning which might be adopted. Firstly, there are theorems about the specification and these are of the form:

$Decls \mid Pred \vdash Conclusion$

A proof of such a theorem is a demonstration that its conclusion really does follow from its hypotheses. In general, a proof is constructed by reasoning from the hypotheses, giving a justification for each step that is made, and arriving finally at the desired conclusion. Secondly, there are circumstances such as precondition calculations when we obtain a complicated expression and need to simplify the statement whilst retaining its meaning. When we perform a simplification the justification of each step must come with an assurance that the new predicate is equivalent to the old.

Although the two styles may sound quite different they both rely on the same underlying system of logic. The way in which the rules of the game are presented will vary from text to text, but the objective remains the same. The following sections attempt to give a flavour of proofs and simplifications.

Reasoning may be carried out at many different levels depending on how rigorous we are trying to be. An informal proof progresses by inspired leaps which are justified by appealing to generally accepted facts and to intuition. Such a proof can be very successful in the task of assuring ourselves and others that a theorem is true, and is extremely useful for giving an understanding of why theorems hold.

At the other end of the scale is the completely formal proof, the kind that must be constructed in order to convince a machine-based proof tool. A fixed set of rules must be strictly applied to justify each step. A formal proof, particularly one which has been verified by a machine, confers great authority and confidence. However, the proof itself may be very detailed and difficult to follow, so that someone trying to read the proof might be convinced more by a belief that the machine must be right than by an understanding of the proof.

An informal proof is not really a proof unless it is possible to give a corresponding formal proof which provides detailed (formal) justification of all the supposedly obvious statements which are used to justify the larger steps of the informal proof. Probably the best way to construct completely formal proofs is to construct informal proofs whose steps correspond to human mind sized inferences, with machine assistance to provide the subproofs which justify these steps.

The aim of this chapter is to introduce the idea of theorems and their proofs, concentrating on what theorems mean and why we might believe them. In what follows we adopt the approach of informal but informed reasoning, informal in that we do not introduce a complete system of formal laws, informed in that our justifications should appeal to knowledge of such things as how to tell when two expressions are equivalent, how to deal with quantified formulae, and how to use general laws about sets, relations, functions and sequences. The following sections provide the groundwork for this informed reasoning and give examples of its use.

9.5   Reasoning with propositions

In previous chapters we have seen many examples of propositions and how they can be combined to give new propositions using the logical operators, $\wedge$, $\vee$, $\neg$, $\Rightarrow$ and $\Leftrightarrow$. One of the basic requirements for carrying out proofs is the ability to manipulate and simplify propositions. In the exercises of Section 2.2.1 truth tables were used to show the equivalence of certain propositions. For example, using small letters p, q and r to denote arbitrary propositions, we can show by constructing a truth table that $p \wedge (q \vee r)$ is equivalent to $(p \wedge q) \vee (p \wedge r)$:

p	q	r	$p \wedge (q \vee r)$		$(p \wedge q)$	$\vee$	$(p \wedge r)$
T	T	T	T	T	T	T	T
T	T	F	T	T	T	T	F
T	F	T	T	T	F	T	T
T	F	F	F	F	F	F	F
F	T	T	F	T	F	F	F
F	T	F	F	T	F	F	F
F	F	T	F	T	F	F	F
F	F	F	F	F	F	F	F

since the fourth and seventh columns of truth values are identical. This uses the known truth tables for $\wedge$ and $\vee$ and shows that whatever the particular truth values of p, q and r either $p \wedge (q \vee r)$ and $(p \wedge q) \vee (p \wedge r)$ are both true or they are both false. So the two are equivalent. Again, if we consider the expression:

$$p \wedge (q \vee r) \Leftrightarrow (p \wedge q) \vee (p \wedge r)$$

we shall find that the column of the truth table beneath the $\Leftrightarrow$ symbol consists of Ts only:

p	q	r	$p \wedge (q \vee r)$		$\Leftrightarrow$	$(p \wedge q)$	$\vee$	$(p \wedge r)$
T	T	T	T	T	T	T	T	T
T	T	F	T	T	T	T	T	F
T	F	T	T	T	T	F	T	T
T	F	F	F	F	T	F	F	F
F	T	T	F	T	T	F	F	F
F	T	F	F	T	T	F	F	F
F	F	T	F	T	T	F	F	F
F	F	F	F	F	T	F	F	F

thus it is reasonable to assert the law in the form:

$$p \wedge (q \vee r) \Leftrightarrow (p \wedge q) \vee (p \wedge r)$$

but in fact we shall use a new symbol $\equiv$ to indicate that we think of this as a law rather than just a proposition. Thus we write:

$$p \wedge (q \vee r) \equiv (p \wedge q) \vee (p \wedge r)$$

If two propositions are equivalent we can safely replace one by the other at any point in a proof. To find whether two propositions are equivalent it is always possible to use the truth table method. However, this is rather cumbersome and tedious, and the truth tables may become very large. Instead we can build up a collection of known equivalences (such as the one above) and use them to justify proof steps whenever a proposition of the right shape is encountered. They can also be used to justify new equivalences. For example, suppose we know that the following two equivalences hold:

(i) $p \wedge (q \vee r) \equiv (p \wedge q) \vee (p \wedge r)$

(ii) $p \wedge p \equiv p$

and we also suspect that $a \wedge (a \vee b)$ is equivalent to $a \vee (a \wedge b)$. This could be confirmed using a truth table, but another method is to use (i) and (ii) as follows:

$$
\begin{array}{ll}
a \wedge (a \vee b) & \\
\equiv (a \wedge a) \vee (a \wedge b) & \text{[using (i)]} \\
\equiv a \vee (a \wedge b) & \text{[using (ii)]}
\end{array}
$$

Starting with $a \wedge (a \vee b)$ we use (i) to expand the statement to the equivalent expression on the second line. This is done by matching $a \wedge (a \vee b)$ with the left hand side of (i), which gives both p and q the value a and r the value b. We now notice that the first part of the new expression is $(a \wedge a)$ which can be simplified using equivalence (ii) to just a. This is all that is needed to prove the equivalence. In setting down the argument we have used $\equiv$ at the beginning of a line to indicate that it is equivalent to the proposition of the previous line. The comment at the right hand side of a line gives the justification for that step. In this example the letters a and b were used to stand for arbitrary propositions to avoid confusion with p and q. We could just as well state the result:

$$p \wedge (p \vee q) \equiv p \vee (p \wedge q)$$

Not all laws are equivalences; one proposition may follow as the result of another without the two being equivalent. For instance, from $p \wedge q$ we can deduce q on its own; one way to confirm this is to construct the truth table for the expression $p \wedge q \Rightarrow q$:

p	q	$p \wedge q$	$\Rightarrow$	q
T	T	T		T
T	F	F		T
F	T	F		T
F	F	F		T

Thus we may assert as a law:

(iii) $p \wedge q \Rightarrow q$

or, by analogy with equivalence laws, we might use a special symbol $\Rrightarrow$ and write it thus:

(iii) $p \wedge q \Rrightarrow q$

Laws of this kind (as well as equivalences) can be used when proving a conclusion from hypotheses. It is not necessary that each line in a proof should be equivalent to the previous one, but it must follow as a consequence of one or more previous lines. The hypotheses may be used at any stage in a proof.

Suppose we now wish to show that from $p \wedge (q \wedge r)$ we can deduce r. Using (iii) we know that $q \wedge r$ follows, and by (iii) again r follows from this. A deductive argument of this kind might be set down in the following way:

(1)	$p \wedge (q \wedge r)$	H
(2)	$q \wedge r$	1, Law (iii)
(3)	r	2, Law (iii)

The numbers in brackets label the lines of the proof so we can refer to them later. At line 1 we write down the hypothesis we are starting with (the H on the right indicates this is a hypothesis). At line 2 we deduce $q \wedge r$. The justification on the right says how this has been done: law (iii) has been applied to line 1. Finally, we obtain r by another application of law (iii), this time to line 2. We might write this slightly less formally in the form:

$p \wedge (q \wedge r)$
$\Rrightarrow q \wedge r$ [using (iii)]
$\Rrightarrow r$ [using (iii)]

The two examples of proofs given above show the two different styles of argument that it will be convenient to use, equivalences and deductions. The collection of laws that we will work with are given in the next section. To emphasise the importance of these laws we introduce some special notation. A law which is an equivalence, such as $\neg \neg p \equiv p$, will be presented:

$$\frac{\neg \neg p}{p} \quad DN$$

The double line between the two expressions denotes an equivalence, and the law is given a name, in this case DN for 'double negative'. A law which works in one direction only will be written with a single line, for example:

$$\frac{p \wedge q}{p} \quad \wedge E$$

Some unidirectional laws require more than one incoming proposition (premise) for their application; in such cases, the premises are separated by commas above the line. An equivalence law can be applied to the whole of a previous line of a proof, or to a part of a previous line, that part being replaced by the equivalent form in the new line which is generated. A unidirectional law may only be applied to the whole of previous lines of the proof as premises in order to make a new line of the proof. Our informal proofs which took the forms of a chain of equivalences, in the first case, and a chain of deductions in the second place, are rather special, though frequently occurring, cases of the more general notion of a proof. A proof may use any previous line as a premise, whilst the chaining proofs use only the immediately preceding line at each stage.

9.5.1   Some propositional laws

We now give a useful collection of laws concerning propositions, and the names by which they will be known. They are presented together without a great deal of explanation to provide a section for reference. The examples of the next section show how the laws may be used and readers new to propositional reasoning are encouraged to become more familiar with the laws by attempting the exercises.

Laws for $\wedge$

$$\frac{p \wedge q}{p} \wedge E1 \qquad \frac{p \wedge q}{q} \wedge E2 \qquad \frac{p \, , \, q}{p \wedge q} \wedge I$$

The first two rules are sometimes called elimination rules and show that from $p \wedge q$ we can deduce p on its own or q on its own. The third rule shows how to introduce a conjunction when we have proofs of the two component propositions already.

$$\frac{p \wedge p}{p} \wedge Id \qquad \frac{p \wedge q}{q \wedge p} \wedge C \qquad \frac{p \wedge (q \wedge r)}{(p \wedge q) \wedge r} \wedge A$$

These three laws are equivalences and they express some properties about $\wedge$ introduced in Chapter 2, namely idempotence, commutativity and associativity.

Laws for $\vee$

$$\frac{p}{p \vee q} \vee I1 \qquad \frac{q}{p \vee q} \vee I2$$

$$\frac{p \vee q, p \Rightarrow r, q \Rightarrow r}{r} \vee E \qquad \frac{p \vee q}{\neg \, (\neg \, p \wedge \neg \, q)} \vee Equiv$$

The most complicated of these is the third rule which shows how we can deduce some result r from a disjunction, $p \lor q$. The idea is that if we can show both that r follows from p and that r also follows from q, then if one of p,q holds r must certainly hold.

As with $\land$, $\lor$ is idempotent, commutative and associative. The proof of these properties from the given laws is left as an exercise.

Laws for $\Rightarrow$

$$\frac{p \Rightarrow q \, , \, p}{q} \Rightarrow E \qquad\qquad \begin{array}{c} [p] \\ \vdots \\ q \\ \hline p \Rightarrow q \end{array} \Rightarrow I \qquad\qquad \frac{p \Rightarrow q}{\neg p \lor q} \Rightarrow Equiv$$

The introduction law for $\Rightarrow$ uses a new notation. Its meaning is as follows: if by assuming p we can show that q is also true then we can say that p implies q. Thus we deduce $p \Rightarrow q$. The notation $[p]$ means that p is an assumption. It can be introduced at any point in a proof and used from then on until the step of $\Rightarrow I$ which 'uses it up'. This is referred to as the scope of the assumption. The scope of an assumption will be indicated in a proof by a vertical bar at the right hand side. Example 4 in the next section shows how this is done. Sometimes more than one assumption with nested scopes may be necessary.

Laws for $\neg$

$$\frac{\neg\neg p}{p} \; DN \qquad\qquad \begin{array}{c} [p] \\ \vdots \\ q \land \neg q \\ \hline \neg p \end{array} \neg I$$

The $\neg$ introduction rule says that if by assuming p we arrive at some contradiction $q \land \neg q$, then our original assumption p must have been incorrect and we deduce $\neg p$. This rule is used in the form of argument known as Proof by Contradiction. To prove some proposition we first make an assumption that its opposite is true and show that this leads to a contradiction. Then $\neg I$ can be used to negate the offending assumption thus establishing the desired result. This method is used in Example 6 in the next section.

Law for $\Leftrightarrow$

$$\frac{p \Leftrightarrow q}{(p \Rightarrow q) \land (q \Rightarrow p)} \Leftrightarrow Equiv$$

Other useful laws

$$\frac{p \wedge (q \vee r)}{(p \wedge q) \vee (p \wedge r)} \; Dist1 \qquad\qquad \frac{p \vee (q \wedge r)}{(p \vee q) \wedge (p \vee r)} \; Dist2$$

$$\frac{p \wedge (p \vee q)}{p} \; Abs1 \qquad\qquad \frac{p \vee (p \wedge q)}{p} \; Abs2$$

These are the distribution and absorption laws which are often very useful when simplifying statements.

Laws for *true* and *false*

The simplest propositions are *true*, which expresses a property true in all circumstances, and *false* which is false in all situations. We shall find it useful to have some rules which apply to these very simple propositions:

$$\frac{p \wedge \neg p}{false} \; F \; Equiv \qquad\qquad \frac{p \vee \neg p}{true} \; T \; Equiv$$

It can never be the case that both p and $\neg p$ hold together, so $p \wedge \neg p$ is equivalent to just *false*. Similarly, either a proposition p is true or its negation $\neg p$ is. So $p \vee \neg p$ is equivalent to *true*.

9.5.2   Examples using laws for propositions

1. There are a number of useful facts about *true* and *false* which can be proved using the given laws. For example:

$$\frac{p \wedge true}{p} \; TF1 \qquad \frac{p \wedge false}{false} \; TF2 \qquad \frac{p \vee true}{true} \; TF3$$

$$\frac{p \vee false}{p} \; TF4 \qquad \frac{\neg \, true}{false} \; TF5$$

We give an equivalence proof for *TF1* and leave the rest as an exercise.

$$
\begin{aligned}
& p \wedge true \\
& \equiv p \wedge (p \vee \neg p) \qquad\qquad\qquad\qquad\qquad\qquad [T \; Equiv] \\
& \equiv p \qquad\qquad\qquad\qquad\qquad\qquad\qquad\qquad\quad [Abs1]
\end{aligned}
$$

The equivalence for *true* is used to expand the original proposition, and the result is then simplified by applying one of the absorption laws.

2. Prove the following law: $\dfrac{p \wedge \neg q}{p \vee q}$

This time the statements are not equivalent – we have to show that the bottom one can be derived from the top one. Notice that if $p \wedge \neg q$ is true then both p is true and $\neg q$ is true. And if p is true, so is $p \vee q$. This leads immediately to the proof below. The fact that $\neg q$ is also true plays no part in the proof.

(1)	$p \wedge \neg q$	H
(2)	p	$1, \wedge E1$
(3)	$p \vee q$	$2, \vee I1$

3. Show the equivalence of $p \Rightarrow q$ and $\neg q \Rightarrow \neg p$.

We need to prove an equivalence about an implication. We already know one equivalence about implication which is given by the law $\Rightarrow Equiv$. This transforms an implication into an expression involving $\neg$ and $\vee$. Applying this to $p \Rightarrow q$ would give $\neg p \vee q$ and to $\neg q \Rightarrow \neg p$ gives $\neg \neg q \vee \neg p$. If we can show that these two are equivalent the proof is complete.

This strategy is captured in the proof below. The first step transforms $p \Rightarrow q$ to its known equivalent. The middle steps massage the expression into the correct form for changing back to the implication $\neg q \Rightarrow \neg p$.

$$
\begin{array}{ll}
p \Rightarrow q & \\
\equiv \neg p \vee q & [\Rightarrow Equiv] \\
\equiv q \vee \neg p & [\vee C] \\
\equiv \neg \neg q \vee \neg p & [DN] \\
\equiv \neg q \Rightarrow \neg p & [\Rightarrow Equiv]
\end{array}
$$

This result is known as the contra-positive law which we will refer to as CP.

4. Show that from $p \vee r \Rightarrow q$ we can deduce $p \Rightarrow q$. Once established we can use this as a new law: $\dfrac{p \vee r \Rightarrow q}{p \Rightarrow q}$

The proof of this law shows the use of the $\Rightarrow I$ rule. The conclusion we are aiming at is an implication, $p \Rightarrow q$. If from an assumption of p we can prove q then $\Rightarrow I$ allows us to deduce $p \Rightarrow q$.

(1)	$p \vee r \Rightarrow q$	H
(2)	p	A
(3)	$p \vee r$	$2, \vee I1$
(4)	q	$1, 3, \Rightarrow E$
(5)	$p \Rightarrow q$	$2, 4, \Rightarrow I$

Firstly in this proof we write down the hypothesis $p \vee r \Rightarrow q$. Then, in accordance with the strategy above we assume p and aim to prove q. Line

3 follows by using $\vee$ introduction, giving us $p \vee q$, which is the expression on the left of the implication at line 1. These two together allow us to deduce q by $\Rightarrow$ elimination. Finally, the step of $\Rightarrow$ introduction uses up the assumption p by making p the left hand side of a new implication.

5. Simplify: $p \wedge ((q \Rightarrow \neg p) \vee q)$

This time we need to find an expression equivalent to the one given. We do not know exactly what we are aiming at, but suspect there is a simpler way of saying the same thing. This is often the case when simplifying a precondition.

The expression is of the form $a \wedge (b \vee c)$, so we can start by using the law of distributivity to expand it. The expression contains an implication which can be equivalently expressed in terms of $\vee$ and $\neg$. The advantage of this is that distributivity can again be used to expand the first part of the expression (see the fourth line of the proof). So far the expression seems to be getting more complicated rather than simpler, but now the opportunity arises to rewrite the sub-expression $p \wedge \neg p$ as *false*. The next proof line simplifies further by using one of the rules about *false*. By the sixth line the expression is starting to look more manageable, but it is not yet in its simplest form. If we use the law of distributivity again the expression can be repacked to the equivalent version of line 7. Further simplification using properties of *true* leads to the final line. The original cumbersome proposition is equivalent to simply p.

$$
\begin{aligned}
&p \wedge ((q \Rightarrow \neg p) \vee q) \\
&\equiv (p \wedge (q \Rightarrow \neg p)) \vee (p \wedge q) &&[Dist1] \\
&\equiv (p \wedge (\neg q \vee \neg p)) \vee (p \wedge q) &&[\Rightarrow Equiv] \\
&\equiv ((p \wedge \neg q) \vee (p \wedge \neg p)) \vee (p \wedge q) &&[Dist1] \\
&\equiv ((p \wedge \neg q) \vee false) \vee (p \wedge q) &&[F\ Equiv] \\
&\equiv (p \wedge \neg q) \vee (p \wedge q) &&[TF4] \\
&\equiv p \wedge (\neg q \vee q) &&[Dist1] \\
&\equiv p \wedge true &&[T\ Equiv] \\
&\equiv p &&[TF1]
\end{aligned}
$$

It would have been possible to start the simplification by expanding the implication and concentrating first on simplifying the second part of the expression. In fact, this would lead to a shorter proof. Try this way as an exercise.

6. Finally we give an example to show how the rule of $\neg I$ may be used, giving a proof by contradiction to establish: $\dfrac{p \wedge \neg q}{\neg (p \wedge q)}$

The strategy is to assume the opposite of what we wish to prove (done at line 2), aim to establish a contradiction (line 5) and then apply the ¬ introduction rule.

$$
\begin{array}{lll}
(1) & p \wedge \neg\, q & H \\
(2) & p \wedge q & A \\
(3) & q & 2, \wedge E2 \\
(4) & \neg\, q & 1, \wedge E2 \\
(5) & q \wedge \neg\, q & 3, 4, \wedge I \\
(6) & \neg\, (p \wedge q) & 2, 5, \neg I
\end{array}
$$

When the ¬ introduction rule is applied the justification gives the line number of the assumption we are blaming, and that of the line on which the contradiction appears. As with the rule of ⇒ introduction, when using ¬ introduction the scope of the assumption being blamed is ended.

In this example the goal we wished to prove was itself the negation of another proposition. The technique of proof by contradiction can still be used if the goal does not have a negated format. To prove proposition p, assume its opposite, ¬ p, and show this leads to a contradiction. Then use the law ¬ I to negate the assumption, giving ¬ ¬ p. By the law of double negation this is equivalent to the required goal, p.

Exercise 9.8 ◇ Use truth tables to confirm the absorption laws.

Exercise 9.9 Prove the equivalences for *true* and *false* from Example 1.

Exercise 9.10 Use the equivalences for *true* and *false* to simplify

(i) *true* ∨ *false*

(ii) *true* ∧ *false*

(iii) (*false* ∨ (¬ (p ∧ q) ∧ (*true* ∨ p))) ∨ *true*

(iv) $p \Rightarrow p$

(v) *false* ⇒ p

Exercise 9.11 Using the alternative method suggested, prove the equivalence of Example 5.

Exercise 9.12 Using the laws given so far, prove the idempotence, commutativity and associativity of ∨. Recall that these properties are:

$$
\frac{p \vee p}{p} \; \vee Id \qquad\qquad \frac{p \vee q}{q \vee p} \; \vee C \qquad\qquad \frac{p \vee (q \vee r)}{(p \vee q) \vee r} \; \vee A
$$

(Hint: express the ∨ statement in terms of ∧ and ¬ , and use the equivalences for ∧.)

Exercise 9.13 ⋄ Prove De Morgan's laws:

$$\frac{\neg\,(p \wedge q)}{\neg\,p \vee \neg\,q} \quad DM1 \qquad\qquad \frac{\neg\,(p \vee q)}{\neg\,p \wedge \neg\,q} \quad DM2$$

Exercise 9.14 Prove the following laws:

(i) $\dfrac{p \wedge q}{p \vee q}$ (ii) $\dfrac{p \Leftrightarrow q}{\neg\,p \Rightarrow \neg\,q}$ (iii) $\dfrac{p \wedge (q \wedge r)}{(p \wedge q) \wedge (p \wedge r)}$

(iv) $\dfrac{p \Rightarrow (q \vee r)}{(p \Rightarrow q) \vee (p \Rightarrow r)}$ (v) $\dfrac{q \vee (p \wedge q)}{q}$ (vi) $\dfrac{p}{\neg\,(\neg\,p \wedge \neg\,q)}$

9.6   Reasoning with predicates

The next stage is to introduce some laws for dealing with predicates. These can then be used in combination with the laws of the last section to provide the basic logical reasoning power we require. In general it is not possible to check whether a quantified statement is true or false using truth tables. Quantified variables may range over infinite sets so we cannot confirm the truth of a quantified statement by checking what happens for each possible value of the variable. It is therefore vital to have a collection of laws to allow proofs involving quantified statements. Here, each law is introduced with an informal description of what it means. The laws presented are just a selection of the useful results that might be called upon for predicate reasoning. Again, we can use these laws to prove new ones as required.

It is worth noting that when we use quantifiers there is no universally applicable method of determining whether a theorem can be proved or disproved, though it can be shown (by mathematical argument about the system of predicate logic) that if there is indeed a proof we would eventually find it by a systematic search through all possible proof lines deducible from the hypotheses. This theoretical result is, in general, of no great practical significance when we are faced with finding a proof, since we do not know in advance that there is a proof, and a systematic search through all possible lines of argument could take a very long time in any case.

9.6.1   Free variables and bound variables

To be able to state the laws for predicate calculus, some new concepts must be introduced. In a quantified statement, such as $\forall\,x : T \bullet p$ or $\exists\,x : T \bullet p$, we say that the variable x is bound by the quantification. Any mention of x within the predicate, p, will refer to the x marking the slot in the quantification, unless it is bound again by a nested quantification. A variable which is not bound is said to be free. For example, in the statement:

$$\exists\,x : \mathrm{N} \bullet x = 2 * y$$

the variable x is bound, but y is free since it is not captured by any quantification. The statement:

$$\forall\, y : \mathbf{N} \bullet \exists\, x : \mathbf{N} \bullet x = 2 * y$$

has both x and y as bound variables. Sometimes the same variable name can appear in more than one situation. For example, consider:

$$y = 2 * x \wedge \exists\, x : \mathbf{N} \bullet x > y$$

In this statement y is certainly free, but what about x? The first time x occurs it is free, but in the second part of the statement, it occurs as the bound variable. This shows that a variable can occur both free and bound within a single statement.

Some of the following laws only hold if a certain variable is *not* free in some statement p. We write:

$$x \backslash p$$

to mean 'x is not free in p'. If $x \backslash p$ and $x \backslash q$ then x is also not free in the compound statements $\neg\, p,\ p \wedge q,\ p \vee q,\ p \Rightarrow q$.

Variables are also bound when they are declared in set expressions. For example, in:

$$\{\, n : \mathbf{N} \mid \exists\, m : \mathbf{N} \bullet n = m * max \,\}$$

the variable n is introduced as a means of describing the set and is bound within the set expression. It also happens that the predicate part of the definition introduces another bound variable, m. Within this definition max is free; if we were working in the context of a specification it would presumably have been declared earlier.

9.6.2   Substitution

A quantified statement such as $\forall\, x : T \bullet p$ says that the property p holds for any element of the correct type, T. We may wish to consider the predicate p with a particular value substituted for x. If t is a term (of type T), that is to say, t is a correctly formed expression composed of constants, operator symbols, functions and so on, then the expression:

$$p[t/x]$$

denotes the predicate p with all free occurrences of x replaced by t. For example, if p is the predicate:

$$x > 10$$

then $p[12/x]$ (which can be read, 'p with 12 for x') is the statement $12 > 10$. This happens to be true. We could also write such substitutions as $p[1/x]$ which is equivalent to the false statement, $1 > 10$. Again, if p is the predicate:

$$x \in S \lor \forall x : T \bullet x \notin S$$

then:

$$p[t/x]$$

is the predicate:

$$t \in S \lor \forall x : T \bullet x \notin S$$

Notice that the bound occurrence of x does not change. A problem can arise when substituting a term which contains variables; this may be illustrated by considering the substitution of $x + 1$ for y in the predicate $\exists x : \mathrm{N} \bullet y \leq x$. If we substitute $x + 1$ for the free occurrence of y obtaining:

$$\exists x : \mathrm{N} \bullet x + 1 \leq x$$

then clearly something is wrong because the x which was free in the term $x+1$ has become trapped by the quantification in the predicate. Thus when substitutions are made it is required that none of the free variables of the term to be substituted should be trapped by quantifiers in the predicate. The problem can always be cured by renaming the quantified variables in the predicate; we shall assume that whenever we write $p[t/x]$ in the laws which follow then such renaming is done where necessary.

9.6.3   Laws for quantifiers

Since quantified statements are themselves propositions in that they are either true or false, the laws for propositions can be applied to them. For example, if we know that:

$$(\forall x : T \bullet p) \land (\forall x : U \bullet q)$$

the $\land$ elimination law could be used to deduce:

$$\forall x : T \bullet p$$

Again, given:

$$\exists y : T \bullet r$$

the rule for double negation says this is equivalent to:

$$\neg \neg (\exists y : T \bullet r)$$

Equivalences can also be used within a quantification, so this is also equivalent to:

$$\exists y : T \bullet \neg \neg r$$

Now we introduce some laws specifically for quantified statements.

A law for $\forall$

If we know that a property is true for all elements of a certain type then we can deduce that it is true for any particular term of that type. This is captured by the specialisation rule:

$$\frac{(\forall x : T \bullet p),\ t \in T}{p[t/x]} \quad SP$$

For example, suppose we know that $\forall n : \mathbf{N} \bullet n \geq 0$ then since we know that 10 is indeed a member of $\mathbf{N}$ we can deduce $10 \geq 0$ in the particular case of the number 10.

Laws for $\exists$

Saying that a property is true for at least one element of a type is the same as saying that it cannot be false for all elements:

$$\frac{\exists x : T \bullet p}{\neg \, \forall x : T \bullet \neg p} \quad Def\ \exists$$

The above rule defines existential quantification in terms of universal quantification. We can also introduce $\exists$ directly using the following law. If p holds for some term t, then there certainly exists some element for which it is true.

$$\frac{p[t/x],\ t \in T}{\exists x : T \bullet p} \quad \exists\, I$$

Thinking of p as a proposition with a vacant slot, the top line of this law is just p with its slot filled by some term t. The law says that if p is true for this particular term, then we can deduce that $\exists x : T \bullet p$. So, for example, since we know that $5 > 0$ and that $5 \in \mathbf{N}$, we can deduce that $\exists n : \mathbf{N} \bullet n > 0$.

A law that we will use frequently is the One Point Rule. This says that if we have an existentially quantified statement, part of which gives us an exact value for the quantified variable, then the quantification can be removed, replacing the variable by its known value wherever it appears. This law is often used in the simplification of preconditions; here it is:

$$\frac{\exists\, x : S \bullet (p \wedge x = t)}{t \in S \wedge p[t/x]} \quad (x \backslash t) \quad \textit{One Point Rule}$$

So, for example, $\exists\, n : \mathbf{N} \bullet (n < 10 \wedge n = 2 * 3)$ is equivalent to $2 * 3 \in \mathbf{N} \wedge 2 * 3 < 10$. The first part merely checks that the term is a member of the correct set. This requirement can usually be confirmed easily leaving just the predicate in which the substitution has been made, in this case $2 * 3 < 10$.

Laws for renaming quantified variables

Because quantified variables are only place holders marking vacant slots we can chose different ones without altering the meaning of the statement (providing the new name does not clash with any existing free variables):

$$\frac{\forall\, x : T \bullet p}{\forall\, y : T \bullet p[y/x]} \quad (y \backslash p, y \backslash T) \quad R\forall$$

$$\frac{\exists\, x : T \bullet p}{\exists\, y : T \bullet p[y/x]} \quad (y \backslash p, y \backslash T) \quad R\exists$$

So, $\forall\, x : \mathbf{N} \bullet \exists\, y : \mathbf{N} \bullet y > x$ is equivalent to $\forall\, m : \mathbf{N} \bullet \exists\, n : \mathbf{N} \bullet n > m$.

Laws for splitting quantified predicates

The following laws show how a proposition within a quantification can be split under separate quantifications:

$$\frac{\forall\, x : T \bullet p \wedge q}{\forall\, x : T \bullet p \wedge \forall\, x : T \bullet q} \quad Q1 \qquad \frac{\exists\, x : T \bullet p \vee q}{\exists\, x : T \bullet p \vee \exists\, x : T \bullet q} \quad Q2$$

$$\frac{\exists\, x : T \bullet p \Rightarrow q}{\forall\, x : T \bullet p \Rightarrow \exists\, x : T \bullet q} \quad Q3 \qquad \frac{\forall\, x : T \bullet p \Rightarrow q}{p \Rightarrow \forall\, x : T \bullet q} \quad (x \backslash p) \quad Q4$$

$$\frac{\forall\, x : T \bullet p \Rightarrow q}{(\exists\, x : T \bullet p) \Rightarrow q} \quad (x \backslash q) \quad Q5 \qquad \frac{(\forall\, x : T \bullet p) \vee (\forall\, x : T \bullet q)}{\forall\, x : T \bullet p \vee q} \quad Q6$$

$$\frac{\forall\, x : T \bullet p \Rightarrow q}{(\forall\, x : T \bullet p) \Rightarrow (\forall\, x : T \bullet q)} \quad Q7 \qquad \frac{\exists\, x : T \bullet p \wedge q}{(\exists\, x : T \bullet p) \wedge (\exists\, x : T \bullet q)} \quad Q8$$

Laws for changing the order of quantification

Where two quantifiers occur together it is sometimes possible to change the order of quantifications. These laws show when it is safe to do so:

$$\frac{\forall\, x : S \bullet \forall\, y : T \bullet p}{\forall\, y : T \bullet \forall\, x : S \bullet p} \quad (x\backslash T, y\backslash S) \quad Q9$$

$$\frac{\exists\, x : S \bullet \exists\, y : T \bullet p}{\exists\, y : T \bullet \exists\, x : S \bullet p} \quad (x\backslash T, y\backslash S) \quad Q10$$

$$\frac{\exists\, x : S \bullet \forall\, y : T \bullet p}{\forall\, y : T \bullet \exists\, x : S \bullet p} \quad (x\backslash T, y\backslash S) \quad Q11$$

Laws for *true* and *false*

The laws given earlier for *true* and *false* can be extended to quantified statements:

$$\frac{\forall\, x : T \bullet \mathit{true}}{\mathit{true}} \quad TF6 \qquad\qquad \frac{\exists\, x : T \bullet \mathit{false}}{\mathit{false}} \quad TF7$$

Laws for quantification over non-empty sets

Finally, here are some laws which may be used when quantifying over a set T, known to be non-empty. The first two laws show how to deal with superfluous quantification. The third says that if a property is known to be true of all elements of T then there is certainly some element of T with that property. The last law shows how two existential quantifications connected by implication may be joined.

$$\frac{\forall\, x : T \bullet p}{p} \quad (x\backslash p,\ T \text{ non-empty}) \quad S\forall$$

$$\frac{\exists\, x : T \bullet p}{p} \quad (x\backslash p,\ T \text{ non-empty}) \quad S\exists$$

$$\frac{\forall\, x : T \bullet p}{\exists\, x : T \bullet p} \quad (T \text{ non-empty}) \quad Q12$$

$$\frac{(\exists\, x : T \bullet p) \Rightarrow (\exists\, x : T \bullet q)}{\exists\, x : T \bullet p \Rightarrow q} \quad (T \text{ non-empty}) \quad Q13$$

9.6.4 Examples using laws for predicates

Here are some examples of reasoning using the laws for predicates (and those for propositions too).

1. Show that:
$$\frac{\forall\, x : T \bullet p \Rightarrow q}{(\forall\, x : T \bullet \neg\, q) \Rightarrow (\forall\, x : T \bullet \neg\, p)}$$

We first use an equivalence about propositions (the contra-positive law) to transform the proposition within the quantification. Then one of the laws on splitting up quantifications can be applied:

$$
\begin{array}{lll}
(1) & \forall\, x : T \bullet p \Rightarrow q & \text{H} \\
(2) & \forall\, x : T \bullet \neg\, q \Rightarrow \neg\, p & CP \\
(3) & (\forall\, x : T \bullet \neg\, q) \Rightarrow (\forall\, x : T \bullet \neg\, p) & Q7
\end{array}
$$

2. Show that: $\dfrac{\forall\, x : T \bullet p}{\neg\, \exists\, x : T \bullet \neg\, p}$

This is an equivalence very similar to the law, *Def* $\exists$. If we use the law of double negation twice to introduce $\neg$, we will then be able to use *Def* $\exists$ to reach the required form:

$$
\begin{array}{ll}
\forall\, x : T \bullet p & \\
\quad \equiv \neg\,\neg\,\forall\, x : T \bullet p & [DN] \\
\quad \equiv \neg\,\neg\,\forall\, x : T \bullet \neg\,\neg\, p & [DN] \\
\quad \equiv \neg\, \exists\, x : T \bullet \neg\, p & [Def\ \exists]
\end{array}
$$

3. Show that: $\dfrac{\forall\, x : T \bullet p \wedge q}{p \wedge \forall\, x : T \bullet q}$ ($x \backslash p$, T non-empty)

Here we have to show that, assuming the side-condition of x not being free in p holds, we can split up the quantification as shown. We can use law Q1 to split up a universal quantification with $\wedge$. Then the assumption that x is not free in p allows us to dispense with that redundant quantification:

$$
\begin{array}{ll}
\forall\, x : T \bullet p \wedge q & \\
\quad \equiv (\forall\, x : T \bullet p) \wedge (\forall\, x : T \bullet q) & [Q1] \\
\quad \equiv p \wedge \forall\, x : T \bullet q & [S\forall\ \ (x \backslash p\, T,\ \text{non-empty})]
\end{array}
$$

4. Show that: $\dfrac{\forall\, x : T \bullet p \vee q}{p \vee \forall\, x : T \bullet q}$ ($x \backslash p$)

We do not have an equivalence which allows us to split up $\forall\, x : T \bullet p \vee q$ directly, but if we rewrite the $\vee$ statement in terms of $\Rightarrow$ we should be able to progress by using the laws for universal quantification with $\Rightarrow$:

$$
\begin{array}{ll}
\forall\, x : T \bullet p \vee q & \\
\quad \equiv \forall\, x : T \bullet \neg\,\neg\, p \vee q & [DN] \\
\quad \equiv \forall\, x : T \bullet \neg\, p \Rightarrow q & [\Rightarrow Equiv] \\
\quad \equiv \neg\, p \Rightarrow \forall\, x : T \bullet q & [Q4\ \ (x \backslash \neg\, p)]
\end{array}
$$

$$\equiv \neg \neg p \lor \forall x : T \bullet q \qquad\qquad [\Rightarrow Equiv]$$
$$\equiv p \lor \forall x : T \bullet q \qquad\qquad [DN]$$

Note that to apply law Q4 we have to show that its side-condition $x \backslash \neg p$ is met. This is satisfied since we know that $x \backslash p$ and this means that $x \backslash \neg p$ also.

Exercise 9.15 $\diamond$ Say which occurrences of the variables x and y are free and which are bound in the following:

   (i) $(\exists y : \mathbb{N} \bullet y > 2) \land (\forall x : \mathbb{N} \bullet x + 1 > x)$

   (ii) $x = 2 * y$

   (iii) $(\exists y : \mathbb{N} \bullet y > 2) \land (\exists x : \mathbb{N} \bullet x > y)$

   (iv) $\forall x : \mathbb{N} \bullet ((\exists y : \mathbb{N} \bullet y > x) \land x = 2 * y)$

Exercise 9.16 Laws Q6, Q7, Q8 and Q11 are not equivalences; they work in one direction only. Give examples to show in each case why an equivalence would not be appropriate. (Hint: you need to find a situation where the bottom line of the law is true, but the top is false.)

Exercise 9.17 $\diamond$ Laws Q9, Q10 and Q11 have side-conditions that $x \backslash T$ and $y \backslash S$. Find examples where S and T do not obey these conditions (that is, S is an expression with free occurrences of y and T has free occurrences of x) to show why these conditions are necessary.

Exercise 9.18 Refer to Section 2.2.3 where the possibility of changing the order of quantifications is discussed. Is there any conflict between what was said there and laws Q9, Q10 and Q11?

Exercise 9.19 Prove the following laws:

   (i) $\dfrac{\exists x : T \bullet p \lor q}{p \lor \exists x : T \bullet q}$ $(x \backslash p, T$ non-empty$)$

   (ii) $\dfrac{\exists x : T \bullet p \land q}{p \land \exists x : T \bullet q}$ $(x \backslash p)$

   (iii) $\dfrac{\exists x : T \bullet p \Rightarrow q}{p \Rightarrow \exists x : T \bullet q}$ $(x \backslash p, T$ non-empty$)$

9.7   A library of laws

To be able to prove theorems about Z specifications we need more than just the basic logical laws. We need laws which tell us how to deal with the various constructs encountered in a specification, such as numbers, sets, relations, functions and sequences. Some of the properties that are needed are commonly used results of arithmetic or basic set theory. For instance, we might happily use the fact that $x + 0 = x$ for any number x, or that $S \subseteq S$ for any set S. Other properties may seem a little less obvious. It may be that:

$$\mathrm{dom}\, f \cap \mathrm{dom}\, g = \emptyset \Rightarrow f \oplus g = f \cup g$$

is just the property needed to complete a certain proof. But is it true? In theory, all laws such as these can be proved from their Z definitions, but in practice it would be very tedious to go back to first principles every time. What is needed is a library of useful laws which, having been proved once, can be used by everyone without fear of unsoundness. Such a collection of basic laws for Z is contained in the *The Z Notation: A Reference Manual* [Spi92]. This is an excellent starting point for anyone proving theorems in Z. We do not reproduce the library of laws here. There are several hundred laws in the reference manual but only a few will be needed for our introductory examples.

Whilst the library contains quite a number of laws it will always be the case that some results we require do not appear in it. This does not necessarily mean that we are mistaken in thinking that the property really is a law, but the library is finite and cannot contain everything. When this happens it is possible to prove the missing law using the Z definitions and the existing laws. Here is the selection of laws which will be useful in the following proofs.

Firstly, a general property of set membership. An element is a member of a set exactly when it obeys the defining predicate of the set:

$$\frac{z \in \{x : X \mid p\}}{z \in X \wedge p[z/x]} \qquad\qquad [L1]$$

For instance, saying that $n \in \{x : Even \mid x > 8\}$ is equivalent to saying $n \in Even \wedge n > 8$.

Next we have a selection of laws taken from the reference manual. They hold for all sets S, T and relations f, g. The first of these is an equivalence concerning sets:

$$\frac{S \subseteq T}{S \in \mathbb{P}\, T} \qquad\qquad [L2]$$

The rest are facts about sets and relations. No hypotheses are needed to establish them, so they could be stated either as deduction laws with the part above the line empty, or as equivalences with *true*. To save space we just state the facts themselves:

$$\emptyset \subseteq S \qquad\qquad\qquad\qquad\qquad\qquad\qquad\qquad\qquad\qquad [L3]$$
$$x \notin \emptyset \qquad\qquad\qquad\qquad\qquad\qquad\qquad\qquad\qquad\qquad\quad [L4]$$
$$\text{dom } \emptyset = \emptyset \qquad\qquad\qquad\qquad\qquad\qquad\qquad\qquad\qquad [L5]$$
$$\text{ran } \emptyset = \emptyset \qquad\qquad\qquad\qquad\qquad\qquad\qquad\qquad\quad\; [L6]$$
$$\text{dom } (f \cup g) = \text{dom } f \cup \text{dom } g \qquad\qquad\qquad\quad [L7]$$
$$S \vartriangleleft (f \cup g) = (S \vartriangleleft f) \cup (S \vartriangleleft g) \qquad\qquad\quad\; [L8]$$

The first two are simple laws about sets. The second two say that the domain and range of the empty relation must themselves both be empty. *L7* says that taking the union of two relations and then finding the resulting domain is equivalent to finding the domains of the two relations first and putting them together. Finally, taking the union of two relations and then subtracting part of the domain is equivalent to performing the domain subtraction on the relations separately and unioning the results together.

The following laws are not in the reference manual, although *L9* is really just another way of stating *L4*:

$$\frac{x \in \emptyset}{\textit{false}} \qquad\qquad\qquad\qquad\qquad\qquad\qquad\qquad\qquad [L9]$$

and here are some facts about the empty set:

$$\forall\, x : \emptyset \bullet p \qquad\qquad\qquad\qquad\qquad\qquad\qquad\qquad\; [L10]$$
$$\emptyset \in \mathbb{P}\, S \qquad\qquad\qquad\qquad\qquad\qquad\qquad\qquad\quad [L11]$$
$$\emptyset \in S \rightarrowtail T \qquad\qquad\qquad\qquad\qquad\qquad\qquad\quad [L12]$$

We now go on to show how laws *L9* to *L12* can be proved from the given laws. The first three are simple, but the fourth will require more work. For the first we are required to show equivalence with *false*; for the remaining three we take the approach that to establish a statement as a fact it is sufficient to show that it is equivalent to *true*.

Proof of law *L9*

$$\frac{x \in \emptyset}{\textit{false}}$$

We start with $x \in \emptyset$ and use a law about *true* to add the conjunct *true*. For any x we know from *L4* that $x \notin \emptyset$ is always equivalent to *true* and so we replace *true* in the following line. This gives a self-contradictory statement which is equivalent to *false*.

$$x \in \emptyset$$
$$\equiv x \in \emptyset \wedge \mathit{true} \qquad\qquad\qquad [TF1]$$
$$\equiv x \in \emptyset \wedge x \notin \emptyset \qquad\qquad\qquad [L4]$$
$$\equiv \mathit{false} \qquad\qquad\qquad [F\ Equiv]$$

Proof of law $L10$

$$\forall\, x : \emptyset \bullet p$$

Remember that declaring $x : S$ for any set S is equivalent to saying that x is of the underlying type of S, and also that it is a member of S itself. For instance, declaring $n : Even$ is the same as $n : \mathbb{N} \mid n \in Even$. Using this we can start to work on the proof, taking X to be the generic type of the empty set. To allow more explanation of what is happening in the proof we add comments in square brackets.

$$\forall\, x : \emptyset \bullet p$$
$$\equiv \textit{[Expanding the type abbreviation for } \emptyset \textit{]}$$
$$\forall\, x : X \mid x \in \emptyset \bullet p$$
$$\equiv \textit{[Rewriting the quantified expression]}$$
$$\forall\, x : X \bullet x \in \emptyset \Rightarrow p$$
$$\equiv \textit{[Using the law we have just proved]}$$
$$\forall\, x : X \bullet \mathit{false} \Rightarrow p \qquad\qquad\qquad [L9]$$
$$\equiv \textit{[Using a property of false]}$$
$$\forall\, x : X \bullet \mathit{true} \qquad\qquad\qquad [\text{Ex. }9.10(v)]$$
$$\equiv \textit{[Using predicate law for true]}$$
$$\mathit{true} \qquad\qquad\qquad [TF6]$$

Proof of law $L11$

$$\emptyset \in \mathbb{P}\, S$$

We prove this law by showing that $\emptyset \in \mathbb{P}\, S$ is equivalent to *true* for any set S. We need to show that the empty set is a member of $\mathbb{P}\, S$. Law L2 says that being a member of $\mathbb{P}\, S$ is equivalent to being a subset of S, so we can use this rule to obtain an equivalent goal. We are then left to prove that the empty set is a subset of S, and this is true by law $L3$. This justification is presented as follows:

$$\emptyset \in \mathbb{P}\, S$$
$$\equiv \emptyset \subseteq S \qquad\qquad\qquad [L2]$$
$$\equiv \mathit{true} \qquad\qquad\qquad [L3]$$

Proof of law $L12$

$$\emptyset \in S \rightarrowtail T$$

This law says that the empty relation can be regarded as a partial injective function. To show it is true we need to show that $\emptyset$ obeys the requirements for being a partial function and for being injective. Recall that a function must have no element of its domain related to more than one element of the range. The empty relation certainly satisfies this since it relates no elements at all. To be injective no element in the range can be related to more than one element of the domain. Again, the empty set fits the bill.

We may feel satisfied with this level of justification, but can if required set down a more rigorous proof. This turns out to be quite lengthy, but we give it in full detail as an example. The strategy follows the explanation above; we use the definition of what it is to be a partial injective function and then show that the empty set meets the requirements.

$\emptyset \in S \rightarrowtail T$

   $\equiv$ *[Replacing $\rightarrowtail$ with its definition]*

   $\quad \emptyset \in \{f : S \nrightarrow T \mid \forall x, y : \mathrm{dom}\, f \bullet f\, x = f\, y \Rightarrow x = y\}$

   $\equiv$ *[Membership of a set is equivalent to satisfying the set predicate]*

   $\quad \emptyset \in S \nrightarrow T \wedge \forall x, y : \mathrm{dom}\, \emptyset \bullet \emptyset\, x = \emptyset\, y \Rightarrow x = y$ $\hfill [L1]$

   $\equiv$ *[The domain of the empty function is the empty set]*

   $\quad \emptyset \in S \nrightarrow T \wedge \forall x, y : \emptyset \bullet \emptyset\, x = \emptyset\, y \Rightarrow x = y$ $\hfill [L5]$

   $\equiv$ *[Universal quantification over the empty set is vacuously true]*

   $\quad \emptyset \in S \nrightarrow T \wedge \mathit{true}$ $\hfill [L10]$

   $\equiv$ *[Property of true]*

   $\quad \emptyset \in S \nrightarrow T$ $\hfill [TF1]$

   $\equiv$ *[Now use the definition of $\nrightarrow$]*

   $\quad \emptyset \in \{f : S \leftrightarrow T \mid \forall x : S;\, y, z : T \bullet$

   $\quad\qquad (x \mapsto y) \in f \wedge (x \mapsto z) \in f \Rightarrow y = z\}$

   $\equiv$ *[Again, membership is equivalent to satisfying the set predicate]*

   $\quad \emptyset \in S \leftrightarrow T \wedge$

   $\quad \forall x : S;\, y, z : T \bullet (x \mapsto y) \in \emptyset \wedge (x \mapsto z) \in \emptyset \Rightarrow y = z$ $\hfill [L1]$

   $\equiv$ *[Using the definition of $\leftrightarrow$]*

   $\quad \emptyset \in \mathbb{P}(S \times T) \wedge$

   $\quad \forall x : S;\, y, z : T \bullet (x \mapsto y) \in \emptyset \wedge (x \mapsto z) \in \emptyset \Rightarrow y = z$

   $\equiv$ *[A powerset includes the empty set]*

   $\quad \mathit{true} \wedge$

   $\quad \forall x : S;\, y, z : T \bullet (x \mapsto y) \in \emptyset \wedge (x \mapsto z) \in \emptyset \Rightarrow y = z$ $\hfill [L11]$

$\equiv$ *[Property of true]*
$$\forall x : S; \, y, z : T \bullet (x \mapsto y) \in \emptyset \land (x \mapsto z) \in \emptyset \Rightarrow y = z \qquad [TF1]$$

$\equiv$ *[The empty set cannot have any members]*
$$\forall x : S; \, y, z : T \bullet \mathit{false} \land \mathit{false} \Rightarrow y = z \qquad [L9]$$

$\equiv$ *[Property of false]*
$$\forall x : S; \, y, z : T \bullet \mathit{false} \Rightarrow y = z \qquad [TF2]$$

$\equiv$ *[Property of true]*
$$\forall x : S; \, y, z : T \bullet \mathit{true} \qquad [Ex. \ 9.10(v)]$$

$\equiv$ *[Property of true]*
$$\mathit{true} \qquad [TF6]$$

This proof shows that the empty function satisfies the conditions for being a partial function, and for being injective. If in the future we need to use these properties we will know immediately that they are true because of the detailed proof given here. This proof is long because each small step has been made explicit. It is often convenient to take several small steps together on a single line of a proof, as long as this does not obscure what is happening.

Another point to note is that the proof has been presented in one large chunk. With hindsight it is often possible to see a better structure for a proof. We could, for instance, have first proved that:

$$\emptyset \in S \nrightarrow T$$

as a separate theorem. This result would then have been available to use in the proof of the main theorem. The same work has to be done, but it is split into more tractable steps.

9.8   Examples of reasoning about a specification

In this section we consider some examples from the Football Identity Scheme specification. Theorems are stated and then proved using the laws introduced in this chapter. Some proof steps are given informal justifications only in an attempt to make the proofs easier to follow.

9.8.1   An initialisation theorem

Earlier, we saw the statement of this theorem:

$$\vdash \exists \mathit{Fid}' \bullet \mathit{InitFid}$$

and its expansion to:

$$\vdash \exists\, members' : ID \nrightarrow PERSON;\; banned' : \mathbb{P}\,ID \mid$$
$$banned' \subseteq \mathrm{dom}\ members' \bullet$$
$$members' = \emptyset \wedge banned' = \emptyset$$

We can now give a fuller justification of it. Remember that the syntax here is equivalent to:

$$\vdash \exists\, members' : ID \nrightarrow PERSON;\; banned' : \mathbb{P}\,ID \bullet$$
$$banned' \subseteq \mathrm{dom}\ members' \wedge members' = \emptyset \wedge banned' = \emptyset$$

The goal is a statement quantifying over *members'* and *banned'* and which has explicit values for these variables (namely, $\emptyset$ in both cases). We can therefore use the One Point Rule twice to obtain a simpler, equivalent goal. Remember that to apply the One Point Rule we must:

(a) show that the terms we are substituting are members of the correct types;

(b) substitute these known terms into the predicate wherever they occur.

From (a) we obtain two parts of a new equivalent goal, namely:

$$\emptyset \in ID \nrightarrow PERSON$$
$$\emptyset \in \mathbb{P}\,ID$$

From (b) we obtain a further requirement, $\emptyset \subseteq \mathrm{dom}\,\emptyset$, so that we now have the goal:

$$\vdash \emptyset \in ID \nrightarrow PERSON \wedge \emptyset \in \mathbb{P}\,ID \wedge \emptyset \subseteq \mathrm{dom}\ \emptyset$$

The application of the One Point Rule may seem complicated, but the rule is so useful that it is worth getting to know the technique.

We can now use some of the laws of previous sections to prove each of the three parts of our goal. In fact, we have done all the work already. The first part follows immediately by law L12. Similarly the second part is true as a result of L11. The third part follows from L3. Hence the goal is true.

9.8.2   Simplifying a precondition

Remember that the precondition of an operation describes the set of starting states from which the operation is guaranteed to perform correctly. A precondition is calculated by removing the after-state variables from the declaration part of the schema describing the operation and existentially quantifying them in the predicate part. So, for the schema:

$$\begin{array}{l} \underline{\quad AddMember \quad\quad\quad\quad\quad\quad\quad\quad\quad\quad\quad\quad\quad\quad\quad\quad\quad} \\ \quad Fid;\ Fid' \\ \quad applicant?:PERSON \\ \quad id!:ID \\ \overline{\quad applicant? \notin \mathrm{ran}\ members} \\ \quad id! \notin \mathrm{dom}\ members \\ \quad members' = members \cup \{id! \mapsto applicant?\} \\ \quad banned' = banned \end{array}$$

the precondition is given by:

$$\begin{array}{l} \underline{\quad PreAddMember \quad\quad\quad\quad\quad\quad\quad\quad\quad\quad\quad\quad\quad\quad\quad} \\ \quad Fid \\ \quad applicant?:PERSON \\ \overline{\quad \exists\, Fid';\ id!:ID \bullet} \\ \quad\quad applicant? \notin \mathrm{ran}\ members\ \wedge \\ \quad\quad id! \notin \mathrm{dom}\ members\ \wedge \\ \quad\quad members' = members \cup \{id! \mapsto applicant?\}\ \wedge \\ \quad\quad banned' = banned \end{array}$$

When a precondition is found in this way it is often the case that the predicate part of the schema is more complicated than it need be and that it can be simplified using equivalences. Remember that the schema, *Fid*, is included in the declaration part of the precondition schema. This means that the variables of *Fid* are visible and that its predicate is available and may be used at any stage during the simplification. We start the simplification of the precondition predicate by first expanding the reference to *Fid'*:

$$\exists\, members':ID \nrightarrow PERSON;\ banned':\mathbb{P}\,ID;\ id!:ID \bullet$$
$$\quad banned' \subseteq \mathrm{dom}\ members'\ \wedge$$
$$\quad applicant? \notin \mathrm{ran}\ members\ \wedge$$
$$\quad id! \notin \mathrm{dom}\ members\ \wedge$$
$$\quad members' = members \cup \{id! \mapsto applicant?\}\ \wedge$$
$$\quad banned' = banned$$

The quantified variables *members'* and *banned'* are given explicit values and so the One Point Rule can be applied to both of these. This is not true of *id!*. It is not given a value and so the One Point Rule is not applicable. Applying the rule we get:

$$\exists\, id!:ID \bullet$$

$members \cup \{id! \mapsto applicant?\} \in ID \rightarrowtail PERSON \wedge$
$banned \in \mathbb{P} ID \wedge$
$banned \subseteq \mathrm{dom}\ (members \cup \{id! \mapsto applicant?\}) \wedge$
$applicant? \notin \mathrm{ran}\ members \wedge$
$id! \notin \mathrm{dom}\ members$

$\equiv$ *[Fid ensures banned $\in \mathbb{P} ID$ so that requirement is redundant]*

  $\exists id! : ID \bullet$

   $members \cup \{id! \mapsto applicant?\} \in ID \rightarrowtail PERSON \wedge$
   $banned \subseteq \mathrm{dom}\ (members \cup \{id! \mapsto applicant?\}) \wedge$
   $applicant? \notin \mathrm{ran}\ members \wedge$
   $id! \notin \mathrm{dom}\ members$ [Using *Fid*]

$\equiv$ *[Property of domains]*

  $\exists id! : ID \bullet$

   $members \cup \{id! \mapsto applicant?\} \in ID \rightarrowtail PERSON \wedge$
   $banned \subseteq \mathrm{dom}\ members \cup \mathrm{dom}\ \{id! \mapsto applicant?\} \wedge$
   $applicant? \notin \mathrm{ran}\ members \wedge$
   $id! \notin \mathrm{dom}\ members$ [*L7*]

$\equiv$ *[Fid ensures banned $\subseteq \mathrm{dom}\ members$]*

  $\exists id! : ID \bullet$

   $members \cup \{id! \mapsto applicant?\} \in ID \rightarrowtail PERSON \wedge$
   $applicant? \notin \mathrm{ran}\ members \wedge$
   $id! \notin \mathrm{dom}\ members$

This is not the end of the road; we pause to consider the way forward. So far, progress has been made using the One Point Rule and facts from *Fid*. There is another tactic which is often useful in these situations. If one conjunct can be shown to follow as a result of the others it can be omitted since it adds no further information. We could justify this with the following rule:

$$\frac{p \wedge q}{p} \quad (q \text{ follows from } p)$$

Note that the side-condition, in effect, requires a subproof. In our case, we can use this technique to remove the conjunct:

$$members \cup \{id! \mapsto applicant?\} \in ID \rightarrowtail PERSON$$

We know from *Fid* that $members \in ID \rightarrowtail PERSON$. The other conjuncts tell us that $id! \notin \mathrm{dom}\ members$ and $applicant? \notin \mathrm{ran}\ members$. This means that we are adding a completely new pair to an injective function, so the result must itself be an injective function. This is the very property given by the first conjunct which has therefore been shown to be redundant. This leaves:

$\exists\, id! : ID \bullet$
  $applicant? \notin \text{ran } members \land$
  $id! \notin \text{dom } members$
    $\equiv [id!$ *does not appear in the first conjunct]*
      $applicant? \notin \text{ran } members \land$
      $\exists\, id! : ID \bullet id! \notin \text{dom } members$ [Ex. 9.19(ii)]

Both parts of this remaining predicate are necessary. We could obtain a further slight simplification by noting that the second part is true exactly when dom *members* is not the whole of *ID*; then and only then will there exist a suitable *id!* not in dom *members*. So we are left with the predicate:

$applicant? \notin \text{ran } members \land \text{dom } members \neq ID$

The simplified version of the schema describing the precondition is thus:

```
┌─ PreAddMember ─────────────────────────────────────
│ Fid
│ applicant? : PERSON
├────────────────────────────────────────────────────
│ applicant? ∉ ran members
│ dom members ≠ ID
└────────────────────────────────────────────────────
```

So for the *AddMember* operation to work successfully it is necessary that the applicant is not already a member and that there is an *ID* left to allocate.

9.8.3 Proving a property of a specification

We wish to prove that adding a member to the system, followed by immediately deleting the same member leaves the state of the system unchanged. The statement of this theorem is:

$AddMember \,_9^\circ\, DeleteMember \mid id! = id? \vdash \Xi Fid$

This states that if the *AddMember* operation is composed with *DeleteMember*, ensuring that the identifier output from the first is the one that will be input to the second, then we can prove that *Fid* remains unchanged.

The schema ΞFid is used in the theorem as a predicate. We must first check that the variables it declares are in scope, and this involves investigating the expression to the left of the turnstile. Remember that the schema:

$AddMember \,_9^\circ\, DeleteMember \mid id! = id?$

is obtained by identifying the after-state variables of *AddMember* with the before-state variables of *DeleteMember* and hiding them. This gives the following schema:

```
┌─ AddandDelete ────────────────────────────────────
│ ΔFid
│ applicant? : PERSON
│ id? : ID; id! : ID
├────────────────────────────────────────────────────
│ ∃ Fid″ •
│         applicant? ∈ ran members ∧
│         id! ∉ dom members ∧
│         members″ = members ∪ {id! ↦ applicant?} ∧
│         banned″ = banned ∧
│         id? ∈ dom members″ ∧
│         id? ∉ banned″ ∧
│         members′ = {id?} ⊲ members″ ∧
│         banned′ = banned″ ∧
│         id! = id?
└────────────────────────────────────────────────────
```

If we expand *Fid″* this becomes:

```
┌─ AddandDelete ────────────────────────────────────
│ ΔFid
│ applicant? : PERSON
│ id? : ID
│ id! : ID
├────────────────────────────────────────────────────
│ ∃ members″ : ID ⇸ PERSON; banned″ : ℙ ID •
│         banned″ ⊆ dom members″ ∧
│         applicant? ∈ ran members ∧
│         id! ∉ dom members ∧
│         members″ = members ∪ {id! ↦ applicant?} ∧
│         banned″ = banned ∧
│         id? ∈ dom members″ ∧
│         id? ∉ banned″ ∧
│         members′ = {id?} ⊲ members″ ∧
│         banned′ = banned″ ∧
│         id! = id?
└────────────────────────────────────────────────────
```

The inclusion of Δ*Fid* ensures that its variables are in scope and that the relationship between them required by *Fid* holds. Since this is the case we can safely interpret Ξ*Fid* on the right of the turnstile as a predicate.

The predicate part of the hypothesis is an existentially quantified statement which can be simplified using the One Point Rule. This gives the equivalent predicate:

$members \cup \{id! \mapsto applicant?\} \in ID \twoheadrightarrow PERSON$
$banned \in \mathbb{P}\, ID$
$banned \subseteq dom(members \cup \{id! \mapsto applicant?\})$
$applicant? \in ran\ members$
$id! \notin dom\ members$
$id? \in dom\ (members \cup \{id! \mapsto applicant?\})$
$id? \notin banned''$
$members' = \{id?\} \triangleleft (members \cup \{id! \mapsto applicant?\})$
$banned' = banned$
$id! = id?$

With the expansion and simplification carried out so far we can rewrite the statement of the theorem as follows:

$\Delta Fid;\ applicant? : PERSON;\ id? : ID;\ id! : ID\ |$
   $members \cup \{id! \mapsto applicant?\} \in ID \twoheadrightarrow PERSON$
   $banned \in \mathbb{P}\, ID$
   $banned \subseteq dom(members \cup \{id! \mapsto applicant?\})$
   $applicant? \in ran\ members$
   $id! \notin dom\ members$
   $id? \in dom\ (members \cup \{id! \mapsto applicant?\})$
   $id? \notin banned''$
   $members' = \{id?\} \triangleleft (members \cup \{id! \mapsto applicant?\})$
   $banned' = banned$
   $id! = id?$

$\vdash$

   $members' = members \land banned' = banned$

We must now show how the conclusion follows from the hypotheses. The fact that $banned' = banned$ follows immediately since it *is* one of the hypotheses. For the other part we start by using another of the hypotheses and argue as follows:

$members' = \{id?\} \triangleleft (members \cup \{id! \mapsto applicant?\})$
   $\equiv$ *[Since id! = id? from the hypotheses]*
       $members' = \{id!\} \triangleleft (members \cup \{id! \mapsto applicant?\})$
   $\equiv$ *[Using law L8]*
       $members' = (\{id!\} \triangleleft members) \cup (\{id!\} \triangleleft \{id! \mapsto applicant?\})$
   $\equiv$ *[If id! is removed from dom\{id! \mapsto applicant?\} nothing is left]*

$$members' = \{id!\} \lhd members \cup \emptyset$$
$$\equiv \textit{[Adding in empty set has no effect]}$$
$$members' = \{id!\} \lhd members$$
$$\equiv \textit{[Since id! is not in } \mathrm{dom}\ members\textit{]}$$
$$members' = members$$

So the goal follows from the hypotheses as required.

Exercise 9.20 If $S \mathrel{\hat{=}} [x : \mathbb{N}]$ calculate and simplify the preconditions of:

(i)

```
Op1
ΔS
x′ = x − 1
```

(ii)

```
Op2
ΔS
x′ = x + 1
```

(iii)

```
Op3
ΔS
(x = 0 ∧ x′ = 0)
∨
(x > 0 ∧ x′ = x − 1)
```

Exercise 9.21 ⋄ Calculate and simplify the precondition of operation *DeleteMember*.

Exercise 9.22 Is it true that *DeleteMember* ⨾ *AddMember* ⊢ Ξ*Fid*?

Exercise 9.23 Give a detailed proof for the theorem:

$$f : X \nrightarrow Y;\ x : X;\ y : Y \mid$$
$$x \notin \mathrm{dom}\ f$$
$$y \notin \mathrm{ran}\ f$$
$$\vdash$$
$$f \cup \{x \mapsto y\} \in X \nrightarrow Y$$

9.9   Further reading

In this chapter we have taken a somewhat informal approach to formal reasoning, since our purpose was to provide an introduction to the ideas and show their relevance in the context of formal specification. Nevertheless, the laws and proofs provided here do give a flavour of formal reasoning and of the level of detail required in a completely formal development. There are many books about logic which treat formal systems of reasoning from a more formal point of view; [Lem90] and [NS85] are good examples. Also, [WL88] may be consulted, especially the first chapter; the treatment is of course directed towards the use of formal reasoning in the context of software specification and development, and so is particularly valuable for our current purposes. It gives a very readable introduction to formal systems and presents a system of natural deduction. A system of reasoning with equivalences is given in [MV94]. An approach to defining a deductive system specifically for Z which includes laws for reasoning with schemas is given in the Z standard [BN92]. More information on the theory and practice of proof in Z can also be found in [Wor93].

Chapter 10

From specification to program: data and operation refinement

We have seen how the Z notation may be used to capture precisely a specification of the functional properties of a system to be developed. We have also seen how proofs about specifications arise and how they may be carried through formally. We now begin to think about how a specification might be used as the starting point for a process which has as its end point a computer program which behaves according to that specification. The process is often thought of as having two phases known as design and implementation; in as far as this is a useful distinction, the division is between major decisions about how a working system is to be produced, and the filling in of the details down to the level of individual instructions in a suitable programming language in accordance with those design decisions. Even when an informal (but systematic) approach to design and implementation is adopted, formal specification is worthwhile because the attempt to capture requirements in a precise mathematical language forces us to think much more carefully about those requirements, and thus some improvement in the quality of the end product should be possible. However, if highly reliable software is to be produced then the development method must also be formal since we must be able to validate rigorously each of the steps of the process, perhaps with the aid of a computerised proof assistant. Within the Z community the development method is usually referred to as refinement, since it is based on an underlying more precise notion of refinement which we shall explain in detail in the present chapter. The need to demonstrate that proposed refinements do indeed have the necessary properties will generate proof obligations, so that the ideas presented in the previous chapter will again be put to good use.

In this book our main emphasis is on specification; we would be happy to think that our readers were able to express themselves in Z with confidence after reading our book. Whole books could be written, and indeed are being written, about refinement, and the topic is very much a subject of continuing research, though many of the central ideas are by no means new. In this chapter and the following one we aim to do no more than to introduce the important issues and point the reader to where more information may be found. In the present chapter we look at the ideas of data refinement and operation refinement: here we are concerned with how the data might be represented in ways more amenable to computer processing. In the next chapter we look at how programming language instructions may be derived which will cause the machine to perform the operations in accordance with their more concrete descriptions.

10.1　What is refinement?

Suppose that a client and a system designer have agreed upon the formal specification of a system. What must now be done in order to fulfil a contract to supply an implemented system in accordance with this specification? Our answer here is that an implementor must do the following:

- Find a way to represent the states of the system as described by the specification (abstract states) within the machine (concrete states), and record the relationship between abstract states and corresponding concrete states.

- Provide for each system operation (abstract operation) a corresponding operation on the concrete states (concrete operation).

- Provide a program for the computer system which will cause the machine to perform the concrete operations when required to do so.

Note that the concrete states must be formally defined, since we must express the precise relationship between abstract and concrete states; this is necessary so that we can prove that the concrete operations are correct realisations of the abstract operation they purport to implement. The concrete states must be immediately representable in the machine, and so must be constructed using the kinds of data structures provided by the programming language we intend to use. This implies that in the last analysis we depend on a formal description of the programming language in order to know the properties of the data structures it provides and the effect upon those data structures of the programming language instructions. We also have to rely on the correctness of the compiler which translates the program into lower-level code.

We said earlier that the whole process of production of a correct implementation from a specification is often referred to as refinement; this usage is by extension of a more precise notion of refinement. Remember that a Z specification says nothing about the sequence of abstract operations which might occur; it merely describes each operation of the system as a change of state, from one valid state to another. Though the data undergoes a change of representation, as we move from abstract to concrete, each concrete operation must in some precise sense correctly mimic its abstract counterpart; expressing this more formally, we must provide for each abstract operation a concrete operation which refines it.

Of course, we must now make clear what we mean when we say that a concrete operation refines an abstract operation. Before we do this however, it will be helpful to define two simpler notions of refinement:

- firstly, for relations in the usual Z sense

- secondly, for operations on the same (abstract or concrete) state

There are two general requirements which will be manifested in slightly different ways in each of the three cases: we say that R is refined by S, which is written $R \sqsubseteq S$, if:

- when R is applicable then so is S

- when R is applicable but S is applied then the result is consistent with R

We call these criteria Applicability and Correctness, respectively. To put it another way, we say that R is refined by S if S has a domain of application at least as large as that of R and acts in accordance with R, though possibly reducing choice, within the domain of R.

An important property of refinement is transitivity, which is to say that for each of the different kinds of refinement mentioned above:

- if $R \sqsubseteq S$ and $S \sqsubseteq T$ then $R \sqsubseteq T$

This means that as we move from specification to implementation we can pass through intermediate levels of refinement in the secure knowledge that the final implementation will be correct so long as we maintain correctness between successive levels.

In the following two subsections we describe refinement of relations and of operations where no change of representation is concerned. The remainder of the chapter will then describe the notion of refinement where such a change of representation must be taken into account.

Exercise 10.1 ⋄ Argue that transitivity of refinement follows from the Applicability and Correctness criteria.

10.1.1   Refinement of relations

In the case of relations $Rel1$ and $Rel2$, both of type $X \leftrightarrow Y$, we say that $Rel1$ is refined by $Rel2$, written $Rel1 \sqsubseteq Rel2$, when the following two properties hold, corresponding respectively to the Applicability and Correctness criteria:

- dom $Rel1 \subseteq$ dom $Rel2$

- (dom $Rel1$) $\lhd Rel2 \subseteq Rel1$

which is to say that whenever $Rel1$ relates an x in X to some ys in Y then $Rel2$ relates that same x to some ys in Y and what is more the set of ys in the case of $Rel2$ is a non-empty subset of the set of ys in the case of $Rel1$.

As a first very simple example, suppose we have the sets *Shape* and *Colour* defined as follows:

$$Shape == \{round, square\}$$
$$Colour == \{red, blue, green\}$$

and the relations $R1$ and $R2$ defined thus:

$$R1 == \{blue \mapsto round, blue \mapsto square, red \mapsto round, red \mapsto square\}$$
$$R2 == \{red \mapsto round, blue \mapsto round, green \mapsto round\}$$

then $R1 \sqsubseteq R2$, since $R2$ extends the domain of $R1$ to allow for all three colours but reduces the choice of shape for colours within the domain of $R1$.

Another example might be drawn from the retail world. Suppose a chain of stores marketing fabrics of various kinds produces a catalogue which makes the following claim:

> All our stores keep in stock every item included in this catalogue, though in some cases a restricted range of colours will be available; we constantly add new lines and you may find new fabrics in the stores which are not yet included in the catalogue.

If we consider the relations:

$$BrentCrossStock : Fabric \leftrightarrow Colour$$

which corresponds to which fabrics are available in which colours in a certain store of the chain, and:

$$Catalogue : Fabric \leftrightarrow Colour$$

which corresponds to which fabrics are available in which colours according to the catalogue, then the claim guarantees that:

- dom *Catalogue* ⊆ dom *BrentCrossStock*

- (dom *Catalogue*) ◁ *BrentCrossStock* ⊆ *Catalogue*

which is exactly:

    Catalogue ⊑ *BrentCrossStock*

In Figure 10.1 we give a pictorial representation of the general situation when we have two relations R and S of type $X \leftrightarrow Y$ with $R \sqsubseteq S$. We show an element of X which is related by R to four elements of Y, but related by S to only two of those four elements.

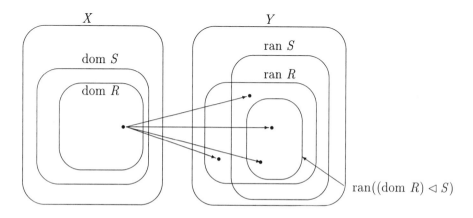

Figure 10.1: $R \sqsubseteq S$, where R, S are of type $X \leftrightarrow Y$, say

Here we have tried to illustrate the various possibilities which can arise: see the Exercise below.

Exercise 10.2 ◇ Give an example of precisely the situation illustrated in Figure 10.1; that is to say, define suitable instances of X, Y, R and S. Note that the uppermost of the four elements of Y must be related by S to some element of X other than the one shown, since it is in the range of S but not in the range of (dom R) ◁ S.

10.1.2   Refinement of operations on the same state

Turning now to the refinement relation for operations described by schemas referring to the same state, abstract or concrete, we may recast the Applicability and Correctness criteria as follows: we say that $Op1 \sqsubseteq Op2$ when:

- pre $Op1 \vdash$ pre $Op2$

- pre $Op1 \wedge Op2 \vdash Op1$

Recall that pre Op applies existential quantification to the after state components and any output variables of Op; furthermore, when we write a schema on the left of $\vdash$, its declarations are treated as declarations whose scope is the whole theorem, and when a schema is written on the right of $\vdash$, its variables must already be declared and only its predicate is used. The two theorems given above may thus be expressed informally as follows:

- When $Op1$ is applicable so is $Op2$.

- When $Op1$ is applicable in state S and $Op2$ is applied, relating S to state S', then $Op1$ also relates S to S'.

Comparing this definition with that for refinement of relations, we see that the set of states satisfying pre Op for an operation Op is the analogue of the domain of a relation. A simple example will make clear what is going on. Consider the following two schemas which describe very simple operations on a state whose only component is x:

$$
\begin{array}{l}
\underline{\quad ChooseSmaller \quad} \\
\hline
x, x', y?, z! : \mathbb{N} \\
\hline
0 < x' < x \\
z! \leq x + y?
\end{array}
$$

$$
\begin{array}{l}
\underline{\quad AlwaysOne \quad} \\
\hline
x, x', y?, z! : \mathbb{N} \\
\hline
x' = 1 \\
z! = 2 + y?
\end{array}
$$

Informally, whenever $\exists x' : \mathbb{N} \bullet 0 < x' < x$, we know that $2 \leq x$ and then $x' = 1$ is a particular value which satisfies the requirement that $0 < x' < x$; if we go on to choose $z' = 2 + y?$ then this also satisfies $z' \leq x + y?$. Now, arguing more formally, we must first show that $ChooseSmaller \sqsubseteq AlwaysOne$. Then the requirement that pre $ChooseSmaller \vdash$ pre $AlwaysOne$ amounts to:

$$
\begin{array}{l}
x, y? : \mathbb{N} \mid \\
\qquad \exists x', z! : \mathbb{N} \bullet 0 < x' < x \wedge z! \leq x + y? \\
\vdash \\
\qquad \exists x', z! : \mathbb{N} \bullet x' = 1 \wedge z! = 2 + y?
\end{array}
$$

Since explicit non-negative integer values are given for the existentially quantified variables x' and $z!$ in the conclusion of the theorem, there is nothing to prove; in fact:

$$x, y? : \mathbb{N} \vdash \text{pre } AlwaysOne$$

The requirement that pre *ChooseSmaller* $\wedge$ *AlwaysOne* $\vdash$ *ChooseSmaller* expands to:

$$x, x', y?, z! : \mathbb{N} \mid$$
$$\quad \exists x', z! : \mathbb{N} \bullet 0 < x' < x \wedge z! \leq x + y?$$
$$\quad x' = 1$$
$$\quad z! = 2 + y?$$
$$\vdash$$
$$\quad 0 < x' < x$$
$$\quad z! \leq x + y?$$

where the vertical stacking signifies conjunction where that is appropriate, a convention we shall use throughout this chapter. From $\exists x', z! : \mathbb{N} \bullet 0 < x' < x$ we may deduce that $1 < x$ or equivalently $2 \leq x$. From $x' = 1$ we can then deduce that:

$$0 < x' < x$$

Taking $z! = 2 + y?$ together with $2 \leq x$ we may then deduce:

$$z! \leq x + y?$$

Exercise 10.3 $\diamond$ Consider the three relations:

$$R == \{x, y, z, n1, n2 : \mathbb{N}_1 \mid x = n1 * z \wedge y = n2 * z \bullet x \mapsto y\}$$
$$S1 == \{x, y : \mathbb{N} \mid x = y > 0\}$$
$$S2 == \{x, n : \mathbb{N} \mid n > 0 \bullet x \mapsto n * x\}$$

Show that $R \sqsubseteq S1$ and that $R \sqsubseteq S2$. Also argue that neither of $S1$ and $S2$ is a refinement of the other.

Exercise 10.4 $\diamond$ Consider the two operations described by the following schemas:

```
┌─ IncludeInput ─────────────────────────────────────
│ x, x' : ℙ N
│ y?, z! : N
├────────────────────────────────────────────────────
│ y? ∉ x; y? ∈ x'
│ ∅ ⊂ x ⊂ x'; z! ∈ x' \ x
└────────────────────────────────────────────────────
```

IncludeLeqInput

$x, x' : \mathbb{P}\,\mathbb{N}$
$y?, z! : \mathbb{N}$

$y? \notin x$
$x' = x \cup \{z : \mathbb{N} \mid z \leq y?\}$
$z! = y?$

Show that *IncludeInput* $\sqsubseteq$ *IncludeLeqInput*. If we replace $y? \notin x$ by $0 \notin x$ in the predicate of *IncludeLeqInput*, is this still a refinement of *IncludeInput*?

10.2   Data refinement

As was said at the beginning of the previous section, the first major step towards creating an implementation of a specification is to make decisions about how the abstract data structures are to be represented in such a way that a computer can more readily manipulate them. This part of the process, including the formal documentation of the relationship between abstract and concrete states, is known as data refinement. In general, the programming language to be used will not provide the abstract data structures directly, though certain languages, the object-oriented languages and most functional languages, provide the means to separate the specification of the properties of an abstract data type from the details of its implementation. Even if we took this kind of approach, we would still at some point have to implement the required operations on the data types; this would again be a matter of finding more concrete, simpler representations for the data so that necessary operations could be performed on these simpler data structures simulating the effect of the operations defined for the abstract data types.

Let us assume then, for the moment, that we wish to implement our systems in a language which, besides a range of basic data types, has only rather simple structured data types such as arrays and record types.

10.2.1   An example data refinement

We are going to take as an example a data refinement for the Football Identity Scheme, described in Chapter 9. We impose a further constraint on the abstract state however, recognising that it will only be possible to handle a finite number of members. We assume that a maximum membership is declared:

$\quad\mid$ $maxmems : \mathbb{N}_1$

and we define the abstract state schema thus:

```
┌─ FidFScheme ─────────────────────────────────
│ members : ID ⤖ PERSON
│ banned : ℙ ID
├──────────────────────────────────────────────
│ banned ⊆ dom members
│ #members ≤ maxmems
└──────────────────────────────────────────────
```

We intend to represent the abstract state using two arrays, *membarr* and *banarr*, where:

- *membarr* is an array of $(ID, PERSON)$ pairs, representing the *members* function.

- *banarr* is an array of positive integers, each of which points to an element of *membarr*, signifying that the member corresponding to that index is banned.

We illustrate the intended representation in Figure 10.2. Here the banned members are *Joe Hooly*, *Sandra Skintight* and *Bill Vandal*. Note that it is important to distinguish between the names of abstract components and those of concrete components; we shall have to say how these two classes of components are related, so we cannot afford any confusion of names. Formally speaking, for the purposes

banarr	
index	ℕ
1	4
2	5
3	2

membarr		
index	*ID*	*PERSON*
1	WW8901	Tom Cobbley
2	WW8903	Bill Vandal
3	WW9001	Daisy Widden
4	WW9002	Joe Hooly
5	WW9004	Sandra Skintight
6	WW9007	Joan Brewer

Figure 10.2: Concrete data structures for the Football Identity Scheme

of the present data refinement, we regard an array of elements of type X as a total function from an interval $1..upb$ to X, for some non-negative integer upb. This is equivalent to saying that an array is a sequence, in the usual Z sense of sequences. However we also want to impose a constraint on the arrays we use: distinct elements should contain distinct values, or more formally, arrays will be injective sequences. The set of injective sequences of elements of type X is defined:

$$\text{iseq } X \ == \ \text{seq } X \cap (\mathbb{N} ⤖ X)$$

We can now define the concrete state of the Football Identity Scheme as follows:

CFidFScheme
$membarr : \mathrm{iseq}(ID \times PERSON)$
$banarr : \mathrm{iseq}\,\mathbb{N}$

ran $membarr \in ID \rightarrowtail PERSON$
ran $banarr \subseteq 1..\#membarr$
$\#membarr \leq maxmems$

---

where the constraints provided in the predicate ensure that:

- the set of $(ID, PERSON)$ pairs held in *membarr* represents a partial injection from ID to $PERSON$, which is what the *members* function is.

- all the positive integers held in *banarr* are in the range from 1 up to the size of *membarr*.

Now we give the relationship between abstract and concrete states:

Retr
FidFScheme
CFidFScheme

$members = \mathrm{ran}\,membarr$
$banned = \mathrm{dom}(membarr (\!| \mathrm{ran}\,banarr |\!))$

The predicate expresses the two constraints:

- The set of $(ID, PERSON)$ pairs contained in *membarr* corresponds to the function *members*.

- The *IDs* of banned members are the first elements of those $(ID, PERSON)$ pairs in *membarr* at positions whose indices are held in *banarr*.

The constraints of *CFidFScheme* ensure that every concrete state represents precisely one abstract state. The relationship between abstract and concrete states is usually known as the retrieve relation: in our case the relation is a total function from concrete to abstract, which is to say that each concrete state corresponds to just one abstract state.

We must provide some initial concrete states, intended to correspond to initial abstract states. Thus we define:

InitCFidFScheme
CFidFScheme$'$

$membarr' = \langle\rangle;\ banarr' = \langle\rangle$

---

which in fact defines a unique initial concrete state in which both arrays are empty.

Exercise 10.5 ◇ Confirm that $membarr' = \langle\rangle$ and $banarr' = \langle\rangle$ are consistent with the $CFidFScheme'$ constraints:

     ran $membarr' \in ID \rightarrowtail PERSON$

     ran $banarr' \subseteq 1..\#membarr'$

     $\#membarr' \leq maxmems$

Exercise 10.6 Prove that: $CFidFScheme \vdash \#banarr \leq \#membarr$

Exercise 10.7 ◇ We said that the retrieve relation $Retr$ was a total function from concrete to abstract states, in that each concrete state corresponds to one and only one abstract state, but there are in general many concrete states which represent any given abstract state. Show how this is possible in the case of $Retr$.

10.2.2   The Initial States Theorem

The first important property which must be proved for a data refinement is that every initial concrete state corresponds under the retrieve relation to an initial abstract state. In the present case, given that $Retr$ is functional, this may be expressed formally in the following theorem:

$$InitCFidFScheme \wedge Retr' \vdash InitFidFScheme$$

Note that $Retr'$ is included on the left hand side (rather than $Retr$) because $InitFidFScheme$ and $InitCFidFScheme$ refer to dashed states. Expanding the theorem for the case at hand, we must show that:

     $FidFScheme'$; $CFidFScheme'$ |
         $membarr' = \langle\rangle$
         $banarr' = \langle\rangle$
         $members' = $ ran $membarr'$
         $banned' = \mathrm{dom}(membarr' (\!| \text{ ran } banarr' \,|\!))$

     $\vdash$

         $members' = \emptyset \wedge banned' = \emptyset$

Using the values for $members'$ and $banned'$ from the hypothesis, the goal becomes:

     ran $membarr' = \emptyset$

     $\mathrm{dom}(membarr' (\!| \text{ ran } banarr' \,|\!)) = \emptyset$

which does indeed hold, since $membarr'$ is the empty sequence.

Exercise 10.8 Assuming that the empty sets are of suitable types, prove that:

   (i)   ◇ $\mathrm{dom}\,\emptyset = \emptyset$ and $\mathrm{ran}\,\emptyset = \emptyset$

   (ii)   for any set S, $\emptyset(\!| S \,|\!) = \emptyset$

   (iii)   for any relation R, $R(\!| \emptyset \,|\!) = \emptyset$

10.3   Operation refinement

The next major step towards providing a correct implementation of a specification is to provide concrete operations for each of the abstract operations. It will of course be necessary to prove for each concrete operation that it is a refinement of the corresponding abstract operation. This will give rise to two theorems in each case, an Applicability Theorem and a Correctness Theorem, corresponding to the two refinement criteria introduced earlier.

10.3.1   An example operation refinement

We consider the *AddMember* operation for the Football Identity Scheme. We give its slightly changed definition here for easy reference:

```
┌─ AddFMember ────────────────────────────────────
│ ΔFidFScheme
│ applicant? : PERSON; id! : ID
├──────────────────────────────────────────────────
│ applicant? ∉ ran members
│ id! ∉ dom members
│ members' = members ∪ {id! ↦ applicant?}
│ banned' = banned
└──────────────────────────────────────────────────
```

When the applicant is not already a member, a new identity code is assigned to the applicant who is then entered as a member together with this code. The operation does not affect the blacklist of banned members.

It is not difficult to guess what needs to be done in order to simulate this operation using the concrete representation proposed in the previous section:

```
┌─ CAddFMember ───────────────────────────────────
│ ΔCFidFScheme
│ applicant? : PERSON; id! : ID
├──────────────────────────────────────────────────
│ applicant? ∉ ran(ran membarr)
│ id! ∉ dom(ran membarr)
│ membarr' = membarr ⌢ ⟨(id!, applicant?)⟩
│ banarr' = banarr
└──────────────────────────────────────────────────
```

Given an applicant who is not already a member, an appropriate $(ID, PERSON)$ pair is added at the end of *membarr*. The array *banarr* is unchanged.

The Applicability criterion for refinement will require that in some sense the concrete operation is applicable whenever the abstract operation is applicable. Thus we need to know the preconditions of the two operations. That for *AddMember* was calculated in Chapter 9: we now have an extra constraint because

the number of members after the addition of the new member must not exceed
maxmems. (See Exercise 10.9 below.) The precondition is thus represented by
the following schema, where the predicate is given in simplified form:

```
┌─ PreAddFMember ──────────────────────────────
│ FidFScheme; applicant? : PERSON
├──────────────────────────────────────────────
│ applicant? ∉ ran members
│ dom members ≠ ID
│ #members < maxmems
└──────────────────────────────────────────────
```

To find the precondition for *CAddFMember* we simplify the predicate of:

```
┌─ PreCAddFMember ─────────────────────────────
│ CFidFScheme
│ applicant? : PERSON
├──────────────────────────────────────────────
│ ∃ CFidFScheme'; id! : ID •
│     applicant? ∉ ran(ran membarr)
│     id! ∉ dom(ran membarr)
│     membarr' = membarr ⁀ ⟨(id!, applicant?)⟩
│     banarr' = banarr
│     #membarr' ≤ maxmems
└──────────────────────────────────────────────
```

(The reader may find it useful to refer back to Chapter 9, where the One Point
Rule was used in order to simplify pre *AddFMember*.) Using the One Point Rule,
the predicate may be written:

∃ *id!* : *ID* •

$$membarr \frown \langle(id!, applicant?)\rangle \in iseq(ID \times PERSON) \tag{1}$$
$$banarr \in iseq\,\mathbb{N} \tag{2}$$
$$ran(membarr \frown \langle(id!, applicant?)\rangle) \in ID \nrightarrow PERSON \tag{3}$$
$$ran\,banarr \subseteq 1..\#(membarr \frown \langle(id!, applicant?)\rangle) \tag{4}$$
$$applicant? \notin ran(ran\,membarr) \tag{5}$$
$$id! \notin dom(ran\,membarr) \tag{6}$$
$$\#(membarr \frown \langle(id!, applicant?)\rangle) \leq maxmems \tag{7}$$

The values of the dashed components, given by the two equalities under the existential quantification in the schema, have been substituted throughout the other
conjuncts; this accounts for conjuncts [5],[6],[7] here. Conjuncts [3] and [4] come
from the state invariant for *CFidFScheme'*, and conjuncts [1] and [2] arise from
the requirements of the One Point Rule and express the fact that the new values
must belong to the sets of which they are declared to be members.

Conjunct [2] follows immediately from *CFidFScheme*, and so is redundant here. Also from *CFidFScheme* we know that ran *banarr* $\subseteq$ 1..#*membarr*, so ran *banarr* must indeed be contained in the larger interval given in [4]. Conjunct [5] can be taken outside the quantification since it does not refer to *id!*. Conjunct [7], since (*membarr* $\frown$ $\langle(id!, applicant?)\rangle$) is one element longer than *membarr*, is equivalent to:

$$\#membarr < maxmems$$

which can be moved outside the quantification. This leaves the following predicate:

applicant? $\notin$ ran(ran *membarr*)	[8]
#*membarr* < *maxmems*	[9]
$\exists\, id! : ID \bullet$	
$\quad membarr \frown \langle(id!, applicant?)\rangle \in \text{iseq}(ID \times PERSON)$	[10]
$\quad \text{ran}(membarr \frown \langle(id!, applicant?)\rangle) \in ID \rightarrowtail PERSON$	[11]
$\quad id! \notin \text{dom}(\text{ran}\, membarr)$	[12]

If neither *applicant?* nor *id!* appear within *membarr*, which is required by [8] and [12], then adding them at the end of the array preserves both the injectivity of the sequence and the injectivity of the set of pairs which forms its range, so that [10] and [11] are redundant. All that remains is:

$$applicant? \notin \text{ran}(\text{ran}\, membarr)$$
$$\#membarr < maxmems$$
$$\exists\, id! : ID \bullet id! \notin \text{dom}(\text{ran}\, membarr)$$

and again, this is equivalent to:

$$applicant? \notin \text{ran}(\text{ran}\, membarr)$$
$$\#membarr < maxmems$$
$$\text{dom}(\text{ran}\, membarr) \neq ID$$

Exercise 10.9 ◇ Check that adding the new constraint #*members* < *maxmems* does not affect anything else during the simplification of the precondition of *AddFMember*.

Exercise 10.10 Give a more formal argument, modelled on the simplification of the precondition of *AddFMember* in Chapter 9, to replace the informal argument for the simplification of the precondition of *CAddFMember* just presented.

10.3.2   The Applicability Theorem

As we said earlier, the preconditions are needed when proving the theorems concerning operation refinement. The first of these is the Applicability Theorem which states that the concrete operation can be applied safely whenever it would be safe to apply the abstract version:

$$PreAddFMember \land Retr \vdash PreCAddFMember$$

This may be read as follows: if *FidFScheme* and *applicant?* satisfy the precondition of the *AddFMember* operation, and *CFidFScheme* represents *FidFScheme*, then *CFidFScheme* and *applicant?* must satisfy the precondition for the corresponding concrete operation *CAddFMember*. In order to use *PreCAddFMember* as a predicate in the conclusion it is necessary to check that the variables which it declares are in scope and of the correct type: in fact *PreCAddFMember* declares *CFidFScheme* and *applicant?*, and both of these are included in the hypotheses of the theorem. Expanding the theorem gives:

$$FidFScheme;\ applicant? : PERSON;\ CFidFScheme\ |$$

$applicant? \notin \mathrm{ran}\ members$	[H1]
$\mathrm{dom}\ members \neq ID$	[H2]
$\#members < maxmems$	[H3]
$members = \mathrm{ran}\ membarr$	[H4]
$banned = \mathrm{dom}(membarr \! (\! | \ \mathrm{ran}\ banarr \ | \!))$	[H5]

$\vdash$

$applicant? \notin \mathrm{ran}(\mathrm{ran}\ membarr)$	[G1]
$\#membarr < maxmems$	[G2]
$\mathrm{dom}(\mathrm{ran}\ membarr) \neq ID$	[G3]

For the first part of the goal, [G1]:

$applicant? \notin \mathrm{ran}\ members$	[from H1]
$\Rightarrow applicant? \notin \mathrm{ran}(\mathrm{ran}\ membarr)$	[from H4]

for the second part of the goal, [G2]:

$\#membarr = \#(\mathrm{ran}\ membarr)$	[*membarr* is injective, from *FidFScheme*]
$= \#members$	[from H4]
$< maxmems$	[from H3]

and for the third part of the goal, [G3]:

$\mathrm{dom}(\mathrm{ran}\ membarr)$	
$= \mathrm{dom}\ members$	[from H4]
$\neq ID$	[from H2]

10.3.3   The Correctness Theorem

It remains to be shown that the concrete operation behaves correctly. Since the retrieve relation is functional, the Correctness Theorem may be stated:

$$PreAddFMember \land Retr \land CAddFMember \land Retr' \vdash AddFMember$$

This may be read as follows:

- if *FidFScheme* and *applicant?* satisfy the precondition of *AddFMember*

- and if *CFidFScheme* represents *FidFScheme*

- and if *CAddFMember* is applied yielding a state *CFidFScheme'*, which represents *FidFScheme'*, and output *id!*

- then, for input *applicant?*, the state change *FidFScheme* to *FidFScheme'* and the output *id!* are consistent with *AddFMember*

We could also express the Correctness Theorem by saying that the image of the concrete operation, as seen through the retrieve function, is consistent with the abstract operation. We look now at the details of the theorem in the present case. Once again, *AddFMember* is a schema and the variables it declares must be in scope. The declarations in *AddFMember* are those of *FidFScheme* and *FidFScheme'* (found in *Retr* and *Retr'* respectively), plus *applicant?* and *id!* (declared in *PreAddFMember* and *CAddFMember* respectively). The predicate of *AddFMember* states that:

$$applicant? \notin \operatorname{ran} members$$
$$id! \notin \operatorname{dom} members$$
$$members' = members \cup \{id! \mapsto applicant?\}$$
$$banned' = banned$$

For the first conjunct we have:

$applicant? \notin \operatorname{ran}(\operatorname{ran} membarr)$	[from *CAddFMember*]
$\Rightarrow applicant? \notin \operatorname{ran} members$	[from *Retr*]

The second conjunct follows similarly, and for the third conjunct:

$members'$	
$= \operatorname{ran} membarr'$	[from *Retr'*]
$= \operatorname{ran}(membarr \frown \langle(id!, applicant?)\rangle)$	[from *CAddFMember*]
$= \operatorname{ran} membarr \cup \{(id!, applicant?)\}$	[properties of ran and $\frown$]
$= members \cup \{id! \mapsto applicant?\}$	[from *Retr*]

The argument for the fourth conjunct is left as an exercise.

Exercise 10.11 ◇ The necessary argument for the fourth conjunct above goes like this:

$banned'$

$\quad = \mathrm{dom}(\ membarr' (\!| \ \mathrm{ran}\ banarr'\ |\!) \ )$ [*Why*1]

$\quad = \mathrm{dom}(\ membarr' (\!| \ \mathrm{ran}\ banarr\ |\!) \ )$ [*Why*2]

$\quad = \mathrm{dom}(\ membarr (\!| \ \mathrm{ran}\ banarr\ |\!) \ )$ [*Why*3]

$\quad = banned$ [*Why*4]

Supply the justifications *Why*1, *Why*2, *Why*3 and *Why*4.

Exercise 10.12 ◇ Consider the *FidFScheme* operation:

```
┌─ BanFMember ─────────────────────────────────
│ ΔFidFScheme
│ miscreant? : ID
├──────────────────────────────────────────────
│ miscreant? ∈ (dom members) \ banned
│ banned' = banned ∪ {miscreant?}
│ members' = members
└──────────────────────────────────────────────
```

Using the same retrieve relation as before, propose a corresponding concrete operation *CBanFMember*, and prove the appropriate applicability and correctness theorems.

10.4   Further discussion and summary

Our example of data and operation refinement showed how we may represent data in a way which is more suitable for translation into programming language code. Often the distance between the level of specification and that of the programming language is too great for this to be accomplished in a single step. In this case one or more intermediate levels may be interposed: between each level and the next more concrete level of representation we must define a retrieve relation and we must define the more concrete versions of operations as refinements of their more abstract counterparts.

The *FidFScheme* example also used a data refinement for which the retrieve relation was a total function from the concrete to the abstract. In general the retrieve relation may be either a partial function from concrete to abstract, or even a relation in the most general sense. In the partial function case, we may well ask why we would choose not to restrict the concrete states so that they all do represent abstract states. However, in some cases it is difficult to express these constraints succinctly; in any case, the refinement criteria will ensure that the concrete states visited by the concrete system all do indeed represent abstract states, so it is only a question of making explicit or leaving implicit such constraints. In the case that the retrieve relation is not functional, the refinement theorems have to be made more complicated: we do not introduce this extra complexity here since it is usually possible and more convenient to make the relation functional from concrete to abstract.

We summarise now the theorems which have to be proved for a proposed data and operation refinement, where AS and CS are the abstract and concrete states respectively, assuming a functional retrieve relation, $Retr$:

- Initial States Theorem:

$$InitCS \wedge Retr' \vdash InitAS$$

  which is to say that every initial concrete state must represent an initial abstract state;

- Applicability Theorems: for each concrete operation COp corresponding to abstract operation AOp,

$$\text{pre } AOp \wedge Retr \vdash \text{pre } COp$$

  which is to say that whenever the abstract operation is applicable in a given abstract state then the concrete operation must be applicable in any concrete state representing the abstract state;

- Correctness Theorems: for each concrete operation COp corresponding to abstract operation AOp,

$$\text{pre } AOp \wedge Retr \wedge COp \wedge Retr' \vdash AOp$$

  which is to say that whenever the concrete operation is applied in a state representing an abstract state for which the abstract operation is applicable, then the action of the concrete operation gives rise to a concrete state which represents an abstract state which could have resulted from the action of the abstract operation, and in the case that there is output from the operations the output produced by the concrete system is a possible output of the abstract operation.

It is perhaps worth stating again what is claimed for an implementation which is a refinement of a specification, and equally what is not claimed. We consider only the case where the retrieve relation is functional. The concrete system must set out from a state which represents a valid initial abstract state. At each step a concrete operation is chosen and this must simulate the corresponding abstract operation in the sense made precise by the refinement theorems. So at each stage the concrete system enters a state which represents an abstract state which could have been reached by applying the corresponding sequence of abstract operations. Figure 10.3 illustrates the sequence of events. Note that the operations may have

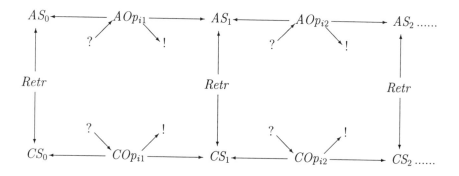

Figure 10.3: Simulation of abstract system by concrete system

inputs and outputs but we have not considered any change of representation here. It is certainly not claimed that every succession of abstract operations may be simulated by a succession of corresponding concrete operations. Remember that the concrete operations may reduce non-determinism at every step: thus only a subset of possible next steps is available to the concrete system after each operation is applied. Referring to the figure, in state CS_1 representing AS_1 the concrete system must offer all operations COp_i for which AS_1 satisfies pre AOp_i; however, at this point the abstract system might also have entered state AS_1', $AS_1' \neq AS_1$, but operations COp_j for which AS_1' satisfies pre AOp_j are not necessarily offered.

Exercise 10.13 Propose a data refinement for the Word-For-Word system described in Chapter 7, define the concrete operations and prove all the necessary theorems. One possibility is to keep two arrays of words, one of native, one of foreign words, and two arrays of integer sequences, one array giving the indices of foreign words which correspond to given native words, the other giving the indices of native words corresponding to given foreign words.

10.5 Further reading

More examples of data and operation refinement may be found in [WM90] and [Wor93].

Chapter 11

From specification to program: operation decomposition

We can look upon data and operation refinement, as we have described it in the previous section, as that part of the development process which corresponds to the design phase of the traditional software life-cycle; it involves choosing ways of representing the abstract data structures which will be more amenable to computer processing, and the translation of abstract operations into corresponding concrete operations. However, those concrete operations are still expressed in the language of schemas and describe only the relationship amongst the components of before and after states; in general this does not make explicit how such changes of state are to be achieved by executing instructions within the repertoire of the computer system upon which the specified system is to be implemented. Operation decomposition is precisely this process of conversion of descriptions of state changes into executable instruction sequences. For the purposes of our discussion of operation decomposition in the present chapter we shall assume that the reader has some experience with a programming language such as BASIC (preferably a structured dialect) or Pascal.

It might be supposed that operation decomposition could be carried through to the level of individual programming language instructions wholly within the Z notation by using the schema calculus, perhaps with the addition of further schema operators, the decomposition process continuing until schemas were produced corresponding directly to programming language instructions. After all, a schema such as:

$$
\begin{array}{|l}
\hline
\mathit{Incr} \underline{} \\
x, x', y, y' : \mathbb{N} \\
\hline
x' = x + y \\
y' = y \\
\hline
\end{array}
$$

would seem to translate to:

```
x := x + y
```

in a language such as Pascal[1], so this appears to be a feasible approach. There are, however, various objections to such a scheme. Most importantly, the schema calculus would have to be expanded to include further operators; in particular we would need an iteration operator, corresponding to traditional loop constructs (such as the `repeat` ... `until` ... of Pascal). We might be tempted to include several other operators to correspond to the facilities provided in different programming languages, some of which would be inappropriate when carrying out a development towards a target language which lacked certain features. In fact the structure of programming languages would be imported into the Z notation, which would be undesirable: remember that Z is a language for describing requirements formally, whilst programming languages describe sequences of computer executable instructions. Again, we might consider allowing schemas to be defined recursively, but then we complicate the mathematics which underpins the Z notation, which is equally undesirable.

The path which we shall pursue here, rather than allowing the structure of programming languages to influence that of Z, allows schemas to be incorporated into programs. We shall henceforth use the word program in an extended sense: wherever a sequence of instructions would be syntactically correct in the programming language, we allow instead a Z schema which relates before and after values of some of the variables which are in scope at that point in the program. In a schema, a plain variable signifies a before value and a dashed variable signifies an after value of a corresponding program variable. We cannot expect the computer to execute a program which contains Z schemas, of course, and the goal of operation decomposition will be to produce a program from which all schemas have been removed. We can only replace a schema by programming language text when the change of state described by the schema is of such a simple kind that it does indeed correspond to an instruction or a group of instructions in that language. At intermediate stages a schema will usually be replaced by further, usually simpler schemas, bound together by the constructs of the programming language; for example, a schema might be replaced by a conditional construct, an `if` .. `then` .. `else` .. construct, in which the arms of the conditional are again schemas. In later sections of the chapter we shall give rules for each of the constructs of the programming language, which tell us when it is possible to introduce the constructs concerned as replacements for schemas.

Anyone familiar with the history of programming methodology will be aware of the ideas which came to be known as structured programming. One important strand within structured programming was the use of pseudocode; that is to say, natural language phrases were incorporated into computer programs in order to

---

[1] We use a typewriter font here, and throughout the chapter whenever we write programming language code, in order to distinguish it from Z.

describe, albeit informally, what was to be done at certain points without giving details of how it was to be done. Executable programs were progressively developed by expanding these natural language phrases, and this process was known as stepwise refinement. It was also suggested that programs could be constructed by making formal statements about the relationships amongst the program variables before and after certain operations, and then finding ways to bridge the gaps between these formal statements, for example by providing intermediate formal statements, allowing those gaps to be narrowed. The development methods which have been proposed for taking Z specifications through to executable programs are based on these ideas which have been common currency within the computer science community for some twenty years; what we shall describe in the remainder of this section is essentially an adaptation of those ideas to the Z style of specification. One very important point to note is that the methods proposed put the emphasis on calculating correct refinements rather than validating refinement guesses. The style of development which we describe here is based upon the work done by IBM Hursley in collaboration with the Programming Research Group, Oxford University [Wor87, Wor89]. Since the first edition of the present book, John Wordsworth has published a book [Wor93] based on this work; we have made some small changes in the refinement rules given later in this chapter in the light of the presentation in Wordsworth's book.

As we said earlier in Chapter 10, we shall assume that our target programming language is a traditional flow-of-control language which includes the following facilities:

- Declarations, serving to introduce variables and to give them types (thus allowing certain types of errors, such as mis-spelt variable names, or inconsistently typed expressions to be detected); some mechanism for delimiting the scope of declarations will also be assumed.

- Assignment, which is to say that variables are thought of as names for boxes, or locations, where values may be stored from time to time as the computation proceeds (but note that we shall assume that a variable may not name different locations during its lifetime, and that different variables may not refer to the same location).

- Sequencing, often represented by ';', meaning that one action is to be followed by another action.

- Alternation, in which tests are made in order to determine which of two (or in some cases more) actions is to be executed next.

- Iteration, which involves interleaving of tests and actions until some overall test fails.

- Function and procedure definitions, which allow us to encapsulate in the programming language frequently useful sequences of actions; in the case of a function, these actions may not change the value of any variable other than those which it uses for its own private purposes, and which are otherwise invisible.

We assume that the reader has an intuitive understanding of these features of traditional programming languages as a result of familiarity with at least one such language. Following the lead of researchers in this area, when we want to present short pieces of programming language code we shall use a language based upon Dijkstra's Guarded Command Language, which distils the essence of the flow-of-control style while preserving much of the non-determinism to be found in specifications. We shall call this language Ω (pronounced 'omega'); we do not claim that Ω is exactly Dijkstra's language, and in particular we make no assumptions about how the meaning of Ω programs might be defined. Where relevant we shall show how the theory applies to more familiar languages with their deterministic control structures. We shall not give a detailed syntax for Ω; we will in fact invent notation, along the lines of existing languages, as needed and without further comment. We have no wish to add yet another brick to the computer language Tower of Babel.

In the following sections we shall look at the usage of each of the features listed above: we shall show how we may define each of the control structures and we shall illustrate the refinement rules which arise from these definitions. Before doing so we enunciate an extremely important general principle: whenever a schema, representing an operation yet to be refined, occurs in a program then its position within the text of the program is such that when called upon to act its precondition is always satisfied. We call this the Precondition Principle. When such a schema is replaced by a refinement within a program which conforms to this principle then the resulting program will also conform to the principle.

We shall assume that whenever a schema occurs as part of a program, then it includes declarations for all the variables which are free in its predicate part. In order to apply some of the refinement rules it will be necessary to normalise such schemas, in the sense that the declaration part should contain only type information whilst the predicate includes all the relevant constraints. We shall also assume that this normalisation process includes using only plain (that is to say, un-dashed) occurrences of variables which are constrained not to change. Thus a normalised schema takes the form:

$$
\begin{array}{|l}
\hline
\ \mathit{Opn} \underline{\hspace{8cm}} \\
\ \Delta[\rho_1]; \ \Xi[\rho_2] \\
\hline
\ \mathit{OpnPred} \\
\hline
\end{array}
$$

where ρ_1, ρ_2 are disjoint lists of distinct variables and their types, where ρ_1 declares the variables which may change, ρ_2 those which may not, and only plain versions of ρ_2 variables occur in *OpnPred*. We use Δ and Ξ here to indicate this, though strictly speaking in Z they may only prefix schema names.

We do not give proper definitions of the meanings of the constructs of Ω, but rather we give rules which say how those constructs may be used to refine certain schemas; after all, this is all we need to know in order to be able to use the language. Of course, if we furnished our language with a definition of the meaning of its programs, using a recognised style of semantic definition, we would ultimately be obliged to show that these rules were valid; however we shall not undertake this here. Of course programs also need to be translated into machine code for the computer on which they are to be executed; this is in effect another process of refinement, involving further data refinement in order to use the very primitive data structures available at machine code level, and also involving further operation decomposition in order to use the instruction set of the machine. The integrity of implementations of specifications ultimately depends on the existence of trustworthy compilers or interpreters for the languages we use. In the end, it is only sensible to use a language which has a formal definition and for which there is a compiler or interpreter which has been proved to conform to that formal definition.

11.1   Declarations

As we have remarked earlier, a Z specification does not usually describe the outermost level of the system. We suppose that there is a driver program which runs the system; this driver determines, or discovers, which operation is to happen next at each stage. The concrete state definition will be translated into global declarations in the programming language, so that the components of the concrete state will be in scope throughout the driver program and in particular will be in scope for the initialisation of the system and for the operations of the system, as described by their corresponding schemas. Indeed, the driver program must only make access to these components within the code for the initialisation and operation schemas. Axiomatic definitions will also become global declarations. When we come to implement the operations in the programming language, extra working space variables will usually be needed; this will give rise to local declarations.

For the kind of system we have considered in this book, where we imagine that each operation is selected from a menu by the user of the system, and each of the operations is made total, the driver program might take the form illustrated in Figure 11.1. This also serves to show the form of most of the constructs of the language Ω:

- The brackets $|[$ and $]|$ delimit the scope of declarations; many languages use **begin** and **end** for this purpose.

```
|[
    AxiomaticDefs;
    ConcreteStateTypeDecls;
    InitSys;
    type Choice = (Quit, Op1, Op2, ..., OpN);
    |[ chosen : Choice; MakeFirstChoice;
        do /* ConcreteStateInvariant */
            chosen /= Quit -->
                if chosen = Op1 -->
                        |[ Op1InOutDecls;
                            GetOp1Inputs; Op1; SendOp1Outputs ]|
                [] chosen = Op2 -->
                        |[ Op2InOutDecls;
                            GetOp2Inputs; Op2; SendOp2Outputs ]|
                .....
                [] chosen = OpN -->
                        |[ OpNInOutDecls;
                            GetOpNInputs; OpN; SendOpNOutputs ]|
                fi;
                MakeNextChoice
        od;
    ]|;
    Goodbye
]|
```

Figure 11.1: An example driver program

- The semicolon is used as a separator between statements to be executed sequentially, and/or between declarations.

- The conditional construct if ...   [] ...   [] ...   ...   fi may have any number of arms, each of which consists of a test and a corresponding action.

- The loop construct do ...   od has a body which consists of a test and an action, execution terminating when the test is false.

In the driver program, which is an extended program in that it contains both programming language code and schemas, we have used the typewriter font to indicate actual programming language symbols or places where code is already written. The operations of the system are still represented by schemas, here shown in the usual font for schemas. The sections of code concerned are as follows:

- `AxiomaticDefns` is the translation of any axiomatic definitions in the specification; it might also include further ancillary definitions found to be useful during the process of operation decomposition; it could also include giving specific values to global variables, where only a type or a range of values is stated in the specification.

- `ConcreteStateTypeDecls` is the translation of the declarations of the components of the concrete state and `/* ConcreteStateInvariant */` is a (non-executable) comment in the programming language corresponding to the constraints expressed in the predicate part of the concrete state definition; note that the types of the components of the concrete state should correspond directly to types in the programming language.

- *InitSys* is the initialisation of the system.

- `MakeFirstChoice` is the code which elicits and records the first choice made from the menu.

- `GetOp1Inputs` and `SendOp1Outputs` handle the inputs and outputs of the operation *Op1*; local declarations `Op1InOutDecls` declare the input and output variables needed for *Op1*; similarly for *Op2*, ..., *OpN*.

- `MakeNextChoice` elicits a further choice from the menu.

- `Goodbye` closes the session.

Of course the schemas *Op1*, *Op2*, ..., *OpN* must also be replaced by code before the driver program is executable. The driver serves as starting point and context for these operation decompositions; note that variables declared in the operation schemas are in the (Ω-)scope of the declarations `ConcreteStateTypeDecls`, and of the appropriate local declarations `Op1InOutDecls`, ..., `OPNInOutDecls`.

11.2   Using local variables

It will often happen that the refinement of an operation requires the use of extra variables whose scope should be restricted to the section of the program corresponding to that refinement. As a very simple example where auxiliary variables may be introduced to advantage, consider the (normalised) operation:

```
___ Swapxy _____
  Δ[x, y : T]
 _____
  x' = y ∧ y' = x
```

We certainly cannot use:

```
x := y; y := x
```

as its translation, for the original value of x would be lost before it could be assigned to y. However, suppose we introduce a new variable z:

```
___ SwapxyUsingz _____
  Δ[x, y, z : T]
 _____
  z' = x ∧ x' = y ∧ y' = z'
```

Now *SwapxyUsingz* may clearly be correctly translated by:

```
z := x; x := y; y := z
```

and then we can translate *Swapxy* by:

```
|[ z:T; z := x; x := y; y := z ]|
```

where the scope of z is confined to this piece of code. (There are, of course, other refinement mechanisms involved in this translation, which we have not yet introduced, but we hope that in this simple case the point at issue can be appreciated.) Here we were able to translate an operation by using an extra variable; this is a generally useful technique, embodied in the following rule:

Refinement Rule: introduce local variables

For a normalised operation Op (in which all the free variables of the predicate part are declared in the declaration part) we have:

$$\begin{array}{c}\_\_\_ Op _____ \\ \Delta[\rho_1]; \Xi[\rho_2] \\ _____ \\ OpPred \end{array} \quad \sqsubseteq \quad |[\ \texttt{Rho3};\quad \begin{array}{c}\_\_\_ OpExtraVars _____ \\ \Delta[\rho_1; \rho_3]; \Xi[\rho_2] \\ _____ \\ OpPred \end{array} \quad]|$$

where `Rho3` is the Ω declaration corresponding to ρ_3. (We assume that the list of declarations ρ_1; ρ_2; ρ_3 does not include any variable more than once.)

Note that since Op is a normalised schema its predicate $OpPred$ will not have any free occurrences of the new variables of ρ_3. When we come to refine $OpExtraVars$, we are thus free to set dashed ρ_3 variables as necessary in order to achieve the effect of Op; on the other hand we can make no assumptions about initial values of ρ_3 variables, and so we are not at liberty to constrain the plain ρ_3 variables in any way.

Exercise 11.1 ◇ Confirm that $SwapxyUsingz$ is a refinement of:

$$SwapxyExtraVars \cong [\Delta[x, y, z : T]; \Xi[\rho] \mid x = y' \wedge y = x']$$

whilst:

$$[\Delta[x, y, z : T]; \Xi[\rho] \mid z = x \wedge x' = y \wedge y' = z]$$

is not a refinement of $SwapxyExtraVars$. Also confirm that:

$$SwapxyUsingz \sqsubseteq SwapPart1 \, \S \, SwapPart2$$

where:

$$SwapPart1 \cong [\Delta[x, z : T]; \Xi[y : T; \rho] \mid z' = x \wedge x' = y]$$
$$SwapPart2 \cong [\Delta[y : T]; \Xi[x, z : T; \rho] \mid y' = z]$$

11.3   Reducing the frame

We have seen that a refinement may make use of extra variables, but there are also circumstances in which a refinement may restrict attention to a proper subset of the components of the operation to be refined. For example, if there had been extra unchanging variables[2] in the $Swapxy$ schema above, as follows:

```
  ___ Swapxy1 _____
 |  Δ[x, y : T]; Ξ[ρ]
 |_____
 |  x' = y ∧ y' = x
 |_____
```

since the new values x' and y' do not depend on the unchanging variables ρ, anything which serves as a refinement of $Swapxy$ will also serve as a refinement of $Swapxy1$ so long as we can be sure that refinement cannot affect the values of variables not mentioned in the operation which it refines. (This is where we need to know that distinct variables may not refer to the same location; if such equivalences were admitted we could inadvertently change a variable which does not appear amongst the declarations of a schema being refined.) This can be generalised to any case where the constraints on the dashed variables are independent of certain of the variables in scope. Thus we have the following rule:

---

[2]Such variables would be those in scope at the point where the swap was needed.

Refinement Rule: reducing the frame

In the case that the predicate of a normalised operation Op can be written as the conjunction of $Rho2and3Pred$ and $Rho1and2Pred$ where $Rho2and3Pred$ constrains only the Ξ variables, whilst $Rho1and2Pred$ relates the before and after values of the Δ variables and a subset ρ_2 of the Ξ variables, then we may discard the remaining Ξ variables and the conjunct $Rho2and3Pred$ and refine the simpler schema; that is to say:

$$
\begin{array}{|l}
\hline Op \\\hline
\Delta[\rho_1]; \Xi[\rho_2; \rho_3] \\\hline
Rho2and3Pred \\
Rho1and2Pred \\\hline
\end{array}
\quad \sqsubseteq \quad
\begin{array}{|l}
\hline OpFewerVars \\\hline
\Delta[\rho_1]; \Xi[\rho_2] \\\hline
Rho1and2Pred \\\hline
\end{array}
$$

The point here is that any change to the ρ_1 variables is not constrained by the ρ_3 variables; the predicate $Rho2and3Pred$ is part of the precondition of the operation since it contains no dashed variables and thus will always be true when the operation is called upon to act. This rule relies upon the requirement that no piece of code in Ω may change the values of any variables not mentioned. When we use the rule above we speak of 'reducing the frame'.

11.4   Assignment

Whenever an operation to be refined gives expressions for the dashed components in terms of the undashed components using only functions guaranteed to produce values under the precondition of the operation, and also the types of the components are sufficiently primitive, then there will be an opportunity to use assignment(s) in the programming language as the refinement. For example, suppose we have to refine:

$$
\begin{array}{|l}
\hline OddsAndSquares \\\hline
\Delta[odd, sq, : \mathbb{Z}]; \Xi[\rho] \\\hline
odd' = odd + 2 \\
sq' = sq + odd \\\hline
\end{array}
$$

We shall suppose that Ω has multiple assignments, so that we can immediately give the following translation:

```
odd, sq := odd + 2, sq + odd
```

For assignment we have the following Refinement Rule:

Refinement Rule: assignment to simple variables

$$
\boxed{
\begin{array}{l}
\underline{\quad MultiAssign \quad} \\
\Delta[x_1 : T_1; \, ...; \, x_n : T_n]; \, \Xi[\rho] \\
\hline
x_1' = e_1 \wedge ... \wedge x_n' = e_n \\
Pred
\end{array}
}
\qquad \sqsubseteq \; \texttt{x1,...,xn := e1,...,en}
$$

where the types $T_1, ..., T_n$ are simple types, where the *es* are expressions which involve the plain *xs* and the variables of ρ, and can be immediately translated into Ω, the es being the corresponding translations, and where *Pred* is any further constraining predicate. The empty assignment, corresponding to $n = 0$, is written `skip`.

Few of the traditional programming languages have such a multiple assignment facility, of course, but we can always achieve the effect of multiple assignments with single assignments by using sufficient extra local variables to hold initial values. Thus, translation to a sequence of single assignments could be done entirely automatically. In the example above, we could replace the multiple assignment by:

```
|[sq0, odd0 : int;
  odd0 := odd; sq0 := sq;
  odd := odd0 + 2; sq := sq0 + odd0 ]|
```

slavishly following the most primitive and obvious method. On the other hand, we can manage without extra variables as follows:

```
sq := sq + odd; odd := odd + 2
```

but even this optimisation could be automatically discovered. *Swapxy* is another example where multiple assignment could be used; the translation to single assignment using an extra variable could be automatically generated.

In the Assignment Rule given above we said that the expressions should be immediately translatable into Ω. We assume that Ω has the usual arithmetic operators, but in addition if the necessary function definitions are given then function applications could also occur in such expressions.

We said that our programming language was to include array types. An array is interpreted mathematically as a function of type $\mathbb{N} \nrightarrow X$, where X is the type of the individual elements. In a traditional programming language, we expect to be able to make assignments which change a single element of an array, for example:

```
a[j] := m + n
```

and this clearly corresponds to:

$$a' = a \oplus \{j \mapsto m + n\}$$

Thus, we could give a slightly more general form of the Assignment Rule: we could allow the equation for some x_i to take the form:

$$x_i' = x_i \oplus \{j \mapsto e\}$$

assuming x_i is of appropriate type, which would correspond to:

```
...,xi[j],... := ...,e,...
```

within the multiple assignment in Ω, where e is the translation of expression e. Such translations should only be used, of course, when the precondition of the operation which requires such an array assignment ensures that the array index concerned is within the bounds of the array.

11.5   Sequencing

If we can find a way to achieve the effect of an operation by a two-stage process, then there will be an opportunity to use sequencing in the programming language when refining that operation. That is to say, for operation Op, suppose that we can find operations $Op1$ and $Op2$ so that:

- $Op1$ is always applicable when Op is applicable.

- Within the domain of Op, whenever $Op1$ is applied, any resulting state is acceptable to $Op2$.

- Within the domain of Op, if $Op1$ is applied and then $Op2$ is applied to the resulting state, then the combined effect is always compatible with that of Op.

In that case, the effect of Op can be achieved by performing $Op1$ followed by $Op2$, which is written as $Op1$; $Op2$ in Ω. Expressing the conditions formally:

Refinement Rule: sequencing

$$Op \sqsubseteq Op1;\ Op2$$

provided the following conditions are satisfied:

$$\text{pre } Op \vdash \text{pre } Op1$$
$$\text{pre } Op \wedge Op1 \vdash (\text{pre } Op2)'$$
$$\text{pre } Op \wedge Op1 \wedge Op2' \vdash Op[''/']$$

where $Op[''/']$ means Op with all dashed variables replaced by corresponding doubly dashed variables.

These conditions fulfil the Precondition Principle and ensure that it is safe to further refine $Op1$ and $Op2$, since any after state to which a refinement of $Op1$ might give rise will be acceptable as a before state for $Op2$, and thus will be acceptable to any refinement of $Op2$.

The sequencing symbol of Ω should not be confused with the symbol for schema composition, though there is a close relationship between the two; indeed $Op1;\ Op2$ is a refinement of $Op1\ _9^o\ Op2$ provided that:

$$\text{pre } (Op1\ _9^o\ Op2) \wedge Op1 \vdash (\text{pre } Op2)'$$

As an example of refinement using sequencing, we consider an operation which is intended to find the position of a largest element of a sequence of natural numbers:

$$
\begin{array}{|l}
\hline
\quad FindMaxPos \underline{\hspace{6cm}} \\
\ \Delta[maxel : \mathbb{N}];\ \Xi[a : \text{seq}\,\mathbb{N}] \\
\hline
\ \#a > 0 \\
\ \forall\, n : 1..\#a \bullet a(maxel') \geq a(n) \\
\ 1 \leq maxel' \leq \#a \\
\hline
\end{array}
$$

Now we want to refine $FindMaxPos$ by using a well-tried method; namely to initialise a local variable which will indicate how much of the array has been so far examined, and then to try to move the value of that variable forwards through the array until the whole of the array has been taken into account. We shall call this local variable *sofar* and our first refinement step is:

$$FindMaxPos \sqsubseteq\ |[\ \texttt{sofar:int};$$

$$
\begin{array}{|l}
\hline
\quad FindMaxPosPlus \underline{\hspace{3cm}} \\
\ \Delta[maxel, sofar : \mathbb{N}]; \\
\ \Xi[a : \text{seq}\,\mathbb{N}] \\
\hline
\ \#a > 0 \\
\ \forall\, n : 1..\#a \bullet a(maxel') \geq a(n) \\
\ 1 \leq maxel' \leq \#a \\
\hline
\end{array}
\ ]|
$$

Now we claim that $FindMaxPosPlus$ may be refined[3] thus:

$$FindMaxPosPlus \sqsubseteq Initialise;\ Complete$$

where the two new schemas are defined:

$$
\begin{array}{|l}
\hline
\quad Initialise \underline{\hspace{7cm}} \\
\ \Delta[maxel, sofar : \mathbb{N}];\ \Xi[a : \text{seq}\,\mathbb{N}] \\
\hline
\ MaxelGreatestSofar' \\
\hline
\end{array}
$$

---

[3]It may be worth pointing out that the method of computation we are developing will resolve the possible non-determinism in the value of *maxel'* by choosing the earliest integer in the range $1..\#a$ for which $\forall\, n : 1..\#a \bullet a(maxel') \geq a(n)$.

```
┌─ Complete ──────────────────────────────────────────────────
│ Δ[maxel, sofar : N]; Ξ[a : seq N]
├─────────────────────────────────────────────────────────────
│ sofar' = #a
│ ΔMaxelGreatestSofar
└─────────────────────────────────────────────────────────────
```

where we make the further definition:

```
┌─ MaxelGreatestSofar ────────────────────────────────────────
│ maxel, sofar : N;  a : seq N
├─────────────────────────────────────────────────────────────
│ #a > 0
│ 1 ≤ maxel ≤ sofar ≤ #a
│ ∀ n : 1..sofar • a(maxel) ≥ a(n)
└─────────────────────────────────────────────────────────────
```

That is to say:

- *Initialise* establishes the condition *MaxelGreatestSofar*.

- *Complete* maintains the condition *MaxelGreatestSofar* whilst setting *sofar* to the length of the array *a*.

Now pre *FindMaxPosPlus* and pre *Initialise* both reduce to $\#a > 0$; for a non-empty sequence there always is a greatest element[4], so the conditions on *maxel'* and *sofar'* which these two schemas require in fact constrain neither the sequence *a* nor the incoming values of *maxel* and *sofar*. Thus the first of the three proofs, namely that:

$$\text{pre } FindMaxPosPlus \vdash \text{pre } Initialise$$

is trivial. The condition pre *Complete* reduces to *MaxelGreatestSofar*, so that *Initialise* can only give rise to states which are acceptable to *Complete*. Thus the second proof will go through:

$$\text{pre } FindMaxPosPlus \wedge Initialise \vdash (\text{pre } Complete)'$$

Finally, any state resulting from the action of *Complete* clearly complies with the requirements of *FindMaxPosPlus* since *Complete* ensures that *sofar'* = #a and that *MaxelGreatestSofar'*. Thus we can prove that:

$$\text{pre } FindMaxPosPlus \wedge Initialise \wedge Complete'$$
$$\vdash FindMaxPosPlus['' /']$$

---

[4] We are relying on a theorem about sequences which we shall not prove here; a library of such theorems would normally be available to the specifier, as explained in Chapter 9.

The reader will probably have guessed that the method envisaged here is to replace *Complete* by a loop; the property *MaxelGreatestSofar* will form an invariant, that is a property whose truth is preserved by the action of that loop. We shall see the details of this when we come to examine the use of loops for refinement. Meanwhile, *Initialise* must give rise to a state in which the invariant is satisfied before *Complete* goes into action, and one simple way to achieve this is to set both *sofar'* and *maxel'* to 1, giving the refinement:

$$Initialise \sqsubseteq \boxed{\begin{array}{l} \_InitRef _____ \\ \Delta[maxel, sofar : \mathbb{N}]; \\ \Xi[a : \text{seq } \mathbb{N}] \\ \hline \#a > 0 \\ sofar' = maxel' = 1 \end{array}}$$

$$\sqsubseteq \text{ sofar,maxel := 1,1}$$

Exercise 11.2 ◇ Give the proof that *Initialise* ⊑ *InitRef*, where the two schemas are defined as above, and in this case the symbol ⊑ stands for refinement of an operation with no change of representation of the state.

11.6 Alternation

The alternation construct which our language Ω provides allows us to test for certain conditions and then to refine under stronger constraints on incoming states. We give the following Refinement Rule:

Refinement Rule: alternation

For predicates *Guard₁*, *Guard₂*, ..., *Guardₙ* which express relationships amongst the plain variables of *Op*:

$Op \sqsubseteq$

```
    if Guard_1 --> Guard₁ ∧ Op
    [] Guard_2 --> Guard₂ ∧ Op
    ......
    [] Guard_n --> Guardₙ ∧ Op
    fi
```

provided the following condition is satisfied:

   pre *Op* ⊢ *Guard₁* ∨ ... ∨ *Guardₙ*

where `Guard_1`, `Guard_2`, ..., `Guard_n` are the Ω translations of the guards *Guard₁*, *Guard₂*, ..., *Guardₙ*.

We assume that these guards are sufficiently simple to be immediately translated into logical expressions in Ω. The condition on the guards may be expressed informally as follows: whenever Op is applicable, at least one of the guards is true. In some languages, if the guards are at all complex it may not be possible to write the corresponding code at those points, and in such cases some preliminary setting of local Boolean variables may be necessary; we shall not look at this in detail here. It may seem surprising that the choice of guards is only constrained by the single condition expressed above; in fact, what we should aim to achieve when we introduce an alternation construct is to distinguish cases each of which is easier to implement because of the extra constraint concerned. If we choose a guard, say $Guard_i$, which is too strong we could find that:

$$\text{pre } (Guard_i \wedge Op) \vdash false$$

In this case, however, we also have:

$$\text{pre } Op \vdash \neg \ Guard_i$$

which means that the test `Guard_i` will always fail and therefore the corresponding alternative will never be chosen and is in fact redundant. Though harmless, this is of course undesirable. As a special case corresponding to the usual `if` ... `then` ... `else` ... `end` found in many languages, we can have exactly two alternatives guarded by $Guard$ and $\neg \ Guard$ respectively, for some choice of $Guard$. Note that the proviso given in the Refinement Rule is trivially satisfied since $Guard \vee \neg \ Guard$ is always true. Again, we need to make a judicious choice of $Guard$ so that two useful cases are distinguished.

As an example we take an operation which could form the body of the loop which $Complete$, defined earlier, will require. It is defined thus:

$$
\begin{array}{|l}
\hline
\text{\_\_} IncrSofar \text{_____} \\
\Delta[sofar, maxel : \mathbb{N}]; \ \Xi[a : \text{seq} \, \mathbb{N}] \\
\Delta MaxelGreatestSofar \\
sofar' = sofar + 1 \\
\hline
\end{array}
$$

This operation will only be used when $sofar$ is strictly less than the length of a; indeed:

$$IncrSofar \vdash 1 \leq sofar < \#a$$

The operation requires that $sofar$ should be increased, whilst $MaxelGreatestSofar$, the invariant, is maintained, so that it will be necessary to adjust $maxel$ appropriately; that is to say, we shall refine $IncrSofar$ as follows:

$$IncrSofar \sqsubseteq MoveSofar; \ AdjustMaxel$$

where we define:

```
┌─ MoveSofar ──────────────────────────────────────────
│ Δ[sofar : N]; Ξ[a : seq N; maxel : N]
├──────────────────────────────────────────────────────
│ MaxelGreatestSofar
│ 1 ≤ sofar < #a
│ sofar' = sofar + 1
│ 1 ≤ maxel < sofar' ≤ #a
│ ∀ n : 1..(sofar' − 1) • a(maxel) ≥ a(n)
└──────────────────────────────────────────────────────
```

which increases *sofar* by 1, thereby disturbing the invariant, and we define:

```
┌─ AdjustMaxel ────────────────────────────────────────
│ Δ[maxel : N]; Ξ[a : seq N; sofar : N]
├──────────────────────────────────────────────────────
│ 1 ≤ maxel < sofar ≤ #a
│ ∀ n : 1..(sofar − 1) • a(maxel) ≥ a(n)
│ MaxelGreatestSofar'
└──────────────────────────────────────────────────────
```

which adjusts *maxel* in order to restore the invariant. The necessary proofs are easily carried through and are left as an exercise. (Note that in the *AdjustMaxel* schema above, and in later schemas, where we write *MaxelGreatestSofar'* all dashed occurrences of Ξ-declared variables should be replaced by plain occurrences.) Within *AdjustMaxel* there are two cases to consider:

- When the element at index *sofar* is greater than the greatest element so far encountered, then *maxel* must be moved to this new index.

- When the element at index *sofar* is no greater than the greatest element so far encountered, then *maxel* can remain unchanged.

The operation *AdjustMaxel* may thus be refined:

```
AdjustMaxel ⊑
        if a[sofar] > a[maxel] --> MoveMaxel
        [] a[sofar] =< a[maxel] --> LeaveMaxel
        fi
```

where the two new schemas are defined as:

```
┌─ MoveMaxel ──────────────────────────────────────────
│ Δ[maxel : N]; Ξ[a : seq N; sofar : N]
├──────────────────────────────────────────────────────
│ 1 ≤ maxel < sofar ≤ #a
│ ∀ n : 1..(sofar − 1) • a(maxel) ≥ a(n)
│ MaxelGreatestSofar'
│ a(sofar) > a(maxel)
└──────────────────────────────────────────────────────
```

___ *LeaveMaxel* _____

$\Delta[maxel : \mathbb{N}]; \; \Xi[a : \text{seq} \, \mathbb{N}; \; sofar : \mathbb{N}]$

$1 \leq maxel < sofar \leq \#a$
$\forall \, n : 1..(sofar - 1) \bullet a(maxel) \geq a(n)$
MaxelGreatestSofar'
$a(sofar) \leq a(maxel)$
_____

Turning our attention to *MoveMaxel*, note that:

$$\text{pre } MoveMaxel \wedge MoveMaxel \vdash maxel' = sofar$$

Here is an informal argument: *MoveMaxel* requires that $a(sofar)$ is larger than any earlier element of a, so only the choice of $maxel' = sofar$ ensures that $a(maxel')$ is larger or equal to all elements up to $sofar$, which is required by *MaxelGreatestSofar'*, which is part of the predicate of *MoveMaxel*.

Now consider *LeaveMaxel*. Combining the first and third lines of its predicate we see that:

$$LeaveMaxel \vdash \forall \, x : 1..sofar \bullet a(maxel) \geq a(x)$$

so that *MaxelGreatestSofar'* is satisfied by taking $maxel' = maxel$, as we expected. However, note that there could be other indices within the range $1..sofar$ which would also satisfy this constraint, so if we choose to set $maxel' = maxel$ this is in general reducing the non-determinism of the operation. To put it another way, if we add the constraint $maxel' = maxel$ to the predicate of *LeaveMaxel* then the result is a refinement of *LeaveMaxel*. This refinement can then be rewritten:

___ *LeaveMaxelRef* _____

$\Xi[a : \text{seq} \, \mathbb{N}; \; sofar, maxel : \mathbb{N}]$

$1 \leq maxel < sofar \leq \#a$
$\forall \, n : 1..(sofar - 1) \bullet a(maxel) \geq a(n)$
MaxelGreatestSofar'
$a(sofar) \leq a(maxel)$
_____

and we can now further refine *AdjustMaxel* as follows:

$AdjustMaxel \sqsubseteq$

```
            if a[sofar] > a[maxel] --> maxel := sofar
            [] a[sofar] =< a[maxel] --> skip
            fi
```

by application of the Assignment Refinement Rule.

The Refinement Rule we gave above for alternation is perhaps the simplest such rule, but there are other alternation rules which can be derived from it which in some cases may be easier to work with. For example, if the operation we wish to refine can easily be expressed as a disjunction we can use the following rule:

Derived Refinement Rule: alternation

$Op_1 \vee Op_2 \vee ... \vee Op_n \sqsubseteq$
    if preOp_1 --> Op_1
    [] preOp_2 --> Op_2

    ......

    [] preOp_n --> Op_n
    fi

where preOp_1, preOp_2, ..., preOp_n are the Ω translations of the preconditions pre Op_1, pre Op_2, ..., pre Op_n.

An informal justification for this rule could be given as follows. If we check that the current state of a computation satisfies the precondition of one of the disjuncts, say Op_i, then any state resulting from applying Op_i will satisfy the requirements of $Op_1 \vee Op_2 \vee ... \vee Op_n$ since it satisfies the requirements of one of its disjuncts.

Exercise 11.3 ⋄ Give an argument which shows that the Derived Alternation Rule given at the end of the text of this section can indeed be derived from the earlier alternation rule. You may wish to show that:

$$\text{pre} \ (Op_1 \vee Op_2 \vee ... \vee Op_n) \vdash \text{pre} \ Op_1 \vee \text{pre} \ Op_2 \vee ... \text{pre} \ Op_n$$

and that for any Op and $OtherOp$:

$$\text{pre} \ Op \wedge (Op \vee OtherOp) \sqsubseteq Op$$

11.7 Iteration

We said earlier that the operation *Complete* could be achieved by repeatedly executing *IncrSofar* until the condition $sofar = \#a$ is satisfied. This will happen within a finite number of iterations since $sofar \le \#a$ at every stage, but each iteration increases $sofar$ by 1. We shall refine *Complete* as follows:

$$Complete \sqsubseteq \textbf{do} \ \texttt{sofar < \#a} \ \texttt{-->} \ IncrSofar \ \textbf{od}$$

where, as before:

$IncrSofar \ \hat{=}$
    $[\Delta[sofar, maxel : \mathbb{N}]; \ \Xi[a : \text{seq} \ \mathbb{N}] \ |$
        $\Delta MaxelGreatestSofar \wedge sofar' = sofar + 1]$

but this refinement is justified by the following Refinement Rule:

Refinement Rule: iteration

$$
\boxed{\begin{array}{l} \underline{Loop} \\[2pt] \dfrac{\Delta[\rho_1];\ \Xi[\rho_2]}{\Delta Inv} \\[6pt] Goal' \end{array}} \quad \sqsubseteq\ \texttt{do Guard --\textgreater} \quad \boxed{\begin{array}{l} \underline{Body} \\[2pt] \dfrac{\Delta[\rho_1];\ \Xi[\rho_2]}{\Delta Inv} \\[6pt] Change \end{array}}\ \texttt{od}
$$

provided that:

$$Inv \wedge Guard \vdash \text{pre } Body$$
$$Body \wedge Guard \vdash 0 \le Var' < Var$$
$$Inv \wedge \neg\, Guard \vdash Goal$$

where:

- *Inv*, *Guard* and *Goal* are schemas with declaration part $\rho_1;\ \rho_2$
- Guard is the Ω translation of the predicate of *Guard*
- *Change* is a further constraint relating the before and after values of the variables for the operation *Body*
- *Goal* is a predicate which expresses the salient property which the loop is intended to achieve
- *Var* is a suitably chosen integer-valued expression in the plain variables

Thus, in order to use a loop to implement an operation we must identify an invariant property, something which is true initially and again true when a goal state has been achieved, and we must identify a further condition which, taken together with the invariant, is sufficient to describe all that is required of goal states. Having done this, the negation of this terminating condition is used as the guard, whilst the body of the loop will be an operation with the same declaration part, which also preserves the invariant, but makes some change which ensures that a goal state is definitely nearer to being realised. This nearness to realisation is measured by an integer-valued expression, known as the variant; we must be able to show that the value of the variant is strictly decreased by the action of the body, but that the body can never cause it to go negative. Expressing all of this rather less formally, the invariant is a property which the body preserves, so that however many times the body may be executed the invariant is not disturbed, whilst the existence of the variant ensures that the body cannot be executed for ever.

Returning now to our example, we see that:

- the invariant for *Complete* and for *IncrSofar* is *MaxelGreatestSofar*
- corresponding to *Change* we have here $sofar' = sofar + 1$

- for *Goal* we need $sofar = \#a$

The expression $\#a - sofar$ will serve as a variant since, expanding $IncrSofar \wedge sofar < \#a$ to form the hypothesis, we have:

$\Delta[sofar, maxel : \mathbb{N}]; \; \Xi[a : \text{seq} \, \mathbb{N}] \mid$
$\Delta\, MaxelGreatestSofar$
$sofar' = sofar + 1$
$sofar < \#a$
$\qquad \vdash 0 \leq \#a' - sofar' < \#a - sofar$

In fact $\Delta\, MaxelGreatestSofar$ is superfluous here since we can prove:

$\Delta[sofar, maxel : \mathbb{N}]; \; \Xi[a : \text{seq} \, \mathbb{N}] \mid$
$sofar' = sofar + 1$
$sofar < \#a$
$\qquad \vdash 0 \leq \#a' - sofar' < \#a - sofar$

We can now give a complete refinement of *FindMaxPos*:

FindMaxPos
$\qquad \sqsubseteq$
$\qquad \mid\lbrack$ sofar : int; *FindMaxPosPlus* $\rbrack\mid$
$\qquad \sqsubseteq$
$\qquad \mid\lbrack$ sofar : int; *Initialise*; *Complete* $\rbrack\mid$
$\qquad \sqsubseteq$
$\qquad \mid\lbrack$ sofar : int
$\qquad\qquad$ sofar,maxel := 1,1;
$\qquad\qquad$ do sofar < #a ->
$\qquad\qquad\qquad$ *MoveSofar*; *AdjustMaxel*
$\qquad\qquad$ od $\rbrack\mid$
$\qquad \sqsubseteq$
$\qquad \mid\lbrack$ sofar : int
$\qquad\qquad$ sofar,maxel := 1,1;
$\qquad\qquad$ do sofar < #a -->
$\qquad\qquad\qquad$ sofar := sofar + 1;
$\qquad\qquad\qquad$ if a(sofar) > a(maxel) --> maxel := sofar
$\qquad\qquad\qquad$ [] a(sofar) =< a(maxel) --> skip
$\qquad\qquad\qquad$ fi
$\qquad\qquad$ od $\rbrack\mid$

Exercise 11.4 ⋄ For the proposed refinement of *Complete* prove the theorem corresponding to the proviso $Inv \wedge Guard \vdash \text{pre } Body$ given in the Refinement Rule.

11.8   Functions and procedures

The translation of axiomatic definitions might well involve the definition of functions in the programming language, and the refinement of the bodies of these functions might result in new refinement subproblems. Again, we may find that we want to define functions on the concrete state which allow the concrete operations to be described more succinctly and with greater clarity. During the operation decomposition phase we may identify further useful functions, as a result of recognising recurring patterns of evaluation.

Most traditional programming languages also allow procedure definitions: for our purposes, the distinction between a function and a procedure is that whereas a procedure may cause a change of state a function may only compute a value without causing any state change. Just as we might recognise recurring patterns of evaluation, we might also identify recurring patterns of state changes, and this is where procedure definitions could be useful.

Turning a state change operation into a procedure definition in effect gives that operation a name in the programming language which can be used to invoke the action corresponding to that operation at different points in the program. In general a procedure will take various parameters, allowing a call of the procedure to be tailored to differing situations. Recognising that the opportunity exists for making useful procedure definitions is of course a traditional part of the programmer's craft; it involves abstracting from a set of situations which have something significant in common. We shall not look at the details of how procedure definitions may be introduced during operation decomposition; the complexities which arise from the different possible parameter passing mechanisms would take us beyond the scope of this introductory text.

Looking to further horizons, the function and the procedure are only the most primitive of encapsulation mechanisms available in modern programming languages; they allow us to encapsulate groups of instructions, whereas the object-oriented languages allow encapsulation related to the data which is manipulated by the program and the allowable operations upon that data. In order to implement a specification in an object-oriented language much thought would be devoted to how the abstract state might be split up into objects, and what would be the required operations upon those objects. Thought would also be devoted to identifying classes which abstract from the particular objects identified as necessary in an effort to generalise, so that different objects may be viewed as instances of the same class. This activity would take place mainly in the data refinement phase, whilst the operation decomposition phase would be mainly concerned with refining the definitions of the functions and procedures identified as necessary for the classes proposed at the data refinement stage. Clearly if we are ever to produce large system implementations by refinement we have to find ways of constructing software platforms well above the level of individual assignment instructions, conditionals and loops. We need to be able to make use of existing specifications and their refinements, and to be able to incorporate specifications of subsystems. The object-oriented languages offer the prospect that in some cases it may be possible to find off-the-shelf classes already defined, perhaps in a basic, very general library or one more specialised to certain kinds of applications. There is some hope that the combination of formal specification and object-oriented design and implementation could form part of a framework for worthwhile software re-use. Much research remains to be done in this area.

11.9   An example of operation decomposition

As an example of operation decomposition we shall consider how we might develop code in Ω for the Football Identity Scheme. We shall not give all the details of this development, but at various stages we shall leave the reader to attend to the finer points. We first give a quick summary of the specification, giving only the formal part here for the sake of brevity.

- Given sets: $[ID, PERSON]$

- Data type definition:

$$REPORT ::= Ok \mid TooManyMembers \mid$$
$$AlreadyMember \mid NotMember \mid AlreadyBanned$$

- Axiomatic definitions:

$$\mid\ maxmems : \mathbb{N}$$

- The abstract state:

- Operations:

$$TotalAddMember \,\widehat{=}\, (AddMember \wedge Success)$$
$$\vee\ ErrorTooManyMembers$$
$$\vee\ ErrorAlreadyMember$$
$$TotalBanMember \,\widehat{=}\, (BanMember \wedge Success)$$
$$\vee\ ErrorAlreadyBanned$$
$$\vee\ ErrorNotMember$$

with suitable further definitions for the schemas occurring on the right hand side of these definitions of the total operations.

We give the expansion of *TotalAddMember*:

TotalAddMember

$\Delta FidFScheme$
$applicant? : PERSON$
$id! : ID;\ rep! : REPORT$

$(applicant? \notin ran\ members \wedge \#members < maxmems \wedge$
$\qquad members' = members \cup \{id! \mapsto applicant?\} \wedge$
$\qquad id! \notin dom\ members \wedge rep! = Ok)$

$\vee$

$(applicant? \in ran\ members \wedge members' = members \wedge$
$\qquad rep! = AlreadyMember)$

$\vee$

$(\#members = maxmems \wedge members' = members \wedge$
$\qquad rep! = TooManyMembers)$

$banned' = banned$

We shall leave the definition of *TotalBanMember* as an exercise for the reader.

When we come to consider the matter we realise that the concrete state *CFidFScheme*:

CFidFScheme

$membarr : iseq(ID \times PERSON)$
$banarr : iseq \mathbb{N}$

$ran\ membarr \in ID \nrightarrow PERSON$
$ran\ banarr \subseteq 1..\#membarr$
$\#membarr \leq maxmems$

---

does not contain quite enough information, and could usefully have some extra components. In a programming language an array is normally a fixed-length area of storage; at any given time during execution it is often the case that only part of that area contains useful information. We propose the extra components *mtop* and *btop* which will represent high-water marks for the arrays *membarr* and *banarr* respectively. We also have to have some way of generating new *IDs* when the operation is invoked: we suppose that there is a function:

$idgen : \mathbb{N} \nrightarrow ID$

$0..maxmems \subseteq dom\ idgen$

---

which generates a different *ID* for each natural number up to *maxmems*. (An example of a suitable *idgen* might be a function which takes a given integer, converts this to an n-digit integer introducing leading zeros if necessary and combines this with a two letter club identifier code, giving an $(n+2)$-character identifier, where n is chosen so that the range of values $1..maxmems$ can be accommodated.) We append a new constraint to the concrete state which expresses the fact that the *IDs* in use at any moment are those which correspond to the first *mtop* elements of the sequence generated by *idgen*. In summary, we define a new concrete state as follows:

$$
\begin{array}{|l}
\underline{\quad CFidFScheme_1 \quad\rule{5cm}{0pt}} \\
\; CFidFScheme \\
\; mtop, btop : \mathbb{N} \\
\hline
\; btop = \#banarr;\; mtop = \#membarr \\
\; \mathrm{dom}(\mathrm{ran}\; membarr) = idgen(\!|\; 1..mtop\; |\!) \\
\end{array}
$$

The new initial state is specified thus:

$$
\begin{array}{|l}
\underline{\quad InitCFidFScheme_1 \quad\rule{4cm}{0pt}} \\
\; CFidFScheme_1' \\
\hline
\; membarr' = \langle\rangle \\
\; banarr' = \langle\rangle \\
\end{array}
$$

which of course implies that $mtop' = btop' = 0$ initially. Corresponding to *TotalAddMember* we propose the following concrete operation:

$$
\begin{array}{|l}
\underline{\quad CTotalAddMember \quad\rule{4cm}{0pt}} \\
\; \Delta CFidFScheme_1 \\
\; applicant? : PERSON \\
\; id! : ID;\; rep! : REPORT \\
\hline
\; (applicant? \notin \mathrm{ran}(\mathrm{ran}\; membarr) \wedge mtop < maxmems \wedge \\
\qquad membarr' = membarr \oplus \{mtop + 1 \mapsto (id!, applicant?)\} \wedge \\
\qquad mtop' = mtop + 1 \wedge \\
\qquad id! = idgen(mtop + 1) \wedge rep! = Ok) \\
\; \vee \\
\; (applicant \in \mathrm{ran}(\mathrm{ran}\; membarr) \wedge membarr' = membarr \wedge \\
\qquad rep! = AlreadyMember) \\
\; \vee \\
\; (mtop = maxmems \wedge membarr' = membarr \wedge \\
\qquad rep! = TooManyMembers) \\
\; banarr' = banarr \\
\end{array}
$$

which we normalise as follows, to conform with the refinement rules given earlier:

     NTotalAddMember _____

       $\Delta[membarr : \mathbb{N} \nrightarrow (ID \times PERSON)$;

           $mtop : \mathbb{N}$

           $id! : ID; \; rep! : REPORT]$;

       $\Xi[banarr : \mathbb{N} \nrightarrow \mathbb{N}; \; btop : \mathbb{N}; \; applicant? : PERSON]$

       $\Delta CFidFScheme_1$

       $(applicant? \notin \mathrm{ran}(\mathrm{ran} \; membarr) \wedge mtop < maxmems \; \wedge$

           $membarr' = membarr \oplus \{mtop + 1 \mapsto (id!', applicant?)\} \; \wedge$

           $mtop' = mtop + 1 \; \wedge$

           $id!' = idgen(mtop + 1) \wedge rep!' = Ok)$

       $\vee$

       $(applicant? \in \mathrm{ran}(\mathrm{ran} \; membarr) \wedge membarr' = membarr \; \wedge$

           $rep!' = AlreadyMember)$

       $\vee$

       $(mtop = maxmems \wedge membarr' = membarr \; \wedge$

           $rep!' = TooManyMembers)$

Here we include the input variable *applicant?* with the Ξ variables because we do not expect these to have their value changed, and we include output variables, *id!* and *rep!* amongst the Δ variables because they will be given values by the operation.

Exercise 11.5 $\diamond$ The intended retrieve relation between the abstract and concrete states may be expressed informally as follows:

(i) the pairings of ID to PERSON which correspond to the membership of the scheme are exactly the items recorded in the *membarr* sequence

(ii) the items in the *banarr* sequence are the indexes corresponding to banned members in the *membarr* sequence

Express these properties of the retrieve relation formally in a schema.

Exercise 11.6 $\diamond$ Give an expanded definition of *TotalBanMember*, and then give the corresponding concrete operation *CTotalBanMember* using the same retrieve relation. Go on to give a normalised version *NTotalBanMember*.

11.9.1   Translating the concrete state definition

We take the outline driver program given earlier in Figure 11.1 as our model; in Figure 11.2 we adapt it for the present system and fill in some detail relating to a possible representation of the types *ID* and *PERSON*. Appropriate values for

```
|[ /* Football Identity Scheme */

    /* Axiomatic and ancillary declarations */
    maxmems : int = ?;
    idlen, plen : int = ?, ?;
    type ID = [1:idlen]char;
    type PERSON = [1:plen]char;
    type IPpair = record id:ID, per:PERSON;
    type REPORT = (Ok,TooManyMembers,AlreadyMember,NotMember);
    function idgen(m : int)ID = |[ IdgenBody ]|;

    /* Concrete state declarations */
    membarr : [1:maxmems]IPpair; banarr : [1:maxmems]int;
    mtop, btop : int;

    /* Initialise system */
    mtop, btop := 0, 0;

    /* Perform operations */
    type Choice = (Quit, AddMember, BanMember);
    |[ chosen : Choice;
       MakeFirstChoice;
       do /* Concrete state invariant */
           /* membarr[1:mtop] injective from ID to PERSON */
           /* all values in banarr[1:btop] less than mtop */
           /* no duplicates in membarr[1:mtop] or banarr[1:btop] */
           chosen /= Quit -->
               if chosen = AddMember -->
                   |[ applicant? : PERSON; id! : ID; rep! : REPORT;
                      get applicant?; NTotalAddMember;
                      send id!, rep! ]|
               [] chosen = BanMember -->
                   |[ ban? : ID; rep! : REPORT;
                      get ban?; NTotalBanMember; send rep!  ]|
               fi;
               MakeNextChoice
        od;
      ]|;
    Goodbye
]|
```

Figure 11.2: Driver for Football Identity Scheme

maxmems, `idlen` and `plen` would be filled in when the system is tailored to the requirements of a given football club. The details of a suitable `idgen` function must also be supplied; we shall not concern ourselves with this, nor with the precise mechanism for obtaining from the user the choices of the next operations to be performed.

11.9.2   Translating a concrete operation

We now signpost the way towards the code for the operation *CTotalAddMember* in the following series of exercises.

Exercise 11.7 ⬦ We can reduce the frame for *NTotalAddMember*, noting that *btop* is unchanged, and that the values of *membarr'*, *mtop'*, *id*! and *rep*! do not depend on *btop*. Give the reduced schema *RTotalAddMember*.

Exercise 11.8 ⬦ The reduced schema *RTotalAddMember* can be expressed as a disjunction of three schemas:

$$RTotalAddMember \; \hat{=}$$
$$NormalAddMember \lor ErrorTooManyMembers \lor ErrorAlreadyMember$$

Write out these three schemas, reducing the frame where possible.

Exercise 11.9 ⬦ For the moment suppose there were a function:

```
occurs2nd(p:PERSON,a:[]IPpair)bool = |[ Occ2Body ]|
```

in Ω which tests if a given **PERSON** occurs as second element at some index in an array of **IPpairs**, delivering a Boolean value. Convert the disjunction of three schemas from the previous exercise into a conditional construct with three alternatives and suitable guards, making use of `occurs2nd`.

Exercise 11.10 ⬦ Each of the arms of the conditional in the previous exercise can be refined using an assignment. Write out these assignments.

Exercise 11.11 ⬦ Now instead of making use of the function `occurs2nd`, consider refining *RTotalAddMember* as follows:

$$RTotalAddMember \sqsubseteq$$
```
             |[ memtest : bool;
```
$$SetMemtest;$$
$$RTAMwithMemtest \;]|$$

where we define:

$$
\begin{array}{|l}
\hline
\_\,SetMemtest \_\!\!\!\_\!\!\!\_ \\
\;\Delta[memtest : Bool]; \\
\;\Xi[applicant? : PERSON;\; membarr : \mathbb{N} \nrightarrow (ID \times PERSON] \\
\hline
\;memtest' = Yes \Leftrightarrow \exists\, i : 1..mtop \bullet second(membarr\; i) = applicant? \\
\hline
\end{array}
$$

$$
\begin{array}{|l}
\hline
\_\,RTAMwithMemtest \_\!\!\!\_\!\!\!\_ \\
\;\Xi[memtest : Bool]; \\
\;RTotalAddMember \\
\hline
\;memtest = Yes \Leftrightarrow \exists\, i : 1..mtop \bullet second(membarr\; i) = applicant? \\
\hline
\end{array}
$$

where we suppose that the type *Bool* is defined:

$$Bool ::= Yes \mid No$$

and we think of *Yes* and *No* as the Boolean values in Ω. Argue that the refinement given above is valid. (Note: *second* is a Z library function which selects the second element of a pair.)

Exercise 11.12 ◇ The schema *SetMemtest* can be implemented using a loop construct, rather as *FindMAxPos* was. Derive the appropriate loop and carry out all the relevant proofs.

Exercise 11.13 ◇ The schema *RTAMwithMemtest* can again be implemented using an alternation construct; do so making use of the value of memtest in the guards.

11.10   Further reading

In this chapter and the previous one we have presented the main ideas of refinement. In particular we have introduced the notion that a program may contain within it subspecifications which say what effect is to be achieved at certain points but do not give programming language instructions which produce that desired effect. We have suggested only minor extensions to the Z notation for the purposes of writing such subspecifications, but we should recognise that a notation which is ideally suited to formal specification at the most abstract level might be somewhat different from a notation for describing the finer details of an algorithm.

Several researchers have suggested that a notation in which pre- and postconditions are given separately, rather than the Z schema notation with its single predicate, is preferable when we want to describe subspecifications. A notation of the following form has been proposed:

$$frame : [pre, post]$$

where *frame* is a sequence of variable names (the ones which may be changed), and *pre* and *post* are the pre- and post-conditions. We have not used this notation in our presentation because we did not want to introduce, in what is meant to be a brief introduction, a whole new raft of notation with rather incompatible conventions. However the reader should be aware that this is an important strand of development within the Z research community. Certainly the new notation makes it easier to express certain refinement laws. From a methodological point of view, the emphasis is placed on the calculation of refinements, in contrast to inspired guesswork followed by confirmation by proof. Such calculations would be made by appeal to laws drawn from a rich repertory of refinement laws which have been discovered and tabulated. The notation and its associated methodology have come to be known as the Refinement Calculus. More information about the Refinement Calculus may be found in [Mor88] and [Mor94].

As we said on an earlier occasion, the ideas involved in operation decomposition are not entirely new, and may be traced back to Dijkstra [Dij76] and Hoare [Hoa69]. Other books which are concerned with the process of developing programming language code from pre- and post-assertions are [Gri81, Dij88, Dro89] and there are several others.

Chapter 12

From theory to practice

In the previous chapters we have introduced the idea of using a mathematical notation, based on set theory and logic, for the description of computer systems as an aid to understanding their function before they are actually produced. We have shown how one particular notation, Z, allows the structuring of specifications by means of schemas. We have set down a way in which these schemas can be used to describe a system in terms of its state, duly constrained by invariants, and the ways in which that state is affected by those operations which the system must provide in order to be useful. We have also shown how schemas may be used to factor out re-usable components of the specification, and how separation of concerns may also be addressed by such means. The notion of proof based on the ability to reason about specifications due to their mathematical nature has also been introduced. Finally we have given a flavour of the ways in which the rigorous development of actual programs from Z specifications can be approached.

In this final chapter we now turn to some of the peripheral issues which surround the application of this method of specification to the craft of software development, and reflect on successes and failures.

12.1 The place of formal methods

In Chapter 1 we introduced the notion of the software life-cycle, and it now seems appropriate to return to this and examine the places where Z is likely to be useful. The main emphasis of this book has been on the specification of particular solutions to information processing needs, so it would be natural to assume that Z is applicable only during the specification phase of the software life-cycle. However, experience has shown that the ability to build a mathematical model of a system prior to embarking on costly programming activity can be very helpful at the point where the customer's requirements are still being studied. The need to write precisely concerning what is meant by the operations required by a user can cause many points of clarification to arise. The fewer of these left outstanding, the less the scope for error in subsequent stages. Z is thus helpful as a requirements analysis technique. We comment later on the possible uses of Z in conjunction with a prototyping approach.

In Chapters 10 and 11 we examined some of the ways in which progress may be made from specification towards actual program code. This is usually associated with the design and implementation phases of the life-cycle. The scope of Z would therefore seem to be centred upon the specification phase, but extending to either side.

In addition to these phases where Z may be gainfully employed there is an obvious, if second order, effect on the testing process. Given that increased precision in the production stages will reduce the number of errors left to be discovered at the subsequent testing phases, it seems obvious that testing could perhaps be reduced, or made more productive in some way. It should be noted that large and complex software systems such as operating systems may require thousands of hours of testing on a variety of large and expensive computers in order to persuade the manufacturer that a new version is not unacceptably less reliable than the previous one. This process can cost hundreds of thousands of pounds for each new version produced, and even a small reduction in this cost is very attractive. It would seem feasible to use formal specifications to direct the testing process into those corners of the operational envelope of the system where errors are most likely to lurk. Some success has been recorded with this approach for hardware [Scu88] but no general scheme is yet available.

12.2   Notes for new users

The luxury of being able to start up a 'green field' software development project complete with its own new techniques is one very seldom enjoyed in the industry at the time of writing, and as the body of existing software continues to grow it seems to be ever less likely. Users of software products expect (and deserve) some kind of continuity, and so products must be corrected and extended and offered on other computers. Thus, new development can be seen as a special case of maintenance. Any new technique must be applicable to the improvement of existing practice, so the enthusiastic proponent of Z is faced with the immediate challenge of introducing the technique to an existing product in an environment where other methods are already current practice.

Deprived of the opportunity to create a brand new environment within which (formally) to build sparkling new products, what can realistically be attempted, and what are the pitfalls?

In point of fact, most products do have an eventual replacement timescale, albeit often a long one. This may be due to structural decay of the product, due to long years of incremental change, or to the user interface becoming outdated, or to the desire to re-implement completely because of the need to move to a new computer architecture. There are thus points where new design techniques may be applied. A word of caution is in order here: the use of any new technique requires time to allow working practices to develop in ways appropriate to the local environment, and a major new development to tight timescales may not be the best place to attempt this local tailoring.

Perhaps the most frequently encountered objection to the adoption of formal methods is that mathematics is too difficult. We hope that this book goes some way towards dispelling this myth through its use of simple set theory and first year undergraduate logic. We suspect that the real issue is one which has been called 'mathsfear', which has at least two manifestations. The first of these concerns the designer or implementer who, after a successful career using the craft methods common to the software industry, is suddenly faced with the unfamiliar, along with all the attendant risks of failure and feelings of inadequacy. Worse yet, production of specifications of hand-crafted products might mean that the painfully acquired intimate knowledge of the product, which may be the practitioner's real value to his or her employer, is now to be made generally available. The second area of repressed concern may lie with the leader of the team, who may fear that engineers trained in a mathematical notation will be able to produce documents which a traditional, craft trained manager will be incapable of understanding. Experience of the industry shows that very few managers actually read documents produced by technical staff and that this fear is thus largely illusory. Nevertheless, imagined fears remain fears, and as such are liable to hinder the adoption of formal methods.

For the reasons outlined above it is suggested that formal (and any other) methods are best introduced into an organisation by means of pilot projects. Experience has shown that such projects can generate small groups of skilled practitioners, and that the spread of techniques through an organisation is often related to the movement of personnel, who take with them ideas which work.

Set against this, it must be pointed out that achievement of a critical mass of expertise can be difficult and important. If documents containing formal text are to be reviewed, then the participants in the reviews must be trained to read them. Where external reviewers, perhaps from other projects, are involved this can be a problem.

A section of a product which is being redeveloped may serve as the vehicle for formal methods so long as it is accepted that other parts of the system, to which the formally defined component will be interfaced, will probably have no formal definition. A team size of three to five seems to be in order so that the work of all can readily be shared to maximise the spread of understanding.

12.3   Effects of formal methods

Experience has shown that the successful use of formal methods requires more than just the training of staff. Indeed, the application of any new method or tool seems to be greatly eased by the provision of adequate support. The process of applying new and unfamiliar notions in an environment where critical and possibly hostile forces exist can be made much more effective at an early stage if a consultant, working perhaps half time on the pilot project, is available. The rôle of the consultant is to provide an answering service for queries concerning notation and technique, and to provide interpretation of results and reassurance that all is well to local management.

An inevitable consequence of the application of rigorous mathematical analysis to the specification phase of a project is the calling into question of many of the assumptions made thus far concerning the objectives of the project. This is actually a good thing, as it helps to remove errors and ambiguities at an early stage. The alternative is the postponement of these issues until, ultimately, the person writing actual program code must make potentially expensive decisions. However, this remedial work is not a feature of projects which do not use formal methods, and hence adequate time is seldom included in the project plans. It can only be prudent therefore to ensure that provision for such effort is made within a Z pilot project, to avoid later criticism due to apparent delay. It should be noted that experience with use of formal methods shows that the extra investment in correcting errors and ambiguities at the earliest possible stage is handsomely repaid by significant reduction in total errors discovered over the whole development cycle, with consequent reduction in total cost. (This can amount to a figure as large as 9%, as in the IBM CICS case, which is outlined later in this chapter.) The feed-forward effect also appears to reduce the time and effort required at the detailed design and coding stages, resulting in an overall project duration similar to that normally anticipated, despite an extended specification phase.

One of the ways in which the use of formal methods such as Z can alter the process of producing computer systems is through its effect on such review or inspection activities as are carried out as part of the project. It has been noted [Fag76] that the discovery and rectification of faults in software is amenable to adaptations of the inspection processes more normally associated with 'physical' engineering disciplines. That is, a document or piece of software is subjected to a methodical analysis, with defects being noted for subsequent correction. It is all too easy during a review to become sidetracked by the syntactic aspects of the document, especially one written in natural langauge. The presence of mathematical text seems to help the review team to rise above this. This may simply be due to the increased information content of the document. The presence of statements which now have unambiguous meaning (or at least clearly defined ambiguity) allows the review process to focus on the meaningful content and rise above mere quibbling about syntax. This may well cause any remedial work identified to be more significant, which will mean that more time and effort will be required to complete it. It is important to remember that the purpose of review is to find errors, rather than merely to achieve some semblance of progress through the completion of a particular stage in a development process by some set time. The manager responsible for the activity may be under strong, even financial, pressure to achieve sign off and hence completion of the review item. It is important for user projects to understand that the extra work generated at early reviews is a benefit due to the use of formal methods, rather than a justification for their abandonment. Again, the first time user of formal methods would be well advised to ensure that review staff are alive to this prospect and make time available to cope with it. It may also be beneficial to discuss these effects with quality assurance staff to ensure that review or inspection criteria and checklists take advantage of the use of formal methods.

It is suggested that the introduction of Z falls naturally into three major phases. First, the notation and method of producing specifications is taught and applied, initially to existing problems and then to a small, pilot development. Second, when confidence in the use of the notation is fairly general, some reasoning is applied, perhaps in a limited fashion; calculation of the pre-conditions of operations is a fruitful area. Finally, the proof skills acquired during phase two are applied to the rigorous development of program code from specifications, if this is demonstrably cost-justifiable. The size of the task of producing a fully proven system should not be underestimated. Indeed, at the present state of the technology it is probably only justifiable for critical components of systems such as secure or life critical systems. However the savings due to reduced testing requirements will certainly offset the costs of proof, but it is not yet clear to what extent.

Because the cost of proof may be high, two cases for the application of formal methods may be discerned. In the critical system case, the primary concern is absolute conformance to specification, with cost a secondary issue. Large sums of money will be spent on providing the necessary personnel with the mathematical skills required to allow the painstaking task of producing programs which will adhere strictly to the given specification. Typical applications might be aircraft autopilots, medical treatment systems or nuclear reactor controllers. It should also be borne in mind that embedded elements of systems which are apparently non-critical may be so expensive to correct in the event of subsequent discovery of faults as to justify similar treatment. The second case justifies the use of formal methods on the basis of productivity, where the primary goals are reduction in development time and overall cost, as opposed to the absolute elimination of divergence from specification. In this scenario little or no proof may actually be done, with the mathematics being used to encourage early confrontation of problems and to facilitate clear concise communications within the team. The differences implied by these two scenarios should be borne in mind when starting to apply formal methods; the neophyte should ensure that the objectives of the work are clearly understood.

12.4 Relationship to other methods

As we have indicated in the preface, Z is not the only notation or method which aims to confer a degree of formality and rigour upon the software development process. There are other members of the family, some closely related, such as VDM [Jon86, JS90], and some more distant cousins too, as exemplified by CSP [Hoa85] and OBJ [GW88]. Space does not permit a detailed examination of any of these other techniques, each of which has its strengths and weaknesses and its advocates and critics. Perhaps it will suffice to note the more commonly encountered branches of the family.

12.4.1 State-based techniques

Notations such as Z and VDM encourage the construction of a model of a system or problem in terms of sets, maps, sequences, predicates and all the other items of the tool kit. VDM has both contributed to and drawn upon the development of Z, and is thus a close cousin. These are the techniques most widespread in industrial use, and arguably the most readily grasped.

The B notation [Abr96] offers the prospect of machine assistance in the rigorous production of programs from specifications, and it shares many of the characteristics of Z and VDM.

12.4.2 Algebraic techniques

Notations such as OBJ [GW88] allow the description of a system and its constituent parts by means of sets of equations which capture behaviour directly, rather than using sets and the like in order to build a mathematical model. Proponents of these techniques claim that a more abstract description of a system is thus achieved since the specifier is not constrained merely to choose from sets, relations, functions, sequences and so forth. Further, machine proof techniques are claimed to be simplified by the theoretical features of this style of specification.

Offset against this, more structuring of the specification at an early stage seems to be required in a fashion which begins to suggest a particular implementation, and the actual equations can be quite difficult to construct until substantial experience is gained. The elegant handling of error cases, greatly aided by schema calculus in Z, seems difficult to achieve. Industrial usage is limited as yet. We note that versions of OBJ under development appear to draw on Z experience of the benefits of packaging mathematics in boxes within natural language text.

12.4.3   Process algebras

Z encourages the construction of a model of a system in terms of mathematical data structures and of the static and dynamic constraints on them. By contrast, the process algebras exemplified by CSP (Communicating Sequential Processes) [Hoa85] and CCS (Calculus of Communicating Systems) [Mil89] allow a system to be modelled by a collection of processes which communicate one with another.

Both the model-based and the process algebraic approaches offer ways of formalising aspects of systems: in some cases the one offers a clearer initial understanding, and in some cases the other. There also seem to be occasions when the use of one follows the use of the other during the design process; for instance, an abstract description of a hotel reservation system might be made using Z, with CSP being used to realise a design which requires communication between geographically separated computers.

Thus the question of whether to use Z or CSP, and in what order, may appear to be a thorny one. We believe that software engineers can benefit from knowledge of both, and should use their judgement as to which to apply to specific parts of the problem in hand. An analogy for this might be the use of Boolean algebra to design the digital elements of an electronic system, alongside the use of phasor analysis when reasoning about the analogue parts of the system. In both cases, the two techniques complement each other and thus form valuable parts of the professional engineer's training.

Overall, we suggest that model-based techniques such as Z currently offer the best introduction to the use of formal techniques in software engineering.

12.4.4   Structured analysis methods

At the time of writing one of the visible manifestations of the growing concern for the efficiency of the software engineering process is the level of interest in methods based on the Yourdon/de Marco approach, often supported by so-called computer aided software engineering (CASE) tools [BO85].

This family of methods encourages the initial approach to the definition of a system via its context and the data flows into it and from it. Analysis is then directed in such a fashion as to identify sub-components and the flows of data between them. Some of the members of this family of methods then prescribe ways of producing program modules corresponding to these sub-components. (The MASCOT method, although not normally considered to be a member of the Yourdon family, has many similarities [Mas]).

It may seem that the choice must be made between formal methods and structured methods, especially as the examples given in this book are of high-level specifications of systems such as might typically be used to illustrate the production of data flow diagrams. However our experience with graphical methods suggests that, whilst they allow the rapid gaining of insights into the structure of problems and possible solutions, they may fall short when precise capture of behaviour is required. We suggest that the two techniques can be used in partnership, where data flow diagramming is used to structure a specification, and Z used to capture the required behaviour of the components. An alternative approach, which has been found useful in practice, is to capture system requirements using Z, and then to use this information to draw data flow diagrams. This has been found especially helpful where the data flow diagram is difficult to produce because issues remain open concerning the functioning of the desired system. Further, the use of Z to produce a terse and fairly flat specification of functional requirements can yield considerable insight without incurring the costs associated with building and then changing a highly structured initial specification.

Work has also been undertaken on the integration of SSADM and Z [PWM93], the translation of data flow diagrams to and from Z [Ran90] and the use of entity relationship models as a basis for Z specifications [SA90].

12.4.5   Object-oriented methods

Arguably the most prominent current trend in software development is that of object orientation. Whilst originally conceived as a program structuring concept in the Simula-67 [Kir89] language, the ideas of class and object have subsequently been applied (*inter alia*) to program design and, more recently, systems and problem analysis techniques. In the case of the latter there have emerged both fresh notations and methods as well as derivatives or extensions of earlier efforts, particularly in the structured methods sphere. A number of object-oriented styles and derivatives of Z have been described and used [SBC92], and we do no more than direct the reader there for further information on these.

Advocates of object orientation claim that it provides a radically new approach to the contemplation of problems by allowing the construction of models which correspond more closely with their real world counterparts, whilst also providing inheritance as an additional abstraction mechanism.

At a less dramatic level it may be claimed that gains in initial understanding and subsequent maintenance are to be had from the close grouping of items of data and the operations which are allowed to manipulate them which arise from the use of the class/object concepts. It could be argued that this is rather more of a packaging issue.

We believe that time will be the judge of this trend in software engineering, but would wish to note in passing that recent experience with a moderately sized case study in Object Z gave rise to the feeling that object-oriented analysis seems to require early deconstruction of the problem into objects. One consequence of this is a slight hindrance to the process of considering and capturing system-wide invariants, which we believe to be a particularly precious and often overlooked benefit of the Z approach. We cannot thus claim wholehearted enthusiasm for the object-oriented approach to specification.

12.5   Prototyping

There is currently a lively debate within the industry regarding the merits of prototyping as a means of eliciting customer requirements. Using this approach, an informal notion of the user's needs are taken as the basis for an implementation, which is typically built using special purpose languages and tools. The user is thus able to try some portion of a solution, or a facsimile thereof, at an early stage. This offers feedback to the design team and allows iteration towards a solution. Since the user's perceived requirement may differ from the actual requirement, and since the very existence of a solution system may in turn change that requirement, it is argued that prototyping is more likely to yield an eventual solution with a high probability of satisfying the user.

It has been suggested that the notion of formal specification runs counter to the idea of prototyping, in that it requires the construction of a more or less complete description of a system before any implementation is begun. We would like to note that there are certain classes of system, notably those where the interface between the computer and the user represents a high proportion of the total system, where the processes involved, such as choice of colours and positioning of items on a display are as yet insufficiently well understood as to admit complete formalism. Prototyping can play a valuable rôle in such situations. Equally, there are classes of system where prototyping is an unsatisfactory approach; the example of an aircraft flight control system springs to mind. Such classes of system need a very high degree of assurance of predictable and well-understood behaviour, which seems more likely to be achieved through systematic exploration of mathematical properties than through user reaction.

We also suggest that all prototyping involves a specification phase, even if only a vestigial one. The user requirement, however vague and informal, will certainly require some study before the intuitive ideas of possible solutions spring to mind. When these ideas do occur, how are they to be captured? Where the functions of the system are apparently simple and seem to correspond well to intuitive notions it may be fairly straightforward to work from these notions, and rely on the user's interaction with the prototype to confirm them. We suggest that functions of systems are frequently much more complex than intuition suggests, and that reliance on intuition alone can lead to dangerous misunderstanding which even the simplest of formal specifications could call into question. For example, consider the handling of annual subscriptions to a sports club. Seemingly, this is a trivial issue, yet we have direct experience of a system where attempts to capture correctly the procedures to be adopted when:

- the subscription rate changes

- a subscription is paid in advance

- an overdue subscription is paid

have required several iterations even when a Z specification has been produced. We suggest, from some experience of using prototyping languages, that a mathematical formalism has a place as a way of capturing pre-prototype ideas.

To put this another way, perhaps, one of the tasks confronting the formal specifier is the reinterpretation of a document in terms that a user can understand and hence dispute or verify. The nature of Z, with its strong emphasis on the use of natural language text, is a great help in this area. Nevertheless, the production of prototype implementations is potentially a very convincing way to explore the behaviour of a specification with its eventual user, and it is in that combination that we suggest formal specification and prototyping offer the most synergy.

12.6 Support tools

It is clearly possible to apply the Z notation without recourse to any graphical technology more complex than pencil and paper. However, most software development organisations make use of word-processing facilities for the production of documents, and it is thus desirable to be able to do likewise with formal specifications. This is the basic formal methods support tool set, namely assistance with editing and printing. The immediate problem is the provision of mathematical type fonts. The particular solution adopted will depend very much on the local environment, but many of the systems available demonstrate their academic history by being Unix based. One example of these is the LaTeX system used in the production of the text for this book, including all the mathematics. Versions of this package are also available for IBM Personal Computers and compatible systems, and the Apple Macintosh series. The widespread availability of personal computers and workstations with bit-mapped graphical displays and laser printers has eased considerably the display and editing of documents containing mathematical symbols.

Given the ability to edit and print Z documents it may also be attractive to produce cross reference listings automatically, showing where particular schemas are defined and used. This aids the maintenance of large specifications.

The precise syntax of Z allows the use of computer-based checking tools. These may simply identify syntactic errors or check that the usage of the objects referred to by the different parts of the specification is correct with respect to their types. The *fuzz* package produced by Mike Spivey (of the Programming Research Group, Oxford University) is a typical example.

Any major project will produce large numbers of documents, and it is helpful to be able to manage the existence of multiple versions of these, along with their relationships to other informal documents and related program code components. For this, some kind of database and configuration management system is required. To fit in with local methods it may be desirable to integrate this system with others, perhaps provided by a CASE tool system.

The great advantage of mathematical methods of specification lies with the ability to reason about specifications. Currently, the provision of tools to support this reasoning is still a research topic. Although not strictly a Z tool, the B notation [Abr96] and its supporting tool set may be indicative of the sorts of tools which may become more widespread.

12.7   Case histories

There are now many instances where Z and other formal methods have been used in the development of computer systems. It is clearly impossible to list them all, but two representative examples are given here.

12.7.1   The CICS product

The best documented example of the use of Z, and indeed of any formal method, is possibly that of the IBM Hursley Laboratory and its application of Z to the Customer Information and Control System (CICS). This product is used by IBM customers for the development and provision of interactive applications such as on-line reservation services and automated bank transaction systems. CICS organises the message flow between users' terminals and the application programs proper, and provides logging and other features to assist in recovery from system breakdowns. It thus shares many of the facilities of a typical real time operating system, and is a very substantial software product, consisting of around 500,000 lines of source program code. The product itself is in widespread use in financial and commercial systems across the whole of the western world.

In broad terms, the study of Z at Hursley began in 1981 [CNS87], and to date over 200 staff have been trained to read or write Z. The most recent experiences show that substantial reductions in the number of errors encountered during the coding and test stages can be made, at the cost of some extra work during the early phases of the life-cycle. This figure may be as much as 40% overall [NC88]. To date, about one-tenth of the lines of code required for a new version of the system have been developed using Z, and an overall cost saving of around 9% has been reported. Use of formal proof is currently limited to the simplification of pre-conditions of operations, and refinement into program is carried out informally, making extensive use of group review mechanisms. Much of the benefit is thus derived from the use of the notation as a documentation, communication and thinking aid.

Future work is likely to include the development of methods and tools to support the introduction of proof techniques, and to increase the usage of Z generally across the product. One is tempted to speculate on the equation which relates the cost of testing and validating a system produced by conventional means, plus the cost of correcting errors found by users, with the alternative costs of proof. Could it be that IBM might one day offer a version of CICS which meets conventional engineering standards, in that it will be offered as fault free?

12.7.2   The Inmos T800 Floating Point Transputer

Background

The original Inmos Transputers did not provide support for floating point arithmetic in hardware. During 1985/6 a project to add support for floating point arithmetic for the IMS T800 version of the Transputer was begun. The slow progress being made by the 'informal' methods team plus Inmos's close links with Oxford University Programming Research Group, where much research into the use of formal methods has been carried out, led Inmos to set up a group to develop a formal approach to the problem.

Approach adopted

The procedure for building a proven implementation was broadly as follows.

- To begin with, a formal specification of the IEEE floating point standard was made using the Z notation. The agreement of this with the informal IEEE specification was necessarily achieved by inspection.

- From this initial specification a decomposition process led to the production of smaller units of specification. In conjunction with this the mathematics necessary to recombine these smaller units into a specification which was provably equivalent to the original were produced.

- Next, occam [Lim88] programs were written which were shown to satisfy the decomposed specifications.

- Using a semi-automatic transformation tool developed at Oxford University to check that the programs remained unchanged from the functionality viewpoint, the programs were then manipulated to optimise performance.

- Finally the occam code was used as input to a software suite which resulted in definitions of the microcode required.

Discussion

A number of features of this experience are worthy of note. First, the Z technique used for the initial specification work has been seen to convey advantages to software projects in a number of cases, including the CICS project at IBM, but here is a well-documented case of its relevance in the VLSI field. Second, occam lends itself to this type of rigorous approach because it is a language designed from the beginning to possess those attributes which are necessary to allow the manipulation of programs in this way. Third, the availability of a software suite to aid the production of VLSI was clearly a great help. The project as a whole represents the successful blending of a number of techniques which have not had a very wide exposure beyond the research field in some cases. It is also interesting to note that the errors which appeared in the first silicon were traced to transcription errors by humans, a clear indication of the desirability of machine support all through the design process.

Benefits

- The total development time was considerably less than a similar project using informal methods, due to the enormous amount of effort needed to verify an informally produced design after the fact. An estimated improvement of 25% in time to market was made.

- The path from specification to product is comprehensively documented (of necessity), greatly assisting future enhancement.

- The first silicon produced contained a very small number of errors, and these were mostly traced to human transcription errors.

12.7.3   A cautionary tale

It may be deemed unwise to include a horror story concerning the application of formal methods at this point, but we believe that wisdom often proceeds from the study of failure. A certain team – they shall remain anonymous – began to apply a formal method to the development of Product A. Besides making a formal notation available, a method for producing formal specifications and then pseudocode was developed, along with inspection and review procedures for quality assurance purposes. As anticipated, the specification and design of Product A took longer than it might have, had formal methods not been used, but the coding was accomplished more easily than usual, leading to completion on schedule. The product passed its acceptance trial with flying colours. Indeed, no errors whatsoever were detected during the trial, which was certainly not the case with competing products.

The method was then applied to a successor, Product B. By this time, the original formal methods enthusiasts were no longer around, partly due to corporate reorganisation. The management team for B were perhaps less sympathetic to the use of formal methods, and reviews were expected to be completed by deadlines, rather than being used to identify problems early in the design. As a result, the formal aspects of the design were only sketchily done, and most of the actual design done via the pseudocode. A total commitment to the use of object-oriented programming was also made, regardless of concerns over possible performance penalties. Product B was late, faulty and deficient in performance, and these faults were laid squarely at the door of formal methods.

Needless to say, plans for any Products C and D made no mention of formal methods, yet many experienced engineers involved with Products A and B remain convinced of the utility of such methods.

The moral of this tale would seem to be that projects can fail due to many reasons, with the blame not always attributed to the real cause. Formal methods practitioners, beware!

12.8   Useful sources

As we made clear at the start, this book is written with the express purpose of introducing the notion of formal methods through the example of Z. The bibliography contains a list of publications giving more information about Z, and about other specification methods and notations.

It is often beneficial to share experiences and receive news of developments in a particular field by meeting with other users. There is a Z User Group, details of which may be obtained from:

> The Industrial Liaison Secretary,
> Oxford University Computing Laboratory,
> 8-11 Keble Road,
> OXFORD,
> OX1 3QD,
> UK.

An electronic newsletter called Z FORUM exists, with the aim of disseminating useful items of news to the Z community. Receipt of this obviously requires access to electronic mail, and may be requested by sending a mail message to `zforum-request@comlab.ox.ac.uk`.

Oxford University also plays host to a World Wide Web site and a portion of this is given over to Z matters. The URL is `http://www.comlab.ox.ac.uk`. We suggest that the best way to improve understanding of the craft of specification is to read examples, preferably of good specifications. These may be found in copies of relevant conference proceedings, and many examples are available in the form of monograph papers from the Computing Laboratory at Oxford University. IBM Hursley Laboratories have made many parts of the CICS specification available [HW90, MW90, Hou90, Bly90, Kin90]. A compendium of case studies is offered in [Hay93].

12.9   Future possibilities

Z is currently in industrial use on a number of products. Industrial users often want standardisation as a way of minimising potential sources of confusion and of maximising the availability of useful tools and ready trained staff. As noted in Chapter 1, we await the production of the British Standard for Z. Meanwhile, tool builders would seem able to consider [Spi92] as strongly indicative of the technical content of the standard. Authors and readers of specifications are unlikely to be led astray by what we offer here.

Nevertheless, research on Z continues. Several institutions are studying ways to extend Z to offer a more natural fit with the object-oriented programming paradigm, for instance, and work is continuing at the Programming Research Group in Oxford on the combination of Z with CSP to allow the natural description of systems where concurrency is an issue. The whole topic of refinement has seen substantial research progress even during the time taken to produce this book. Work on proof support tools proceeds, and early examples have been shown of systems capable of generating programs and proofs at the same time. The widespread availability of such systems could well alter the balance of the proof versus testing argument.

Appendix A: Solutions to exercises

Chapter 2

Exercise 2.1

(i) *{Finland, Sweden}*

(ii) *{Belgium, France, Germany, Italy, Luxemburg, Netherlands, Denmark, Greece, Ireland, United Kingdom, Spain, Portugal }*

(iii) *{France, Germany, Italy, Denmark, Greece, Ireland, United Kingdom, Spain, Portugal }*

(iv) $\emptyset$

(v) *{Denmark, Norway, Iceland}*

(vi) $\emptyset$

Exercise 2.2

If $x \in A \cup (B \cup C)$ then $x \in A$ or $x \in B \cup C$.

(a) if $x \in A$ then $x \in A \cup B$ and so $x \in (A \cup B) \cup C$

(b) if $x \in B \cup C$ then $x \in B$ or $x \in C$

    (i) if $x \in B$ then $x \in A \cup B$ and so $x \in (A \cup B) \cup C$

    (ii) if $x \in C$ then $x \in (A \cup B) \cup C$

So in all cases $x \in (A \cup B) \cup C$. Hence, $A \cup (B \cup C) \subseteq ((A \cup B) \cup C$. Together with the argument in the question, this gives $A \cup (B \cup C) = (A \cup B) \cup C$. Similarly:

(a) If $x \in (A \cap B) \cap C$ then $x \in A \cap B$ and $x \in C$. If $x \in A \cap B$ then $x \in A$ and $x \in B$, so $x \in B \cap C$ and $x \in A \cap (B \cap C)$. Therefore $(A \cap B) \cap C \subseteq A \cap (B \cap C)$.

(b) If $x \in A \cap (B \cap C)$ then $x \in A$ and $x \in B \cap C$. If $x \in B \cap C$ then $x \in B$ and $x \in C$, so $x \in A \cap B$ and $x \in (A \cap B) \cap C$. Therefore $A \cap (B \cap C) \subseteq (A \cap B) \cap C$.

Hence $A \cap (B \cap C) = (A \cap B) \cap C$

323

Exercise 2.3

(i) If $x \in A \cap (B \cup C)$ then $x \in A$ and $x \in B \cup C$. If $x \in B \cup C$ then $x \in B$ or $x \in C$

    (a) if $x \in B$ then, since $x \in A$, $x \in A \cap B$ and also $x \in (A \cap B) \cup (A \cap C)$

    (b) if $x \in C$ then, since $x \in A$, $x \in A \cap C$ and also $x \in (A \cap B) \cup (A \cap C)$

So in either case $x \in (A \cap B) \cup (A \cap C)$. Hence $A \cap (B \cup C) \subseteq (A \cap B) \cup (A \cap C)$. The other part of the argument goes similarly. If $x \in (A \cap B) \cup (A \cap C)$ then either $x \in A$ and $x \in B$ or $x \in A$ and $x \in C$; now:

    (a) if $x \in A$ and $x \in B$ then $x \in B \cup C$ also, so $x \in A \cap (B \cup C)$

    (b) if $x \in A$ and $x \in C$ then $x \in B \cup C$ also, so again $x \in A \cap (B \cup C)$

Thus $(A \cap B) \cup (A \cap C) \subseteq A \cap (B \cup C)$.

Exercise 2.4

(i) if $x \in A$ then, trivially, $x \in A$. Hence $A \subseteq A$.

(ii) Since $\emptyset$ has no members, $x \in \emptyset \Rightarrow x \in A$ is always true. Therefore $\emptyset \subseteq A$.

(iii) If $x \in A$ then $x \in A$ or $x \in B$. So $A \subseteq A \cup B$.

(iv) If $x \in A \cap B$ then $x \in A$ and $x \in B$. So $A \cap B \subseteq A$.

(v) If $x \in A \setminus B$ then $x \in A$ and $x \notin B$. So $A \setminus B \subseteq A$.

Exercise 2.5

(i) *UAWYZBU*

(ii) *UVYXU*

(iii) *UAWYVU*

(iv) *UXYZBU*

Exercise 2.6

(i)

p	q	$p \Rightarrow q$	$\neg p \vee q$
T	T	T	F T
T	F	F	F F
F	T	T	T T
F	F	T	T T

(ii)

p	q	r	$(p \wedge q)$	$\wedge$ r	p	$\wedge$ $(q \wedge r)$
T	T	T	T	T	T	T
T	T	F	T	F	F	F
T	F	T	F	F	F	F
T	F	F	F	F	F	F
F	T	T	F	F	F	T
F	T	F	F	F	F	F
F	F	T	F	F	F	F
F	F	F	F	F	F	F

(iii)

p	q	r	$(p \vee q)$	$\wedge$ r	$(p \wedge r)$	$\vee$	$(q \wedge r)$
T	T	T	T	T	T	T	T
T	T	F	T	F	F	F	F
T	F	T	T	T	T	T	F
T	F	F	T	F	F	F	F
F	T	T	T	T	F	T	T
F	T	F	T	F	F	F	F
F	F	T	F	F	F	F	F
F	F	F	F	F	F	F	F

(iv)

p	q	$\neg p$	$\vee$	$(p \wedge q)$	$\neg p$	$\vee$ q
T	T	F	T	T	F	T
T	F	F	F	F	F	F
F	T	T	T	F	T	T
F	F	T	T	F	T	T

Exercise 2.7

p	q	$(p \Leftrightarrow q)$	$(p \Rightarrow q)$	$\wedge$	$(q \Rightarrow p)$
T	T	T	T	T	T
T	F	F	F	F	T
F	T	F	T	F	F
F	F	T	T	T	T

Exercise 2.8

Suppose that $p \Rightarrow q$ is true and that q is false. If p were true, then (since q is false) $p \Rightarrow q$ would also be false, which contradicts our first assumption. Hence p must be false.

Exercise 2.9

(i) if $p \Leftrightarrow q$ is true, then $\neg p \Leftrightarrow \neg q$ is true

(ii) if $p \Leftrightarrow q$ is true and p is true, then q is true

(iii) if $p \Leftrightarrow q$ is true and q is true, then p is true

(iv) if $p \Leftrightarrow q$ is true and p is false, then q is false

(v) if $p \Leftrightarrow q$ is true and q is false, then p is false

Exercise 2.10

Ordinary usage of 'if' often implies 'only if' as well. For example:

> *if it's a sunny day then we will go for a picnic*

might well be interpreted as:

> *if it's a sunny day we will go for a picnic and if not we won't*

so the given sentence might well be captured in logical symbols as either $p \Rightarrow q$ or $(p \Rightarrow q) \wedge (\neg p \Rightarrow \neg q)$, the latter being equivalent to $p \Leftrightarrow q$.

Exercise 2.11

(i) there is a person who never speaks to any of his neighbours

(ii) everyone knows someone who lives alone

(iii) there is a country whose capital is not its largest city

Exercise 2.12

(i) $\forall g : girl \bullet g \ is \ nice \Rightarrow \exists s : sailor \bullet g \ loves \ s$
   or alternatively:
   $\exists s : sailor \bullet \forall g : girl \bullet girl \ is \ nice \Rightarrow g \ loves \ s$

(ii) $\neg (\forall g : thing \bullet g \ glisters \Rightarrow g \ gold)$

(iii) $\forall c : city \bullet c \ is \ a \ European \ capital \wedge c \neq Paris$
   $\Rightarrow Paris \ is \ more \ romantic \ than \ c$

(iv) $\exists r : region \bullet r \ is \ in \ Asia \wedge$
   $\forall c : country \bullet c \ is \ European \Rightarrow rainfall \ r > 5 * (rainfall \ c)$

Exercise 2.13

$\exists\, x : X \bullet (\exists\, y : Y \bullet x \text{ and } y \text{ are related})$

states that there is some value of x for which:

$\exists\, y : Y \bullet x \text{ and } y \text{ are related}$

and this in turn states that for some value of y, x and y are related. This is simply saying that x and y are related for some particular values of x and of y. This would be the same if the order of quantification were reversed. That is, the original statement is equivalent to:

$\exists\, y : Y \bullet (\exists\, x : X \bullet x \text{ and } y \text{ are related})$

Exercise 2.14

(i) every person has a parent

(ii) there is a person who is everyone's parent

(iii) the second proposition is stronger than the first, and we have here an example of following law:

$$\exists\, x : X \bullet \forall\, y : Y \bullet P \;\Rightarrow\; \forall\, y : Y \bullet \exists\, x : X \bullet P$$

Exercise 2.15

(i) *PrimeNumbers* ==
$\qquad \{n : integer \mid n > 0 \wedge$
$\qquad\qquad \forall\, p, q : integer \bullet p > 0 \wedge q > 0 \Rightarrow$
$\qquad\qquad\quad n = p * q \Rightarrow$
$\qquad\qquad\qquad ((p = 1 \wedge q = n) \;\vee\; (p = n \wedge q = 1))\}$

(ii) *ShakespeareHistorical* ==
$\qquad \{p : play \mid p \text{ is by Shakespeare} \wedge p \text{ is based upon historical events}\}$

(iii) *ToryEnclave* ==
$\qquad \{pc : constituency \mid$
$\qquad\qquad pc \text{ has Tory MP} \wedge$
$\qquad\qquad \forall\, nc : constituency \bullet nc \text{ borders } pc \Rightarrow \neg\,(nc \text{ has Tory MP})\}$

(iv) *Biographies* ==
$\qquad \{b : book \mid$
$\qquad\qquad \exists\, p : person \bullet b \text{ is the story of } p's \text{ life} \wedge$
$\qquad\qquad b \text{ is in English}\}$

(v) *PostWarAutobiographies* ==
      $\{b : Biographies \mid$
          b *is written by its subject* $\wedge$ b *published after* $1945\}$

(vi) *Misanthropists* ==
      $\{p : person \mid$
          $\forall n : person \bullet n$ *is neighbour of* $p \Rightarrow p$ *does not speak to* $n\}$

Exercise 2.16

(i) *CoPrimes* ==
      $\{n, m : number \mid$
          $n > m \wedge \neg \, (\exists p, q, r : number \bullet p > 1 \wedge n = p * q \wedge m = p * r)\}$

(ii) *TopOfThePops* ==
      $\{g : groupname; \ t : title; \ d : date \mid$
          $g's$ *recording of* d *was a best selling single recorded after* $1950 \wedge$
          d *is Saturday of the week when* $g's$ *recording of* t *sold most copies*$\}$

(iii) *GrandNationalWinners* ==
      $\{h : horse; \ r : rider; \ t : trainer; \ y : year \mid$
          h *won Grand National in year* $y \wedge$
          r *rode* h *in Grand National in year* $y \wedge$
          t *trained* $h \wedge y > 1950\}$

Exercise 2.17

FirstDivisionFixtures ==
      $\{f, g : club \mid f \in FirstDivision \wedge g \in FirstDivision \wedge f \neq g\}$

Exercise 2.18

(i) *CoPrimeSets1* ==
      $\{s : set \ of \ numbers \mid$
          $\forall f : number \bullet f > 1 \Rightarrow$
             $\neg \, (\forall e : number \bullet e \in s \Rightarrow \exists q : number \bullet e = q * f)\}$

(ii) *CoPrimeSets2* ==
      $\{s : set \ of \ numbers \mid$
          $\forall p, q : number \bullet (p \in s \wedge q \in s \wedge p \neq q) \Rightarrow$
             $\neg \, (\exists f, r, s : number \bullet f > 1 \wedge p = f * r) \wedge q = f * s))\}$

Chapter 3

Exercise 3.1

$ToNative \;==\; KnownToNative \cup UnknownToNative$

where:

$KnownToNative \;==$
    $\{\,Vocab, Vocab' : set\ of\ (Native,\ Foreign);$
      $f? : Foreign;\ ns! : set\ of\ Native;\ rep! : Message \mid$
          $Vocab \in WellFormedVocabs$
          $\wedge\ Vocab' = Vocab$
          $\wedge\ f? \in OrthoForeign$
          $\wedge\ ns! = \{n : Native \mid (n, f?) \in Vocab\}$
          $\wedge\ ns! \neq \emptyset \wedge rep! = Ok\}$
$UnknownToNative \;==$
    $\{\,Vocab, Vocab' : set\ of\ (Native,\ Foreign);$
      $f? : Foreign;\ ns! : set\ of\ Native;\ rep! : Message \mid$
          $Vocab \in WellFormedVocabs$
          $\wedge\ Vocab' = Vocab$
          $\wedge\ f? \in OrthoForeign$
          $\wedge\ ns! = \{n : Native \mid (n, f?) \in Vocab\}$
          $\wedge\ ns! = \emptyset \wedge rep! = WordNotKnown\}$
$TotalToNative \;==\; ToNative \cup ToNativeError$

where:

$ToNativeError \;==$
    $\{\,Vocab, Vocab' : set\ of\ (Native,\ Foreign);$
      $f? : Foreign;\ ns! : set\ of\ Native;\ rep! : Message \mid$
          $Vocab \in WellFormedVocabs$
          $\wedge\ Vocab' = Vocab$
          $\wedge\ f? \notin OrthoForeign$
          $\wedge\ ns! = \emptyset$
          $\wedge\ rep! = ErrorInInput\}$

Exercise 3.2

$FalseFriends \ ==$
$\qquad \{ Vocab, Vocab' : set\ of\ (Native,\ Foreign);$
$\qquad\quad falsefr! : set\ of\ (Native,\ Foreign) \mid$
$\qquad\qquad\qquad Vocab \in WellFormed Vocabs$
$\qquad\qquad\qquad \wedge\ Vocab' = Vocab$
$\qquad\qquad\qquad \wedge\ falsefr! = \{n : Native; f : Foreign \mid$
$\qquad\qquad\qquad\qquad\qquad n\ verysimilarto\ f$
$\qquad\qquad\qquad\qquad\qquad \wedge\ \exists f1 : Foreign \bullet (n, f1) \in Vocab$
$\qquad\qquad\qquad\qquad\qquad \wedge\ \exists n1 : Native \bullet (n1, f) \in Vocab$
$\qquad\qquad\qquad\qquad\qquad \wedge\ (n, f) \notin Vocab\}\}$

So the words concerned are known to the vocabulary, are very similar, but do not correspond in meaning.

Exercise 3.3

$[Date,\ Event]$

We model Diary as a pair consisting of a current date and a set of $(Date,\ Event)$ pairs representing engagements.

$Diary \ == \ \{currentdate : Date;\ engs : set\ of\ (Date,\ Event)\ pairs \mid$
$\qquad\qquad\qquad \forall d : Date;\ e : Event \bullet (d, e) \in engs \Rightarrow d \geqslant currentdate\}$

The following messages may be output:

$Message \ == \ \{Ok,\ BadDate,\ NewDay,\ NoEngagements\}$

(i) $AddEng \ ==$
$\qquad \{diary, diary' : Diary;\ d? : Date;\ f? : Event;\ r! : Message \mid$
$\qquad\qquad \exists c : Date;\ e : set\ of\ (Date,\ Event)\ pairs \bullet$
$\qquad\qquad\quad diary = (c, e)$
$\qquad\qquad\quad \wedge \neg\ (d?\ is\ before\ c)$
$\qquad\qquad\quad \wedge\ diary' = (c, e \cup \{(d?, f?)\})\}$

(ii) $DateList \ ==$
$\qquad \{diary, diary' : Diary;\ d? : Date;\ l! : set\ of\ Event;\ r! : Message \mid$
$\qquad\qquad \exists c : Date;\ e : set\ of\ (Date,\ Event)\ pairs \bullet$
$\qquad\qquad\quad diary = (c, e)$
$\qquad\qquad\quad \wedge\ diary' = diary$
$\qquad\qquad\quad \wedge \neg\ (d?\ is\ before\ c)$
$\qquad\qquad\quad \wedge\ l! = \{f : Event \mid (d?, f) \in e\}$
$\qquad\qquad\quad \wedge\ l! \neq \emptyset$
$\qquad\qquad\quad \wedge\ r! = Ok\}$

(iii) We assume a function *next d* which takes a date and gives the following day's date:

$$
\begin{aligned}
DayEnd \ = = \ \{ &diary, diary' : Diary;\ r! : Message\ | \\
&\exists\, c : Date;\ e : set\ of\ (Date,\ Event)\ pairs \bullet \\
&diary = (c, e) \\
&\wedge\ diary' = (next\ c, e \setminus \{f : Event\ |\ (c, f) \in e\}) \\
&\wedge\ r! = NewDay\}
\end{aligned}
$$

The system is initialised by inputting the current date; the set of engagements is taken to be empty.

$$
InitDiary\ = = \ \{diary' : Diary;\ c? : Date\ |\ diary' = (c?,\ \emptyset)\}
$$

Summary of operations:

Operation	Inputs/Outputs	Precondition
AddEng	*d? : Date*	$\neg\,(d?\ is\ before\ c)$
	e? : Event	
	r! : Message	
DateList	*d? : Date*	$\neg\,(d?\ is\ before\ c)$
	l! : set of Event	
	r! : Message	$\{f : Event\ |\ (d?, f) \in e\} \neq \emptyset$
NewDay	*r! : Message*	*true*

If the input date has already gone, *AddEng* records an error:

$$
\begin{aligned}
AddEngErr\ = = \ \{ &diary, diary' : Diary;\ d? : Date;\ f? : Event;\ r! : Message\ | \\
&\exists\, c : Date;\ e : set\ of\ (Date,\ Event)\ pairs \bullet \\
&diary = (c, e) \\
&\wedge\ d?\ is\ before\ c \\
&\wedge\ diary' = diary \\
&\wedge\ r! = BadDate\}
\end{aligned}
$$

For the *DateList* operation, a possible error occurs when the date entered is already past:

$$
\begin{aligned}
DateListErr\ = = \\
\{ &diary, diary' : Diary;\ d? : Date;\ l! : set\ of\ Event;\ r! : Message\ | \\
&\exists\, c : Date;\ e : set\ of\ (Date,\ Event)\ pairs \bullet \\
&diary = (c, e) \\
&\wedge\ diary' = diary \\
&\wedge\ d?\ is\ before\ c \\
&\wedge\ l! = \emptyset \\
&\wedge\ r! = BadDate\}
\end{aligned}
$$

Another case which may require comment is when the output set is empty:

$DateListEmpty$ ==
　　$\{diary, diary' : Diary; d? : Date; l! : set\ of\ Event; r! : Message\ |$
　　　　$\exists c : Date;\ e : set\ of\ (Date,\ Event)\ pairs\ \bullet$
　　　　　$diary = (c, e)$
　　　　　$\wedge\ diary' = diary$
　　　　　$\wedge \neg (d?\ is\ before\ c)$
　　　　　$\wedge\ l! = \{f : Event\ |\ (d?, f) \in e\} = \emptyset$
　　　　　$\wedge\ r! = NoEngagements\}$

The total operations are:

$$AddEngTotal \ == \ AddEng \cup AddEngErr$$
$$DateListTotal \ == \ DateList \cup DateListErr \cup DateListEmpty$$
$$DayEndTotal \ == \ DayEnd$$

Chapter 4

Exercise 4.1

(i) $\{\emptyset, \{0\}, \{1\}, \{0, 1\}\}$

(ii) $\{\emptyset\}$

(iii) $\{\emptyset, \{\emptyset\}\}$

(iv) $\{\emptyset, \{\emptyset\}, \{\{1\}\}, \{\emptyset, \{1\}\}\}$

Exercise 4.3

For each of the n elements of X there are two possibilities: either it appears in a particular subset or it does not. So there are 2^n possible subsets of X and so $\mathbb{P}\,X$ has 2^n members.

Exercise 4.5

(i) $\{\emptyset, \{round\}, \{round,\ square\}\}$

(ii) $\{\emptyset, \{round\}, \{square\}\}$

(iii) $\{\emptyset, \{\{round\}\}\}$

(iv) $\{\emptyset, \{\emptyset\}, \{\{\{round\}\}\}, \{\emptyset, \{\{round\}\}\}\}$

Exercise 4.7

(i) Incorrect. The empty set must be of type $\mathbb{P}\,X$ for some X, and so can never be of the same type as individual integers.

(ii) Correct.

(iii) Incorrect. A basic type declaration introduces a completely new type. In the example, y cannot be both an integer and an $OUTPUT$.

Exercise 4.11

Each possible pair has n choices for its first element and m choices for its second element. Thus there are $n * m$ possible pairs and so $X \times Y$ has $n * m$ members.

Exercise 4.13

(i) $onloan,\ notonloan : \mathbb{P}(BOOK \times \mathbb{Z})$

$notonloan\ =\ library \setminus onloan$

(ii) $issued : \mathbb{P}(USERS \times (BOOK \times \mathbb{Z}))$

$\forall\, copy : (BOOK \times \mathbb{Z}) \bullet$
$copy \in onloan \Leftrightarrow (\exists\, u : USERS \bullet (u, copy) \in issued)$

$\forall\, u, v : USERS;\ copy : (BOOK \times \mathbb{Z}) \bullet$
$(u, copy) \in issued \wedge (v, copy) \in issued \Rightarrow u = v$

Exercise 4.15

$Odd\ ==\ \{x : \mathbb{Z} \mid \exists\, y : \mathbb{Z} \bullet y \geqslant 0 \wedge x = 2 * y + 1\}$
$numpair : Odd \times Odd$
$\forall\, n, m : \mathbb{Z} \bullet numpair = (n, m) \Rightarrow n \geqslant m$

Exercise 4.17

(i) $node(Neil, unk, unk)$

(ii) $node(Jonathan, node(John, unk, unk), node(Mollie, unk, unk))$

(iii) $node(Ben,$
$\qquad node(Ian, unk, unk),$
$\qquad node(Jane,$
$\qquad\qquad node(John, node(Percy, unk, unk), node(Alice, unk, unk)),$
$\qquad\qquad node(Mollie, unk, unk)$
$\qquad\qquad)$
$\qquad)$

Exercise 4.20

$$BINTREE ::= binnode \langle\!\langle BINTREE \times BINTREE \rangle\!\rangle$$
$$endnode \langle\!\langle \mathbb{Z} \rangle\!\rangle$$

$$binnode(binnode(endnode5, binnode(endnode3, endnode6)),$$
$$endnode11)$$

Exercise 4.21

(i) 2

(ii) 1

(iii) −1

(iv) 2

Exercise 4.23

$$m \mathinner{\ldotp\ldotp} n \;=\; \{x : \mathbb{Z} \mid m \leqslant x \leqslant n\}$$

Exercise 4.24

(i) $\forall x, y : \mathbb{Z} \bullet x > y \Rightarrow x - y > 0$
       $\forall x, y : \mathbb{Z} \mid x > y \bullet x - y > 0$

(iv) $\forall a, b : \mathbb{Z} \bullet a < b \Rightarrow (\exists m : \mathbb{Z} \bullet m \in a \mathinner{\ldotp\ldotp} b \wedge (\exists n : \mathbb{Z} \bullet m = 2 * n))$
       $\forall a, b : \mathbb{Z} \mid a < b \bullet (\exists m : \mathbb{Z} \mid m \in a \mathinner{\ldotp\ldotp} b \bullet (\exists n : \mathbb{Z} \bullet m = 2 * n))$

Exercise 4.26

(i) $\{pair : \mathbb{Z} \times \mathbb{Z} \mid (\exists i : (1 \mathinner{\ldotp\ldotp} s) \bullet pair = (i, i))\}$

(ii) $\{i : (1 \mathinner{\ldotp\ldotp} 8) \bullet (i, i)\}$

Exercise 4.29

(i)

$$\begin{array}{|l}
\hline
evensize : \mathbb{P}\,\mathbb{Z} \\
\hline
\exists\, m : \mathbb{N}_1 \bullet \#evensize = m * 2 \\
\end{array}$$

Exercise 4.30

(i) *origin* $==$ $(0,0)$

Exercise 4.34

$$\underline{\hspace{1cm}[X]\hspace{1cm}}$$
$$\_ \subset \_ : \mathbb{P}(\mathbb{P}\,X \times \mathbb{P}\,X)$$
$$\forall S, T : \mathbb{P}\,X \bullet S \subset T \Leftrightarrow (\forall s : S \bullet s \in T \wedge S \neq T)$$

Exercise 4.36

The definition does not uniquely define *singleton* for each instantiation of X. For instance, if X is instantiated with $\mathbb{Z}$, then *singleton* could be $\{-1\}$, $\{0\}$, $\{1\}$...

Chapter 5

Exercise 5.2

(i) *rides'* $=$ *rides* $\cup \{(Kate, Bicycle)\}$

(ii) *rides'* $=$ *rides* $\setminus \{(Ben, Unicycle)\}$

(iii) *rides'* $= \{p : Potters;\ w : WheeledVehicles \mid$
$$(p, w) \in rides \wedge w \neq Bicycle \bullet (p, w)\}$$

Exercise 5.3

(i) $\{\emptyset, \{(0, blue)\}, \{(0, green)\}, \{(1, blue)\}, \{(1, green)\},$
$\{(0, blue), (0, green)\}, \{(0, blue), (1, blue)\}, \{(0, blue), (1, green)\},$
$\{(0, green), (1, blue)\}, \{(0, green), (1, green)\}, \{(1, blue), (1, green)\},$
$\{(0, blue), (0, green), (1, blue)\}, \{(0, blue), (0, green), (1, green)\},$
$\{(0, blue), (1, blue), (1, green)\}, \{(0, green), (1, blue), (1, green)\},$
$\{(0, blue), (0, green), (1, blue), (1, green)\}\}$

(ii) $\{\emptyset[A \times A]\}$

(iii) $\mathbb{Z} \leftrightarrow \mathbb{Z} \times \mathbb{Z}$

Exercise 5.5

(i) dom *plays* = {*Ashkenazy, Williams, David, Huw, Alice, Kate*}
   ran *plays* = {*piano, guitar, violin, trumpet, flute*}
   dom *worksby* = {*piano, guitar, harpsichord, trumpet, flute, violin*}
   ran *worksby* = {*hammering, plucking, blowing, bowing, scraping*}

(ii) dom *plays* has type $\mathbb{P}$ *People*
   ran *plays* has type $\mathbb{P}$ *Instruments*
   dom *worksby* has type $\mathbb{P}$ *Instruments*
   ran *worksby* has type $\mathbb{P}$ *Actions*

Exercise 5.7

(i) $domain = \{n : \mathbb{N} \mid \exists\, m : \mathbb{N} \bullet n = 2 * m\}$
   $range = \mathbb{N}$

(iii) $domain = \emptyset[X]$
   $range = \emptyset[X]$

Exercise 5.8

$$(\mathbb{Z} \times \mathbb{Z}) \leftrightarrow \mathbb{Z}$$

$$\begin{array}{|l}
pairsum : (\mathbb{Z} \times \mathbb{Z}) \leftrightarrow \mathbb{Z} \\
\hline
\forall\, x, y, z : \mathbb{Z} \bullet ((x, y), z) \in pairsum \Leftrightarrow z = x + y
\end{array}$$

Exercise 5.10

$plays^{\sim}$ = {*piano* ↦ *Ashkenazy, guitar* ↦ *Williams,*
   violin ↦ *David, trumpet* ↦ *Huw,*
   flute ↦ *Alice, piano* ↦ *Alice, piano* ↦ *Kate*}
dom $plays^{\sim}$ = {*piano, guitar, trumpet, violin, flute*}
ran $plays^{\sim}$ = {*Ashkenazy, Williams, David, Huw, Alice, Kate*}
$worksby^{\sim}$ = {*hammering* ↦ *piano, plucking* ↦ *guitar,*
   plucking ↦ *harpsichord, blowing* ↦ *trumpet,*
   blowing ↦ *flute, bowing* ↦ *violin, scraping* ↦ *violin*}
dom $worksby^{\sim}$ = {*hammering, plucking, blowing, bowing, scraping*}
ran $worksby^{\sim}$ = {*piano, guitar, harpsichord, trumpet, flute, violin*}

Exercise 5.12

(ii)

$$\begin{aligned}
\operatorname{ran}(R^\smile) &= \{x : X \mid \exists\, y : Y \bullet y \mapsto x \in R^\smile\} \\
&= \{x : X \mid \exists\, y : Y \bullet x \mapsto y \in R\} \\
&= \operatorname{dom} R
\end{aligned}$$

Exercise 5.14

(i) $\operatorname{ran}(\{Kate\} \lhd rides)$

(ii) $\operatorname{dom}(rides \rhd \{Bicycle, Tricycle\})$

(iii) $\{Ben, Huw\} \lhd rides \rhd \{Bicycle\}$

Exercise 5.15

(i)

$$\begin{aligned}
&\operatorname{dom}(S \lhd R) \\
&\quad = \{x : X \mid \exists\, y : Y \bullet x \mapsto y \in (S \lhd R)\} \qquad\qquad \text{[defn of dom]} \\
&\quad = \{x : X \mid \exists\, y : Y \bullet x \in S \wedge x \mapsto y \in R\} \qquad\quad \text{[defn of } \lhd] \\
&\quad = \{x : X \mid x \in S \wedge \exists\, y : Y \bullet x \mapsto y \in R\} \\
&\qquad\qquad\qquad\qquad\qquad\qquad\quad \text{[} y \text{ not quantified in } x \in S] \\
&\quad = \{x : X \mid x \in S\} \cap \{x : X \mid \exists\, y : Y \bullet x \mapsto y \in R\} \quad \text{[set theory]} \\
&\quad = S \cap (\operatorname{dom} R) \qquad\qquad\qquad\qquad\qquad\qquad\qquad \text{[using defns]}
\end{aligned}$$

Exercise 5.17

(i) $\{2 \mapsto 4, 3 \mapsto 3, 3 \mapsto 4, 4 \mapsto 2\}$

(ii) $\{1 \mapsto 3, 2 \mapsto 2, 2 \mapsto 3, 3 \mapsto 1\}$

(iii) $\{1 \mapsto 1, 2 \mapsto 2, 2 \mapsto 3, 3 \mapsto 3, 3 \mapsto 2, 4 \mapsto 4\}$

(iv) $\{1 \mapsto 4, 2 \mapsto 3, 2 \mapsto 2, 3 \mapsto 2, 3 \mapsto 3, 4 \mapsto 1\}$

Exercise 5.19

(ii)

$$
\begin{aligned}
Q \,{}_9^\circ\, Q^\sim & \\
&= \{x : X; y : Y \mid x \mapsto y \in Q \land y \mapsto x \in Q^\sim \bullet x \mapsto x\} && \text{[defn of }{}_9^\circ\text{]} \\
&= \{x : X; y : Y \mid x \mapsto y \in Q \bullet x \mapsto x\} && \text{[defn of } Q^\sim\text{]} \\
&= \{x : X \mid \exists y : Y \bullet x \mapsto y \in Q \bullet x \mapsto x\} && \text{[using Ex. 4.25]} \\
&= \{x : X \mid x \in \mathrm{dom}(Q) \bullet x \mapsto x\} && \text{[defn of dom]} \\
&= \{x : (\mathrm{dom}\ Q) \bullet x \mapsto x\} && \text{[rewriting]} \\
&= \mathrm{id}[\mathrm{dom}\ Q] && \text{[defn of id]}
\end{aligned}
$$

Exercise 5.21

(i) $\{Bicycle\}$

(ii) $\{Ben\}$

Exercise 5.23

(i) $rides(\!| \ \{Huw, Ben\} \ |\!)$

Exercise 5.25

(i)

$$
\begin{aligned}
R(\!|\ S \cup T\ |\!) & \\
&= \{x : X; y : Y \mid x \in S \cup T \land x \mapsto y \in R \bullet y\} && \text{[defn of } (\!|\ |\!)\text{]} \\
&= \{x : X; y : Y \mid (x \in S \lor x \in T) \land x \mapsto y \in R \bullet y\} && \\
& && \text{[defn of } union\text{]} \\
&= \{x : X; y : Y \mid (x \in S \land x \mapsto y \in R) \lor && \\
& \quad\quad (x \in T \land x \mapsto y \in R) \bullet y\} && \\
&= \{y : Y \mid \exists x : X \bullet (x \in S \land x \mapsto y \in R) \lor && \text{[using Ex. 4.25]} \\
& \quad\quad (x \in T \land x \mapsto y \in R)\ \bullet y\} && \\
&= \{y : Y \mid (\exists x : X \bullet (x \in S \land x \mapsto y \in R)) \lor && \text{[pred calc]} \\
& \quad\quad (\exists x : X \bullet (x \in T \land x \mapsto y \in R))\} && \\
&= \{y : Y \mid (\exists x : X \bullet x \in S \land x \mapsto y \in R)\} \cup && \text{[set theory]} \\
& \quad \{y : Y \mid (\exists x : X \bullet x \in T \land x \mapsto y \in R)\} && \\
&= R(\!|\ S\ |\!) \cup R(\!|\ T\ |\!) && \text{[defn of } (\!|\ |\!)\text{]}
\end{aligned}
$$

(ii) This is not a law. Consider:

$$R = \{1 \mapsto 1, 2 \mapsto 1\}$$
$$S = \{1\}$$
$$T = \{2\}$$

So that:

$$R(\!| S \cap T |\!) = R(\!| \emptyset |\!) = \emptyset$$

but:

$$R(\!| S |\!) \cap R(\!| T |\!) = \{1\} \cap \{1\} = \{1\}$$

If we try to construct a proof as in (i), we obtain a conjunction within the existential quantifier. It is not in general possible to split this into two quantified expressions in the same way.

Exercise 5.27

(i) $\{a \mapsto 1, b \mapsto, c \mapsto 3, d \mapsto 3, e \mapsto 2\}$

(ii) $\{a \mapsto 2\}$

Exercise 5.29

Each element of the domain is related to exactly one element of the range.

Exercise 5.31

(i)

$$\begin{array}{|l}
plustwo : \mathbb{Z} \to \mathbb{Z} \\ \hline
\forall x : \mathbb{Z} \bullet plustwo\ x = x + 2
\end{array}$$

dom $plustwo = \mathbb{Z}$
ran $plustwo = \mathbb{Z}$

(iii)

$$\begin{array}{|l}
squareroot : \mathbb{Z} \nrightarrow \mathbb{Z} \\ \hline
\forall x : \mathbb{Z}; y : \mathbb{N} \bullet squareroot\ x = y \Leftrightarrow y * y = x
\end{array}$$

dom $squareroot = \{x : \mathbb{N} \bullet x^2\}$
ran $squareroot = \mathbb{N}$

Exercise 5.32

(i)

$$Squares \ == \ \{x : \mathbb{Z} \bullet x^2\}$$

$$\begin{array}{|l}
squareroot : Squares \to \mathbb{Z} \\
\hline
squareroot = \{x : \mathbb{Z} \bullet x^2 \mapsto x\}
\end{array}$$

Exercise 5.35

$$X \rightarrowtail Y \ == \ \{f : X \nrightarrow Y \mid f^\sim \in Y \nrightarrow X\}$$

f satisfies the new definition

$$\begin{aligned}
&\Leftrightarrow && f \in X \nrightarrow Y \wedge f^\sim \in Y \nrightarrow X \\
&\Leftrightarrow && f \in X \nrightarrow Y \wedge f^\sim \in Y \leftrightarrow X \wedge && \text{[defn of $\nrightarrow$]}\\
& && \forall\, y : Y; x_1, x_2 : X \bullet (y \mapsto x_1 \in f^\sim \wedge y \mapsto x_2 \in f^\sim) \Rightarrow x_1 = x_2 \\
&\Leftrightarrow && f \in X \nrightarrow Y \wedge f \in X \leftrightarrow Y \wedge \\
& && \forall\, x_1, x_2 : X; y : Y \bullet (x_1 \mapsto y \in f \wedge x_2 \mapsto y \in f) \Rightarrow x_1 = x_2 \\
&\Leftrightarrow && f \in X \nrightarrow Y \wedge && \text{[using functionality of f]}\\
& && \forall\, x_1, x_2 : X; y : Y \bullet f\, x_1 = y \wedge f\, x_2 = y \Rightarrow x_1 = x_2 \\
&\Leftrightarrow && f \in X \nrightarrow Y \wedge \\
& && \forall\, x_1, x_2 : X \bullet \exists\, y : Y \bullet f\, x_1 = y \wedge f\, x_2 = y \Rightarrow x_1 = x_2 \\
&\Leftrightarrow && f \in X \nrightarrow Y \wedge && \text{[f is a function]}\\
& && \forall\, x_1, x_2 : \mathrm{dom}\, f \bullet f\, x_1 = f\, x_2 \Rightarrow x_1 = x_2
\end{aligned}$$

Exercise 5.37

$(X \rightarrowtail Y) \cap (X \to Y)$ is the set of all injective functions from X to Y which are also total on X. It is therefore another way of defining $X \rightarrowtail Y$.

Exercise 5.39

There is no partial surjective function from *LET* to *NUM* since both have the same number of elements.

$$\{a \mapsto 1, b \mapsto 2, c \mapsto 3, d \mapsto 4, e \mapsto 5\} \in LET \nrightarrow\!\!\!\!\rightarrow NUM$$

Exercise 5.41

(i) $\{x : \mathbb{Z} \bullet 2x \mapsto x\}$

(ii) $\{x, y : \mathbb{Z} \mid x = 2y \lor x = 2y + 1 \bullet x \mapsto y\}$

(iii) $\{x : \mathbb{Z} \bullet x \mapsto x + 1\}$

Exercise 5.43

$$X \rightarrowtail Y \;==\; (X \twoheadrightarrow Y) \cap (X \rightarrowtail Y)$$

Exercise 5.48

inverse of	function	total	injective	surjective	finite
$\rightarrow$			✓	✓	
$\twoheadrightarrow$			✓		
$\rightarrowtail$	✓		✓	✓	
$\rightarrowtail\!\!\!\!\rightarrow$	✓		✓		
$\rightarrow\!\!\!\twoheadrightarrow$		✓	✓	✓	
$\twoheadrightarrow$		✓	✓		
$\rightarrowtail\!\!\rightarrow$	✓	✓	✓	✓	
$\twoheadrightarrow$			✓		✓
$\rightarrowtail\!\!\!\!\twoheadrightarrow$	✓		✓		✓

Exercise 5.50

(i) *shopprice'* = *shopprice* $\oplus \{i \mapsto p\}$

(ii) *shopprice'* = *shopprice* $\oplus \{i \mapsto 2 * (shopprice \; i)\}$

Exercise 5.51

(i) first is instantiated with $\mathbb{Z}, \mathbb{Z} \times \mathbb{Z}$

(ii) first is instantiated with $\mathbb{Z}, \mathbb{Z}$ and second is instantiated with $\mathbb{P}\,\mathbb{Z}, \mathbb{Z} \times \mathbb{Z}$

(iii) first has not been fully instantiated since $\emptyset$ is itself generically defined

(iv) first is instantiated with $\mathbb{Z}, \mathbb{P}\,\mathbb{Z}$ and with $\mathbb{Z} \times \mathbb{P}\,\mathbb{Z}, \mathbb{Z}$

Exercise 5.54

$$
\begin{array}{|l}
\hline
\_\_[X, Y, Z]_____ \\
\text{dom} : (X \leftrightarrow Y) \to \mathbb{P}\, X \\
\text{ran} : (X \leftrightarrow Y) \to \mathbb{P}\, Y \\
\_^{\sim} : (X \leftrightarrow Y) \to (Y \leftrightarrow X) \\
\lhd : (\mathbb{P}\, X \times (X \leftrightarrow Y)) \to (X \leftrightarrow Y) \\
\rhd : ((X \leftrightarrow Y) \times \mathbb{P}\, Y) \to (X \leftrightarrow Y) \\
\vartriangleleft : (\mathbb{P}\, X \times (X \leftrightarrow Y)) \to (X \leftrightarrow Y) \\
\vartriangleright : ((X \leftrightarrow Y) \times \mathbb{P}\, Y) \to (X \leftrightarrow Y) \\
\_\,\substack{\circ\\\circ}\,\_ : ((X \leftrightarrow Y) \times (Y \leftrightarrow Z)) \to (X \leftrightarrow Z) \\
\_(\!|\ \_\ |\!) : ((X \leftrightarrow Y) \times \mathbb{P}\, X) \to \mathbb{P}\, Y \\
\hline
\forall P : X \leftrightarrow Y;\ Q : Y \leftrightarrow Z;\ S : \mathbb{P}\, X;\ T : \mathbb{P}\, Y \ \bullet \\
\quad \text{dom}\, P \ = \ \{x : X \mid \exists y : Y \bullet x \mapsto y \in P\} \\
\quad \text{ran}\, P \ = \ \{y : Y \mid \exists x : X \bullet x \mapsto y \in P\} \\
\quad\quad P^{\sim} \ = \ \{x : X; y : Y \mid x \mapsto y \in P \bullet y \mapsto x\} \\
\quad S \lhd P \ = \ \{x : X; y : Y \mid x \in S \wedge x \mapsto y \in P\} \\
\quad R \rhd T \ = \ \{x : X; y : Y \mid y \in T \wedge x \mapsto y \in P\} \\
\quad S \vartriangleleft P \ = \ \{x : X; y : Y \mid x \notin S \wedge x \mapsto y \in P\} \\
\quad P \vartriangleright T \ = \ \{x : X; y : Y \mid y \notin T \wedge x \mapsto y \in P\} \\
\quad P\,\substack{\circ\\\circ}\,Q \ = \ \{x : X; y : Y; z : Z \mid x \mapsto y \in P \wedge \\
\quad\quad\quad\quad\quad\quad\quad\quad\quad\quad\quad y \mapsto z \in Q \bullet x \mapsto z\} \\
\quad P(\!|\ S\ |\!) \ = \ \{x : X; y : Y \mid x \in S \wedge x \mapsto y \in P \bullet y\} \\
\hline
\end{array}
$$

Exercise 5.55

(i) $\{i : \mathbb{N} \bullet i \mapsto i + 1\}$

(ii) $\{i, j : \mathbb{N} \mid i + j = 6 \bullet (i, j) \mapsto (i + 1, j)\}$

(iii) $\{i : \mathbb{N};\ S : \mathbb{P}\,\mathbb{N} \mid i \in S \bullet (i, S) \mapsto S \setminus \{i\}\}$

(iv) $\{i : \mathbb{N};\ S : \mathbb{P}\,\mathbb{N} \mid (i, S) \mapsto S \setminus \{i\}\}$

Exercise 5.57

f maps each number i to its complement j in $n + 1$, that is, $i + j = n + 1$.

$f \,\substack{\circ\\\circ}\, g$ reverses the order in which range elements are indexed by the integers of the domain: if g is:

$$\{1 \mapsto r_1, 2 \mapsto r_2, \ldots, n - 1 \mapsto r_{n-1}, n \mapsto r_n\}$$

then $f \,\substack{\circ\\\circ}\, g_n$ is:

$$\{n \mapsto r_1, n - 1 \mapsto r_2, \ldots, 2 \mapsto r_{n-1}, 1 \mapsto r_n\}$$

Exercise 5.58

(i) $\{1 \mapsto 1, 2 \mapsto 1, 3 \mapsto 1\}$

(ii) $\{1 \mapsto 3, 2 \mapsto 2, 3 \mapsto 1\}$

(iii) $\{1 \mapsto \{Ben, Kate\}, 2 \mapsto \{Alice, Huw\}\}$

Exercise 5.60

(i) yes

(ii) no: sequences start at index 1

Exercise 5.61

$$\text{seq}_1 \, X \;==\; \text{seq} \, X \setminus \{\langle\rangle\}$$

Exercise 5.63

$$\text{iseq} \, X \;==\; \text{seq} \, X \cap (\mathbb{N} \rightarrowtail X)$$

Exercise 5.65

(i) $\langle Alice, Huw, Ben \rangle$

(ii) $\langle Huw, Kate, Alice \rangle$

(iii) $\langle Kate, Alice \rangle$

(iv) $\{2 \mapsto Alice, 3 \mapsto Huw\}$

Exercise 5.67

$$
\begin{array}{l}
\underline{[X]}\\[-0.3em]
\hline
rev : \text{seq} \, X \to \text{seq} \, X \\
\hline
\forall s : \text{seq} \, X \bullet rev \, s = (\lambda \, i : 1 .. \#s \bullet (\#s + 1) - i) \,\overset{\circ}{\underset{9}{}}\, s
\end{array}
$$

$$
\begin{aligned}
rev \, rev \, s &= (\lambda \, i : 1 .. \#s \bullet (\#s + 1) - i) \,\overset{\circ}{\underset{9}{}}\, (\lambda \, i : 1 .. \#s \bullet (\#s + 1) - i) \,\overset{\circ}{\underset{9}{}}\, s \\
&= (\lambda \, i : 1 .. \#s \bullet (\#s + 1) - ((\#s + 1) - i)) \,\overset{\circ}{\underset{9}{}}\, s \\
&= (\lambda \, i : 1 .. \#s \bullet i) \,\overset{\circ}{\underset{9}{}}\, s \\
&= \text{id}[\text{dom} \, s] \,\overset{\circ}{\underset{9}{}}\, s \\
&= s
\end{aligned}
$$

Exercise 5.70

$$\boxed{\begin{array}{l} [X] \\ \hline \cap, \cup : \mathbb{P}(\mathbb{P}\,X) \to \mathbb{P}\,X \\ \hline \forall\, S : \mathbb{P}(\mathbb{P}\,X) \bullet \cap S = \{x : X \mid \forall\, s : S \bullet x \in s\} \wedge \\ \qquad\qquad\qquad\qquad\ \cup S = \{x : X \mid \exists\, s : S \bullet x \in s\} \end{array}}$$

Exercise 5.71

$$\boxed{\begin{array}{l} [X] \\ \hline \_in\_ : X \leftrightarrow \mathrm{bag}\,X \\ \hline \forall\, x : X;\ b : \mathrm{bag}\,X \bullet x\ in\ b \Leftrightarrow x \in \mathrm{dom}\,b \end{array}}$$

Exercise 5.73

$unit = [\![dinner\_plate, soup\_bowl, wine\_glass, egg\_cup, mug]\!]$

$count\ unit\ dinner\_plate = 12$

$count\ unit\ soup\_bowl = 8$

$count\ unit\ wine\_glass = 6$

$count\ unit\ egg\_cup = 4$

$count\ unit\ mug = 7$

The value of $count$ is 0 for all other kitchen items. The set representation is:

$$\{dinner\_plate \mapsto 12, soup\_bowl \mapsto 8, wine\_glass \mapsto 6, egg\_cup \mapsto 4, mug \mapsto 7\}$$

Chapter 6

Exercise 6.1

$[Copy, Book, Reader, Category]$

$$\boxed{\ limit : Category \to \mathbb{N}}$$

$$\begin{array}{l} \underline{\ CatLibrary} \\ stock : Copy \twoheadrightarrow Book \\ issued : Copy \twoheadrightarrow Reader \\ shelved : \mathbb{F}\,Copy \\ readers : \mathbb{F}\,Reader \\ categ : Reader \twoheadrightarrow Category \\ \hline shelved \cup \mathrm{dom}\,issued = \mathrm{dom}\,stock \\ shelved \cap \mathrm{dom}\,issued = \emptyset \\ \mathrm{ran}\,issued \subseteq readers \\ \forall\, r : readers \bullet \#(issued \rhd \{r\}) \leq (limit\ (categ\ r)) \\ \mathrm{dom}\,categ = readers \end{array}$$

Exercise 6.2

[*User, Word*]

```
┌─ LogSys ──────────────────────────────────────
│  password : User ↠ Word
│  regd : 𝔽 User
│  active : 𝔽 User
│ ─────────────────────────────────────────────
│  active ⊆ regd = dom password
└───────────────────────────────────────────────
```

Exercise 6.3

[*Copy, Book, Reader*]

```
┌─ Issue ────────────────────────────────────────
│  stock, stock' : Copy ↠ Book
│  issued, issued' : Copy ↠ Reader
│  shelved, shelved' : 𝔽 Copy
│  readers, readers' : 𝔽 Reader
│  categ, categ' : Reader ↠ Category
│  c? : Copy
│  r? : Reader
│ ──────────────────────────────────────────────
│  shelved ∪ dom issued = dom stock
│  shelved' ∪ dom issued' = dom stock'
│  shelved ∩ dom issued = ∅
│  shelved' ∩ dom issued' = ∅
│  ran issued ⊆ readers
│  ran issued' ⊆ readers'
│  ∀ r : readers • #(issued ▷ {r}) ≤ (limit (categ r))
│  ∀ r : readers' • #(issued' ▷ {r}) ≤ (limit' (categ r))
│  dom categ = readers
│  dom categ' = readers'
│  c? ∈ shelved
│  r? ∈ readers
│  #(issued ▷ {r?}) < (limit (categ r))
│  issued' = issued ⊕ {c? ↦ r?}
│  shelved' = shelved \ {c?}
│  stock' = stock
│  readers' = readers
│  categ' = categ
└───────────────────────────────────────────────
```

Exercise 6.4

(a) *issued'* assigns *r?* at most *maxloans* books

(b) *issued'* is equal to *issued* plus the new loan to $r?$, $(c? \mapsto r?)$

(c) $c?$ is in *shelved* and therefore cannot be in dom *issued* (since these are disjoint)

(d) *issued'* assigns exactly one more copy to $r?$ than does *issued*

(e) *issued'* assigns $r?$ at most *maxloans* books, so *issued* assigns $r?$ at most *maxloans* -1 books, that is, $\#(issued \rhd \{r?\}) < maxloans$

Exercise 6.5

$$shelved \cup \text{dom } issued = \text{dom } stock \wedge$$
$$shelved \cap \text{dom } issued = \emptyset \wedge$$
$$\text{ran } issued \subseteq readers \wedge$$
$$\forall r : readers \bullet \#(issued \rhd \{r\}) \leq maxloans \wedge$$
$$\text{dom } readerloans = readers \wedge$$
$$\forall r : readers \bullet readerloans\ r = \#(issued \rhd \{r\})$$

Exercise 6.6

(i)

```
┌─ Deregistration ─────────────────────────────────
│ password, password' : User ↦ Word
│ regd, regd' : F User
│ active, active' : F User
│ u? : User
│ p? : Word
├──────────────────────────────────────────────────
│ active ⊆ regd
│ active' ⊆ regd'
│ regd = dom password
│ regd' = dom password'
│ u? ∉ active
│ (u? ↦ p?) ∈ password
│ password' = password \ {u? ↦ p?}
│ regd' = regd \ {u?}
│ active' = active
└──────────────────────────────────────────────────
```

In order to show that *active'* $\subseteq$ *regd'* $=$ dom *password'*:

(a) *active* is a subset of *regd*

(b) *active'* is equal to *active*, therefore *active'* is a subset of *regd*

(c) *regd* is included in *regd'*, therefore *active'* is a subset of *regd'*

(d) *regd* is equal to dom *password*

(e) *regd'* is equal to *regd* $\cup$ {*u*?}

(f) dom *password'* is equal to dom(*password* $\cup$ {*u*? $\mapsto$ *p*?}) which is equal to (dom *password*) $\cup$ {*u*?}

(g) therefore *regd'* = dom *password'*

Exercise 6.7

The only difference when this version of the schema is expanded is that the predicate limiting readers' loans is given as:

$$\forall r : Readers \bullet readerloans\ r = \#(issued \rhd \{r\})$$

whereas in the previous version r ranged over the set *readers* (that is, the registered readers). However, the constraint on the range of *issued* ensures that any unregistered reader has no books issued. And since $0 \le maxloans$, the two versions are equivalent.

Exercise 6.8

```
┌─ LibStock ──────────────────────────────────
│ stock : Copy ⇸ Book
│ issued : Copy ⇸ Reader
│ shelved : 𝔽 Copy
├─────────────────────────────────────────────
│ shelved ∪ dom issued = dom stock
│ shelved ∩ dom issued = ∅
└─────────────────────────────────────────────
```

```
┌─ LibReaders ────────────────────────────────
│ readers : 𝔽 Reader
│ readerloans : Reader ⇸ ℕ
├─────────────────────────────────────────────
│ dom readerloans = readers
└─────────────────────────────────────────────
```

```
┌─ LibraryXtra ───────────────────────────────
│ LibStock
│ LibReaders
├─────────────────────────────────────────────
│ ran issued ⊆ readers
│ ∀ r : readers • readerloans r = #(issued ▷ {r}) ≤ maxloans ∧
└─────────────────────────────────────────────
```

Exercise 6.9

$$
\boxed{\begin{array}{l}
\underline{S'} \\
x', y' : \mathbb{N} \\
\hline
x' < y'
\end{array}}
$$

$$
\boxed{\begin{array}{l}
\underline{T} \\
x, y, x', y' : \mathbb{N} \\
g? : \mathbb{N} \\
\hline
x < y \\
x' < y' \\
x < g? < y \\
x' > x \lor y' < y
\end{array}}
$$

The third line of the predicate implies that $x < y$, so the first line may be omitted.

Exercise 6.10

(i)

$$
\boxed{\begin{array}{l}
\underline{Onloan} \\
\Xi Library \\
r? : Reader \\
s! : \mathbb{F}\ Copy \\
\hline
r? \in readers \\
s! = \mathrm{dom}(issued \rhd \{r?\})
\end{array}}
$$

(ii)

$$
\boxed{\begin{array}{l}
\underline{DeregReader} \\
\Delta Library \\
r? : Reader \\
\hline
r? \in readers \setminus \mathrm{ran}\ issued \\
readers' = readers \setminus \{r?\} \\
stock' = stock \\
issued' = issued \\
shelved' = shelved
\end{array}}
$$

Exercise 6.12

```
┌─ AddCopyError ─────────────────────────────────────────────
│ ΞLibrary
│ b? : Book
│ rep! : Report
├───────────────────────────────────────────────
│ dom stock = Copy
│ rep! = AllCopyIdsUsed
└───────────────────────────────────────────────
```

Exercise 6.13

p	q	r	$(p \wedge q)$	$\vee$	$(\neg p \wedge r)$		$(p \Rightarrow q)$	$\wedge$	$(\neg p \Rightarrow r)$	
T	T	T	T	T	F	F	T	T	F	T
T	T	F	T	T	F	F	T	T	F	T
T	F	T	F	F	F	F	F	F	F	T
T	F	F	F	F	F	F	F	F	F	T
F	T	T	F	T	T	T	T	T	T	T
F	T	F	F	F	T	F	T	F	T	F
F	F	T	F	T	T	T	T	T	T	T
F	F	F	F	F	T	F	T	F	T	F

(i)   (a) $b? \in \text{ran } stock \Rightarrow rep! = FurtherCopyAdded$ so if $b? \in \text{ran } stock$ then we
know that $rep! = FurtherCopyAdded$

(b) if $rep! = NewTitleAdded$ then we must have
$NewTitleAdded = FurtherCopyAdded$ but this contradicts the fact that
$NewTitleAdded \neq FurtherCopyAdded$

(c) hence we conclude that $rep! \neq NewTitleAdded$

(ii) Similar to (i).

Exercise 6.14

(i) $ExpandS \vee ExpandT \cong [x, y, z : \mathbb{Z} \mid 0 \leq x < y \vee 0 \leq y < z]$

(ii) $x = 1, y = 2, z = -1$ satisfies $ExpandS \vee ExpandT$ but not $SorT$.

(iii) The problem is that the first part of the predicate of $ExpandS \vee ExpandT$ can
be satisfied – and thus the whole predicate, since it is a disjunction, can be
satisfied – without constraining z to be a non-negative integer. In $SorT$ the
declaration $z : \mathbb{N}$ requires z to be non-negative.

Exercise 6.15

```
┌─ LoanTransaction ──────────────────────────────
│ ΔLibrary
├────────────────────────────────────────────────
│ stock' = stock; readers' = readers
└────────────────────────────────────────────────
```

```
┌─ Registration ─────────────────────────────────────────
│ ΔLibrary
├────────────────────────────────────────────────────────
│ stock' = stock; issued' = issued; shelved' = shelved
└────────────────────────────────────────────────────────
```

Exercise 6.16

```
┌─ NormalIssue ──────────────────────────────────
│ ΔLibrary
│ c? : Copy; r? : Reader
│ rep! : Report
├────────────────────────────────────────────────
│ c? ∈ shelved; r? ∈ readers
│ #(issued ▷ {r?}) < maxloans
│ issued' = issued ⊕ {c? ↦ r?}
│ stock' = stock; readers' = readers
│ rep! = Ok
└────────────────────────────────────────────────
```

```
┌─ IssueError ───────────────────────────────────────────
│ ΞLibrary
│ c? : Copy; r? : Reader
│ rep! : Report
├────────────────────────────────────────────────────────
│ (r? ∈ readers ∧ #(issued ▷ {r?}) = maxloans ∧
│                 rep! = ReaderHasMaxLoans) ∨
│ (r? ∉ readers ∧ rep! = ReaderNotRegistered) ∨
│ (c? ∈ dom issued ∧ rep! = CopyAlreadyIssued)
└────────────────────────────────────────────────────────
```

This may be rewritten:

```
┌─ IssueError ───────────────────────────────────────────
│ ΞLibrary
│ c? : Copy; r? : Reader
│ rep! : Report
├────────────────────────────────────────────────────────
│ (((r? ∈ readers ∧ #(issued ▷ {r?}) = maxloans)
│                 ⇒ rep! = ReaderHasMaxLoans) ∧
│  (r? ∉ readers ⇒ rep! = ReaderNotRegistered))
│ ∨
│ (c? ∈ dom issued ∧ rep! = CopyAlreadyIssued)
└────────────────────────────────────────────────────────
```

Note that only the first disjunction may be replaced by conjunction. The second one does not match the pattern $(p \wedge q) \vee (\neg p \wedge q)$ needed for the equivalence.

Exercise 6.17

Either $rep! = ReaderHasMaxLoans$ or $rep! = CopyAlreadyIssued$. One possibility is to define:

```
┌─ AlreadyIssued ────────────────────────────────
│ issued : Copy ⇸ Reader
│ c? : Copy
│ r? : Reader
│ rep! : Report
├────────────────────────────────────────────────
│ r? ∈ readers
│ #(issued ▷ {r?}) ≠ maxloans
│ c? ∈ dom issued
│ rep! = CopyAlreadyIssued
└────────────────────────────────────────────────
```

The predicate of *IssueError* is:

$$(r? \in readers \wedge \#(issued \triangleright \{r?\}) = maxloans \wedge rep! = ReaderHasMaxLoans) \vee$$
$$(r? \notin readers \wedge rep! = ReaderNotRegistered) \vee$$
$$(r? \in readers \wedge \#(issued \triangleright \{r?\}) \neq maxloans \wedge$$
$$c? \in dom\ issued \wedge rep! = CopyAlreadyIssued)$$

This may be simplified using the equivalence in the text to:

$$(r? \notin readers \Rightarrow rep! = ReaderNotRegistered) \wedge$$
$$(r? \in readers \Rightarrow$$
$$((\#(issued \triangleright \{r?\}) = maxloans \Rightarrow rep! = ReaderHasMaxLoans) \wedge$$
$$(\#(issued \triangleright \{r?\}) \neq maxloans \Rightarrow (c? \in dom\ issued \wedge$$
$$rep! = CopyAlreadyIssued))))$$

Using $p \Rightarrow ((q \Rightarrow r) \wedge (\neg q \Rightarrow s)) \Leftrightarrow (((p \wedge q) \Rightarrow r) \wedge ((p \wedge \neg q) \Rightarrow s)))$:

$$r? \notin readers \Rightarrow rep! = ReaderNotRegistered \wedge$$
$$(r? \in readers \wedge \#(issued \triangleright \{r?\}) = maxloans) \Rightarrow rep! = ReaderHasMaxLoans \wedge$$
$$(r? \in readers \wedge \#(issued \triangleright \{r?\}) \neq maxloans)$$
$$\Rightarrow (c? \in dom\ issued \wedge rep! = CopyAlreadyIssued)$$

Exercise 6.19

```
┌─ DiscardBookCopy ──────────────────────────────────────────
│ ΔLibrary
│ b? : Book; c? : Copy
├────────────────────────────────────────────────────────────
│ (c? ↦ b?) ∈ stock
│ #(stock ▷ {b?}) > 2
│ c? ∈ shelved
│ shelved' = shelved \ {c?}
│ stock' = {c?} ◁ stock
│ issued' = issued; readers' = readers
└────────────────────────────────────────────────────────────
```

$DiscardCopy \mathrel{\widehat{=}} DiscardBookCopy \setminus \{c?\}$

```
┌─ DiscardCopy ──────────────────────────────────────────────
│ ΔLibrary
│ b? : Book
├────────────────────────────────────────────────────────────
│ #(stock ▷ {b?}) > 2
│ ∃ c : Copy •
│       (c ↦ b?) ∈ stock ∧
│       c ∈ shelved ∧
│       shelved' = shelved \ {c} ∧
│       stock' = {c} ◁ stock
│ issued' = issued; readers' = readers
└────────────────────────────────────────────────────────────
```

```
┌─ NotMoreThanTwo ───────────────────────────────────────────
│ ΞLibrary
│ b? : Book; rep! : Report
├────────────────────────────────────────────────────────────
│ #(stock ▷ {b?}) ≤ 2
│ rep! = NoCopyToDiscard
└────────────────────────────────────────────────────────────
```

```
┌─ AllIssued ────────────────────────────────────────────────
│ ΞLibrary
│ b? : Book; rep! : Report
├────────────────────────────────────────────────────────────
│ b? ∈ ran stock
│ ∀ c : Copy • stock c = b? ⇒ c ∉ shelved
│ rep! = AllCopiesIssued
└────────────────────────────────────────────────────────────
```

$TotalDiscardCopy \mathrel{\widehat{=}} (DiscardCopy \wedge Success) \vee NotMoreThanTwo \vee AllIssued$

Exercise 6.20

The necessary *FurtherConstraint* is as follows:

$b? \in \operatorname{ran} stock; \; c \in shelved$

Exercise 6.21

$ReaderLostContact \mathrel{\widehat{=}} RemoveBooks \mathbin{\substack{\circ \\ 9}} RemoveReader$

─── *RemoveBooks* ───────────────
$\Delta Library$
$r? : Reader$
─────────────────────
$r? \in readers$
$issued' = issued \mathbin{\rhd} \{r?\}$
$stock' = (\operatorname{dom}(issued \mathbin{\rhd} \{r?\})) \mathbin{\lhd} stock$
$shelved' = shelved$
$readers' = readers$

─── *RemoveReader* ───────────────
$\Delta Library$
$r? : Reader$
─────────────────────
$r? \in readers$
$readers' = readers \setminus \{r?\}$
$stock' = stock$
$issued' = issued$
$shelved' = shelved$

─── *ReaderLostContact* ───────────────
$\Delta Library$
$r? : Reader$
─────────────────────
$\exists Library'' \bullet$
$\qquad r? \in readers \;\wedge$
$\qquad issued'' = issued \mathbin{\rhd} \{r?\} \;\wedge$
$\qquad stock'' = (\operatorname{dom}(issued \mathbin{\rhd} \{r?\})) \mathbin{\lhd} stock \;\wedge$
$\qquad shelved'' = shelved \;\wedge$
$\qquad readers'' = readers \;\wedge$
$\qquad r? \in readers'' \;\wedge$
$\qquad readers' = readers'' \setminus \{r?\} \;\wedge$
$\qquad r? \in readers'' \;\wedge$
$\qquad readers' = readers'' \setminus \{r?\} \;\wedge$
$\qquad stock' = stock'' \;\wedge$
$\qquad issued' = issued'' \;\wedge$
$\qquad shelved' = shelved''$

which simplifies to:

ReaderLostContact ────────────────────

$\Delta Library$
$r? : Reader$

$r? \in readers$
$readers' = readers \setminus \{r?\}$
$issued' = issued \rhd \{r?\}$
$stock' = (\text{dom}(issued \rhd \{r?\})) \lhd stock$
$shelved' = shelved$

Exercise 6.23

PreEnterNewCopy ────────────────────

$Library$
$b? : Book$

$\exists Library' \bullet$
$\qquad (\exists c : Copy \mid c \notin \text{dom } stock \bullet$
$\qquad\qquad\qquad stock' = stock \oplus \{c \mapsto b?\} \wedge$
$\qquad\qquad\qquad shelved' = shelved \cup \{c\}) \wedge$
$\qquad issued' = issued \wedge$
$\qquad readers' = readers$

Expanding the predicate gives:

$\exists stock' : Copy \nrightarrow Book;\ issued' : Copy \nrightarrow Reader;\ shelved' : \mathbb{F}\ Copy;$
$\quad readers' : \mathbb{F}\ Reader;\ c : Copy \bullet$
$\qquad shelved' \cup \text{dom } issued' = \text{dom } stock' \wedge$
$\qquad shelved' \cap \text{dom } issued' = \emptyset \wedge$
$\qquad \text{ran } issued' \subseteq readers' \wedge$
$\qquad \forall r : readers' \bullet \#(issued' \rhd \{r\}) \leq maxloans \wedge$
$\qquad c \notin \text{dom } stock \wedge$
$\qquad stock' = stock \oplus \{c \mapsto b?\} \wedge$
$\qquad shelved' = shelved \cup \{c\} \wedge$
$\qquad issued' = issued \wedge$
$\qquad readers' = readers$

Since the quantified variables are all given explicit values (and all are declared correctly) we can remove the quantification and replace each occurrence of a dashed variable with its given value. (The justification for this is known as the One Point Rule which is discussed in Chapter 9.)

$(\exists\, c : Copy \bullet$
$(shelved \cup \{c\}) \cup (\mathrm{dom}\ issued) = \mathrm{dom}(stock \oplus \{c \mapsto b?\})\ \wedge$
$(shelved \cup \{c\}) \cap (\mathrm{dom}\ issued) = \emptyset\ \wedge$
$c \notin \mathrm{dom}\ stock)\ \wedge$
$\mathrm{ran}\ issued \subseteq readers\ \wedge$
$\forall\, r : readers \bullet \#(issued \rhd \{r\}) \le maxloans$

We have also moved the parts of the predicate not involving c outside the remaining quantification and it can now be seen that these parts follow immediately from *Library*. We now argue as follows:

(a) from *Library*:

$$shelved \cup (\mathrm{dom}\ issued) = \mathrm{dom}\ stock$$

(b) adding c into both sides gives:

$$(shelved \cup \{c\}) \cup (\mathrm{dom}\ issued) = (\mathrm{dom}\ stock) \cup \{c\}$$

(c) since $\mathrm{dom}(stock \oplus \{c \mapsto b?\}) = (\mathrm{dom}\ stock) \cup \{c\}$ we have:

$$(shelved \cup \{c\}) \cup (\mathrm{dom}\ issued) = \mathrm{dom}(stock \oplus \{c \mapsto b?\})$$

Finally:

(a) we can rewrite the second predicate within the quantification as:

$$(shelved \cap (\mathrm{dom}\ issued) = \emptyset) \wedge (\{c\} \cap (\mathrm{dom}\ issued) = \emptyset)$$

the first part of which follows immediately from *Library*

(b) If $c \notin \mathrm{dom}\ stock$ then $c \notin \mathrm{dom}\ issued$ since $\mathrm{dom}\ stock$ contains all of $\mathrm{dom}\ issued$. Hence $\{c\} \cap (\mathrm{dom}\ issued) = \emptyset$.

We are left with:

```
┌─ PreEnterNewCopy ─────────────────────────────
│  Library
│  b? : Book
│ ──────────
│  ∃ c : Copy • c ∉ dom stock
└───────────────────────────────────────────────
```

Exercise 6.25

Let $x' = x$, $z! = x + 1$ and $y' = y$. Then:

$x + 1 \le x' + 1$	[in fact they are equal]
$x' + 1 = x + 1 \le z! = x + 1$	[again, they are equal]
$z! = x + 1 \le y - 1$	[by assumption]
$y' - 1 \le y - 1$	[equal again]

Exercise 6.27

The definition for *ListenerDetails* could be something such as:

```
┌─ ListenerDetails ──────────────────────────────────
│ name, address : String
├────────────────────────────────────────────────────
│ slength name ≤ 40; slength address ≤ 80
└────────────────────────────────────────────────────
```

Then the *ChangeAddress* operation on *ListenerDetails* would be:

```
┌─ ChangeAddress ────────────────────────────────────
│ ΔListenerDetails
│ newaddr? : String
│ rep! : Report
├────────────────────────────────────────────────────
│ slength newaddr? ≤ 80 ⇒
│         (address' = newaddr? ∧ rep! = AddressChanged)
│ slength newaddr? > 80 ⇒
│         (address' = address ∧ rep! = AddressTooLong)
└────────────────────────────────────────────────────
```

The framing schema is then:

```
┌─ ΦListenerDetails ─────────────────────────────────
│ ΔAudioLib
│ ΔListenerDetails
│ lisnid? : ListenerId
├────────────────────────────────────────────────────
│ lisnid? ∈ dom listeners
│ θListenerDetails = listeners lisnid?
│ listeners' = listeners ⊕ {lisnid? ↦ θListenerDetails'}
└────────────────────────────────────────────────────
```

Finally the system level operation is defined as follows:

$$ChangeListenerAddress \mathrel{\widehat{=}}$$
$$\exists \Delta ListenerDetails \bullet$$
$$[\Delta AudioLib \mid stock' = stock; \; out' = out]$$
$$\wedge \; \Phi ListenerDetails \wedge ChangeAddress$$

Chapter 7

Exercise 7.1

The given sets of the specification are:

$$[Copy, Book, Reader]$$

There is a maximum number of books which any reader may have on loan at one time:

```
│ maxloans : ℕ
```

The state of the system is recorded in the schema, *Library*:

Library

$stock : Copy \nrightarrow Book$
$issued : Copy \nrightarrow Reader$
$shelved : \mathbb{F}\, Copy$
$readers : \mathbb{F}\, Reader$

$shelved \cup \mathrm{dom}\, issued = \mathrm{dom}\, stock$
$shelved \cap \mathrm{dom}\, issued = \emptyset$
$\mathrm{ran}\, issued \subseteq readers$
$\forall r : readers \bullet \#(issued \rhd \{r\}) \leq maxloans$

Initially the library has no stock and no readers:

InitLibrary

$Library'$

$stock' = \emptyset$
$issued' = \emptyset$
$shelved' = \emptyset$
$readers' = \emptyset$

The operation *Issue* issues a copy of a book to a registered reader:

Issue

$\Delta Library$
$c? : Copy$
$r? : Reader$

$c? \in shelved$
$r? \in readers$
$\#(issued \rhd \{r?\}) < maxloans$
$issued' = issued \oplus \{c? \mapsto r?\}$
$stock' = stock$
$readers' = readers$

The operation *Return* represents a reader returning a book to the library:

Return

$\Delta Library$
$c? : Copy$

$c? \in \mathrm{dom}\, issued$
$issued' = \{c?\} \lhd issued$
$shelved' = shelved \cup \{c?\}$
$stock' = stock$
$readers' = readers$

The act of adding a copy of a book to stock is captured in *EnterNewCopy*:

EnterNewCopy
$\Delta Library$
$b? : Book$

$\exists\, c : Copy \mid c \notin \text{dom } stock \bullet$
$\qquad stock' = stock \oplus \{c \mapsto b?\} \wedge$
$\qquad shelved' = shelved \cup \{c\}$
$issued' = issued$
$readers' = readers$

Removing a copy of a book from stock is represented by *FromStock*:

FromStock
$\Delta Library$
$c? : Copy$

$c? \in shelved$
$stock' = \{c?\} \vartriangleleft stock$
$issued' = issued$
$shelved' = shelved \setminus \{c?\}$
$readers' = readers$

The system may be interrogated to find which books are on loan to a given reader:

ReaderHas
$\Xi Library$
$r? : Reader$
$loans! : \mathbb{F}\ Copy$

$r? \in readers$
$loans! = \text{dom}(issued \vartriangleright \{r?\})$

The system can also tell us who has a particular copy of a book:

WhoHasCopy
$\Xi Library$
$c? : Copy$
$r! : Reader$

$c? \in \text{dom } issued$
$r! = issued\ c?$

A new reader may register with the library:

```
┌─ Register ──────────────────────────────────────────
│ ΔLibrary
│ r? : Reader
├─────────────────────────────────────────────────────
│ r? ∉ readers
│ readers' = readers ∪ {r?}
│ stock' = stock
│ issued' = issued
│ shelved' = shelved
└─────────────────────────────────────────────────────
```

A reader's registration may be cancelled:

```
┌─ Cancel ────────────────────────────────────────────
│ ΔLibrary
│ r? : Reader
├─────────────────────────────────────────────────────
│ r? ∈ readers
│ r? ∉ ran issued
│ readers' = readers \ {r?}
│ stock' = stock
│ issued' = issued
│ shelved' = shelved
└─────────────────────────────────────────────────────
```

The operations are summarised in the following table which gives the inputs and outputs for each operation along with its precondition under normal circumstances.

Operation	Inputs/Outputs	Precondition
Issue	$c?$: *Copy*	$c? \in shelved$
	$r?$: *Reader*	$r? \in readers$
		$\#(issued \rhd \{r?\}) < maxloans$
Return	$c?$: *Copy*	$c? \in \text{dom } issued$
EnterNewCopy	$b?$: *Book*	$\text{dom } stock \neq Copy$
FromStock	$c?$: *Copy*	$c? \in shelved$
ReaderHas	$r?$: *Reader*	$r? \in readers$
	$loans!$: $\mathbb{F} \, Copy$	
WhoHasCopy	$c?$: *Copy*	$c? \in \text{dom } issued$
	$r!$: *Reader*	
Register	$r?$: *Reader*	$r? \notin readers$
Cancel	$r?$: *Reader*	$r? \in readers$
		$r? \notin \text{ran } issued$

The following schema provides a report for successful operations:

```
┌─ Success ───────────────────────────────────────────
│ rep! : Report
├─────────────────────────────────────────────────────
│ rep! = Ok
└─────────────────────────────────────────────────────
```

The following schemas describe error cases for the *Issue* operation:

```
┌─ HasMaxLoans ────────────────────────────────────
│ issued : Copy ⇸ Reader
│ readers : 𝔽 Reader
│ r? : Reader
│ rep! : Report
├──────────────────────────────────
│ r? ∈ readers
│ #(issued ▷ {r?}) = maxloans
│ rep! = ReaderHasMaxLoans
└──────────────────────────────────
```

```
┌─ AlreadyIssued ────────────────────────────────────
│ issued : Copy ⇸ Reader
│ c? : Copy
│ r? : Reader
│ rep! : Report
├──────────────────────────────────
│ r? ∈ readers
│ #(issued ▷ {r?}) ≠ maxloans
│ c? ∈ dom issued
│ rep! = CopyAlreadyIssued
└──────────────────────────────────
```

```
┌─ NotRegistered ────────────────────────────────────
│ readers : 𝔽 Reader
│ r? : Reader
│ rep! : Report
├──────────────────────────────────
│ r? ∉ readers
│ rep! = ReaderNotRegistered
└──────────────────────────────────
```

Using these we can build the total issue operation:

$$TotalIssue \;\widehat{=}$$
$$(Issue \land Success) \lor NotRegistered$$
$$\lor\; HasMaxLoans \lor AlreadyIssued$$

The error case for the return operation is if the input copy is not issued:

```
┌─ ReturnError ────────────────────────────────────
│ ΞLibrary
│ c? : Copy
│ rep! : Report
├──────────────────────────────────
│ c? ∉ dom issued
│ rep! = BookNotIssued
└──────────────────────────────────
```

The total return operation is then:

$$TotalReturn \triangleq (Return \land Success) \lor ReturnError$$

A new copy cannot be entered if no copy identifiers are available:

```
┌─ EnterNewCopyError ──────────────────────────────
│ ΞLibrary
│ b? : Book
│ rep! : Report
├──────────────────────────────────────────────────
│ dom stock = Copy
│ rep! = CopyIdsAllUsed
└──────────────────────────────────────────────────
```

This gives the total operation:

$$TotalEnterNewCopy \triangleq$$
$$(EnterNewCopy \land Success) \lor EnterNewCopyError$$

There are two possible cases we may wish to distinguish when attempting to remove a book from stock:

```
┌─ NotInStock ─────────────────────────────────────
│ ΞLibrary
│ c? : Copy
│ rep! : Report
├──────────────────────────────────────────────────
│ c? ∉ dom stock
│ rep! = BookNotStocked
└──────────────────────────────────────────────────
```

```
┌─ CurrentlyIssued ────────────────────────────────
│ ΞLibrary
│ c? : Copy
│ rep! : Report
├──────────────────────────────────────────────────
│ c? ∈ dom stock
│ c? ∈ dom issued
│ rep! = BookCurrentlyIssued
└──────────────────────────────────────────────────
```

These are combined for a total operation:

$$TotalFromStock \triangleq$$
$$(FromStock \land Success) \lor NotInStock \lor CurrentlyIssued$$

The operation to discover how many books a certain reader has will object if that person is not registered:

```
┌─ NotRegistered ──────────────────────────────
│ ΞLibrary
│ r? : Reader
│ rep! : Report
├──────────────────────────────────────────────
│ r? ∉ readers
│ rep! = NotRegisteredReader
└──────────────────────────────────────────────
```

$$TotalReaderHas \;\hat{=}$$
$$(ReaderHas \land Success) \lor NotRegistered$$

We can only discover who has a particular copy if that copy is issued:

```
┌─ NotIssued ──────────────────────────────────
│ ΞLibrary
│ c? : Copy
│ rep! : Report
├──────────────────────────────────────────────
│ c? ∉ dom issued
│ rep! = BookNotIssued
└──────────────────────────────────────────────
```

$$TotalWhoHasCopy \;\hat{=}$$
$$(WhoHasCopy \land Success) \lor NotIssued$$

Someone who is already a registered reader cannot re-register:

```
┌─ AlreadyReader ──────────────────────────────
│ ΞLibrary
│ r? : Reader
│ rep! : Report
├──────────────────────────────────────────────
│ r? ∈ readers
│ rep! = ReaderAlready
└──────────────────────────────────────────────
```

$$TotalRegister \;\hat{=}$$
$$(Register \land Success) \lor AlreadyReader$$

Finally, a reader with outstanding loans cannot be cancelled:

```
┌─ ReaderHasBooks ─────────────────────────────
│ ΞLibrary
│ r? : Reader
│ rep! : Report
├──────────────────────────────────────────────
│ r? ∈ readers
│ r? ∈ ran issued
│ rep! = OutstandingLoans
└──────────────────────────────────────────────
```

$TotalCancel \cong$

$\qquad (Cancel \wedge Success) \vee ReaderHasBooks$

The final stage is a summary of operations:

$TotalIssue \cong$

$\qquad (Issue \wedge Success) \vee NotRegistered$

$\qquad \vee HasMaxLoans \vee AlreadyIssued$

$TotalReturn \cong$

$\qquad (Return \wedge Success) \vee ReturnError$

$TotalEnterNewCopy \cong$

$\qquad (EnterNewCopy \wedge Success) \vee EnterNewCopyError$

$TotalFromStock \cong$

$\qquad (FromStock \wedge Success) \vee NotInStock \vee CurrentlyIssued$

$TotalReaderHas \cong$

$\qquad (ReaderHas \wedge Success) \vee NotReader$

$TotalWhoHasCopy \cong$

$\qquad (WhoHasCopy \wedge Success) \vee NotIssued$

$TotalRegister \cong$

$\qquad (Register \wedge Success) \vee AlreadyReader$

$TotalCancel \cong$

$\qquad (Cancel \wedge Success) \vee NotReader \vee ReaderHasBooks$

Exercise 7.2

$\qquad \_verysimilarto\_ : Native \leftrightarrow Foreign$

$\boxed{\begin{array}{l} \underline{FalseFriends} \\[2pt] \Xi\, WordForWord \\ falsefr! : Native \leftrightarrow Foreign \\ \hline falsefr! = \{n : Native; f : Foreign \mid \\ \qquad\qquad n \in \mathrm{dom}\ Vocab \wedge f \in \mathrm{ran}\ Vocab \\ \qquad\qquad \wedge\ n\ verysimilarto\ f\} \end{array}}$

Exercise 7.3

Pairs such as $(n, fseq1)$ and $(n, fseq2)$, where $fseq1 \neq fseq2$, must be related one way or the other by the ordering, because:

$\qquad \forall x, y : X \bullet x \neq y \Rightarrow x\ rel\ y \vee y\ rel\ x$

according to the definition of *alphorder*. We will have to define an ordering on sequences of *Foreign* words: this can be done by making the empty sequence earlier than any other sequence, making the first element of two given non-empty sequences determine the order in accordance with the order on individual foreign words when those first elements are different, and if that fails to determine an order we compare the tails of the sequences. We can still leave undetermined whether two equal pairs – the case when $fseq1 = fseq2$ – are related or not. So two possibilities, as required by the exercise, are to use an ordering on sequences to determine the order for pairs where the first components are equal and the second components are different, but we can decide that:

(a) $\forall\, n : Native;\ fseq : seq\ Foreign \bullet (n, fseq)\ rel\ (n, fseq)$

(b) or alternatively: $\forall\, n : Native;\ fseq : seq\ Foreign \bullet \neg\, ((n, fseq)\ rel\ (n, fseq))$

Exercise 7.4

$$RequestForeignDict \mathrel{\hat=} ForeignDict \land ReportIfVocabEmpty$$

$$
\begin{array}{|l}
\hline
\_\,ForeignDict \,\rule[0pt]{4cm}{0.4pt}\\
\Xi\, WordForWord\\
dict! : seq(Foreign \times seq\ Native)\\
\hline
dict! = SetInForeignDictOrder\\
\qquad\qquad (\lambda f : Foreign\,WordsKnown \bullet\\
\qquad\qquad\qquad SetInNative\,WordOrder(\,Vocab^{-1}(\!|\ \{f\}\ |\!)\,))\\
\hline
\end{array}
$$

Exercise 7.5

Yes.

Chapter 8

Exercise 8.1

Leaders will need to be identified in a similar way to children, so we should declare a set of identifiers, such as:

$$[LEADERID]$$

We may also want to specify types for the various pieces of information associated with children and leaders. Although many details may eventually be recorded, at this abstract level of specification we want to keep detail down to a minimum. The only essential information at this stage is the age of a child (needed to assign the child to a suitable group). Ages can be represented by $\mathbb{N}$ so we will not need any special definitions. All other information, including names, can be parcelled together and represented by a basic type. We will want different information about children and leaders so in fact we declare two types:

$$[CHILDINFO, LEADERINFO]$$

When it comes to implementation, each element of $CHILDINFO$ could be represented by, for example, a record containing name, address, telephone number and known allergies.

Exercise 8.2

The Camp has fixed age bands which are used to determine the grouping of children. We could use an abbreviation definition for this:

$$Band1 == 5 .. 7$$
$$Band2 == 8 .. 9$$
$$Band3 == 10 .. 11$$
$$Band4 == 12 .. 16$$
$$CampAgeBands == \{Band1, Band2, Band3, Band4\}$$

Each group has a maximum size depending on the associated age band. There are various ways this could be represented. One choice is to define a function which, for each band, returns the maximum group size:

$$maxgpsize == \{Band1 \mapsto 8, Band2 \mapsto 15, Band3 \mapsto 15, Band4 \mapsto 15\}$$

It may be that some time after we have made a choice such as this it becomes apparent that another approach would have made specification easier. This is worth looking out for. At this stage it seems that the likely use will be to determine a maximum size for a given group. So the function looks as if it will be useful.

There is another global maximum: the overall number allowed for any one session:

$$maxsessionsize == 250$$

Exercise 8.3

The abstract approach can be demonstrated most easily with the maximum session size by simply declaring:

$$maxsessionsize : \mathbb{N}$$

Leaving various possibilities open like this is known as non-determinism or under-specification.

There are various ways of specifying the age bands abstractly. One possibility is:

$$
\begin{array}{|l}
CampAgeBands : \mathrm{seq}_1\, \mathbb{P}\, \mathbb{N} \\
\hline
\forall i : \mathrm{dom}\ CampAgeBands \bullet \\
\quad \exists n1, n2 : \mathbb{N} \bullet CampAgeBands\ i = n1 \mathrel{..} n2 \\
\forall i, j : \mathrm{dom}\ CampAgeBands \bullet \\
\quad (CampAgeBands\ i \cap CampAgeBands\ j) \neq \emptyset \Rightarrow i = j \\
\bigcup(\mathrm{ran}\ CampAgeBands) = \\
\quad min\,(\bigcup(\mathrm{ran}\ CampAgeBands)) \mathrel{..} max\,(\bigcup(\mathrm{ran}\ CampAgeBands))
\end{array}
$$

This axiomatic definition declares $CampAgeBands$ in a somewhat different way as a sequence with at least one element. This is because we cannot explicitly name the bands 1 to 4 as we did before since we do not know in advance how many age bands there might be. The first predicate says that each age band is a number range between certain maximum and minimum values. The second predicate says that no two age bands overlap: that is, they are *disjoint*. Thirdly, we use the generalised union operator defined in Exercise 5.70 to state that all the age bands together must form a whole number range between the maximum and minimum ages: the bands are said to *cover* that range. Any collection of sets with these last two properties (that is, the sets are disjoint and the sets cover S for some set S) are referred to as a *partition* of S.

For the final global definition we have:

$$
\begin{array}{|l}
maxgpsize : (\mathrm{ran}\ CampAgeBands) \to \mathbb{N}
\end{array}
$$

Exercise 8.4

(a) Children must be registered and their details obtained. It is therefore likely that a child register to record this information would be a useful state component.

(b) Similarly, a register for leaders might form a second component.

(c) There is also a need for some sort of bookings register to record which children have booked for which session. This is a little more complicated because sessions consist of a number of groups and so we must also consider the allocation of children and leaders to groups.

Exercise 8.5

Following the style of the children's register we can define a state component *lreg* which is a function from $LEADERID$ to the details of a leader. We could put leaders' details into a schema, but since they are all parcelled together within the type $LEADERINFO$ (because we do not need to reference any of them explicitly at this level) it may be simpler to define:

$$
\begin{array}{|l}
\_\,LeaderReg \underline{\hspace{6cm}} \\
lreg : LEADERID \nrightarrow LEADERINFO \\
\hline
\end{array}
$$

Exercise 8.6

$$
\begin{array}{|l}
\underline{\quad InitChildReg \quad\rule{5cm}{0pt}} \\
\quad ChildReg' \\
\hline
\quad creg' = \emptyset \\
\end{array}
$$

$$
\begin{array}{|l}
\underline{\quad InitLeaderReg \quad\rule{5cm}{0pt}} \\
\quad LeaderReg' \\
\hline
\quad lreg' = \emptyset \\
\end{array}
$$

As $creg'$ is defined to be empty, we must check that the empty set satisfies the requirements of $ChildReg'$, that is:

$$\emptyset \in CHILDID \nrightarrow Child$$

This is true since the empty set of the correct type is just the empty function. A similar argument holds for $lreg'$. An initialisation proof is dealt with in some detail in Section 9.8.1.

Exercise 8.7

No. The requirements tell us that each session runs on a particular day and at a particular time (either morning or afternoon). So we will be able to distinguish a session by its date and time.

Exercise 8.8

Within the *Group* schema, children are referred to by their identifiers. We cannot know their ages without reference to the child register. As that register is in a different part of the state, the requirement that all children are in the correct age band cannot be expressed at this level. We need to remember the requirement and add it as a constraint on the combined state later. It is unfortunate that this seemingly group-specific piece of information cannot be captured in the *Group* schema but, when dividing up the state as we have done, there will always be constraints needed at the end to glue the parts together.

Exercise 8.9

First we have an informal statement of the necessary constraints.

(a) No two groups in any one session can have overlapping membership: a child can belong to no more than one group in a session.

(b) The total number of children in a session must not exceed the maximum session size.

Another required property is that all leaders and children involved in a session should be registered in the system. However, we must wait until we have the combined state schema to express this since it involves reference to the child and leader registers.

To formalise the first constraint:

$$\forall \, l1, l2 : \text{dom } session \mid l1 \neq l2 \bullet$$
$$(session \; l1).members \cap (session \; l2).members = \emptyset$$

This says that, considering any two groups (that is, groups identified by different leaders), the intersection of their membership is empty. The notation uses two different kinds of dot. The larger, fat dot is the familiar one used in many set expressions and predicates so far. The second dot is the schema selection operator which projects out the named component from an element of schema type (see Section 6.6.1). In this predicate, *session l1* applies the *session* function to the leader *l1* to obtain the related instance of the schema *Group*. That group's *members* component is then accessed by the schema selection notation: $(session \; l1).members$.

For the second constraint we have:

$$\#(\bigcup\{l : \text{dom } session \bullet (session \; l).members\}) \leq maxsessionsize$$

This again uses the generalised union symbol to join together a whole set of sets, and the two different dots discussed above. In this case, the fat dot indicates that the expression which follows defines the terms that will appear in the resulting set. So, with *l* ranging over all the group leaders in this session, we extract the members of the group associated with *l*. The predicate says that if we join all these sets of members together then the size of the combined set must be no greater than the maximum allowed session size.

There are many different ways of writing these predicates. If yours looks different from these it does not necessarily mean that one of us is wrong!

Exercise 8.10

```
┌─ CampEnergy ──────────────────────────────────
│ ChildReg
│ LeaderReg
│ BookingReg
├────────────────────────────────────────────────
│ ∀ sess : ran breg • ∀ grp : ran(sess.session) •
│     dom sess ⊆ dom lreg ∧
│     grp.members ⊆ dom creg ∧
│     ∀ cid : (grp.members) • (creg cid).age ∈ grp.band
└────────────────────────────────────────────────
```

The predicate says that for any group in any session the following must hold:

(a) all group leaders (identified by dom *sess*) must appear in the leaders' register (dom *lreg*)

(b) all children in a group (*grp.members*) must be in the child register (dom *creg*)

(c) all children in a group are within the group's age band

Again, these requirements may be formalised in many different ways.

Exercise 8.11

```
┌─ InitCampEnergy ─────────────────────────────────────
│  CampEnergy'
│  InitChildReg
│  InitLeaderReg
│  InitBookingReg
└──────────────────────────────────────────────────────
```

Each initialisation has the appropriate register empty. We must check that, with the empty set for *creg'*, *lreg'* and *breg'* the predicate part of *CampEnergy'* is satisfied. As we will see later, a predicate which universally quantifies over the empty set:

$$\forall x : \emptyset \bullet pred$$

is always true. Hence empty registers do represent a valid instance of the initialised *CampEnergy'* state.

Exercise 8.12

Some of the many possible operations are listed in the following table:

Operation	Registers
Register child	*creg*
Alter child details	*creg*
Alter child age	*creg,breg,lreg*
Delete child	*creg,breg*
Add session	*breg*
Add group	*breg,lreg*
Register leader	*lreg*
Alter leader details	*lreg*
Delete leader	*lreg,breg*
Make booking	*breg,creg,lreg*
Delete booking	*breg*
Obtain list of children booked for session	*breg*
Obtain list of children of a particular age band booked for session	*breg*
Obtain list of leaders involved in a session	*breg*
Obtain details of a particular child	*creg*
Obtain age of a particular child	*creg*
Obtain details of a particular leader	*lreg*

Exercise 8.13

```
┌─ SmallAlterChildAge ──────────────────────────────
│ ΔChild
│ c_age? : ℕ
│ r! : Rep
├────────────────
│ age' = c_age?
│ details' = details
│ r! = Success
└───────────────────────────────────────────────────
```

```
┌─ SmallObtainChildDetails ─────────────────────────
│ ΞChild
│ c_info! : CHILDINFO
│ r! : Rep
├────────────────
│ c_info! = details
│ r! = Success
└───────────────────────────────────────────────────
```

```
┌─ SmallObtainChildAge ─────────────────────────────
│ ΞChild
│ c_age! : ℕ
│ r! : Rep
├────────────────
│ c_age! = age
│ r! = Success
└───────────────────────────────────────────────────
```

Exercise 8.14

All operations are total apart from *SmallAlterChildAge*. The precondition of this is:

```
┌─ preSmallAlterChildAge ───────────────────────────
│ Child
│ c_age? : ℕ
├────────────────
│ ∃ Child'; r! : Rep •
│     age' = c_age? ∧
│     details' = details ∧
│     r! = Success
└───────────────────────────────────────────────────
```

Expanding the definition of *Child* the predicate of this becomes:

$$\exists\, age' : 5\,..\,16;\ details' : CHILDINFO;\ r! : Rep \bullet$$
$$age' = c\_age?\ \wedge$$
$$details' = details\ \wedge$$
$$r! = Success$$

This gives explicit values for the variables age', $details'$ and $r!$ within the predicate. These values can be used to replace all reference to age', $details'$ and $r!$ and thus eliminate their quantification. This is a technique seen earlier in the book. It is justified by the One Point Rule which will be described in detail in Section 9.6.3. To apply this rule we must also show that the values given really are suitable values for the variables they replace. In this case we are left with the requirement:

$$c\_age? \in 5 \mathbin{.\,.} 16$$

This shows that we need an error condition:

$$
\boxed{\begin{array}{l}
\underline{\,BadAgeErr\,} \\
\Xi\,Child \\
c\_age : \mathbb{N} \\
r! : Rep \\
\rule{4cm}{0.4pt} \\
c\_age \notin 5 \mathbin{.\,.} 16 \\
r! = AgeOutsideLimits
\end{array}}
$$

One convention that is sometimes used is to append a 0 to the names of partial operations: the total versions will then have the 0 removed. Following that convention here, our original definition of the operation should have been named $SmallAlterChildAge0$ and we can now define:

$$SmallAlterChildAge \mathrel{\widehat{=}} SmallAlterChildAge0 \lor BadAgeErr$$

Exercise 8.15

In the operation of adding a child there is no 'before' *Child* state. Also, it will require the allocation of an identifier not previously known to the system. There are two ways of viewing this: either an identifier may be thought of as being generated within the machine or it could be viewed as being assigned by the operator and entered as input to the operation. If the first view is adopted the development would be:

$$
\boxed{\begin{array}{l}
\underline{\,\Phi2Ca\,} \\
\Delta\,ChildReg \\
Child' \\
\rule{4cm}{0.4pt} \\
\exists\, c : CHILDID \bullet \\
\quad c \notin \mathrm{dom}\,creg \land \\
\quad creg' = creg \oplus \{c \mapsto \theta\,Child'\}
\end{array}}
$$

The promoted operation is:

$$AddChild0a \mathrel{\widehat{=}} \exists\, Child' \bullet \Phi2Ca \land SmallAddChild0$$

Note that since there is no before state of the *Child* schema, only *Child'* should be hidden. The expanded schema is:

```
┌─ AddChild0a ─────────────────────────────────────────────
│ Δ ChildReg
│ c_age? : ℕ
│ c_info? : CHILDINFO
│ r! : Rep
├──────────────────────────────────────────────────────────
│ ∃ age' : 5 .. 16; details' : CHILDINFO •
│       ∃ c : CHILDID •
│             c ∉ dom creg ∧
│             creg' = creg ⊕ {c ↦ θ Child'} ∧
│       c_age? ∈ 5 .. 16 ∧
│       age' = c_age? ∧
│       details' = c_info? ∧
│       r! = Success
└──────────────────────────────────────────────────────────
```

This can be simplified using the One Point Rule to:

```
┌─ AddChild0a ─────────────────────────────────────────────
│ Δ ChildReg
│ c_age? : ℕ
│ c_info? : CHILDINFO
│ r! : Rep
├──────────────────────────────────────────────────────────
│ ∃ c : CHILDID •
│       c ∉ dom creg ∧
│       creg' = creg ⊕ {c ↦ (μ Child' | age' = c_age? ∧
│                                          details' = c_info?)}
│ c_age? ∈ 5 .. 16
│ r! = Success
└──────────────────────────────────────────────────────────
```

We repeat the development for the second possible approach. The framing schema for this is:

```
┌─ Φ2Cb ───────────────────────────────────────────────────
│ Δ ChildReg
│ Child'
│ c? : CHILDID
├──────────────────────────────────────────────────────────
│ c? ∉ dom creg
│ creg' = creg ⊕ {c? ↦ θ Child'}
└──────────────────────────────────────────────────────────
```

Again, the promoted version is:

$$AddChild0b \,\widehat{=}\, \exists\, Child' \bullet \Phi2Cb \land SmallAddChild0$$

After expansion and simplification this is:

```
┌─ AddChild0b ─────────────────────────────────────────
│ Δ ChildReg
│ c? : CHILDID
│ c_age? : ℕ
│ c_info? : CHILDINFO
│ r! : Rep
├──────────────────────────────────────────────────────
│ c? ∉ dom creg
│ creg' = creg ⊕ {c? ↦ (μ Child' | age' = c_age? ∧
│                                    details' = c_info?)}
│ c_age? ∈ 5 .. 16
│ r! = Success
└──────────────────────────────────────────────────────
```

We shall take the latter approach as giving our working versions of $\Phi 2C$ and *AddChild0*: the choice will really depend on the requirements for the system. The second approach gives a slightly simpler specification since it involves less quantification. You may like to note where differences would occur in the continued development if the first approach had been chosen.

Exercise 8.16

```
┌─ DeleteChild0 ───────────────────────────────────────
│ Δ ChildReg
│ c? : CHILDID
│ r! : Rep
├──────────────────────────────────────────────────────
│ c? ∈ dom creg
│ creg' = {c?} ◁ creg
│ r! = Success
└──────────────────────────────────────────────────────
```

Exercise 8.17

The precondition is:

$$\text{pre } DeleteChild0 = \exists\, ChildReg';\ r! : Rep \bullet DeleteChild0$$

This can be expanded:

```
┌─ preDeleteChild0 ────────────────────────────────────
│ ChildReg
│ c? : CHILDID
├──────────────────────────────────────────────────────
│ ∃ creg' : CHILDID ⇸ Child; r! : Rep •
│     c? ∈ dom creg ∧
│     creg' = {c?} ◁ creg ∧
│     r! = Success
└──────────────────────────────────────────────────────
```

Using the One Point Rule this can be simplified to:

$$
\begin{array}{|l}
\underline{preDeleteChild0} \\
\quad ChildReg \\
\quad c? : CHILDID \\
\hline
\quad c? \in \text{dom } creg \\
\hline
\end{array}
$$

Exercise 8.18

We need to check that:

$$\Phi 1\,C \setminus ChildReg' = (\text{pre } \Phi 1\,C) \wedge Child'$$

Expanding the left hand side gives:

$$
\begin{array}{|l}
\underline{\Phi 1\,C \setminus ChildReg'} \\
\quad ChildReg \\
\quad \Delta\,Child \\
\quad c? : CHILDID \\
\hline
\quad \exists\,ChildReg' \bullet \\
\qquad \theta\,Child = creg\ c? \wedge \\
\qquad c? = \text{dom } creg \wedge \\
\qquad creg' = creg \oplus \{c? \mapsto \theta\,Child'\} \\
\hline
\end{array}
$$

The predicate can be rearranged since the first two conjuncts do not contain any quantified variables:

$$
\begin{aligned}
&\theta\,Child = creg\ c? \wedge \\
&c? = \text{dom } creg \wedge \\
&\exists\,ChildReg' \bullet \\
&\qquad creg' = creg \oplus \{c? \mapsto \theta\,Child'\}
\end{aligned}
$$

The third conjunct is true by the One Point Rule since for any *Child'* the resulting *creg'* satisfies *ChildReg'*. So the predicate simplifies to:

$$
\begin{aligned}
&\theta\,Child = creg\ c? \wedge \\
&c? = \text{dom } creg \wedge
\end{aligned}
$$

Taking the calculation of pre $\Phi 1\,C$ from the text, we see that the above result is equivalent to $(\text{pre } \Phi 1\,C) \wedge Child'$.

Exercise 8.19

```
┌─ preΦ2C ──────────────────────────────────────
│ ChildReg
│ c? : CHILDID
├───────────────────────────────────────────────
│ ∃ ChildReg'; Child' •
│       c? ∉ dom creg ∧
│       creg' = creg ⊕ {c? ↦ θ Child'}
└───────────────────────────────────────────────
```

which is equivalent to:

```
┌─ preΦ2C ──────────────────────────────────────
│ ChildReg
│ c? : CHILDID
├───────────────────────────────────────────────
│ c? ∉ dom creg
└───────────────────────────────────────────────
```

We know that the required precondition is equivalent to:

$$(\text{pre } SmallAddChild0 \land \text{pre } \Phi 2C) \setminus Child$$

which gives:

```
┌─ preAddChild0 ────────────────────────────────
│ ChildReg
│ c? : CHILDINFO
│ c_age? : ℕ
│ c_info? : CHILDINFO
├───────────────────────────────────────────────
│ c? ∈ dom creg
│ c_age? ∈ 5 .. 16
└───────────────────────────────────────────────
```

Exercise 8.20

There are two possible error conditions: the input identifier may be in use already and the input age may not be in the correct range. When there is more than one error condition it may seem straightforward to define error conditions for the various cases and use disjunction to join them:

```
┌─ KnownCidErr ─────────────────────────────────
│ ΞChildReg
│ c? : CHILDID
│ r! : Rep
├───────────────────────────────────────────────
│ c? ∈ dom creg
│ r! = CidKnown
└───────────────────────────────────────────────
```

```
┌─ BadAgeRegErr ─────────────────────────────────
│ Ξ ChildReg
│ c_age? : ℕ
│ r! : Rep
├────────────────────────────────────────────────
│ c_age? ∉ 5 .. 16
│ r! = AgeOutsideLimits
└────────────────────────────────────────────────
```

$$AddChild \triangleq AddChild0 \lor KnownCidErr \lor BadAgeRegErr$$

However, there is a point to note here. Defined in this way the operation is non-deterministic: if both errors occur at once the specification does not say which error message is to be given. Only one message is returned, and the specification allows this to be chosen non-deterministically by the system. Once we are aware of this situation, either we may be happy to leave it like that or we may wish to resolve the non-determinism at this level. Some possible ways of doing the latter are:

(a) Decide which error message should take precedence and add additional predicates to ensure that that one is returned if both errors occur.

(b) Make the output a set or sequence of error reports so that any number of errors can be reported.

(c) Have a special error report which covers the combined case.

We choose to leave our non-deterministic operation as it is for now.

Exercise 8.21

Partial operations:

```
┌─ AddLeader0 ─────────────────────────────────
│ Δ LeaderReg
│ l? : LEADERID
│ l_info? : LEADERINFO
│ r! : Rep
├──────────────────────────────────────────────
│ l? ∉ dom lreg
│ lreg' = lreg ⊕ {l? ↦ l_info?}
│ r! = Success
└──────────────────────────────────────────────
```

```
┌─ DeleteLeader0 ──────────────────────────────
│ Δ LeaderReg
│ l? : LEADERID
│ r! : Rep
├──────────────────────────────────────────────
│ l? ∈ dom lreg
│ lreg' = {l?} ◁ lreg
│ r! = Success
└──────────────────────────────────────────────
```

```
┌─ AlterLeaderDetails0 ────────────────────────────────
│ ΔLeaderReg
│ l? : LEADERID
│ l_info? : LEADERINFO
│ r! : Rep
├──────────────────────────────────────────────────────
│ l? ∈ dom lreg
│ lreg' = lreg ⊕ {l? ↦ l_info?}
│ r! = Success
└──────────────────────────────────────────────────────
```

```
┌─ ObtainLeaderDetails0 ───────────────────────────────
│ ΞLeaderReg
│ l? : LEADERID
│ l! : LEADERINFO
│ r! : Rep
├──────────────────────────────────────────────────────
│ l? ∈ dom lreg
│ l! = lreg l?
│ r! = Success
└──────────────────────────────────────────────────────
```

It is now apparent that more reports are needed:

```
┌─ UnknownLidErr ──────────────────────────────────────
│ ΞLeaderReg
│ l? : LEADERID
│ r! : Rep
├──────────────────────────────────────────────────────
│ l? ∉ dom lreg
│ r! = LidNotKnown
└──────────────────────────────────────────────────────
```

Similarly, we have:

```
┌─ KnownLidErr ────────────────────────────────────────
│ ΞLeaderReg
│ l? : LEADERID
│ r! : Rep
├──────────────────────────────────────────────────────
│ l? ∈ dom lreg
│ r! = LidKnown
└──────────────────────────────────────────────────────
```

Total operations:

$$AlterLeaderDetails \mathrel{\hat=} AlterLeaderDetails0 \lor UnknownLidErr$$
$$ObtainLeaderDetails \mathrel{\hat=} ObtainLeaderDetails0 \lor UnknownLidErr$$
$$AddLeader \mathrel{\hat=} AddLeader0 \lor KnownLidErr$$
$$DeleteLeader \mathrel{\hat=} DeleteLeader0 \lor UnknownLidErr$$

Exercise 8.22

Partial operations on groups:

```
┌─ VSmallAddToGroup0 ──────────────────────────────────
│ ΔGroup
│ c? : CHILDID
│ r! : Rep
├──────────────────────────────────────────────────────
│ c? ∉ members
│ #members ≠ maxgpsize band
│ members' = members ∪ {c?}
│ band' = band
│ r! = Success
└──────────────────────────────────────────────────────
```

```
┌─ VSmallDeleteBooking0 ───────────────────────────────
│ ΔGroup
│ c? : CHILDID
│ r! : Rep
├──────────────────────────────────────────────────────
│ c? ∈ members
│ members' = members \ {c?}
│ band' = band
│ r! = Success
└──────────────────────────────────────────────────────
```

```
┌─ VSmallAddNewGroup0 ─────────────────────────────────
│ Group'
│ b? : CampAgeBands
│ r! : Rep
├──────────────────────────────────────────────────────
│ members' = ∅
│ band' = b?
│ r! = Success
└──────────────────────────────────────────────────────
```

Error schemas:

```
┌─ FoundInGroupErr ────────────────────────────────────
│ ΞGroup
│ c? : CHILDID
│ r! : Rep
├──────────────────────────────────────────────────────
│ c? ∈ members
│ r! = ChildAlreadyInSession
└──────────────────────────────────────────────────────
```

```
┌─ GroupFullErr ───────────────────────────────────────
│ ΞGroup
│ r! : Rep
├──────────────────────────────────────────────────────
│ #members = maxgpsize band
│ r! = NoRoomInGroup
└──────────────────────────────────────────────────────
```

```
┌─ NotInGroupErr ─────────────────────────────────
│ ΞGroup
│ c? : CHILDID
│ r! : Rep
├─────────────────────────────────
│ c? ∉ members
│ r! = ChildNotInGroup
└─────────────────────────────────
```

Total operations on groups:

$$VSmallAddToGroup \triangleq VSmallAddToGroup0 \lor FoundInGroupErr$$
$$\lor\ GroupFullErr$$
$$VSmallDeleteBooking \triangleq VSmallDeleteBooking0 \lor NotInGroupErr$$
$$VSmallAddNewGroup \triangleq VSmallAddNewGroup0$$

Exercise 8.23

```
┌─ Φ2G ─────────────────────────────────
│ ΔSession
│ Group'
│ l? : LEADERID
├─────────────────────────────────
│ l? ∉ dom session
│ session' = session ⊕ {l? ↦ θGroup'}
└─────────────────────────────────
```

Exercise 8.24

$$SmallAddToGroup0 \triangleq \exists \Delta Group \bullet \Phi1G \land VSmallAddToGroup$$
$$SmallDeleteBooking0 \triangleq \exists \Delta Group \bullet \Phi1G \land VSmallDeleteBooking$$
$$SmallAddNewGroup0 \triangleq \exists Group' \bullet \Phi2G \land VSmallAddNewGroup$$

Exercise 8.25

```
┌─ Φ1G \ Session' ─────────────────────────────────
│ Session
│ ΔGroup
│ l? : LEADERID
├─────────────────────────────────
│ θGroup = session l?
│ l? ∈ dom session
│ ∃ Session' • session' = session ⊕ {l? ↦ θGroup'}
└─────────────────────────────────
```

The third part of the predicate cannot be eliminated since it is not necessarily true: if the number of participants in a session is already *maxsessionsize* then placing an additional member in a group would not result in a valid session.

$$
\begin{array}{|l}
\underline{\;(\text{pre } \Phi 1\, G) \wedge Group'\;}\rule{4cm}{0pt} \\
Session \\
\Delta\, Group \\
l? : LEADERID \\
\hline
\theta\, Group = session\ l? \\
l? \in \text{dom } session
\end{array}
$$

When calculating the precondition both *Session'* and *Group'* are hidden. The third conjunct is in this case true since it is always possible to find a value for *group'* which makes a valid *session'*; take *group' = session l?* which ensures that *session' = session*.

Promotion of preconditions fails because there is an extra requirement (that the total number of children at a session be within a certain maximum size limit) which can only be expressed at the session level. Hence there are valid instances of group operations which cannot be carried out at the session level.

Exercise 8.26

$$
\begin{array}{|l}
\underline{\;SessionFullErr\;}\rule{4cm}{0pt} \\
\Xi Session \\
r! : Rep \\
\hline
\#\bigcup\{l : \text{dom } session \bullet (session\ l).members\} = maxsessionsize \\
r! = NoRoomInSession
\end{array}
$$

$$
\begin{array}{|l}
\underline{\;UnknownLeaderErr\;}\rule{3.5cm}{0pt} \\
\Xi Session \\
l? : LEADERID \\
r! : Rep \\
\hline
l? \notin \text{dom } session \\
r! = LeaderNotInSession
\end{array}
$$

$$
\begin{array}{|l}
\underline{\;ChildInSessionErr\;}\rule{3.5cm}{0pt} \\
\Xi Session \\
c? : CHILDID \\
r! : Rep \\
\hline
\exists l : \text{dom } session \bullet c? \in (session\ l).members \\
r! = ChildAlreadyInSession
\end{array}
$$

$$
\begin{array}{|l}
\underline{\;KnownLeaderErr\;}\rule{4cm}{0pt} \\
\Xi Session \\
l? : LEADERID \\
r! : Rep \\
\hline
l? \in \text{dom } session \\
r! = LeaderAlreadyInSession
\end{array}
$$

Exercise 8.27

$$SmallAddToGroup \cong SmallAddToGroup0 \lor SessionFullErr \lor$$
$$UnknownLeaderErr \lor ChildInSessionErr$$
$$SmallDeleteBooking \cong SmallDeleteBooking0 \lor UnknownLeaderErr$$
$$SmallAddNewGroup \cong SmallAddNewGroup0 \lor KnownLeaderErr$$

Exercise 8.28

```
┌─ SmallGetChildren ─────────────────────────────────────
│ ΞSession
│ cs! : ℙ CHILDID
│ r! : Rep
├────────────────────────────────────────────────────────
│ cs! = ⋃{l : dom session • (session l).members}
│ r! = Success
└────────────────────────────────────────────────────────
```

Exercise 8.29

```
┌─ Φ1B ──────────────────────────────────────────────────
│ ΔBookingReg
│ ΔSession
│ d? : DATE
│ t? : TIME
├────────────────────────────────────────────────────────
│ (d?, t?) ∈ dom breg
│ θSession = breg (d?, t?)
│ breg' = breg ⊕ {(d?, t?) ↦ θSession'}
└────────────────────────────────────────────────────────
```

```
┌─ Φ2B ──────────────────────────────────────────────────
│ ΔBookingReg
│ Session'
│ d? : DATE
│ t? : TIME
├────────────────────────────────────────────────────────
│ (d?, t?) ∉ dom breg
│ breg' = breg ∪ {(d?, t?) ↦ θSession'}
└────────────────────────────────────────────────────────
```

$$AddSession0 \cong \exists Session' \bullet \Phi2B \land SmallInitSession$$
$$AddNewGroup0 \cong \exists \Delta Session \bullet \Phi1B \land SmallAddNewGroup$$
$$AddToGroup0 \cong \exists \Delta Session \bullet \Phi1B \land SmallAddToGroup$$
$$DeleteBooking0 \cong \exists \Delta Session \bullet \Phi1B \land SmallDeleteBooking$$
$$GetNo0 \cong \exists \Delta Session \bullet \Phi1B \land SmallGetNo$$
$$GetAgeBandNo0 \cong \exists \Delta Session \bullet \Phi1B \land SmallGetAgeBandNo$$

Exercise 8.30

The condition holds since both $\Phi 1B \setminus breg$ and $(\text{pre } \Phi 1B) \wedge Session'$ are equivalent to:

```
┌─ BookingReg ──────────────────────
│ Δ Session
│ d? : DATE
│ t? : TIME
├────────────────────────────────
│ θSession = breg (d?, t?)
│ (d?, t?) ∈ dom breg
└────────────────────────────────
```

Exercise 8.31

```
┌─ SessionUnknownErr ───────────────
│ Ξ BookingReg
│ d? : DATE
│ t? : TIME
│ r! : Rep
├────────────────────────────────
│ (d?, t?) ∉ dom breg
│ r! = UnknownSession
└────────────────────────────────
```

```
┌─ SessionExistsErr ────────────────
│ Ξ BookingReg
│ d? : DATE
│ t? : TIME
│ r! : Rep
├────────────────────────────────
│ (d?, t?) ∈ dom breg
│ r! = SessionExists
└────────────────────────────────
```

$AddSession \mathrel{\widehat{=}} AddSession0 \vee SessionExistsErr$
$AddNewGroup \mathrel{\widehat{=}} AddNewGroup0 \vee SessionUnknownErr$
$AddToGroup \mathrel{\widehat{=}} AddToGroup0 \vee SessionUnknownErr$
$DeleteBooking \mathrel{\widehat{=}} DeleteBooking0 \vee SessionUnknownErr$
$GetNo \mathrel{\widehat{=}} GetNo0 \vee SessionUnknownErr$
$GetAgeBandNo \mathrel{\widehat{=}} GetAgeBandNo0 \vee SessionUnknownErr$

Exercise 8.32

DeleteSession0
$\Delta BookingReg$
$d? : DATE$
$t? : TIME$
$r! : Rep$

$(d?, t?) \in \text{dom } breg$
$(breg\ (d?, t?)).session = \emptyset$
$breg' = \{(d?, t?)\} \lhd breg$
$r! = Success$

SessionNotEmptyErr
$\Xi BookingReg$
$d? : DATE$
$t? : TIME$
$r! : Rep$

$(d?, t?) \in \text{dom } breg$
$\exists\, l : LEADERID;\ g : Group\ |$
$\qquad\qquad (l, g) \in (breg(d?, t?)).session \bullet g.members \neq \emptyset$
$r! = SessionNotEmpty$

$$DeleteSession \ \widehat{=}\ DeleteSession0 \vee SessionUnknownErr \vee$$
$$SessionNotEmptyErr$$

Exercise 8.33

FullAddLeader
$\Delta CampEnergy$
$\Xi ChildReg$
$\Xi BookingReg$
$AddLeader$

We need to check:

$$\forall\, sess : \text{ran } breg' \bullet \forall\, grp : \text{ran } sess \bullet$$
$$\text{dom } sess \subseteq \text{dom } lreg' \wedge$$
$$grp.members \subseteq \text{dom } creg' \wedge$$
$$\forall\, cid : (grp.members) \bullet (creg'\ cid).age \in grp.ageband$$

Since *breg* and *creg* are unchanged, the second two conjuncts follow from their undashed equivalents. The first conjunct:

$$\text{dom } sess \subseteq \text{dom } lreg'$$

holds since:

$$\text{dom } sess \subseteq \text{dom } lreg$$

and the *AddLeader* operation ensures that dom $lreg \subseteq$ dom $lreg'$.

Exercise 8.34

```
┌─ FullDeleteChild0 ──────────────────────────────────────
│ ΔCampEnergy
│ ΞLeaderReg
│ ΞBookingReg
│ DeleteChild
├──────────────────────────────────────────────────────
│ ∀ s : ran breg • ∀ g : ran(s.session) • c? ∉ g.members
└──────────────────────────────────────────────────────
```

```
┌─ ExistingBookingsErr ───────────────────────────────────
│ ΞCampEnergy
│ c? : CHILDID
│ r! : Rep
├──────────────────────────────────────────────────────
│ ∃ s : ran breg • ∃ g : ran(s.session) • c? ∈ g.members
│ r! = BookingsExist
└──────────────────────────────────────────────────────
```

$$FullDeleteChild \cong FullDeleteChild0 \lor ExistingBookingsErr$$

```
┌─ FullDeleteLeader0 ─────────────────────────────────────
│ ΔCampEnergy
│ ΞChildReg
│ ΞBookingReg
│ DeleteLeader
├──────────────────────────────────────────────────────
│ ∀ d? : DATE; t? : TIME • l? ∉ dom((breg (d?, t?)).session)
└──────────────────────────────────────────────────────
```

```
┌─ LeaderWithGroupsErr ───────────────────────────────────
│ ΞCampEnergy
│ l? : LEADERID
│ r! : Rep
├──────────────────────────────────────────────────────
│ ∃ d? : DATE; t? : TIME • l? ∈ dom((breg (d?, t?)).session)
│ r! = LeaderHasGroups
└──────────────────────────────────────────────────────
```

$$FullDeleteLeader \cong FullDeleteLeader0 \lor LeaderWithGroupsErr$$

FullAlterAge0
$\Delta\,CampEnergy$
$\Xi\,LeaderReg$
$\Xi\,BookingReg$
$AlterChildAge$
<hr>
$(\neg\,\exists\,b : CampAgeBands \bullet \{(creg\ c?).age, c\_age?\} \subseteq b) \Rightarrow$
$\quad \forall\,s : \text{ran}\ breg \bullet \forall\,g : \text{ran}(s.session) \bullet c? \notin g.members$

AgeBandBookingsErr
$\Xi\,CampEnergy$
$c? : CHILDID$
$c\_age? : \mathbb{N}$
$r! : Rep$
<hr>
$\neg\,\exists\,b : CampAgeBands \bullet \{(creg\ c?).age, c\_age?\} \subseteq b$
$\exists\,s : \text{ran}\ breg \bullet \exists\,g : \text{ran}(s.session) \bullet c? \in g.members$
$r! = BookingsInOldAgeBand$

$FullAlterAge \;\widehat{=}\; FullAlterAge0 \vee AgeBandBookingsErr$

Chapter 9

Exercise 9.1

(i) $x : \mathbb{N} \vdash \exists\,y : \mathbb{N} \bullet y > x$

Exercise 9.2

(i) No number greater than max is in the range of f.

Exercise 9.4

DeleteMember
$\Delta\,Fid$
$id? : ID$
<hr>
$id? \in \text{dom}\ members$
$id? \notin banned$
$members' = \{id?\} \lhd members$
$banned' = banned$

This prevents a banned member leaving the scheme. Otherwise a banned member could leave and rejoin simply to beat the system.

Exercise 9.7

The variables *members'* and *banned'* are of different types and therefore require different instantiations of ∅. In fact, the Z Reference Manual [Spi92] explains that an expression such as:

$$members' = banned' = \emptyset$$

is equivalent to:

$$members' = banned' \wedge banned' = \emptyset$$

and, as stated above, the first conjunct is not well-typed. However, it is possible to write:

$$members' = \emptyset = banned'$$

since this is equivalent to:

$$members' = \emptyset \wedge \emptyset = banned'$$

giving two occurrences of ∅ which could be instantiated separately.

Exercise 9.8

p	q	$p \wedge (p \vee q)$	p	$p \vee (p \wedge q)$
T	T	T	T	T	T	T
T	F	T	T	T	T	F
F	T	F	T	F	F	F
F	F	F	F	F	F	F

Exercise 9.13

$$\neg (p \wedge q)$$
$$\equiv \neg (\neg \neg p \wedge \neg \neg q) \qquad [DN]$$
$$\equiv \neg p \vee \neg q \qquad [\vee \, Equiv]$$

$$\neg (p \vee q)$$
$$\equiv \neg \neg (\neg p \wedge \neg q) \qquad [\vee \, Equiv]$$
$$\equiv \neg p \wedge \neg q \qquad [DN]$$

Exercise 9.15

(i) *x,y* both bound throughout.

(ii) x,y both free throughout.

(iii) y is bound in the first conjunct; in the second conjunct x is bound and y is free.

(iv) x is bound; y is bound in the first conjunct and free in the second.

Exercise 9.17

Q9. If S is $\mathbb{N}$, T is $\{x\}$ and p is $x = y$, then $\forall x : S \bullet \forall y : T \bullet p$ is true. However, reversing the order of quantification gives: $\forall y : \{x\} \bullet \forall x : \mathbb{N} \bullet x = y$. If the first x is not in the scope of some previous declaration of the correct type then this statement is not even type correct. If there is a correctly typed binding of x in scope then the statement is false since it claims that one particular value is equal to all numbers.

Q10. As before, if T captures x then reversing the order of quantification could well result in a type error. Even if there is a previously declared x of the correct type the rule would be invalid without side-conditions. Suppose S is $\mathbb{N}$, T is $\{x\}$ and p is $y = 0$. Then $\exists x : \mathbb{N} \bullet \exists y : \{x\} \bullet y = 0$ is true. If x has previously been declared, for example $x == 1$, then $\exists y : \{x\} \bullet \exists x : \mathbb{N} \bullet y = 0$ is false.

Q11. As for Q10.

Exercise 9.21

PreDeleteMember

Fid
$id? : ID$

$\exists\, Fid' \bullet$

     $id? \in \operatorname{dom} members \wedge$
     $id? \notin banned \wedge$
     $members' = \{id?\} \vartriangleleft members \wedge$
     $banned' = banned$

Using the One Point Rule the predicate is equivalent to:

     $\{id?\} \vartriangleleft members \in ID \rightarrowtail PERSON \wedge$
     $banned \in \mathbb{P}\, ID \wedge$
     $banned \subseteq \operatorname{dom}(\{id?\} \vartriangleleft members) \wedge$
     $id? \in \operatorname{dom} members \wedge$
     $id? \notin banned$

Fid ensures that the second conjunct holds. Also from Fid, we know that $members \in ID \rightarrowtail PERSON$ and so any subset of $members$ is also an injective function of this type. This leaves:

     $banned \subseteq \operatorname{dom}(\{id?\} \vartriangleleft members) \wedge$
     $id? \in \operatorname{dom} members \wedge$
     $id? \notin banned$

The first of the remaining conjuncts may be rewritten:

$$banned \subseteq (\text{dom } members) \setminus \{id?\}$$

This follows (using a law from the reference manual) if we can show that :

$$(banned \subseteq \text{dom } members) \wedge (banned \cap \{id?\} = \emptyset)$$

The first part of this follows from *Fid* and the second is a consequence of $id? \notin banned$. We are left with:

$$id? \in \text{dom } members \wedge$$
$$id? \notin banned$$

both of which are needed so:

$$
\begin{array}{|l}
\_\text{PreDeleteMember} \_\!\_\!\_\!\_\!\_\!\_\!\_\!\_\!\_\!\_\!\_\!\_\!\_\!\_\!\_\!\_\!\_\!\_\!\_\!\_\!\_\!\_\!\_\!\_\!\_ \\
\quad Fid \\
\quad id? : ID \\
\hline
\quad id? \in \text{dom } members \\
\quad id? \notin banned \\
\end{array}
$$

Chapter 10

Exercise 10.1

Suppose $R \sqsubseteq S$ and $S \sqsubseteq T$. Applicability holds for both of these, so if R is applicable then so is S, and if S is applicable then so is T. Hence, if R is applicable then so is T.

By correctness, if R is applicable and S is applied then the result is consistent with R, and if S is applicable and T is applied then the result is consistent with S. Suppose R is applicable then, using applicability, S is applicable and so is T. If T is applied then the result is consistent with S which in turn must be consistent with R. Hence, if R is applicable and T is applied then the result is consistent with R.

Hence, $R \sqsubseteq T$.

Exercise 10.2

Suppose $X = Y = \mathbb{Z}$ and

$$R == \{1 \mapsto 1, 1 \mapsto 2, 1 \mapsto 3, 1 \mapsto 4\}$$
$$S == \{0 \mapsto 1, 1 \mapsto 2, 1 \mapsto 3\}$$

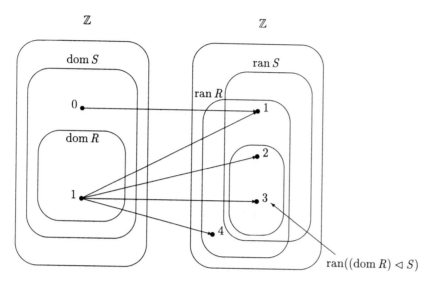

Exercise 10.3

dom R

$= \{x : \mathbb{N}_1 \mid \exists\, y, z, n1, n2 : \mathbb{N}_1 \bullet x = n1 * z \land y = n2 * z\}$

$= \{x : \mathbb{N}_1 \mid \exists : n1, z : \mathbb{N}_1 \bullet x = n1 * z\}$ [could take $(y, n2) = (x, n1)$]

$= \mathbb{N}_1$ [could take $(z, n1) = (x, 1)$]

dom $S1$

$= \{x : \mathbb{N} \mid \exists\, y : \mathbb{N} \bullet x = y \land y > 0\}$

$= \{x : \mathbb{N} \mid x > 0\}$ [One Point Rule]

$= \mathbb{N}_1$

dom $S2$

$= \{x : \mathbb{N} \mid \exists\, n : \mathbb{N} \bullet n > 0\}$

$= \mathbb{N}$ [Predicate is *true*]

Thus, dom $R \subseteq$ dom $S1$ and dom $R \subseteq$ dom $S2$, which are the first requirements if $S1$ and $S2$ are to be refinements of R.

Now, $(\text{dom } R) \lhd S1 = \mathbb{N}_1 \lhd S1 \subseteq R$, since for any $(x, x) \in S1$ with $x > 0$ we can choose $n1 = n2 = x, z = 1$, so that $(x, x) \in R$ also; thus we now know that $R \sqsubseteq S1$.

Similarly, $(\text{dom } R) \lhd S2 = \mathbb{N}_1 \lhd S2 \subseteq R$. For any $(x, n * x) \in S2$, with $x > 0$, we can choose $n1 = 1, z = x, n2 = n$, so $(x, n * x) \in R$. Therefore $R \sqsubseteq S2$.

Since $\neg\,(\text{dom } S2 \subseteq S1)$ we know that $S1$ is not a refinement of $S2$.

However, nor is $S2$ a refinement of $S1$; for example $(2, 4) \in S2$ but $(2, 4) \notin S1$, so $S2$ relates 2 to 4 which is not acceptable to $S1$.

Exercise 10.4

PreIncludeInput _____

$x : \mathbb{P}\,\mathbb{N}$

$y? : \mathbb{N}$

_____

$\exists x' : \mathbb{P}\,\mathbb{N};\ z! : \mathbb{N} \bullet$

$\qquad y? \notin x \wedge y? \in x' \wedge \emptyset \subset x \subset x' \wedge z! \notin x' \setminus x$
_____

The predicate of this simplifies to $y? \notin x \wedge x \neq \emptyset$.

PreIncludeLeqInput _____

$x : \mathbb{P}\,\mathbb{N}$

$y? : \mathbb{N}$

_____

$\exists x' : \mathbb{P}\,\mathbb{N};\ z! : \mathbb{N} \bullet$

$\qquad y? \notin x \wedge x' = x \cup \{z : \mathbb{N} \mid z \le y?\} \wedge z! = y?$
_____

The predicate simplifies to $y? \notin x$. This satisfies the first refinement condition since:

$$PreIncludeInput \vdash y? \notin x$$

Secondly, *PreIncludeInput* $\wedge$ *IncludeLeqInput* expands to:

$x, x' : \mathbb{P}\,\mathbb{N}$

$y? : \mathbb{N}$

$z! : \mathbb{N}$

_____

$y? \notin x$

$x \neq \emptyset$

$x' = x \cup \{z : \mathbb{N} \mid z \le y?\}$

$z! = y?$
_____

From this we need to prove:

$$y? \notin x \wedge y? \in x' \wedge \emptyset \subset x \subset x' \wedge z! \in x' \setminus x$$

(a) The first conjunct comes immediately from the hypotheses.

(b) The second conjunct comes from the hypothesis $x' = x \cup \{z : \mathbb{N} \mid z \le y?\}$ since this set clearly contains $y?$.

(c) From the hypothesis $x \neq \emptyset$ we know that $\emptyset \subset x$.

(d) Since $y? \notin x$ and both $x \subseteq x'$ and $y? \in x'$ we have $x \subset x'$.

(e) $z! = y?$ and $y? \in x'$ and $y? \notin x$. Therefore $z! \in x' \setminus x$.

This confirms that *IncludeInput* ⊑ *IncludeLeqInput*. The precondition of the modified schema is:

$$
\begin{array}{|l}
x : \mathbb{P}\,\mathbb{N} \\
y? : \mathbb{N} \\
\hline
\exists\, x' : \mathbb{P}\,\mathbb{N};\ z! : \mathbb{N} \bullet \\
\quad 0 \notin x \wedge x' = x \cup \{z : \mathbb{N} \mid z \le y?\} \wedge z! = y?
\end{array}
$$

The predicate of this simplifies to $0 \notin x$. For the first refinement condition it would be necessary to show that $0 \notin x$ follows from *PreIncludeInput*, but this cannot be done since $x = \{0\}$ is a perfectly acceptable before state for *PreIncludeInput*. Therefore the modified schema is not a refinement of *IncludeInput*.

Exercise 10.5

We need to show:

$$
\begin{aligned}
&\operatorname{ran} \emptyset \in ID \rightarrowtail PERSON \\
&\operatorname{ran} \emptyset \subseteq 1\,..\,(\#\emptyset) \\
&(\#\emptyset) \le maxmems
\end{aligned}
$$

(a) The first part follows from the fact that $\operatorname{ran} \emptyset = \emptyset$ (Law *L6* in Chapter 9) and $\emptyset \in ID \rightarrowtail PERSON$ (*L12*).

(b) Secondly, $1\,..\,(\#\emptyset) = 1\,..\,0 = \emptyset$ giving $\emptyset \subseteq \emptyset$ which is *true*.

(c) Thirdly, $\#\emptyset = 0$, and 0 must be less than or equal to *maxmems* since *maxmems* is an element of $\mathbb{N}$.

Exercise 10.7

A concrete state in which:

$$
\begin{aligned}
membarr &= \langle(WW8901, Tom), (WW8903, Bill), (WW9001, Daisy)\rangle \\
banarr &= \langle\rangle
\end{aligned}
$$

corresponds to the abstract state in which:

$$
\begin{aligned}
members &= \{WW8901 \mapsto Tom,\ WW8903 \mapsto Bill,\ WW9001 \mapsto Daisy\} \\
banned &= \emptyset
\end{aligned}
$$

Other distinct concrete states corresponding to the same abstract state are all those with *banarr* empty and with *membarr* containing the same elements but in a different order.

Exercise 10.8

(i)

$$\mathrm{dom}(\emptyset[X, Y])$$
$$= \{x : X \mid (\exists\, y : Y \bullet x \mapsto y \in \emptyset)\} \qquad \text{[defn of dom]}$$
$$= \{x : X \mid (\exists\, y : Y \bullet \mathit{false})\} \qquad \text{[defn of $\emptyset$]}$$
$$= \{x : X \mid \mathit{false}\} \qquad \text{[TF7]}$$
$$= \emptyset[X] \qquad \text{[defn of $\emptyset$]}$$

and similarly for ran.

Exercise 10.9

The extra predicate, $\#members < maxmems$, does not contain any of the quantified variables and may therefore be taken outside the quantification. The remaining quantified predicate simplifies as before to:

$$applicant? \notin \mathrm{ran}\ members \wedge$$
$$\mathrm{dom}\ members \neq ID$$

Exercise 10.11

(i) Follows from $Retr'$.

(ii) $banarr' = banarr$ (from $CAddMember$).

(iii) (a) $membarr' = membarr \frown \langle(id!, applicant?)\rangle$ (from $CAddMember$)

(b) So:

$$membarr' (\!| \mathrm{ran}\ banarr' |\!) =$$
$$membarr (\!| \mathrm{ran}\ banarr |\!) \cup$$
$$((\#membarr + 1) \mapsto (id!, applicant?)) (\!| \mathrm{ran}\ banarr |\!)$$

(c) However, $\mathrm{ran}\ banarr \subseteq 1\,..\,\#membarr$ (from $CFidScheme$) so that:

$$\#membarr + 1 \notin \mathrm{ran}\ banarr$$

(d) This means that:

$$((\#membarr + 1) \mapsto (id!, applicant?)) (\!| \mathrm{ran}\ banarr |\!) = \emptyset$$

(e) Hence $membarr' (\!| \mathrm{ran}\ banarr |\!) = membarr (\!| \mathrm{ran}\ banarr |\!)$

(iv) Follows from $Retr$.

Exercise 10.12

```
┌─ CBanFMember ────────────────────────────────────────
│ ΔCFidFScheme
│ miscreant? : ID
├──────────────────────────────────────────────────────
│ miscreant? ∈ dom(ran membarr)
│ miscreant? ∉ dom(membarr ⦇ ran banarr ⦈)
│ ran banarr' =
│         (ran banarr) ∪ dom(membarr ▷ ({miscreant?} × PERSON))
│ membarr' = membarr
└──────────────────────────────────────────────────────
```

(a) **Calculating the preconditions**

```
┌─ PreBanFMember ──────────────────────────────────────
│ FidFScheme
│ miscreant? : ID
├──────────────────────────────────────────────────────
│ ∃ FidFscheme' •
│         miscreant? ∈ (dom members) \ banned ∧
│         banned' = banned ∪ {miscreant?} ∧
│         members' = members
└──────────────────────────────────────────────────────
```

Using the One Point Rule to simplify the predicate gives:

$$members \in ID \nrightarrow PERSON \land$$
$$banned \cup \{miscreant?\} \in \mathbb{P}\, ID \land$$
$$banned \cup \{miscreant?\} \subseteq dom\, members \land$$
$$miscreant? \in (dom\, members) \setminus banned$$

The first and second conjuncts follow from the declarations of *FidFScheme*. The third follows from the declaration of *banned* in *FidFScheme* and from the fourth conjunct since this ensures that *miscreant?* is in dom *members*. This leaves:

```
┌─ PreBanFMember ──────────────────────────────────────
│ FidFScheme
│ miscreant? : ID
├──────────────────────────────────────────────────────
│ miscreant? ∈ (dom members) \ banned
└──────────────────────────────────────────────────────
```

```
┌─ PreCBanFMember ─────────────────────────────────────
│ CFidFScheme
│ miscreant? : ID
├──────────────────────────────────────────────────────
│ ∃ CFidFscheme' •
│         miscreant? ∈ dom(ran membarr) ∧
│         miscreant? ∉ dom(membarr ⦇ ran banarr ⦈) ∧
│         ran banarr' = (ran banarr)∪
│                 dom(membarr ▷ ({miscreant?} × PERSON)) ∧
│         membarr' = membarr
└──────────────────────────────────────────────────────
```

Using the One Point Rule the predicate simplifies to:

$\exists\, banarr' : \mathrm{iseq}\,\mathbb{N} \bullet$
$\quad membarr \in \mathrm{iseq}(ID \times PERSON) \land$
$\quad \mathrm{ran}\, membarr \in ID \rightarrowtail PERSON \land$
$\quad \mathrm{ran}\, banarr' \subseteq 1\,..\,\#membarr \land$
$\quad \#membarr \le maxmems \land$
$\quad miscreant? \in \mathrm{dom}(\mathrm{ran}\, membarr) \land$
$\quad miscreant? \notin \mathrm{dom}(membarr \,(\!|\, \mathrm{ran}\, banarr \,|\!)\,) \land$
$\quad \mathrm{ran}\, banarr' =$
$\qquad (\mathrm{ran}\, banarr) \cup \mathrm{dom}(membarr \rhd (\{miscreant?\} \times PERSON))$

The first two conjuncts and the fourth (which may be taken outside the quantification) follow from *CFidFScheme*. The third conjunct follows from the last since:

$\mathrm{ran}\, banarr \subseteq 1\,..\,\#membarr$

(from *CFidFScheme*), and:

$\mathrm{dom}\, membarr \subseteq 1\,..\,\#membarr$

since *membarr* is a sequence. The fifth and sixth conjuncts may be taken outside the quantification. This leaves:

$miscreant? \in \mathrm{dom}(\mathrm{ran}\, membarr) \land$
$miscreant? \notin \mathrm{dom}(membarr \,(\!|\, \mathrm{ran}\, banarr \,|\!)\,) \land$
$\exists\, banarr' : \mathrm{iseq}\,\mathbb{N} \bullet$
$\quad \mathrm{ran}\, banarr' =$
$\qquad (\mathrm{ran}\, banarr) \cup \mathrm{dom}(membarr \rhd (\{miscreant?\} \times PERSON))$

The third conjunct is true since *banarr* can always be extended to include new members (of the correct type) in its range. We have:

```
┌─ PreCBanFMember ──────────────────────────────
│  CFidFScheme
│  miscreant? : ID
├───────────────────────────────────────────────
│  miscreant? ∈ dom(ran membarr) ∧
│  miscreant? ∉ dom(membarr (| ran banarr |))
└───────────────────────────────────────────────
```

(b) **Applicability**

$PreBanFMember \land Retr \vdash PreCBanFMember$

The declaration part of *PreCBanFMember* is included in the hypotheses. This leaves the goal:

$miscreant? \in \mathrm{dom}(\mathrm{ran}\, membarr) \land$
$miscreant? \notin \mathrm{dom}(membarr \,(\!|\, \mathrm{ran}\, banarr \,|\!)\,)$

Using the identities from *Retr* this is equivalent to:

> *miscreant?* $\in$ dom *members* $\land$
> *miscreant?* $\notin$ *banned*

which follows from *PreBanFMember*.

(c) **Correctness**

> *PreBanFMember* $\land$ *Retr* $\land$ *CBanFMember* $\land$ *Retr'* $\vdash$ *BanFMember*

FidFScheme and *FidFScheme'* are included in *Retr* and *Retr'* respectively. The input, *miscreant?* is declared in *PreBanFMember*. Therefore we may interpret the goal as:

> *miscreant?* $\in$ (dom *members*) $\setminus$ *banned* $\land$
> *banned'* = *banned* $\cup$ {*miscreant?*} $\land$
> *members'* = *members*

As with Applicability, the first conjunct follows from *CBanFMember* and *Retr*. *CBanFMember* ensures that *membarr'* = *membarr* and thus:

> ran *membarr'* = ran *membarr*

The third conjunct follows from this using *Retr* and *Retr'*. For the second conjunct, using *Retr* and *Retr'* we must prove:

> dom(*membarr'* $\lhd$ *banarr'* $\rhd$) = dom(*membarr* $\lhd$ *banarr* $\rhd$) $\cup$ {*miscreant?*}

or, using *CBanFMember*:

> dom(*membarr* $\lhd$ (ran *banarr*)
> $\qquad\qquad\qquad$ $\cup$ dom(*membarr* $\rhd$ ({*miscreant?*} $\times$ *PERSON*)) $\rhd$))
> $\quad$ = dom(*membarr* $\lhd$ (ran *banarr*) $\rhd$) $\cup$ {*miscreant?*}

or, equivalently:

> dom(*membarr* $\lhd$ (ran *banarr*) $\rhd$)$\cup$
> $\qquad$ dom(*membarr* $\lhd$ dom(*membarr* $\rhd$ ({*miscreant?*} $\times$ *PERSON*)) $\rhd$))
> $\quad$ = dom(*membarr* $\lhd$ (ran *banarr*) $\rhd$) $\cup$ {*miscreant?*}

which will follow if we can show that:

> dom(*membarr* $\lhd$ dom(*membarr* $\rhd$ ({*miscreant?*} $\times$ *PERSON*)) $\rhd$))
> $\quad$ = {*miscreant?*}

Suppose that f and g are functions with $g \subseteq f$ then:

> dom(f $\lhd$ dom g $\rhd$)

$$= \mathrm{dom}(g \,(\!|\, \mathrm{dom}\, g \,|\!)) \qquad\qquad [f \text{ acts as } g \text{ on the domain of } g]$$
$$= \mathrm{dom\, ran}\, g \qquad\qquad\qquad\quad [g \text{ maps its domain to its range}]$$

We can apply this result to:

$$\mathrm{dom}(membarr \,(\!|\, \mathrm{dom}(membarr \rhd (\{miscreant?\} \times PERSON)) \,|\!))$$

since $membarr \rhd S \subseteq membarr$ for any set S (of the correct type). Thus we obtain:

$$\mathrm{dom}(\mathrm{ran}(membarr \rhd (\{miscreant?\} \times PERSON)))$$

The set:

$$\mathrm{ran}(membarr \rhd (\{miscreant?\} \times PERSON))$$

consists of all the pairs in the *membarr* array whose first element is *miscreant?*. The domain of this set is either $\emptyset$ (if the set itself is empty) or just $\{miscreant?\}$. We know from *CBanFMember* that $miscreant? \in \mathrm{dom\, ran}\, membarr$ and therefore the domain is $\{miscreant?\}$ as required.

Chapter 11

Exercise 11.1

In order to show that $SwapxyExtraVars \sqsubseteq SwapxyUsingz$ we need to show:

$$\mathrm{pre}\ SwapxyExtraVars \vdash \mathrm{pre}\ SwapxyUsingz$$
$$\mathrm{pre}\ SwapxyExtraVars \wedge SwapxyUsingz \vdash SwapxyExtraVars$$

In the first case, pre $SwapxyUsingz$ reduces to $true$ by application of the One Point Rule. This needs no hypothesis. In the second case, expanding the hypotheses gives:

$$x, x', y, y', z, z' : T; \rho;$$
$$true$$
$$z' = x \wedge x' = y \wedge y' = z'$$

from which we can deduce that $x' = y \wedge y' = x$ which is all we need to establish $SwapxyExtraVars$.

However, the second schema given is not a refinenent since its precondition includes the constraint $z = x$ which cannot be proved from hypothesis pre $SwapxyExtraVars$ since this reduces to $true$.

Finally, $SwapPart1 \,\overset{\circ}{,}\, SwapPart2$ is defined as:

$$\exists x'', y'', z'' : T \bullet SwapPart1['' /'] \wedge SwapPart2['' /]$$

which when expanded becomes:

$$\exists\, x'', y'', z'' : T \bullet [\Delta[x, y, z : T]; \Xi[\rho]\ |$$
$$z'' = x \wedge x'' = y \wedge y'' = y$$
$$\wedge\ y' = z'' \wedge x' = x'' \wedge z' = z'']$$

Using the One Point Rule to eliminate the doubly-dashed variables this reduces to:

$$[\Delta[x, y, z : T]; \Xi[\rho]\ |$$
$$y' = x \wedge x' = y \wedge z' = x]$$

which is equivalent to *SwapxyUsingz*.

Exercise 11.2

First we need to show that:

$$\text{pre } Initialise \vdash \text{pre } InitRef$$

Now, pre *Initialise* is equivalent to:

$$\exists\, a' : \text{seq}\,\mathbb{N}, sofar', maxel' : \mathbb{N} \bullet a = a' \wedge MaxelGreatestSofar'$$

and this reduces to:

$$\#a > 0 \wedge \exists\, sofar', maxel' : \mathbb{N} \bullet 1 \le maxel' \le sofar' \le \#a$$

by the One Point Rule. Also, pre *InitRef* reduces to $\#a > 0$ by applying the One Point Rule. Since $\#a > 0$ is one of the components of the reduced form of pre *Initialise* derived above, the result we need follows immediately.

Secondly, we need to show:

$$\text{pre } Initialise \wedge InitRef \vdash Initialise$$

We only need *InitRef* as hypothesis: this gives us $\#a > 0$, $sofar' = 1$ and $maxel' = 1$, and these values for $sofar'$ and $maxel'$ do indeed satisfy *MaxelGreatestSofar'*. If we substitute these values throughout *MaxelGreatestSofar'* we obtain $1 \le 1 \le 1 \le \#a$, which is certainly true since $\#a > 0$, and $\forall\, n : 1..1 \bullet a(1) \ge a(n)$, which is also true since the only n in the range $1..1$ is 1 itself.

Exercise 11.3

For simplicity let us take the case where we have a disjunction of exactly two operations; the argument can easily be extended to the more general case. From the Alternation Refinement Rule given at the start of the section we can make the refinement:

$$Op_1 \vee Op_2 \sqsubseteq$$
$$\texttt{if preOp\_1 --> } (\text{pre } Op_1 \wedge (Op_1 \vee Op_2))$$

$$\texttt{[] preOp\_2 --> } (\text{pre } Op_2 \wedge (Op_1 \vee Op_2))$$
$$\texttt{fi}$$

provided that we can show that:

$$\text{pre } (Op_1 \vee Op_2) \vdash \text{pre } Op_1 \vee \text{pre } Op_2$$

This follows immediately from rule $Q2$ of Chapter 9.

We now want to simplify the guarded operations. We can show that for any Op and $OtherOp$:

$$\text{pre } Op \wedge (Op \wedge OtherOp) \subseteq Op$$

Informally, when the precondition of Op is satisfied we can always choose to do what Op allows, rather than do anything else which $OtherOp$ might permit. Again using the rules for existential quantification from Chapter 9, we can show that the precondition of pre $Op \wedge (Op \vee OtherOp)$ is equivalent to pre Op. Thus the Applicability requirement for refinement is easily derived. The Correctness requirement is also satisfied because:

$$\text{pre } Op \wedge Op \vdash \text{pre } Op \wedge (Op \vee OtherOp)$$

This can be established using only propositional calculus rules for $\wedge$ and $\vee$.

Thus we can now simplify the refinement as follows:

$$Op_1 \vee Op_2 \sqsubseteq$$
$$\texttt{if preOp\_1 --> } Op_1$$
$$\texttt{[] preOp\_2 --> } Op_2$$
$$\texttt{fi}$$

which is exactly the Derived Rule as required.

Exercise 11.4

Let us first simplify pre *Body*. This is equivalent to:

$$\exists \, sofar', maxel' : \mathbb{N} \bullet$$
$$MaxelGreatestSofar \wedge MaxelGreatestSofar' \wedge sofar' = sofar + 1$$

which can be simplified to:

$$MaxelGreatestSofar \wedge \exists \, maxel' : \mathbb{N} \bullet MaxelGreatestSofar'[sofar + 1/sofar']$$

using the One Point Rule, and using the notation $[sofar+1/sofar']$ to indicate the substitution of $sofar + 1$ for $sofar'$ throughout $MaxelGreatestSofar$. Now, $MaxelGreatestSofar$ is one of the hypotheses, since this is in fact the invariant Inv. The guard $sofar < \#a$, the other hypothesis, ensures that $sofar + 1 \leq \#a$. So if we now expand the existentially quantified part of the simplification of pre *Body* we have:

$$\exists \, maxel' : \mathbb{N} \bullet$$
$$\#a > 0$$
$$1 \leq maxel' \leq sofar + 1 \leq \#a$$
$$\forall n : 1..sofar + 1 \bullet a(maxel') \geq a(n)$$

Now $\#a > 0$ is already part of *MaxelGreatestSofar*, and the remaining conjuncts merely state that there is a greatest element for the range $1..sofar + 1$, where $sofar + 1 \le \#a$. This is a property of arrays (sequences) which is always true.

Exercise 11.5

The retrieve relation is expressed formally as follows:

$$
\begin{array}{|l}
\hline
\_Retr_1 _____ \\
\quad FidFScheme \\
\quad CFidFScheme_1 \\
\hline
\quad members = \mathrm{dom}\, membarr \\
\quad banned = \mathrm{dom}(membarr \restriction (\mathrm{ran}\, banarr \restriction)) \\
\hline
\end{array}
$$

Exercise 11.6

The expanded version of *TotalBanMember* is as follows:

$$
\begin{array}{|l}
\hline
\_TotalBanMember _____ \\
\quad \Delta FidFScheme \\
\quad ban? : ID \\
\quad rep! : REPORT \\
\hline
\quad (ban? \in \mathrm{dom}\, members \wedge ban? \notin banned \\
\qquad banned' = banned \cup \{ban?\} \wedge rep! = Ok) \\
\quad \vee \\
\quad (ban? \notin \mathrm{dom}\, members \wedge banned' = banned \wedge rep! = NotMember) \\
\quad \vee \\
\quad (ban? \in banned \wedge rep! = AlreadyBanned) \\
\quad members' = members \\
\hline
\end{array}
$$

The corresponding concrete operation is:

```
┌─ NTotalBanMember ─────────────────────────────────────────────
│ ΔCFidScheme₁
│ ban? : ID
│ rep! : REPORT
├───────────────────────────────────────────────────────────────
│ (ban? ∈ dom(ran membarr) ∧
│       ban? ∉ dom(membarr (| ran banarr |)) ∧
│       banarr' = banarr ⊕
│             {btop + 1 ↦
│                   μ i : ℕ; p : PERSON | membarr(i) = (ban?, p) • i} ∧
│       btop' = btop + 1 ∧ rep! = Ok)
│ ∨
│ (ban? ∉ dom(ran membarr) ∧
│       banarr' = banarr ∧ btop' = btop ∧ rep! = NotMember)
│ ∨
│ (ban? ∈ dom(membarr (| ran banarr |)) ∧
│       banarr' = banarr ∧ btop' = btop ∧ rep! = AlreadyBanned)
│ membarr' = membarr
└───────────────────────────────────────────────────────────────
```

Finally the normalised version of the concrete operation may be expressed as follows:

```
┌─ CTotalBanMember ─────────────────────────────────────────────
│ Δ[banarr : ℕ ⇸ ℕ; btop : ℕ; rep! : REPORT]
│ Ξ[membarr : ℕ ⇸ (ID × PERSON); mtop : ℕ; ban? : ID]
├───────────────────────────────────────────────────────────────
│ ΔCFidFScheme₁
│ (ban? ∈ dom(ran membarr) ∧
│       banarr' = banarr⊕
│             {btop + 1 ↦ μ i : ℕ; p : PERSON |
│                   membarr(i) = (ban?, p) • i}
│       ∧ btop' = btop + 1 ∧ rep! = Ok)
│ ∨
│ (ban? ∉ dom(ran membarr) ∧
│       banarr' = banarr ∧ btop' = btop ∧ rep! = NotMember)
│ ∨
│ (ban? ∈ dom(membarr (| ran banarr |)) ∧
│       banarr' = banarr ∧ btop' = btop ∧ rep! = AlreadyBanned)
└───────────────────────────────────────────────────────────────
```

Exercise 11.7

Reducing the frame by eliminating *btop* we obtain the following schema:

```
┌─ RTotalAddMember ──────────────────────────────────────────
│ Δ[membarr : ℕ ⇸ (ID × PERSON);
│     mtop : ℕ
│     id! : ID; rep! : REPORT];
│ Ξ[banarr : ℕ ⇸ ℕ; applicant? : PERSON]
├────────────────────────────────────────────────────────────
│ Δ CFidFScheme₁ \ (btop)
│ (applicant? ∉ ran(ran membarr) ∧ mtop < maxmems ∧
│       membarr' = membarr ⊕ {mtop + 1 ↦ (id!', applicant?)} ∧
│       mtop' = mtop + 1 ∧
│       id!' = idgen(mtop + 1) ∧ rep!' = Ok)
│ ∨
│ (applicant? ∈ ran(ran membarr) ∧ membarr' = membarr
│       ∧ rep!' = AlreadyMember)
│ ∨
│ (mtop = maxmems ∧ membarr' = membarr
│       ∧ rep!' = TooManyMembers)
└────────────────────────────────────────────────────────────
```

Note that we cannot reduce the frame further by discarding *banarr* because there is a relationship between *membarr*, which may change, and *banarr*.

Exercise 11.8

The three schemas required are as follows:

```
┌─ NormalAddMember ──────────────────────────────────────────
│ Δ[membarr : ℕ ⇸ (ID × PERSON);
│     mtop : ℕ
│     id! : ID; rep! : REPORT];
│ Ξ[banarr : ℕ ⇸ ℕ; applicant? : PERSON]
├────────────────────────────────────────────────────────────
│ Δ CFidFScheme₁ \ (btop)
│ applicant? ∉ ran(ran membarr)
│ mtop < maxmems
│ membarr' = membarr ⊕ {mtop + 1 ↦ (id!', applicant?)}
│ mtop' = mtop + 1
│ id!' = idgen(mtop + 1); rep!' = Ok
└────────────────────────────────────────────────────────────
```

┌─ *ErrorTooManyMembers* ─────────────────────────
│ $\Delta[id! : ID;\ rep! : REPORT]$;
│ $\Xi[banarr : \mathbb{N} \nrightarrow \mathbb{N};\ member : \mathbb{N} \nrightarrow (ID \times PERSON)$;
│ $mtop : \mathbb{N};\ applicant? : PERSON]$
├──
│ $\Delta CFidFScheme_1 \setminus (btop)$
│ $applicant? \in \mathrm{ran}(\mathrm{ran}\ membarr)$
│ $membarr' = membarr$
│ $rep!' = AlreadyMember$
└──

┌─ *ErrorAlreadyMember* ──────────────────────────
│ $\Delta[id! : ID;\ rep! : REPORT]$;
│ $\Xi[banarr : \mathbb{N} \nrightarrow \mathbb{N};\ member : \mathbb{N} \nrightarrow (ID \times PERSON)$;
│ $mtop : \mathbb{N};\ applicant? : PERSON]$
├──
│ $\Delta CFidFScheme_1 \setminus (btop)$
│ $mtop = maxmems;\ membarr' = membarr$
│ $rep!' = TooManyMembers$
└──

The first of these schemas cannot have the frame reduced, but the other two can be reduced by discarding all the Ξ variables, thus reducing to:

┌─ *ErrorTooManyMembersReduced* ──────────────────
│ $\Delta[id! : ID;\ rep! : REPORT]$;
├──
│ $rep!' = AlreadyMember$
└──

┌─ *ErrorAlreadyMemberReduced* ───────────────────
│ $\Delta[id! : ID;\ rep! : REPORT]$
├──
│ $rep!' = TooManyMembers$
└──

There is no constraint on the values of $id!'$ of course, since no new member is being added, and so no new identity code is needed. We might take the decision to set $id!' = idgen(0)$, and if we add this to the two error schemas we obtain:

┌─ *ErrorTooManyMembersReducedRefined* ───────────
│ $\Delta[id! : ID;\ rep! : REPORT]$
├──
│ $rep!' = AlreadyMember;\ id!' = idgen(0)$
└──

┌─ *ErrorAlreadyMemberReducedRefined* ────────────
│ $\Delta[id! : ID;\ rep! : REPORT]$;
├──
│ $rep!' = TooManyMembers;\ id!' = idgen(0)$
└──

which are of course refinements of the respective operations since they add a constraint to the output values.

Exercise 11.9

$NormalAddMember \lor ErrorTooManyMembers \lor ErrorAlreadyMember$

$\sqsubseteq$

```
        if not(occurs2nd(applicant?,membarr)) and mtop < maxmems
           -->  NormalAddMember
        [] mtop = maxmems -->  ErrorTooManyMembers
        [] occurs2nd(applicant?,membarr) -->  ErrorAlreadyMember
        fi
```

Exercise 11.10

$NormalAddMember \lor ErrorTooManyMembers \lor ErrorAlreadyMember$

$\sqsubseteq$ .. as before ..

$\sqsubseteq$

```
        if not(occurs2nd(applicant?,membarr)) and mtop < maxmems
           --> mtop, id!, membarr[mtop+1] :=
             mtop+1, idgen(mtop+1), (idgen(mtop+1),applicant?)
        [] mtop = maxmems --> rep! := TooManyMembers
        [] occurs2nd(applicant?,membarr)
           --> rep! := AlreadyMember
        fi
```

Exercise 11.11

The point here is that we still have to implement *RTotalAddMember*, but we can make use of the value of *memtest* in *RTAMwithMemtest*; this value is *Yes* when and only when the *applicant?* is already a member.

Exercise 11.12

The loop will use a counter, say j, which counts from 1 up to *mtop*. The variable *memtest* will be initialised to *No*. The guard for the loop will check that *memtest* is (still) *No* and that $j \leq \#membarr$. In the body of the loop, *memtest* is set to *Yes* if $membarr(j)$ corresponds to the *applicant?*. The invariant needed here is:

$$memtest = Yes \Leftrightarrow \exists i : 1..j - 1 \bullet second(membarr\ i) = applicant?$$

The variant for the loop is $\#membarr - j$. The detailed proofs are left to the reader.

Exercise 11.13

We can now refine as follows:

RTAMwithMemtest

⊑
```
if memtest = No and mtop < maxmems
   --> NormalAddMember
[] mtop = maxmems -->  ErrorTooManyMembers
[] memtest = Yes -->  ErrorAlreadyMember
fi
```

Appendix B: The syntax of Z

In the body of the text we have been rather informal about the syntax of the Z notation, giving examples to illustrate usage. We give now a formal syntax for the notation, based on that given in [Spi92]. Indeed, Mike Spivey provided the LaTeX files for his syntax tables, which we acknowledge with thanks. We assume that the reader is familiar with the BNF notation for grammars; some extended notation is used here:

- S sep ... sep S means a series of syntactic units S separated by separators sep.

- S ... S means a series of syntactic units S with no separators (other than blank space).

- Optional syntactic elements are enclosed in slanting square brackets; for example: [Optional].

Certain collections of symbols have a range of binding powers: they are the logical connectives, used in predicates and schema expressions, the special-purpose schema operators, and infix function symbols, used in expressions. The relative binding powers of the logical connectives are indicated by listing them in decreasing order of binding power; the binding powers of infix function symbols are given towards the end. Each production for which a binding power is relevant has been marked with a symbol at the right margin; '< −' marks a symbol which associates to the left - for example, $A \wedge B \wedge C$ means $(A \wedge B) \wedge C$ - and '− >' marks a symbol which associates to the right. Unary symbols are marked with '−'.

We add comments to productions to indicate their significance. Certain features have not been discussed in the present book. These we mark with a '†'; further information is available in [Spi92].

Specification   ::=   **Paragraph NL ... NL Paragraph**

only formal part considered; **NL** means newline

Paragraph   ::=   [Ident, ..., Ident]

declaration of given sets

| Axiomatic-Box
| Schema-Box
| Generic-Box
| Schema-Name [Gen-Formals] $\hat{=}$ Schema-Exp

linear form of schema definition; †schemas can have parameters too

| Def-Lhs == Expression

declaration of constants

| Ident ::= Branch | ... | Branch

data type definition

| Predicate

expressing constraints on global variables

Axiomatic-Box   ::= $\left[\begin{array}{|l}\text{Decl-Part} \\ \hline \text{Axiom-Part}\end{array}\right.$

axiomatic description; optional predicate part

Schema-Box   ::= $\left[\begin{array}{|l}\underline{\text{Schema-Name [Gen-Formals]}} \\ \text{Decl-Part} \\ \hline \text{Axiom-Part}\end{array}\right]$

schema definition; optional predicate part

†can have generic parameters too

Generic-Box   ::= $\left[\begin{array}{l}\overline{\text{[Gen-Formals]}} \\ \text{Decl-Part} \\ \hline \text{Axiom-Part}\end{array}\right]$

generic definition; optional predicate part

Decl-Part	::=	Basic-Decl Sep ... Sep Basic-Decl

declaration part of box form

Axiom-Part	::=	Predicate Sep ... Sep Predicate

predicate part of box form

Sep	::=	;	NL

Basic-Decl	::=	Decl-Name, ..., Decl-Name : Expression

the Expression yields a set or type

	|	Schema-Ref

a declaration may import a schema

Declaration	::=	Basic-Decl; ...; Basic-Decl

Def-Lhs	::=	Var-Name [Gen-Formals]

left-hand side of constant declaration can have parameters

	|	Pre-Gen Ident

prefix definition

	|	Ident In-Gen Ident

infix definition

Branch	::=	Ident

the simple case

	|	Var-Name ⟨⟨Expression⟩⟩

for structured set definitions

Schema-Exp	::=	∀ Schema-Text • Schema-Exp
	|	∃ Schema-Text • Schema-Exp
	|	∃$_1$ Schema-Text • Schema-Exp

schema quantifications; † ∃$_1$ means there exists unique...

	|	Schema-Exp-1

other forms of schema expression

Schema-Exp-1	::=	[Schema-Text]	
			the linear form
	|	Schema-Ref	
			refer to a schema by name
	|	¬ Schema-Exp-1	—
			negation
	|	pre Schema-Exp-1	—
			precondition
	|	Schema-Exp-1 ∧ Schema-Exp-1	< —
			conjunction
	|	Schema-Exp-1 ∨ Schema-Exp-1	< —
			disjunction
	|	Schema-Exp-1 ⇒ Schema-Exp-1	— >
			implication
	|	Schema-Exp-1 ⇔ Schema-Exp-1	< —
			equivalence
	|	Schema-Exp-1 ⌈ Schema-Exp-1	< —
			projection
	|	Schema-Exp-1 \ (Decl-Name, ..., Decl-Name)	< —
			hiding
	|	Schema-Exp-1 ⨟ Schema-Exp-1	< —
			composition
	|	Schema-Exp-1≫Schema-Exp-1	< —
			†piping
	|	(Schema-Exp)	
			bracketing

Schema-Text	::=	Declaration [| Predicate]	
			declaration and optional constraint

Schema-Ref	::=	Schema-Name Decoration [Gen-Actuals] [Decoration]	
			schema name may be decorated; †with parameters if appropriate

Renaming	::=	[Decl-Name/Decl-Name, ..., Decl-Name/Decl-Name]	
			renaming new for old

Predicate	::=	∀ Schema-Text • Predicate	
			universal quantification
	|	∃ Schema-Text • Predicate	
			existential quantification
	|	∃₁ Schema-Text • Predicate	
			†unique existential quantification
	|	**let** Let-Def; ...; Let-Def • Predicate	
			†local definition
	|	Predicate-1	
			other forms

Predicate-1	::=	Expression Rel Expression Rel ... Rel Expression	
			relations may be written in a series
			example: $i \leq j \leq k = n$
	|	Pre-Rel Decoration Expression	
			prefix relation used
	|	Schema-Ref	
			the schema vars must already be in scope; imports predicate part
	|	**pre** Schema-Ref	
			precondition
	|	*true*	
			always true predicate
	|	*false*	
			always false predicate
	|	¬ Predicate-1	
			negation
			$-$
	|	Predicate-1 ∧ Predicate-1	
			conjunction
			$< -$
	|	Predicate-1 ∨ Predicate-1	
			disjunction
			$< -$
	|	Predicate-1 ⇒ Predicate-1	
			implication
			$- >$
	|	Predicate-1 ⇔ Predicate-1	
			equivalence
			$< -$
	|	(Predicate)	
			bracketing

Rel	::=	= | ∈ | In-Rel Decoration	
			relation symbols

| Let-Def | ::= | Var-Name == Expression |
| | | †local definition |

Expression-0	::=	λ Schema-Text • Expression
		lambda form of function
	|	μ Schema-Text [• Expression]
		†unique description: the somevars such that something...
	|	let Let-Def; ...; Let-Def • Expression
		†local definition
	|	Expression

Expression	::=	if Predicate then Expression else Expression
		†conditional
	|	Expression-1

Expression-1	::=	Expression-1 In-Gen Expression-1
		$->$
		infix generic
	|	Expression-2 $\times$ Expression-2 $\times$ ... $\times$ Expression-2
		Cartesian product of sets
	|	Expression-2

Expression-2	::=	Expression-2 In-Fun Expression-2
		$<-$
		infix function application
	|	$\mathbb{P}$ Expression-4
		powerset
	|	Pre-Gen Expression-4
		prefix generic
	|	$-$ Decoration Expression-4
		unary minus
	|	Expression-4 (| Expression-0 |)
		relational image
	|	Expression-3

Expression-3	::=	Expression-3 Expression-4
		function application
	|	Expression-4

Expression-4	::=	Var-Name *[Gen-Actuals]*	
			explicit typing if needed
	|	Number	
			unsigned numbers
	|	Schema-Ref	
			refer to schema by name
	|	Set-Exp	
			set expression
	|	⟨ *[Expression, ..., Expression]* ⟩	
			sequence notation: ⟨⟩ is empty sequence
	|	⟦ *[Expression, ..., Expression]* ⟧	
			bag notation
	|	(Expression, ..., Expression)	
			tuple notation
	|	θ Schema-Name Decoration*[Renaming]*	
			forms tuple with named components from schema
	|	Expression-4 . Var-Name	
			component selection from object of schema type
	|	Expression-4 Post-Fun	
			postfix function application
	|	Expression-4^{Expression}	
			exponentiation
	|	(Expression-0)	
			bracketing
Set-Exp	::=	{ *[Expression, ..., Expression]* }	
			members listed
	|	{ Schema-Text *[• Expression]* }	
			members described by property
Ident	::=	Word Decoration	
			identifiers may include decorations
Decl-Name	::=	Ident | Op-Name	
			names for declared objects
Var-Name	::=	Ident | (Op-Name)	
			an Op–Name needs brackets in certain contexts

Op-Name	::=	_ In-Sym Decoration _
	|	Pre-Sym Decoration _
	|	_ Post-Sym Decoration
	|	_ ⦇ _ ⦈ Decoration
	|	— Decoration

underscores indicate position of arguments

In-Sym	::=	In-Fun | In-Gen | In-Rel

infix symbols

Pre-Sym	::=	Pre-Gen | Pre-Rel

prefix symbols

Post-Sym	::=	Post-Fun

postfix symbols

Decoration	::=	⌈Stroke ... Stroke⌋

multiple decoration possible

Gen-Formals	::=	[Ident, ..., Ident]

formal generic parameters

Gen-Actuals	::=	[Expression, ..., Expression]

actual generic parameters

Here is a list of the classes of terminal symbols used in the grammar, including the standard symbols defined in the Basic Library:

Word	Undecorated name or special symbol
Stroke	Single decoration: ', ?, ! or a subscript digit
Schema-Name	Same as Word, but used to name a schema
In-Rel	Infix relation symbol
	$\neq\ \notin\ \subseteq\ \subset\ <\ >\ \leq\ \geq\ \in\dagger\ \sqsubseteq\dagger$
	prefix† in† suffix† partition†
In-Gen	Infix generic symbol
	$\leftrightarrow\ \rightarrow\ \nrightarrow\ \rightarrowtail\ \nrightarrowtail\ \twoheadrightarrow\ \ntwoheadrightarrow\ \rightarrowtail\ \ntwoheadrightarrowtail\ \twoheadrightarrowtail$

In-Fun   Infix function symbol

Priority 1: $\mapsto$

Priority 2: ..

Priority 3: $+$ $-$ $\cup$ $\setminus$ $\frown$ $\uplus$ $\uplus\dagger$

Priority 4: $*$ div mod $\cap$ $\uparrow\dagger$ $\lceil\,\rceil\,_\S$ $\circ$ $\otimes\dagger$

Priority 5: $\oplus$ $\sharp\dagger$

Priority 6: $\lhd$ $\rhd$ $\lessdot$ $\gtrdot$

Pre-Rel   Prefix relation symbol

disjoint$\dagger$

Pre-Gen   Prefix generic symbol

$\mathbb{P}_1$ id $\mathbb{F}$ $\mathbb{F}_1\dagger$ seq   seq$_1$ iseq   bag

Post-Fun   Postfix function symbol

$\_^\sim$ $\_^*\dagger$ $\_^+\dagger$

Number   Unsigned decimal integer

Bibliography

[Abr96]   J.-R. Abrial. *The B-Book*. Cambridge University Press, Cambridge, 1996.

[Bly90]   D. Blyth. The CICS application programming interface: Temporary storage. IBM Technical Report TR12.301, IBM United Kingdom Laboratories Ltd, Hursley Park, Winchester, Hampshire SO21 2JN, UK, December 1990.

[BN92]   S. M. Brien and J. E. Nicholls. Z base standard. Technical Monograph PRG-107, Oxford University Computing Laboratory, Wolfson Building, Parks Road, Oxford, UK, November 1992. Accepted for standardisation under ISO/IEC JTC1/SC22.

[BO85]   N. D. Birrell and M. Ould. *A Practical Handbook for Software Development*. Cambridge University Press, Cambridge, 1985.

[Boe81]   B. W. Boehm. *Software Engineering Economics*. Prentice Hall, Englewood Cliffs, 1981.

[Bow95]   J. P. Bowen. *Formal Specification and Documentation using Z: A Case Study Approach*. International Thomson Press, London, 1995.

[BS93]   J. P. Bowen and V. Stavridou. Safety-critical systems, formal methods and standards. *IEE/BCS Software Engineering Journal*, 8(4):189–209, July 1993.

[CCEBUE94] Canada Common Criteria Editorial Board (US and Europe). Common criteria for information technology security evaluation, October 1994. CCEB-94/082-084. Version 0.9.

[CNS87]   B. P. Collins, J. E. Nicholls, and I. H. Sørensen. Introducing formal methods: the CICS experience with Z. IBM Technical Report TR12.260, IBM United Kingdom Laboratories Ltd, Hursley Park, 1987.

[Dij72]   E. W. Dijkstra. *Structured Programming.* Academic Press, New York, 1972. Notes on Structured Programming.

[Dij76]   E. W. Dijkstra. *A Discipline of Programming.* Prentice Hall, Hemel Hempstead, 1976.

[Dij88]   E. W. Dijkstra. *A Method of Programming.* Addison-Wesley, Wokingham, 1988.

[Dro89]   G. Dromey. *Program Derivation.* Addison-Wesley, Wokingham, 1989.

[Fag76]   M. E. Fagan. Design and code inspections. *IBM Systems Journal,* 1976.

[Gri81]   D. Gries. *The Science of Programming.* Springer Verlag, New York, 1981.

[GW88]   J. A. Goguen and T. Winkler. *Introducing OBJ3.* SRI International, Menlo Park, 1988.

[Hay93]   I. J. Hayes, editor. *Specification Case Studies.* Prentice Hall, Hemel Hempstead, 2nd edition, 1993.

[Hoa69]   C. A. R. Hoare. An axiomatic basis for computer programming. *Communications of the ACM,* 12, 1969.

[Hoa85]   C. A. R. Hoare. *Communicating Sequential Processes.* Prentice Hall, Hemel Hempstead, 1985.

[Hou90]   I. S. C. Houston. The CICS application programming interface: Automatic transaction initiation. IBM Technical Report TR12.300, IBM United Kingdom Laboratories Ltd, Hursley Park, Winchester, Hampshire SO21 2JN, UK, December 1990.

[HW90]   I. S. C. Houston and J. B. Wordsworth. A Z specification of part of the CICS file control API. IBM Technical Report TR12.272, IBM United Kingdom Laboratories Ltd, Hursley Park, Winchester, Hampshire SO21 2JN, UK, 1990.

[Inc88]   D. C. Ince. *An Introduction to Discrete Mathematics and Formal System Specification.* Oxford University Press, Oxford, 1988.

[Jon86]   C. B. Jones. *Systematic Software Development Using VDM.* Prentice Hall, Hemel Hempstead, 1986.

[JS90]   C. B. Jones and R. C. Shaw. *Case Studies in Systematic Software Development.* Prentice Hall, Hemel Hempstead, 1990.

[Kin90]   S. King. The CICS application programming interface: Program control. IBM Technical Report TR12.302, IBM United Kingdom Laboratories Ltd, Hursley Park, Winchester, Hampshire SO21 2JN, UK, December 1990.

[Kir89]   Bjorn Kirkerud.   *Object-oriented Programming with Simula.* Addison-Wesley, Wokingham, 1989.

[KS89]   S. King and I. H. Sørensen. Specification and design of a library system. In *The Theory and Practice of Refinement: Approaches to the Formal Development of Large-Scale Software Systems*, Oxford, 1989. Butterworths. Unpublished.

[Lem90]   E. J. Lemmon. *Beginning Logic.* Chapman and Hall, 2nd edition, 1990.

[Lim88]   INMOS Limited. *Occam 2 Reference Manual*, 1988.

[Mas]   The Official Handbook of MASCOT, version 3.1, issue 1. Computing Division, Defence Research Agency (Malvern), St. Andrew's Road, Malvern, Worcs. WR14 3PS.

[Mil89]   R. Milner. *Communication and Concurrency.* Prentice Hall, Hemel Hempstead, 1989.

[Mor88]   C. C. Morgan. The specification statement. *ACM Transactions on Programming Languages and Systems (TOPLAS)*, 10(3), July 1988.

[Mor94]   C. C. Morgan. *Programming from Specifications.* Prentice Hall, Hemel Hempstead, 2nd edition, 1994.

[MS91]   B. Q. Monahan and R. C. Shaw. Model-based specifications. In J. A. McDermid, editor, *Software Engineer's Reference Book*, chapter 21. Butterworth-Heinemann, Oxford, UK, 1991.

[MV94]   C. C. Morgan and T. Vickers, editors. *On the Refinement Calculus.* Formal Approaches to Computing and Information Technology series (FACIT). Springer-Verlag, New York, 1994.

[MW90]   P. Mundy and J. B. Wordsworth. The CICS application programming interface: Transient data and storage control. IBM Technical Report TR12.299, IBM United Kingdom Laboratories Ltd, Hursley Park, Winchester, Hampshire SO21 2JN, UK, October 1990.

[NC88]   C. J. Nix and B. P. Collins. The use of software engineering, including the Z Notation, in the development of CICS. *Quality Assurance*, 14(3):103–110, September 1988.

[Neu89]   P. G. Neuman. Risks to the public in computers and related systems. *ACM SIGSOFT, Software Engineering Notes*, 14(2), 1989.

[NS85]   W. H. Newton-Smith. *Logic: An Introductory Course*. Routledge & Kegan Paul, London, 1985.

[Pre92]   R. S. Pressman. *Software Engineering : A Practitioner's Approach*. McGraw-Hill, London, 1992.

[PWM93]   F. Polack, M. Whiston, and K. C. Mander. The SAZ project: Integrating SSADM and Z. In *FME'93: Industrial-strength Formal Methods*, volume 670 of *Lecture Notes in Computer Science*, pages 541–557, New York, 1993. Springer-Verlag.

[Qui69]   W. V. Quine. *Set Theory and its Logic*. Harvard University Press, Harvard, 1969.

[Qui76]   W. V. Quine. *The Ways of Paradox*. Harvard University Press, Cambridge, Mass., 1976.

[Ran90]   G. P. Randell. Translating data flow diagrams into Z (and vice versa). Report no. 90019, RSRE, Ministry of Defence, Malvern, Worcestershire, UK, October 1990.

[SA90]   L. T. Semmens and P. M. Allen. Using entity relationship models as a basis for Z specifications. Technical Report IES1/90, Leeds Polytechnic, Faculty of Information and Engineering Systems, Leeds, UK, 1990.

[SBC92]   S. Stepney, R. Barden, and D. Cooper, editors. *Object Orientation in Z*. Workshops in Computing. Springer-Verlag, 1992.

[Scu88]   G. T. Scullard. Test case selection using VDM. In *VDM88 Conference Proceedings, Lecture Notes in Computer Science*, volume 328, New York, 1988. Springer-Verlag.

[Som92]   I. Sommerville. *Software Engineering*. Addison-Wesley, Wokingham, 4th edition, 1992.

[Spi92]   J. M. Spivey. *The Z Notation: A Reference Manual*. Prentice Hall, Hemel Hempstead, 2nd edition, 1992.

[UMoD89]   Directorate of Standardisation UK Ministry of Defence. Interim defence standard 00-55: Requirements for the procurement of safety critical software in defence equipment, 1989.

[WL88]   J. C. P. Woodcock and Martin Loomes. *Software Engineering Mathematics: Formal Methods Demystified.* Pitman, London, 1988.

[WM90]   J. C. P. Woodcock and C. C. Morgan. Refinement of state-based concurrent systems. In *VDM and Z – Formal Methods in Software Development*, volume 428 of *Lecture Notes in Computer Science*, New York, 1990. Springer-Verlag.

[Woo89]   J. C. P. Woodcock. Mathematics as a management tool: Proof rules for promotion. In *Proc. 6th Annual CSR Conference on Large Software Systems*, Bristol, UK, September 1989.

[Woo90]   J. C. P. Woodcock. *Using Z – Specification, Refinement and Proof.* Programming Research Group, Oxford University, 1990.

[Wor87]   J. Wordsworth. A Z Development Method. Technical report, IBM United Kingdom Laboratories Ltd., Hursley Park, Winchester, Hampshire SO21 2JN,UK, 1987.

[Wor89]   J. B. Wordsworth. A Z Development Method. In *Proceedings of the Workshop on Refinement, The Open University, Milton Keynes*, Oxford, January 1989. Butterworths. Unpublished.

[Wor93]   J. B. Wordsworth. *Software Development with Z: A Practical Approach to Formal Methods in Software Engineering.* Addison-Wesley, Wokingham, 1993.

List of symbols

Index